"With this book Toyin Falola joins a [...] historians who participated in the n[...] I found this book as enjoyable as Tr[...] [...] Russian Revolution. While the scale of the two historical incidents are different, the writing is as close to the guts and as stirring of the senses as any personal history can be. This book also distinguishes itself as a modern classic in which one culture (Yoruba rebellion) is successfully written in the language of another (English). A unique reading experience."

　—Kole Omotoso

"Chronicles the cultures and traditions of Yorubaland of the 1960s, including the predominance of African traditional religions; Christianity; Islam; polygamy; agriculture; education; work ethics; and sacrifice . . . a must-read for scholars of African life-writing, history, sociology, economics, politics, and gender studies, as well as those interested in African, Diaspora, comparative studies, and the autobiographical genre."

　—Adetayo Alabi, University of Mississippi

"'When an old man dies, a library is burned,' said the late Hampate Ba. Book by book, Toyin Falola is building a library for Africa and the world, fashioned from his memories, wit, and wisdom. His are the tales of a generation who came of age at the same time as their nations. The tales are compelling, fierce, and funny, to be read and cherished."

　—Aminatta Forna, author of *The Memory of Love*

"*Counting the Tiger's Teeth* shines astonishing light on a major rebellion so poetically as to make the reader relive the experience with the author. Toyin Falola's indelible memory makes the story fresh and no doubt a unique mirror of a particular teenager with a sharp sensibility."

　—Tanure Ojaide, University of North Carolina at Charlotte

"I read *A Mouth Sweeter Than Salt* with my mouth agape at its mesmerizing storytelling. In his new memoir, Falola again enters the house of amazing tales and emerges with a narrative that is at once captivating and deeply riveting. *Counting the Tiger's Teeth* is proof that we not only survive to tell the tale, but that stories keep us alive."

　—E. C. Osondu, Winner of the Caine Prize for African Writing

# Counting the Tiger's Teeth

## An African Teenager's Story

✦ ✦ ✦

TOYIN FALOLA

The University of Michigan Press
*Ann Arbor*

First paperback edition 2016
Copyright © by Toyin Falola 2014
All rights reserved

Published in the United States of America by
The University of Michigan Press
Manufactured in the United States of America
♾ Printed on acid-free paper

2018   2017   2016   5   4   3

A CIP catalog record for this book is available from the British Library.

ISBN 978–0-472–11948–6 (hardcover)
ISBN 978–0-472–12071–0 (e-book)

ISBN 978-0-472-03656-1 (paper)

*For Pastor, Baba Nihinlola, My Grandfather*

✦ ✦ ✦

Homage to the man who grows old like dust
Homage to wise mentor
Homage to the pathfinder
Homage to life and death
May this homage be accepted:
When the worm pays homage to the earth
The earth opens its mouth to accept it.

Deep in gentle and exacting thoughts
In communion with the massive man above the sky
The patrol officer residing at the periphery of earth and
        heaven
Patrolling the world around, waiting for God to appear.

Fighter on earth
His fury dries up the stream, whirls the huge tree
His breath purifies the wind, as leaves flutter
His words climb to the hilltop
Scattered like mystery
To descend on mountains and wilderness.

The itinerant sage
The ageless man
One who makes a decision
And never looks back
A fighter without remorse.

Honor the valiant hero
Controller of impenetrable forces
Enemy of the agents of darkness
The mighty one who confines the bigger bully to his room
The authority that terrifies with truth
Custodian of heaven's gates
Who sends evil men into hell fire.

Pastor disappeared
To turn into an orisa

Guardian of the roads to heaven
Gatekeeper of the path to the world
Forging along with strength.

Pastor, unwind
Throw small pieces of kola nuts into your mouth
Smoke the pipe
Pretend to fall asleep
Dance to the sounds of drums
Smile gently.

Baba, spring to your feet!
Arise, aged man from heaven
Baba, spring to your feet!
Return to the world
Baba, spring to your feet!
Dogged father, arise!

Pastor, remain calm
I beseech you
When you become the strong wind
Do not fell the tree in my village
When fire covers your body
Do not ravage my house.

I will always respond to your call
Baba's cup of water, sweet water
I will not pronounce evil
May my intentions be virtuous
May my path be calm
May my ways be peaceful.

I inherited your head
The head that calls wealth and it answers
The head that calls children and they answer
The head that calls one person for two hundred to appear
The head that carries no regrets
The head that does not bellow for help.

An ounce of experience is better than a pound of book knowledge.

# Contents

✦ ✦ ✦

# Preface

✦ ✦ ✦

In 1968, I dropped out of high school to join a peasant rebellion, known as the Agbekoya, that continued to 1970. By the end of December 1969, I was no longer a member, but I followed its activities in 1970, until it fizzled out, although it remained in memory and has been forever remembered in oral accounts, even up to today. It has been the subject of a host of academic writings, mainly historical and sociological, and also of poetry and plays. Elements of it, especially the use of juju (powerful magic), continue to dominate people's imaginations and have appeared in some Nollywood movies. This memoir is a small contribution to that moment in history, a way of walking with ancestors, remembering the dead, reminding the living, converting orality into a permanent text, and providing a small nugget about my own experience in life, as limited as it is.

This memoir is neither a complete historical account of this period nor a full account of the rebellion itself. It is just about my own specific experience, a tiny slice of a bigger historical moment of which I was a part. It is certainly the first account from an insider, far different from all the research monographs and articles that are based on public records. I know where the records are dead wrong and where the secret records in the government ministry are, by and large, fabrications by state officials who were reporting what they knew nothing or little about. This memoir is based on the activities of just one wing based at the village of Akanran, southeast of Ibadan. But as this wing also hosted the coordinating headquarters, I was in a position to know virtually all the most important steps and details of the rebellion, including those that never made it to any official or recorded accounts, especially since some political aspects of the rebellion in dealing with state officials were also, for strategic reasons, constructed on the manufacture of deceits to mislead the government.

The event that occupies the entire space of this memoir, the peasant rebellion in the Western Region of Nigeria from 1968 to 1970, was very well known and reported in all the newspapers of the time; the records on it are abundant and can be found in the archives. I went to the archives to read all of the records. I went back to the ministry where I had worked as an administrative officer in 1977 and used my established contacts to enable me to look at all the confidential memos and secret documents that have not even been released to the public. While I read and re-read all the newspapers and records of the time, this memoir owes nothing to them and is not based on their evidence. For me to use those materials for this book is like asking a hen to lay duck eggs or to look for a black goat in the dark.

Rather, this memoir is based on what I saw and heard, what I participated in, and what I suffered. I walked in the shadow of death, as the psalmist would put it, but survived. Not all did, most notably my grandfather Pasitor, whom I wrote about in *A Mouth Sweeter Than Salt*. Pasitor, without fully understanding the consequences of his actions, drafted me into the politics and violence of the post-independence years. The 1960s were a very turbulent time in Western Nigeria, and I observed most of it. In updating my memoir to include the years from 1967 to 1969, my first and most important declaration of gratitude goes to Pasitor, without whom this memoir would not be possible. Leku, my "godmother," also died during the rebellion. I cannot thank her enough, and our relationship requires a separate book.

Many others died, nameless in the records, all totally forgotten, as if they died for nothing. When a hunter sets a trap, using a goat as the bait, he never expects to catch a rabbit. The traps of the dead wasted the goats they used as bait. As Nigeria continues to regress, what we saw as corruption and as government excesses in those days would now make that period a moment of bliss. The leaders that followed those we fought have been worse. While these men were born in a stable, they did not come into the world as horses, but, as they continued to live in the stable, they behaved like horses. We could not ride these horses; rather, they ride us. Today, there is no longer a moral center to create the equivalent

Cover image of a popular magazine in the Yoruba language (August–October 1968), a satire on power, showing how chiefs and politicians exercised extreme power to the extent of being able to behead a poor woman in public and getting away with it. Ministry of Information, Ibadan.

of that peasant rebellion. If change and good government were what the men died for, it is unfortunate that they died at all. *Ile n je eniyan*—the soil consumes human bodies. Such bodies became mere food for the "soil." Assuming they provide nutrients, I simply hope that the new bodies they have nourished and will continue to nourish over time will create a better country. A big plate consumes more food than a small one. If a better country emerges, even if it takes as long as a thousand years, then their memories will be excavated, their place in history will be restored, and they will be treated as heroes in the long history of human suffering. For now, let the truth be told: They died in vain. The evil men survived, and with them, evil; they are the ones whose egos and vanity took the bigger plates. They continue to perfect the art of treachery and deceit; and as they do, they continue to drag down millions of people, give a bad name to their people, and lead Nigeria toward perdition. The words of truth cannot be chained. The dead shall rise again, and, when they do, they will repeat the fight. In that second battle of good against evil, we will win. One day, our frogs will stop jumping backwards.

# CHAPTER 1

# Ogun's Gift

✦ ✦ ✦

In one stroke of the machete, the agile man in his mid-forties cut the frightened, lean-looking dog into two pieces, almost in the middle of its already over-stretched neck. Blood spattered everywhere: on clothes, bodies, sandals, instruments, weapons, plants, and wristwatches. No one cared about the blood that spilled on them; I saw some men even licking the blood that fell on their arms. Some smelled the blood and expressed satisfaction with smiles on their faces. The blood was also on me in tiny speckles, and as it dried it changed color, clashing with my white shirt and khaki shorts.

The atmosphere began to acquire the feel of a carnival—people dancing in small circles here and there, making loud noises, clapping their palms, drumming. I began to dance, too, and to sing along although my eyes and mind were fixed on the center spot where a dead dog lay resting in two pieces with some other objects. The people were overjoyed even if the moment itself was full of gloom and uncertainty. I was worried, nervous in that moment that the end of history was in sight, that the end of the world was near. I would soon be gone, to join my father in heaven, a place of no return. Soon, we would all be dead. Our struggles were for a better life, but the end was death. If the dog was dead, we all would follow, slaughtered like him, to be decapitated, brutalized, violently killed. Only, unlike the dog, we had notice, and we prepared for the fatal and violent end. Let it come. We were eager to invite death.

I was not afraid, for I had no signs in me that induced fear. I was a total stranger to fear. In that year, I had become so immune to fear that I would even cross the road in front of a moving vehicle. As the driver slammed his brakes to avoid crushing me, he would curse me and abuse my mother in a raised and agitated voice. I just moved on, not responding, not worried. Sometimes I would walk into the bush adjoining the road, a place people dreaded because of scorpions and snakes. My conclusions were always tentative, no matter the subject. But I could concentrate, even if the subjects that consumed my mind were too many. I concentrated as I looked at the lifeless dog before me.

I looked different. I was different. I was wearing khaki shorts, called knickers or short trousers by all, with a white short-sleeved shirt. A dirty shirt since I hadn't changed it for some days. I would usually use a hand-kerchief to hide the accumulated dirt on the collar, but on this day even my handkerchief was dirty. Spots of blood from the dog were on my shirt and legs, even on my lips; I cleaned them with my tongue and swallowed the blood. I had tasted blood before—most of the time my own of course, when I injured myself riding a bicycle or playing soccer. Licking or sucking the blood was, I assumed in my childhood, to return it to its source in the body; later on, I did it to stop the bleeding. The dog's blood did not make a difference. Or the difference in taste did not matter.

The songs were endless, the chants got louder, the dancing more intense, and the crowd much bigger. I had to struggle not to be pushed aside or to the back, as many wanted to stay close to the center of the action where the dead dog lay on the ground. As the older men forcefully pushed me back, some even yelling for me to leave, I pressed forward along with the crowd. The struggle for the center stage was a struggle for space. I had a non-negotiable curiosity to know, to see, and an obsession not to miss the slightest detail of this significant moment. I stayed in the innermost ring, sitting down temporarily in the dirt to relieve my aching legs.

To sit down within a crowd was to invite either injury or death. Should the mob be forced to disperse by force or violence, the one who had denied himself the immediate use of his legs would find his head and body flattened by those who collapsed on top of him. I knew that a mob could collapse like a high-rise building, having observed how people fell on one another at a crowded soccer stadium. I had once been transferred like a baton while watching a soccer game at Liberty Stadium, the first modern soccer arena in my city of Ibadan. But on this fateful day, I had no concern for danger, though I didn't sit for long. I avoided being sealed in an envelope, made of thighs and legs, bent knees, and lean and fat buttocks. To fly, learn to stand!

I carried no instruments or weapons, other than the notebook and pen in my pocket. Pasitor, my grandfather, was then opposed to the use of weapons; he avoided carrying a gun, and he did not allow me to put a knife in my pocket. Charms, yes! Potent juju, yes!! Guns and clubs, no!!! Pasitor was a warrior without weapons—his rebellious spirit was in his words, his energy, his diplomacy, and his passion. He interpreted the sixth of the Ten Commandments, which prohibited killing, as allowing the delegation of it to others. All that would soon be history. I was about to see guns, although I never used one. I had had to touch guns, but they were those used by hunters of wild game. I saw others carry weapons, and, as in the case of the executed dog, I had seen the use of weapons. However, I love action, and this was becoming a most exciting moment.

The dog on the ground had stopped breathing. He struggled for quite a while, and it was clear that he did not lack the will to stay alive or to endure. His hind legs protested in death that his body had been severed from his head. The legs could no longer stand erect, but they attempted to stagger and make small movements, until they finally stood still. The drips of fluid from the intestines that were slit open, mixed with blood and producing a range of colors, continued for some time. The odor was not as foul as I had expected, unlike the smell of discharges from human stomachs in latrines. I thought it might be that the smell of the men's bodies overpowered the odor of the dog.

I noticed that the upper part of the dog fought for much longer. The dog's eyes refused to close, looking at those who terminated his life as if to appeal to their guilt or tell them that they were cruel. The dog was not weeping, as human beings do when they suffer a similar fate of anguish or death. No, the eyes looked confident, although the body looked indignant. The front legs could not kick or move. The barking had ceased, and the mouth appeared locked. I did not see a pitiful sight. A dignified dog in death?

The people mourned the dog. There were songs of praise, as if a life lived to the fullest was being celebrated at its finest hour. No one called the dog by his name; rather, he was spoken of in reference to a mighty name: Ogun. The dog had a name, *aja*, the generic name for most dogs. But its stature was elevated that afternoon to *aja* Ogun, that is, Ogun's dog. I had heard all dogs being referred to as *eran* Ogun (Ogun's meal), an indication that they are Ogun's favorite dish, his delicacy. I saw the dish waiting for Ogun, still raw, lying on the ground. Would Ogun feed on it as men fed on cows or devoured wild animals fully roasted and smoked? But nobody was making a bonfire. The dog was lying in two pieces on the ground, being mourned with songs and dancing, with songs especially in praise of the one who cherished it the most: Ogun.

The machete that had done its work was lying on the bare ground close to the dog, a warning that the dog must not contemplate a resurrection any time soon. The dog could either be angry with the person who killed it or forgive that person, but the tool that brought about his end was still very much around, sharpened with skill and great attention. It was not unlikely that the dog had heard men's warnings that if you do not control the sword, you should not seek to discover the person who killed your father. The unclosed eyes of the dog could see the machete, but it needed its body to be rejoined and the strength to get up, pick up the machete, and begin to cut off human heads in revenge. This did not happen, and I had no need to hold my head or plan an escape for fear that the dog would retaliate.

The dead can rise, and when they do they cause surprise and stares. But they never rise to live for long: Their game is to derive joy in the surprise of their quick appearance and disappearance. As they disappear, they become labeled as ghosts, a status that the dead still enjoy since people continue to talk about them. I imagined that the dog had the power to become whole and come back to life, but he did not do so on that fateful day. Men had actually boasted that they could cut a dog in half and re-attach the two parts of its body. There were even names of powerful magicians in the land, tossed around all the time, who had the power to rejoin severed limbs to bodies and reunite any disjointed parts of bodies as long as the soul had not departed. The magicians always experimented with hens, taking off the head of one of them. Then, half-alive and half-dead, it would dance for a while, and the magician would claim victory for making it live again. There were probably magicians who could make the dog come alive, but what would Ogun eat if they did so?

The dog on his own could not return from heaven. Even the powerful juju men in the land could not undo this death. This dog was already consumed by Ogun, which was the reason for the jubilation. What was on the ground, being mourned, had already been accepted by Ogun as a good dinner. The body and the entrails had been carefully relished and eaten slowly. As we sang and danced, Ogun was savoring his meal. Ogun was in no rush, which explains why we stayed there for hours. For Ogun to enjoy the dog, the men added palm oil, the fresh reddish oil from the best tropical palm trees. They added some greens. They even gave Ogun a nice beverage—the intoxicating wine from the palm tree. Palm wine is that delicious drink with the deceptive appearance of skimmed milk. Ogun likes the *ogidi emu*, the undiluted palm wine, taken fresh from the incised palms that discharge their juices into calabash gourds. The gourds had carried the wine to the scene, and were placed close to the head of the dog. Near its tail, very short and now so useless that it could not even fight the flies that were buzzing around the place, were other items—kola nuts, bitter nuts, salt, and cowries. Ogun could eat some of them, like the caffeine-filled kola nuts, or the medicinal bitter kola to relieve the indigestion caused by consuming a whole dog within a couple of minutes. But Ogun could not eat the cowries, those ancient currencies and ritual objects, put beside the dog. Ogun spends money, but he cannot eat it.

It was hard for me to take my eyes off the machete. Not that I thought that someone would pick it up to cut off my head. Africa had never had the machetes later used in Rwanda, those machetes that the Hutu imported in large quantities from China to slaughter their age-old ethnic rivals, the Tutsi. Barbarism was pushed to its ultimate primitive level in the Rwandan civil war, when human beings could be clubbed and sliced to pieces, left to bleed to death while crying and watching their killers. Our Ogun took animals; those from Rwanda took humans. I kept looking at the machete to find the source of its power to overcome the dog. It was usual to go for the neck to kill an animal, since it was certain that the neck would be severed in one attack. Moving to the dog's middle parts to make more cuts, after the decapitation, was to show that an energetic man in combination with a heavy, sharp machete could inflict greater damage. The middle parts contained bones, flesh, and muscles, a stomach, and much more. Delivering a dextrous deadly stroke in the dog's middle parts was not a message to Ogun but a message to men: Acquire power, be energetic, as the person to be cut into pieces in the days ahead was even stronger than this dog.

The dog did not have the Tutsi's look of fear on seeing a machete. No one even kicked the dog with their feet or spat on him as the Hutu and Tutsi did to one another. No one called the dog a cockroach as the Hutu called the Tutsi. A woman even said that the dog was lucky to have been selected to feed Ogun. To feed Ogun was not an act of murder but an act of grace, coming with the sacrificial blood of redemption, and for the devotees, a form of transubstantiation. The machete was not a tool of death, as in the Rwandan genocide, but a tool of liberation and a weapon of rebirth. The machete and the dog, lying side-by-side, looked like two identical twins, happy and blessed. The machete was not an agent of death, but an agent of peace: In doing its deadly job, the machete was preparing the way for peace. The violence brought about by the machete and the death of the dog were for ritual cleansing.

The dog and the machete were joined in spirit, in life and death. Ogun had united them for a good cause. The machete, a piece of iron, belonged to Ogun, who owns all iron objects in the land, even the ore from which the iron was made. The ore and the iron derived their being and materialization from Ogun. The dog, too, belonged to Ogun, as his most cherished meal. Ogun could drink the dog's blood, even doing so as a merciful gesture to human beings whose blood he could also drink with relish. If Ogun owned the machete and owned the dog, the machete was not the brutal tool made in China for the Hutu. I could understand why the dog was not angry with its companion, the machete. Both of them acted out the fulfillment of a prophecy, the actualization of a long-held tradition that both would always be at the service of Ogun with men as priests.

The blood of Jesus, so I heard many times, had cleansed the bodies of the sinners who believe in him and his heavenly father. The blood of the dog was not to cleanse any sinners of their sins, as there were none on that day: Even the man who killed the dog was not a sinner. The men gathered there were all martyrs unafraid to be crucified; even the blood they agreed to shed was not to wash away anyone's sins but to cleanse the world they disliked. The dog was smart to have gone first, like John the Baptist who preceded Jesus Christ. The dog had more power than John the Baptist, and more roles to perform. He had made Ogun full and happy, for no one wanted to confront Ogun's anger. The dog had swapped his own blood for that of the humans, making it possible for one life to save the lives of thousands. Thus, what the dog had experienced was not a murder but a ritual sacrifice. The men who were dancing and rejoicing could see the body of the decapitated dog on the floor, but it was not their bodies that Ogun demanded. The smell was not odious; the spilled blood was not nauseating. No one wanted human blood on their clothes or bodies; neither would they lick it if it accidentally landed on their lips.

The dog's demise had a purpose, although the dog did not volunteer for it. It was not even its business to comply. It was a lucky dog, as we all thought, but this was the perception of men and women and not of animals. Blessed are the animals who allow themselves to be killed and roasted as food either for gods or humans, so do men think. The dogs and goats, sheep and rams have no police, judges, and jail houses for the butchers who terminate their lives. They can make noises and cry, they can taunt and protest, but they cannot arrest the men who kill them. They can look and see, but they provide no philosophical arguments to convince the minds of men that their action is evil. Thus, Ogun's men and women see the dog as Ogun's beef. And Ogun's philosophy, as I knew it, was that a sacrifice was necessary. The dog was the supreme sacrifice. Ogun and men had what they wanted. I observed. And without my observation, the activities of the men and women who took part in a peasant rebellion for three years would be lost, never to be recovered.

Ogun's wish was fulfilled in the evening of October 15, 1968, in the village of Akanran, the headquarters of the Ibadan South District Council area and some twenty miles southeast of Ibadan, the capital of Western State, Nigeria. This was a day of sacrifice. Hundreds of people, mainly men, had been gathering in the village for about three days. It seemed to have been for much longer, for when I arrived on October 14, hundreds were already ahead of me. The houses in the village were not enough for them. They set up camps and tents all over the place, some in the deep farms, some along the paths between the village and the farmlands, some along the little stream that served the village. Emissaries and messages were going back and forth, spies were being coached. There were many whispers. I could see various movements and activities, and I could hear about various plans and schemes. You need to give me a moment before I can tell you what I saw and heard. A sacrifice supercedes a narration, and communion with Ogun and the gods takes precedence over communion with people.

The division of the dog into two was not the beginning of the sacrifice. There were many sacrifices that I did not see or that I was not invited to. No one person could hear all the prayers, listen to all the confessions, smell all the objects involved. They did not see my pact, too, the pact I made with Leku, the woman herbalist, charm maker, and mediator with the spiritual forces who had foretold a war two years earlier.

It was Akanbi Ogundele who broke up all the whispers and side talk with the heavy sound of a gong. *Gbon-gan, gbon-gan, gbon-gan,* the gong sounded the first time. *Pam, pam, pam,* it sounded the second time, much louder. *Gbon-gan, gbon-gan, gbon-gan, gbon-gan,* it kept on sounding uninterupted, for a much longer time. Other gongs began to sound (*ding, dong, dong*), and people began to congregate at the main spot, where the dead dog was placed. I took a gong from a man who looked tired and began to beat it with a rod. I created a musical pattern out if it, which no one could have taken seriously.

After many minutes had gone by, Akanbi Ogundele commanded us to stop, shouting *o tooo! o toooo! o tooo!* (stop! stop! stop!). It was a command that did not obtain instant obedience. Indeed, the sound of the gong became much louder, and Ogundele had to keep yelling *o tooo! o toooo! o tooooo!* his voice developing a musical rhythm. His call for quiet reminded me of the Yoruba refrain: If the drummer being asked to stop refuses to stop beating his drum, it could lead to a fight. Then, one at a time, the beaters stopped, and I stopped too. The silence was temporary, as Ogundele stepped forward to speak in Yoruba, part of which I have translated:

> I, the man that you are looking at
> Three men in one
> The man to reference other men
> My mother is dead,
> My father is not alive
> Natives of heaven
> It is their message that I want to deliver to you all
> And I shall deliver this message now.
> You are not listening to my voice
> You are listening to the voices of the dead
> Noble ancestors who live above the sky.

Yes, a message could be sent from heaven to earth. I have listened to such messages every mid-year as the masquerades roll out, as if from nowhere, to various parts of the city. Human beings have always claimed to be mediators between heaven and earth. There have been many prophets who have received divine revelations, in all ages, then and now, and many more will rise again, competing with the resurrected.

The beginning of the Yoruba, as one of our myths tells us, came to be in heaven where our God (Olodumare) decided to create an entire planet. He gave the assignment to a multi-legged hen who carried a sachet of sand and some seeds. The chicken broke open the sachet and used its legs to spread the sand which became the earth; the seeds were planted to become the plants. Human beings appeared from a void, surviving on the land and the chickens, before they discovered other crops and animals. After this incident, the Yoruba have always seen heaven as close by, and visitations could even be made from heaven to earth and vice versa. Once a year, the Yoruba devote many days to ancestor visitations, as the dead appear in the form of masquerades to offer prayers and blessings and to relay messages from the world beyond.

But Akanbi Ogundele was not a masquerade: He was standing before me, like a man, although he said that he was "three men in one." Akanbi Ogundele did not let us know how his dead parents gave him the message, but I, like others, believed that he received one. People do receive messages from the dead: The dead could bring the messages themselves, relayed by the masquerades. Through trance. Through dreams. Even through another person who appeared without notice, delivered the message, and disappeared into thin air. But the dead could also send their words through a person like Ogundele who had a way of reaching the world beyond us. Nobody in the audience doubted that he could have been sent to us by dead forces. Ogundele reminded his audience:

We have made a sacrifice to Ogun
Ogun, the Lord of Ire
Ogun the flogger
Flog our enemies for us
Don't flog us
Flog the wicked, the unjust
Ogun, the tall man with a big mouth
Thousands of teeth that carve and bite
Ogun, bite our enemies with your teeth of arrows
Carve wicked men into small rocks.

Only the mighty can break rocks, not with machetes and axes, but with something else: supernatural power. Ogundele's associates who were dressed like him did not allow him to finish his praise in honor of Ogun before they interrupted him. My attention shifted to these youthful and energetic men in their twenties and thirties. As their temporary chant leader, holding a flywhisk in his right hand, recited a line, they repeated it after him, creating a chant of praise that could be heard a mile away:

Stop, silence, silence, silence!
My mouth needs your silence
For your ears to listen
To Ogun's honor
All the birds in the forest have stopped singing
All the women have stopped cooking and pounding yam
No cries from babies, no laughter from men
For Ogun has arrived here
Ogun Lakaaye

Lord of hunters and warriors
Lord of the jungle
Master of the thick forest.

The shout of Ogun filled the air. Ogun oooooo, Ogun ooooooo, Ogun ooooo! His name was called upon many times, and the *ooo* sound that ended each call became its own music. The shouting was energetic: Men sweated off weight with the intensity of the movements, their coordinated cacaphony; it was like the ecstasy following a goal in a soccer match after a scoring drought, when the outburst of goalllllllll shakes the stadium and the city.

Ogunoooooo and goallllll are recognizable moments of praise and victory, adulation and joy. Everyone knew Ogun: the god of all iron, the god of all wars, the god of all calamities. Ogun had little competition from other Yoruba gods, and his attributes and those of Olodumare, the High God, often sounded alike. For what Olodumare could do, Ogun was also capable of doing. If Olodumare created the world, Ogun, with his machete, made it habitable—he cleared the land, he made the tools with which to plant food crops, he tamed the wild animals, and he supplied the tools with which to build houses. Who did not know Ogun? Only the person that Ogun did not know.

Ogun was even more feared than Sango, the god of thunder that we worshiped in my lineage. Sango could be insulted or ridiculed during the dry season when he could not use his power of thunder to strike anyone down; or you could insult him during the rain season when he could not conjure fire to burn down your house. Ogun defied all seasons and all places. He was everywhere there was a metal object, from the spoon to carry the food to the mouth, to the car to carry the body from one place to another. From Ogun, there was no escape, even from the farmland where hoes and machetes were used. To shout the name of Ogun was to tremble before him, to realize one's smallness in the cosmos, to acknowledge his presence and might, to respect and fear him. Ogun made no hesitation in striking anyone dead at any time, a fact publicly acknowledged by declarations made to the god that he was always held in awe and fear.

Ogun had to be feared in order for him to show love. He was not benevolent, but rather vengeful: To get his attention, you had to deny him his mighty wrath. To seek his affection, you must avoid making him angry. For his anger was truly devastating: Ogun, who declined to wear real cloths but covered his nakedness with palm fronds, could make a man impotent, deny him a source of livelihood, cause a car to crash and mangle its owner into small pieces easy for a vulture to pounce on. Ogun could inflict maximum damage on women, flattening their breasts, closing their vaginas to prevent urination, intercourse, and childbirth. He loved blood; he could drink it, and he did so to rehydrate. His favorite attire was painted red—not painted by any artist, but soaked in blood. I knew that people were afraid of Ogun, and I could relate to this as I had seen him in action countless times. Ogun had been known to destroy towns, to dry up an entire river, to split a mountain in half. He loved to drink palm wine, but he was not allergic to blood.

I was with Ogun on that day. His presence and majesty were there to see in people's faces, in the intensity of their responses, in their ectasy. I was not a stranger to Ogun, the god and the spirit, alias Lakaaye. I had seen his shrines at various locations in the city and the villages. I had observed his worship at Elepo, my grandfather's village close to my city, Ibadan. I had invoked him in plays and class essays. I had listened to songs and poems about him. When a dog moved close to a road, motorists attempted to kill it as a spontaneous sacrifice to Ogun. The dogs in my city were no fools; like the people, they looked right, left, right before they crossed the roads. For, if they made the mistake of moving near a moving vehicle, they should not expect to be spared. Indeed, the motorist who killed a dog received a warm salutation for providing food for Ogun. Vultures could be tempted to look for carcasses on motorable roads and not get into trouble. A dog knew he must avoid the best bones on the roads and go instead to a refuse dump to eat waste and feces. On that day at Akanran, the Lord was there, fully clad in his costume of blood. On Ogun's wrist, and on the wrists of many on that day, there was raffia, from the palm trees that supplied Ogun's oil and undiluted wine. Ogun loved to dress in raffia or to use it as a highlight on his pants, and many people at Akanran were imitating him.

Ogun had a gentle side, and women prayed to him for children, hunters appealed to him for game. At Akanran, no one was interested in Ogun's pleasant side, the favors he could bestow in connection with reproduction and sexual proclivity. I never heard the lamentation of barren women asking Ogun to cleanse their wombs. Their wombs had all been closed, as the world did not want to welcome another person who would suffer like those already living. No one asked Ogun to remove all the locusts from the farms and restore productivity. They were not looking for food—life was not prosperous, and more food would not make it better.

People were seeking anger, for Ogun to join them in being angry, and to manifest his anger. If Ogun could hurt himself in anger, he was being asked on that day to get angrier, to unleash his full wrath, to sharpen all iron objects, not to cultivate plants or harvest crops, not to fell trees or build house pillars and make roofs, not to clear the forest path to make roads, but to kill. Ogun should kill, and he should allow us to kill. We wanted to kill, not wild game for food, the dog for Ogun, or goats and chickens for food, but human beings. We must kill. It was time to kill.

Ogundele repeatedly appealed to Ogun to kill, to kill on our behalf, and to empower us to kill. Revenge! Peace will come, but not without sacrificing human beings. Our targets: wicked men and their accomplices.

Ogun had no appetite for the blood of the righteous and the credible, the just and the compassionate, the poor, the struggling, the honest ones. "The owner of iron," as his principal cognomen proclaimed, could go on a killing spree. We needed him, as the number of wicked men was on the rise. It was the mission Ogun usually chose for himself, and from which men pleaded to be spared. Men now wanted to send Ogun on an errand to terrorize the men that brought them misery and agony. Ogun did not like to waste human bodies, for he had to consume them, but his stomach was not big enough. As we killed together, we might have to join Ogun in his dinner.

For Ogun to kill on men's behalf, they had to praise him to the high heavens, now his abode. It was Ogun who was expected to send men on errands, but now they were asking the god to work for them. Ogundele's associates, unlike me, knew what they were doing. Ogun was described as "the terrible god" who demanded dogs and blood; the razor who could shave heads and slash throats, the axe who could cut trees to pieces, the sharp knife who feared no muscle. Ogundele had to seek another moment of silence so that he could talk:

> Words are about to fall;
> They hit like rocks
> Words are like eggs;
> When they break, they cannot be restored.
> In the presence of Ogun
> Silence, silence, silence!
> Words of truth
> To bring our final freedom
> Ogun, the conqueror from the hill top
> Will seal the words in blood.

We work for Ogun
Ogun will work for us
After our mission is done
The world will be restored
We cannot restore the world
Without Ogun's help
Without my Lord's sanction.
Ogun, we honor the mighty.

Trust in Ogun was legendary. No one would swear by Ogun's name and embark on a mission of deceit. In the hierachy of the Yoruba Orisa, Ogun was on top. This was a god who respected only two of his peers and looked down on others, even snatching away their wives. One peer was Orunmila, the god of divination—the wisest and all-knowing god. Ogun lacked the personality and temperament of such a gentle god who could do no evil. Always in a hurry, Ogun was prone to making mistakes with his spontaneous actions. Orunmila could calm people down with wise words. The other god that Ogun respected was Esu, the multi-talented, versatile god who monopolized the crucial service of taking sacrifices and offerings to spirits, gods, and goddesses. No matter how powerful Ogun was, and no matter how much prestige he claimed, Esu could sabotage him by refusing to mediate. For the dog that the people killed on that day to reach Ogun's throat, for the blood to soak his garments, Esu had to consent and run the necessary errands. Esu had to carry the food and knives and could deny Ogun the use of them. Ogun was smart enough not to seek to compete with Orunmila and Esu. Ogun also allowed his followers to honor their ancestors like gods.

This was my first encounter with Ogundele, but it was an impressive one. I was not overwhelmed by his presence but rather struck by his passion. His oratorical skills were limited. He delivered Ogun's message in a measured manner, sounding out each line as if his mind was heavy. He was about six feet tall, and his stomach was large. His eyes were red, with eyeballs that appeared about to leave their sockets. He was wearing sandals made of discarded car tires. The soles were about four inches thick. To my mind, he needed those sandals because he needed to negotiate a street full of nails in a casual manner. However, he could still get stuck on painful nails. His pants were neither short nor long. The upper part was covered by his big *dansiki* top. The lower parts of the pants stopped short of reaching the ankles, ending midway between the knees and the feet. So big were the lower parts that a goat could hide on the left and a baby could hide on the right. At one point, I wondered why it did not occur to the dog to run under Ogundele's pants and hide there. I imagined that he was not wearing underwear but another small pair of pants with many pockets in which to hide and store a variety of objects.

Ogundele, sweat all over his body, and with a touch of foam in one corner of his lips, raised his voice and said that this was not the time for people in the audience to make sacrifices to their *ori*, that is, to engage in individualized worship of one's self and soul. He was not wishing anyone bad luck or bad destiny, but he wanted all of them to come together, bound in a collective mission sanctioned by Ogun. They must all pay their dues, give the surgeon the right knife, give the woodcarver the right wood, give the herbalists the correct leaves and roots, and offer the right sacrifices to Ogun. I thought we had already done so, but he was saying otherwise.

I still did not understand the final destination of Ogundele's speech. I was drawn to the sacrifice and the crowd. He was motivating them to fight for a cause bigger than each and every one of them. It was not a prepared speech, so he had no notes to return to. The interruptions were frequent. The mood alternated from soberness and silence to dancing and shouting, from calmness to rowdiness, from calm bearing to angry posturing. At one stage, a small number of people broke off to simply dance to a repetitive song:

A dead dog does not bark
A dead ram does not hook anyone
Here we are
Superior to dead dogs
Superior to dead rams
Ready for battle

These are metaphoric words to convey the impotence of rivals, the conquest of enemies. God has already answered our prayers to overcome, to begin the dawn of a new era that will bring prosperity to all. The small breakaway group was in turn interrupted and dispersed by some elderly men who accused them of a juvenile diversion from the main cause. The main mission, they reminded the group, was for *atunse*, that is, to "repair" the world, to achieve a renewal but with a cost. Thus, I could see people dancing and singing appropriately, while others were accused of not doing so.

Ogundele seized on the word *atunse* to steal a moment yet again. He had never been allowed to finish his talk. There was no script, just a series of spontaneous statements and actions. Now, he changed his talk to a sermon. I did not know why. "The world has turned upside down," he told the crowd. It was not that he wanted the world to return to a golden age when the eyes were located on the knees, when men and women knew their rights, when children were respectful of their parents, and when anybody could eat whatever fruits and grains they wanted. That would be asking for too much, he thought. What he wanted was for the current world to be repaired, to be normalized. It was already broken. According to Ogundele, the world was a pot made of clay, and once broken it could not be put together. But they were gathered to repair the broken pot, he reminded them. Each and every one of them had to locate the broken pieces in scattered locations, far away and even further. After they had collected all the broken pieces, they would have to put them in the same place. They would then have to send for men and women in the land who possessed the wisdom, insight, and knowledge to put the fragments together. It would not be a perfect job since the lines and crevices would be obvious, but the restored pot should be able to serve as a temporary container. If they did not put this broken pot together, all of the people would have to accept the reality of chaos, an angry cosmos, and a world that no one could understand. The world had become a broken pot.

All those who were listening to the speech, including myself and the other partakers in the sacrifice to Ogun, were *atunluse* (those who strive to repair the world). We would soon begin the task, and someone had to tell us what to do. I eagerly awaited my assignment on that day. I was even thinking that there would be a notebook with names, roles, and responsibilities recorded in it for me. Ogundele did not tell me what to do, but I imagined he must have told others. The Yoruba value oratorical skills. To lead, one must be gifted in language, rich in idioms and proverbs. It was most unlikely in my days for the deaf to succeed. Loud and argumentative, the Yoruba would keep talking until their elders called them to order. Ogundele had not been called to order by anyone, but he was constantly interrupted by his peers and others in order for them to energize themselves. Ogundele was not angry at such interruptions as he joined them in singing and dancing. This was not the day when we would sing our own praises, as we later did, but the moment to praise Ogun, the god of iron and also of war.

I wanted to know more about Ogundele, and I did my own research on him later on, behaving like a dog who was patient enough to eat the fattest bone. The Yoruba have a way of presenting historical narratives, *itan*, which gives us an enchanting framework with which to understand Ogundele and others. Anybody who wants to know can collect *itan*, not from archives located far away in secluded places but from the immediate environment. Just ask—the one who does not know will lead you to the one who knows. But *itan* itself will lead you elsewhere—to the realm of the dead, both underground and above the skies. University-based historians quibble a lot, and it is very hard to find two of them who agree on any interpretation. The historians are imposing themselves on the past, which is the source of their problem. *Itan* is imposing itself on the collectors, which is the source of its power. *Tan* is to spread a message, spread it like the gradual flow of lava from a volcano. The ability to engage in *itan* is the power of knowledge, as the hunters say in their song, "*omode lo l'orin, agba lo nitan*"—singing is child's play, storytelling is for adults and the initiated. As if to further enhance its power, *itan* has the capacity to metamorphose into *aroba*, which is the ability of a narrator to combine philosophy with history, to present the past as a living present, to convert events into memory. I understood both, *itan* and *aroba*.

In surrendering to the god Ogun, Ogundele fully accepted the spiritual forces that were beyond himself. As his name implied, the stamp of Ogun was on him from birth, as his parents proclaimed with the name Ogundele that Ogun, the god, had chosen their house as an abode. Having no other choice, his parents chose the cult of Ogun for him.

As a devotee, he accepted chores for Ogun, some perhaps grudgingly and many others voluntarily. When Ogun first intruded into his life, it was through the pain of circumcision. I need not go from one man to another to remove their pants and underwear to know if they are circumcised. All male Yoruba, like Ogundele, were circumcised very early in life, when the pain, minimal or not, could not be remembered in later years. The men and women who wielded the circumcision knives were devotees of Ogun. As they made their cuts, with the little babies crying hard, the blood became yet another fluid for Ogun's consumption. Although it rarely happened, things might go wrong and a baby might not survive the circumcision. Ogun would be angry if the parents mourned their loss for too long or even followed the corpse to the burial site in the forest. Before Ogun could check whether they had been crying for too long, the baby would be hurriedly buried in the jungle so that only a few people could locate its final resting place.

Ogundele survived the circumcision, and he later put his penis to good use, as he was expected to, as the penis is not a bar of soap that diminishes with use. For he had seven wives and nineteen children, three of whom were with us on that day. He did not want to marry seven wives, as I had heard, but a series of misfortunes created good fortune for him. His senior brother, a poor farmer, died and left behind two wives whom Ogundele was asked to acquire. Widow inheritance was not uncommon, even if a new generation of women, and almost all the educated women, kicked against the practice and refused to be inherited. However, in this case no one forced either of the two women to accept a new husband, and both surely agreed to marry Ogundele. Since bridewealth had been paid on them by their late husband, Ogundele did not have to worry about acquiring the resources necessary for him to marry and entertain his guests. He had two wives before fortune smiled on him. It was not unlikely that his senior brother also left him with some other inheritances such as a small area of farmland.

When Ogundele suffered a prolonged illness in his mid-thirties and the sources of his income dried up and loans piled up, he knew that regular medicines, the ones prescribed by "native doctors" who used "native medicine" and those prescribed by *dokita oyinbo* (Western-trained doctors), would not work. Both types of medicine failed to restore his health and dug holes in his pocket. He visited a diviner whose prediction was dire: He must marry a hunchbacked woman. Diviners have a way of prescribing a course that only the strong and determined can pursue. I have heard of cases of diviners telling embattled people to look for a viper's tooth; water collected in the middle of the night from the sea, the Atlantic Ocean, far away from the Yoruba hinterland; the bones of dead corpses; and other even harder to get objects. One ambitious politician, seeking power at all costs, was asked to provide seven live vipers and to collect the first urine of seven new male babies. The bigger the head, the bigger the headache: If the items could not be procured, there was no need of returning to the diviner for remedies, as there were none.

In any case, Ogundele was strong-willed and not known for giving up so easily. Men and women with hunched backs were in short supply. To reverse his misfortune, he would look for a hunchback. There was not a single one in all the schools that I had attended, and I had only seen three during my whole life thus far. I had never spoken to any as of that time, although one, Aliu, was to become a close friend of mine for twenty years after 1977. As the belief goes, without the wrath of a god, a woman could not have given birth to a hunchback.

Ogundele and his friends searched far and wide until they found one, an Ekiti woman from the eastern part of the Yoruba country, the area my wife hails from. As the *itan* confirms, since *itan* has the capacity to affirm and confirm, the parents of the hunchback were very happy to meet a man who was eager to become the husband of a woman who had lost all hope of finding one. They probably had no way of knowing that Ogundele was not doing them a favor but looking for a solution to his big problem. So happy were they that they waived the bridewealth that Ogundele should have paid before taking their daughter as a wife. He took a free wife, a woman with the calmness of a dead sea. I saw her.

Ogundele had now become the husband of five women, testimony that Ogun was actually blessing him and giving him the opportunity to out-produce his enemies with children. Behind his back, he was nicknamed *Oko abuke* (the husband of a hunchback) until he heard about it. While the nickname was originally intended derisively, Ogundele actually fell in love with it. Whereas others would have been angered by it and sought all the means in the world to suppress the nickname, he instead adopted it as one of his signature tunes, an *oriki*. Even on that day at Akanran, with his own mouth and in a confident manner, he told the audience:

I, the husband of one with the hunches
The front hunch stores bees and scorpions
The back hunch stores poisons
Do not invite my anger
Avoid my sanctions
Let the scorpions stay in their reserves
Do not allow the poisons to walk to your side.

Ogundele was able to convert ridicule into a bicycle enabling him to move faster past his detractors. He was now above shame, beyond ridicule.

The senior wives were not jealous of the hunchback, as it is the youngest wife who should spend more days than the others in the master's bedroom. It was her face and body that they could not stand. Her teeth were unevenly spaced. The three front ones were off center and extended out so much that her lips could not cover them. Whenever she spoke, saliva left her mouth in rushes of little droplets that scattered like fallen stars. Her lips could not even serve as an umbrella to cover her mouth. As she spoke, little saliva drops might fall into other people's mouths, or onto their clothes, bodies, and food. It became risky to speak with her at close range since saliva could speed from her mouth to other people's mouths within seconds. Participation in communal eating became a problem, and some of her co-wives would cook and pretend to be full so that there would be no excuse to eat with her. The children of the co-wives stopped eating in the house whenever the hunchback was around. As the gossip went, no one was sure of what the dirty saliva contained, and it was even alleged that it could spread epilepsy and leprosy. The new wife became a pariah. She took everything in silence, like the fish who refuses to open its mouth so that it can never be caught with a hook.

The hunchback woman was also said to have an incurable odor. Ogundele was advised to take her to the Ogunpa River, which runs through the streets of Ibadan, to bathe her. This river travels slowly and has the color of dirt—it is one of the dirtiest of all rivers, not good enough even to wash dirty discarded metal. No one ever drank from the dirty Ogunpa River, which was also a transmitter of countless diseases. People threw their trash into it as we did at Agbokojo, the neighborhood of my birth where my father's house stood close to the river's bank. When Ogundele announced to the hunchback his plan to take her to the Ogunpa, she was furious. No persuasion could make her change her mind. Perhaps Ogundele was confusing ugliness with stupidity. Since the other wives could not stand the hunchback's odor, it was easy for Ogundele to persuade them to join him in forcefully carrying the woman to the river. With excessive force, her legs and hands were tied up with a piece of fabric and her mouth sealed by binding the lips together. She was then carried to the Ogunpa, where she was bathed. When the bathing was over, the sponge, bucket, soap, and other items that had been used were thrown into the river. The women left hurriedly, leaving Ogundele to walk slowly back home with his lovely clean wife, if the water from the dirty Ogunpa River could ever clean anyone. The co-wives went straight to the shower, scrubbing their bodies as if they wanted to remove stains and scars, not wanting to carry with them any traces of the water from the river, and they threw away anything that had touched their bodies while they were there. To taunt the hunchback and to taunt their husband, the co-wives put on the same attire, called *and co*, and applied heavy makeup. When a chicken tries to scratch the ground with both legs, expect a problem to follow.

Ogundele lost on all counts. The odor did not go away. Others in the compound believed it got worse, and they now said openly that the hunchback smelled like urine and feces dumped into the Ogunpa River. Comparing a human being with *ito* (urine) and *igbe* (feces) was such an insult that even the meekest would not take it. An open and prolonged conflict ensued between the hunchback and the other women. None of the women wanted to sleep with their husband. They ridiculed the small vagina of the hunchback, wondering how Ogundele could make any use of it. The enforced bath had enabled them to see all the hunchback's hidden parts. Everybody now knew that her breasts were the size of tangerines. The most rascally of the wives insisted that her husband could never sleep with her anymore, because she did not want the odor of the hunchback to spread to her own body.

Yet fighting the taciturn Ogundele was like throwing stones at a tree that has no fruit. Frustrated and angry, Ogundele secretly saved money to enable him to marry two more wives on the same day just to spite all his other wives. This was how he ended up with seven wives and an *oriki*:

> Ogundele, the husband of the black woman
> Oko abuke, the husband of the light skinned woman
> When Ogundele takes his morning shower
> Seven women carry seven different soaps
> Each begging, "use mine," "use mine."
> Ogundele, three men combined into one.
> The husband of the tall and short
> Lord of the fat and lean, mean and tough
> A friend to the moon, a friend to the sun
> Ogundele uses no whip on any woman
> Only a weakling duels with a woman
> What Ogundele uses is a woman
> To conquer another woman.

As Ogundele grew up, he began to imitate his god, with whom he struck up an everlasting friendship. Ogun approved of his harem, which he saw as a blessing for a man with limited means. The symbol of Ogun was always with Ogundele as he carried a knife in his pocket at all times, kept guns in his house, and worked with iron implements. If he had grown up during the nineteenth century, when the Yoruba fought many wars, Ogundele would have been a warrior. By 1968, the Yoruba had left their wars behind for more than eighty years. Modern armies and police forces had replaced the old warriors. Members of the modern armies and police forces had uniforms and weapons but no philosophy of war to boast about and no god of war to guide them. Ogundele did not have the privileges and status of membership in the modern police and army, but he had a god of war to protect him and a philosophy of war at the same time. Ogundele knew that if you removed the uniforms from the police and the soldiers, they looked no more than weak men. If you took away the guns from them, they were no more than cowards who would die many times before their deaths.

As if Ogundele knew that times of trouble would come, he never gave up on Ogun, thus establishing a permanent connection with this god of war. I never had that connection, as mine was to seek the Christian god who allowed one to do well in school. Ogundele obtained his income through the use of the weapons of reproduction and violence. He had never parted with these weapons in his life. In the city, he worked as a blacksmith, repairing tools, from machetes and hoes for farm work, to knives and axes for domestic use. All these tools could kill, and all needed the support of Ogun before they could maintain their cool tempers. The job was not enough for him, and it could even make him wretched. The days when blacksmiths could make a decent living were over. There were new imported machetes and utensils in all the markets for anyone to buy. A constant supply from abroad made them readily available. People complained that they were not durable—their handles fell apart, their blades quickly became dull, and they rusted too fast—but people would still rather buy another than repair a bad one. Ogundele could not make money from domestic utensils either, as cheaper aluminium pots and pans were readily available, all imported from abroad.

When Ogundele chose to be a blacksmith, he was following a long line of family members in taking up this occupation. His father was a blacksmith, and many of his family members had been blacksmiths too, serving as apprentices to older family members. I wondered why he did not go to school, not even to an elementary school, so that he could make a living with a pen. After all, a pen was still an object of Ogun. In his days, an elementary school diploma would have qualified him for many jobs, at the very least to work as a messenger in the colonial service. I could not speak for Ogundele, and I did not know what Ogundele's father had in mind. His family might have misread the changing nature of the economy, as many people always misread society, not knowing when to give up a craft until they had no money to put food in their bellies. I know that many blacksmiths at Ode Aje, where I lived after the age of ten, spoke of family tradition and pride in the occupations of the past. Some in my elementary school came to school in the morning and joined their parents in the afternoon and at the weekend to practice their crafts.

If Ogundele wanted to serve Ogun as a smith, I wondered why he did not become a goldsmith. Goldsmiths made more money than blacksmiths; they even dressed very well at church on Sundays, and women liked them. The goldsmiths cleaned earrings, necklaces, bracelets, and other pieces of jewelry. They redesigned old ones, refashioned imported ones to meet with local acceptance; they even polished and shined at short notice. The successful ones among them traded in gold and silver jewelry, and they were known in the neighborhood to have spare money that women could borrow. They worked slowly, as if they wanted to catch crickets, to develop a genteel image that attracted women socialites to them. Ogundele knew that this lucrative job existed, and it was one sanctioned by Ogun. Like the blacksmiths, the goldsmiths had their trade guilds, and Ogun was the patron god of both. They joined forces and resources to celebrate the annual Ogun festival in cities and villages. At Akanran on that day, I looked around for goldsmiths, and I found none.

I did not have to ask anyone to find an answer to the question of why Ogundele and the blacksmiths were at Akanran and the goldsmiths were not. It was not as if Ogundele was short of friends; after all, there were, among us, people in other occupations, such as Adio the *fokanaisa* (vulcanizer), Sufi *di telo* (tailor), and Kamoru *aburo lanlodu* (Kamr, landlord's junior brother). Ogundele and all these other folks needed a second job to survive, and the goldsmiths did not. The goldsmiths had a lot to lose: money and women. The poor farmers had very little to lose, and nothing to fear. Ogundele, like many people at Akanran on that day, chose to farm. As they discovered, the government was interested in the farms, not to increase the crop yields, not to help the poor farmers, but to collect tithes and taxes from them. Tolerance, Ogundele and others fully understood, was no weakness. For their eggs to hatch large birds, they had to be patient.

Ogundele and millions of struggling Yoruba farmers, tenant farmers, poor urban dwellers, marginalized artisans, angry cab drivers, and others were now at the mercy of Ogun. They said so, and they acted their part with the sacrifice. We danced to appease Ogun, for he was present, and I believed that there were those who felt his being, his presence. This was not the same as the recitation of Ogun in my school, which was a fake reenactment ceremony. This was not an example of memorization, a lesson in cultural history. Ogun at Akanran was real. I knew then that Ogun was difficult to predict, for no one knew what he would do, how he would do it, and when he would do it. He was accessible, which was why people would call on him, since they knew he would answer. But it was one thing for Ogun to answer a call, and another for him to listen to a wish, and yet another for him to act on it. For Ogun, in his unpredictable aspect, could turn the gun around so that the holder would shoot himself. Ogun could decide to befriend the machete instead of the machete holder so that instead of the machete cutting a piece of wood for its owner, it could choose to cut off the owner's toes and fingers. Ogun could be angry with a hunter, with the result that the hunter, instead of directing the gun at an antelope, would turn it against himself, putting the mouth of the gun in his own mouth, pulling the trigger to discharge the bullets into his own head, which would scatter into pieces for the poor antelope to look at.

As the party in honor of Ogun continued, when a lean-looking teenager fell into a trance, the noise became thunderous. It was as if heaven itself was about to collapse and turn its fallen energy into an enormous noise. More people fell into a trance and more noises were produced, such that my ears began to ache and my chest felt the weight of a heavy load. I did not know the exact number of those who had fallen into a trance, but there were about seven listening to the messages others were relaying. Before then, I had only heard about one person falling into a trance in the celebration of the goddess of Omi (water) at Ibadan and others in one of the Pentecostal churches, like the Christ Apostolic Church or the Cherubim and Seraphim. With so many people falling into a trance, Ogun's visibility was no longer in doubt. He had changed his garments and body and entered into the chosen ones among us. We now had people possessed by Ogun, in a trance, shaking their bodies so hard that I was waiting for heads to leave their necks, for limbs to fall.

The sight of the post-death reaction of the dog now paled into insignificance in comparison to the sight of men and women in a trance, especially a teenager who was only a little older than me. I did not know why Ogun did not possess me—perhaps I did not dance hard enough, sing non-stop at the top of my voice, or display sufficient energy. Or Ogun was a mind reader who knew that my mind was not fully with him, that my spirituality was void and empty. I wanted Ogun to have chosen me if only to know what a trance really was, since I had always doubted it was real. I was jealous of those whom Ogun had chosen. I would talk to the teenager, I promised myself, to discover his feelings. I wanted to know whether trance and madness were similar. I still do not know today.

Ogundele had lost control of the crowd. Or I should say that everybody had now lost control of one another, since we all became no more than observers. Ogun had become the one in control, at center stage. Ogun had mounted many men and women, boys and girls, all as horses, riding them vigorously and hurriedly, to communicate his message to us.

People were listening, saying *ehen* (yes), *ase* (amen), *bee ni ko ri* (may it be so). The invocations to Ogun now became noisy, producing clashes of words and sounds. I believed that no one had expected all these uncontrolled, spontaneous invocations. No one had hoped that many would fall into a trance. Speaking in tongues was always strange to me, and the interpreter was interpreting a language that I did not understand. The interpreters were affirming the hopes of those who were gathered, encouraging them to act, promising them that victory was theirs, and supplying them with words that communicated energy. At Sango worship, which I had often seen, I had heard about how men and women begged Sango to solve the problems of bad health, conflicts in marriages, and the pervasive power of evil. They would even ask Sango to let them dip their hands into their pockets and find money there.

The messengers of Ogun, delivering his message, did not look humble. They were delivering messages with acrobatic displays—jumping up and down, or remaining seated but hitting the ground with their bodies. The teenager even hurt himself, with blood spreading all over his nose and face. A thought crossed my mind: If they put together all those who were in a trance, perhaps they could engage in a wrestling or boxing match. And what would these aggressive competitors do? Would they fight one another to death? In any case, they were separated from each other, different mediums communicating messages that agreed with each other, or I should say messages that the interpreters communicated to us in the same way. It was only the interpreters who knew what those possessed by Ogun were saying, and the possessed were communicating with tumultuous energy. There was vitality in the delivery, urgency in the words, vibrancy in the tone. A woman in a trance spoke so loudly that her voice became hoarse. She did not deliver the words of affection that I was used to in Christian Sunday schools, but, as the interpreters relayed them to us, words of anger. Even small children, some now arriving from where I did not know, looked frightened. Mothers with babies on their backs tightened their long, broad baby wrappers, and the babies' eyes that I saw were wide open. The plants stayed calm, branches and leaves did not shake, and it appeared as if insects refused to crawl. The air was still.

I was becoming a convert but not a devotee of Ogun. Ogun was no longer an anonymous figure, but someone I could identify with at that very hour. I saw a spirit in human flesh, in the faces of those in a trance, the possessed, those about to be possessed, the interpreters relaying messages, the faces of believers, the still trees, the tamed air. Various myths of Ogun crept into my mental universe, not as I had previously regarded them—as folklore, anonymous memory—but now as a combination of truth and magic. One day, I had to compare Ogun with Sango in a discussion with fellow students. We were walking home from high school one hot afternoon when a boy called Sango a god of darkness for choosing to destroy with fire. "No, he was a god of light," I said, for fire terminated darkness. The boy admired Ogun instead, even slamming one of his books on the floor to display courage and energy, to convince me that he and his god had the will to argue, the blood and strength to fight at short notice.

Like this boy, my high school classmate, Ogun was a deviant god. The message of the trance was that of deviance. One interpreter told us Ogun confirmed that so many who saw themselves as living beings were already dead—dead from hunger, abuse, sickness, and poverty—that he wondered why they were afraid of death. If a person was already dead, why preserve the corpse among the living? I had a feeling that Ogun was not calling them cowards—he did not have to use clever words to abuse anyone—but he was telling them that their lives, the way they lived them, were useless to them and others. They had to change from a life of darkness to a life of light. But for the transition to occur, they had to offer Ogun his favorite beverage: blood. I understood that the dog's blood was now insufficient to quench Ogun's thirst, and he was asking for more blood—my blood and that of others. I was ambivalent, thinking that my blood was sweet, that Ogun could drink of it, but I did not want to offer all of it, just a little. If we could all contribute a drop, perhaps a teaspoonful, Ogun should be full and satisfied. Not so. Some had to give up all of their blood, something that I was not prepared to do on that day, although I was not afraid of death.

If Akanran was now Ogun's Kingdom, I kept asking myself whether it was a Kingdom of Good or a Kingdom of Good to Come. The talk of evil and good went on simultaneously. In this kingdom of evil, its people's dogs asked for the second set of bones before finishing the first; their vinegar, full of treachery, was able to catch more flies than honey; gold and perfume were more important than a good name; and their antelopes preferred to wear the clothes and shoes of elephants. We were the good people, but we had no peace, not enough to eat, no electricity, no clean water, no medical services, no money. There was a Kingdom of Evil somewhere else. This I knew, since we had all gathered to fight and demolish this evil kingdom. But we had given a great deal of power to Ogun, and less to ourselves to enable us to fight. Ogun was the one carrying our guns, swords, clubs, bows, and arrows, while we looked at the interpreters telling us how Ogun could jump on horses and lead a cavalry charge.

We were not asking too much of Ogun. Not only did Ogun have a personality imbued with conflict, symbolized as our strong spirit, a spirit stronger than all of us gathered at Akanran, but he reveled in conquests and wars. He was the god of war, the only one. Even when two or more competing parties agreed that Ogun was their only god of war, Ogun had to decide with whom to side, whom to adjudge as the guilty one. For when enemies met, I doubt whether the one that won was the one who had ignored Ogun. He loved such encounters, big ones that led to the spilling of blood. For Ogun claimed victory by conquering men and their wars. For whether a party lost or won, Ogun still had to be thanked.

Mythologies of the past are the performance of the present. The mythologies of anger shaped the minds of men, not in centuries long gone but in 1968. Ogun the mythological was a reality. And the reality was that he could explode in anger. Here was Ogun whose father needed to find a trick to expel him from his own kingdom at Ife to prevent havoc, carefully despatching him to the city of Ire as its king. Ogun, in uncontrollable moments, even killed his own people at Ire—not once but twice. As the myth goes, Ogun killed them the first time because they did not tell him that the palm wine gourds were empty and, the second time, because someone called his name in vain. And when he killed, it was not just one or two people he killed; he kept cutting off heads until he got tired. Just as Ogun exploded on Ire, he also exploded on himself. In a hurry for his sperm to be released into the vagina of Olure, his first wife, he angrily cut the tip of his own penis! Nobody wanted Ogun to explode on them, even if he had chosen not to win a war for them. Others and I myself at Akanran were not just seeking Ogun's support and leadership, his affirmation, his instructions for us to go ahead on a mission whose consequences we did not know; we also wanted to avoid Ogun's exploding on us if he chose to support the other side.

Those in a trance and others in awe of them were now walking away, one by one, followed by a large crowd of chanters. Many were wearing their amulets, some carrying potent charms to protect themselves. As they departed, they were doing so with Ogun in their bodies, in the belief, as the interpreters told us, that our cause was just, that Ogun was on the side of the good forces that we represented, that our values were closer to those the gods have outlined for us, that those who wanted to destroy our world were evil men who must be destroyed. Voices from heaven had told us that we would win because we were just. We were already consuming our chickens before they were cooked and confirming the skin and size of a lion that we were yet to kill.

My destiny and that of Ogun were now joined. Isola, my cognomen, now acquired a more important meaning than my name, Oloruntoyin. Akanran became the small egg that produced the fat chicken. For my name is meant to praise God, the Christian God, in gratitude for His permanence, for His kindness in bringing me into this world, and as a blessing to parents who desired a child. Isola is a declaration that I could leap and fly, be part of an adventure and a misadventure at the same time. There was no longer any thought of turning back for one who had acquired the traits of a tiger, playing with its tail, teasing its essence, behaving like a tiger. Ogun, the dreaded god, had liberated Isola from fear. His messengers, in trances and strange words, told us that Ogun was pleased with me and others. Isola did not know when it had happened, as he himself was now possessed, praising Ogun, the wielder of iron who destroyed many cities and towns, who conjured many men to burn their penises and women to slash open their vaginas, the vengeful god who bit and injured even himself, the pathfinder opening the bush and the jungle to new roads and houses, dividing rivers into halves, the god of war who commanded us to pluck out an eye for an eye. The mission must now begin: It is easy to be in a crowd—I had already done this. And it requires courage to stand alone—I was able to do this as well.

# CHAPTER 2

# Pouches and Pregnancies

✦ ✦ ✦

My mission began in the very early hours of October 17, 1968. I had not slept much as the previous evening rolled into night and then came the sudden arrival of the dawn. Some hours before darkness fell that evening, the crowd began to talk of war. However, the preparations were not publicly announced so as not to scare the women who would lose their husbands, disturb the minds of maidens preparing for their weddings, notify the children about to become orphans, or terrify the cowards, feeble men pretending to be strong in the midst of the courageous. A war council was formed with branches in a dozen locations, mainly village centers located all over what was then known as the Western State of Nigeria. This was a long stretch, from the remote clusters in the lagoon swamps to the peripheries where the Yoruba met other cultures in the east, west, and north, an area big enough to form its own country, which aspiring secessionists were to call the Oduduwa Republic in 1994. At Akanran, we were forming a republic of warriors.

I retreated with Pasitor into the local church, a small building that could, at best, only hold a maximum of fifty people. Akanran was a religiously heterogeneous society, with more Muslims than Christians. The Anglican Church was always struggling to maintain its congregation, and it often fell into a ridiculous insignificance when its members went to the city, Ibadan, to spend the weekend, which they often did. The Yoruba are intensely urban: Akanran was where they planted cocoa and made their money. Ibadan was where they spent the money and flaunted their

Lilliputian prosperity, where they dressed nicely and maintained a better standard of living. No one wore their best dresses in the villages, or even ate their best meals there. They would eat roasted yam in the farms, pounded yam with vegetables in the village, but pounded yam with beef in the city. Even men with two wives put the older one in the village and the younger and more beautiful one in the city.

Whether at Elepo or Akanran, I was always wondering why the missions built churches there. If you were not very observant, you would not notice the church or the mosque in those villages as they were not imposing and contributed little or nothing to the architectural landscape. Even the house of the head of the village was no different from the struggling farmer's house. Of course churches were built, but they were small mud buildings, and they put unpaid pastors to man them, men like my grandfather. The pastors could not live by ministry work alone and had to engage in farming and petty trade. When a pastor left for the city, as he often did, the service was conducted by a mediocre replacement who read the biblical passages assigned to him and delivered silly sermons. In any case, we had more Muslims than Christians, but the majority of them never prayed five times a day—perhaps they prayed twice, very early in the morning and briefly in the evening. If a message was important, a prayer session could be terminated and continue much later, with an apology for keeping Allah waiting. People kneeling down in praise of Allah could easily be diverted.

In October 1968, the church's congregation had been enlarged beyond the church's capacity. It now provided shelter for those who were looking for a temporary place to reside. The size of the "congregation" had expanded, more with pagans—as they were called—than with the *Omo Jesu* (Jesus children). Pasitor, my grandfather on my mother's side, whose occupational name of Pastor was pronounced in Yoruba with an *i* after the *s*, had the privilege of staying in the church although this was not his own ministry, as his based in another village, Elepo. Since my grandfather had been working as a licensed pastor based at Elepo where I began to visit him from 1963, I had become closer to him, like the proverbial child who knows how to wash his hands and dine with elders. He had basically introduced me to village life and farming as well as to rural and city politics. I was able to stay with him in the church, thus avoiding the tents hurriedly built to accommodate the crowd converging on Akanran. The church had no beds, and the pews could not be converted into beds. People sat all over the place, sleeping upright; the lucky ones could rest their backs on walls and benches. Those who sat on the floor used one another for support, as one shoulder touched another. The smell of dried sweat was pungent. The breeze from the outside cooled the space, but it also distributed the smell.

Dawn arrived. Pasitor led me outside the church. We walked along the bush paths, guided by his battery-powered torch, to the house of a senior man. I was asked to wait outside, and Pasitor went in to talk; with whom I did not know. I sat down and fell asleep. When he woke me up, I was actually lying down in the dust in deep sleep. Pasitor instructed me to proceed to Ibadan, where Leku, the famous woman herbalist and a relation, would give me some items to bring back for him. He needed to stay behind. I had carried out several such errands before, moving between him and Iya Lekuleja (shortened to Leku), to collect herbs or deliver oral messages. The mouth and legs were the main telephone lines of that era.

A company had actually been formed, of people of various ages and both sexes, about forty or so in all, all to go on different errands to different places. I did not know what they were asked to do. Neither did they know what I had been asked to do or what the items I needed to collect could be. We had to walk. Pasitor gave me some coins to buy food in the morning, when food sellers in the villages along the way would have prepared the usual breakfast: corn pap and *akara*, fried beans. We messengers could not wait for lorries, avoided main roads, and took a series of smaller roads that led to the city. To reach Leku, I had to walk no less than twenty miles, which would take almost five hours. It took time, not effort, although lorries connected the city with the villages and people hardly walked that distance anymore.

We all proceeded, no one talking, just marching in a long single file, with the person in front holding a torch until the dawn broke and we could see. I knew where I was going, but I did not know what others were doing and why they could not take the lorries that would reach their destinations in thirty minutes to an hour.

I did not eat. I was too much consumed with thoughts to think of food. I was in a company where I did not know what others were up to, and as we moved toward the city the crowd was thinning out, as one person would turn off to the left and another to the right. By the time we reached Aperin on the outskirts of the city, and I made my right turn, I was the only one left. The crowd had dissipated. The population had long since woken up, with people going to their workplaces, students already in schools, and food hawkers everywhere, advertising their products. I was still not hungry. I saw some students, the truants, but I was not interested in them or in school. Here was a different world where the people did not know that a war was being prepared not far away from them, and I had pity on them. I passed along a number of major streets, seeing the crowds but not at all excited about them. Even the newspaper vendors did not attract my attention, as I was not interested in reading the news. I was the intermediary between Pasitor and Leku, the only two people who mattered to me.

I did not see any of my schoolmates along the way, only some who looked like them, boys and girls known as "day students" to differentiate and separate them from those staying in the boarding houses. Parents obsessed with the success of their children never allowed them to be day students, as these were boys and girls who could become truants, fall by the wayside, dropping out of school for months without their parents even knowing about it until it was too late. I was later to establish my own small school for such truants, and, by some kind of miracle, a few of them are successful today.

It was a trying time for the country, going through a civil war between the federal government, headed by General Yakubu Gowon, the president of Nigeria, and Colonel Odumegwu Ojukwu, the president of Biafra. The "day students" had an occupation on both sides: In the new country of Biafra, they were drafted into an all-citizen army, with or without pay, and many perished defending a budding nationalism inspired by a heavily bearded charismatic messiah. On the federal side, they were recruited into a growing federal army, which was later to become the largest in Black Africa. The lure of wages terminated the education of many of these boys, including Kola, my childhood friend. Misguided freedom fighters who could not define nationalism, those who rose within the ranks among them were later to torment millions of Nigerians, including their classmates who had completed their education. Some of the boys on the street on October 17 were to become officers with political power some twenty years later. One actually became the governor of three states, including my own state, between 1986 and 1991, although he was unable to write three correct sentences in English. Life is fate, as long as we are faithful.

I kept walking, passing through various compounds, undeveloped land, small areas of bush, a dump heap. Rather than waving at people, I waved at lizards and birds, looked at insects on the ground, and examined plants here and there. I saw dogs, and my mind went to the one slaughtered the day before. My mind went to the dog and Ogun. Akanran was too aggressive in celebrating Ogun as a god; indeed, the elements of his annual festival, found in all the basic Yoruba texts that I had read, were already being extended. Men and women were supposed to be well dressed, looking happy and prayerful. Not so on October 16. The king of the city must be there, accessible, praying for all, as they prayed for him in return. Not in Akanran—no king was there, and some kings were even presented to us as our enemies who had obstructed the course of our progress and poisoned our happiness. The people would be united, all seeing Ogun as superior to all. In the annual festival, priests would preside. But Akanran did not invite the priesthood of Ogun—priest or no priest, Ogun belonged to us all. In the annual festival, the dog would not be brutally decapitated, but mercifully killed to drain his blood to wash away the evil omens. At Akanran, the blood was on us, sealing our omens, the glue of our sins to our bodies.

When I reached Ojagbo, the city ward where Leku's store was located, she was not to be found. Her store was closed, but not locked. Leku never locked her store; she would only close it to indicate to her customers and visitors that she had gone for the day. Even the rascally would not dare enter Leku's store with all the myths surrounding it and its owner. To threaten to push a boy into Leku's store was enough to frighten him, as boys all believed that it was full of live scorpions and snakes, sorcerers and witches, and other agents of death.

Leku's store was her life. Yet women in adjacent and opposite stores said that she had not been seen for days. There were no traces of her. In the case of most other women traders, emissaries would have been sent to their houses to find out why they were absent from work, usually due to an illness that had befallen them, their husbands, or their children, or some emergency, all calling for the expression of sympathy. However, Leku was not in their league, she did not relate to them, and none would even nurse a desire to find out why she was not at her store. At best, they would say "a a ri iya" (we did not see the elderly woman) and return to their businesses, gesturing to indicate that they were not supposed to know her movements or even bother to find out about her. Leku was not the kind of woman who could be declared missing. Who would steal a burden, carrying a woman who could become a dangerous scorpion, bite you, and then escape? The talk about Leku was always closer to truth than fiction—when everyone was complaining of cold, she was hot; and when they were hot, she was cold; when they were hungry, she was full; and when they were full, she was hungry. She reversed the order of existence, a master of her own rules. When city officials were asking the women around her to buy licenses for their small stores and checking their husbands' tax receipts in front of their wives, they ran past Leku's store. Men who had paid no taxes could just sit around her, and the most powerful tax collectors became powerless, as they were so afraid to come near her, lest their fingers should wither away.

I sat in front of her store, at the point where the two doors met so that no one could enter without pushing me aside. I was disappointed, dejected, and depressed. I fell asleep.

It was a riotous sleep, full of turbulence. I found myself in a deep jungle, far more massive than around Akanran or any village that I had ever seen. It was a jungle without paths to walk or roam as the vines interlocked one tree with another. It had no end, no beginning, no edges, no center. The only entrance to the jungle was through the sky, to be dropped into it like fruit falling off trees. Even then, one had to be lucky to get at the right entrance, the one that led to the ground, as one could drop from the sky but be held by a tree branch. I could see the tops of trees but nothing above them. It was the shaft of sunlight that provided light, but only to a small portion of the area that I could see. Dangerous animals were nearby, and one could hear the roaring of lions. Tigers were actually behind me, and I was terrified. A restless squirrel was hopping onto tree branches, not looking for seeds or nuts to eat, but crying, making sounds that seemed louder than drums. The squirrel was saying something in an animal language, directed to other rodents, small animals and insects close to the tree, and birds and rats that were near enough to hear. Others looked at the squirrel and signaled that they heard and thanked it. As the squirrel made more sounds, it jumped to a lower tree branch, displaying an agility that made me angry that God did not make me a monkey. A few fellow rodents moved near its old abode to feast on what it had left behind and perhaps carried away some abandoned nuts. The squirrel kept moving from one branch to another, looking in all directions—up, down, straight ahead, behind, and toward the center. As it reached the lowest branch, what I saw was rattling: With speed and agility, a python attacked the squirrel, swallowing it in one gulp. No bones were crushed, no flesh was chewed. The squirrel was whole, in the stomach of another being, lodged inside it like a bullet shot into a head.

At last, I understood why the squirrel was so terribly agitated, making sounds, changing locations, looking at all points of the compass, checking underground, raising its head to see things above it: It was warning other small animals that a dangerous and hungry python was on the tree base looking for food. A ruthless, merciless python was ready to attack.

The squirrel saw the python. Why did it not stay at the top of the tree where the python could not reach it? A crawling animal could not compete with a rodent in the game of crossing between tree branches. Why not keep quiet, stay still, and let the python slither away, to look for food in caves and holes where bush rats abound, or go to the wet places, the natural habitat of obese frogs that could no longer leap with any degree of efficiency? No, no, no. The squirrel moved toward the python with its own legs, quick strong hind legs, efficient fingers, reminding me of the saying that what the vulture will eat is provided by death. The squirrel sought death, an avoidable death, moving down to befriend it. My mouth was wide open, big enough for the dead squirrel to actually occupy it; a mouth opened as an expression of wonder and confusion. Flies could enter at will.

Having enjoyed its delicious food, the python revealed itself to me in its full majesty—long, beautiful, shining, sleek. It saw me and made a striking, speedy, and efficient dash at me. Before its final attack, with its long tongue already touching my nose, its eyes popping out, its mouth widely opened revealing powerful jaws and frightening teeth, I woke up, shouting aloud, "*ejo, ejo, ejo*" (snake, snake, snake!). I was all sweaty, mumbling and rambling.

Back in waking life, saviors and sympathizers, mainly store owners who heard my call of *ejo*, rushed toward me with sticks, buckets, firewood, and whatever they could grab. One came with a tin of milk, as if this could kill or crush a big snake to death. A woman hurriedly picked up her baby from the floor and ran away in the opposite direction, to protect her baby and herself from the agitated snake.

"Where is the snake?" "Where is the snake?" "Where did it run to?" "In what direction did it go?" All these questions were coming at once and at the same speed as that of the snake that desired me as a dessert.

"*Ala ni, ala ni,*" I began to shout back that it was a dream, something I saw in my sleep, *ala ni, ala ni, ala ni.* It was a dream, a dream, a dream. The urgency of their actions called for my repetition.

They hissed, rolled their eyes, and called me all sorts of names—a truant; an indolent useless boy; a jobless fool; a mannerless, motherless, fatherless boy; a bastard; and much more. Then came the questions: Why are you not in school? Why are you not learning a trade? What did you come here to steal? Who is your mother, a prostitute? In normal circumstances, a boy under siege would run. I did not run, but I answered one of their questions: "I was looking for Iya Leku." That was the truth, the absolute truth, and I did not plan to fall asleep; the dream, I had no control over. Then and now, I hardly dream, although I have been told that I do, only that I forget. I remember this and a few other dreams, all in moments of distress.

The women asked me to leave immediately, to go and look for my useless mother. The father was always left unmentioned: Women blamed fellow women, attributing what they saw as my transgressions to my poor mother. The women had come to accept that the success of their children depended on them, and those children later paid back their mothers handsomely by taking care of them in old age, far better than they would care for their fathers.

It was time to leave before they took their brooms to hit me, at the same time using curses, two violent actions that were understood to be righteous sanctions. Beatings with sticks, even if more painful, were far more tolerable to me than beatings with brooms, a symbol of dirt. One was not even expected to walk across a piece of broom, made of dry palm fronds, on waking up in the morning, as it was a really bad omen that the day would be messed up, that all transactions would end in failure. Besides, there were those in the city who believed that a man beaten with a broom would become impotent. Before we went to bed, brooms were put away, under the bed, in corners of the house, in backyards, places where the chances of walking over them were nil. When we crossed over a broom, it was not treated as an accident, but as a plot by an enemy to destroy us. A piece of a broom can be soaked in charms, and put on the ground to catch a married woman suspected of cheating on her husband. Should she cross over it, the death of one person would soon be announced: If the woman was truly adulterous, the man who had intercourse with her would die shamelessly before the action was completed, and both would be exposed and she would then die; if she was not adulterous, she would not die. No year passed without talk of a man who died of what was known as *magun* (never climb), a victim of a powerful charm passed on to him through a woman who crossed over a piece of broom.

A full bunch of broom pieces had to be avoided if one piece could cause so much damage. If just one could bring bad fortune, then the whole bundle tied together with a rope at its short handle could bring a bundle of bad luck. You beat a goat with a bundle, drove away hens and cocks disturbing your peace and going after your maize. I did not want to be hit by a whole collection of brooms, one woman hitting you on the head, another on the back, cursing you and your mother as they hit. I deserved it: I had already agitated them with the snake scare. The fear of a snake is second only to the phobia with regard to scorpions. No one wants to have anything to do with either, at any time, at all cost.

I left, as my head instructed my legs to do. It had never occurred to me or Pasitor that I would not find Leku in her store by mid-day. It had never happened before. She was always there, rain or sunshine, attending to men and women looking for herbs, emotionally disturbed people in search of counseling, diviners and their apprentices in pursuit of plants and the bones of various animals to use for medicinal purposes. Many people knew her over the years, or they knew the woman from whom they bought items. But Leku hardly revealed herself, hardly spoke more than a few sentences. She was always in her store, with her clay pipe in her mouth, lit, emitting occasional smoke. Even when she fell asleep, or pretended to be asleep, the pipe was in her mouth.

I lived with Leku at Ode Aje from 1963 to 1965, for most days of the year except when I went to Elepo to see Pasitor, my grandfather who lived there as a part-time preacher and part-time farmer, a respected community leader. Leku was never home during the day—she left at dawn and returned at dusk. She cooked no food, hardly spoke to anybody in the house, smoked her pipe in silence, and kept to herself in her overcrowded room full of dead plants and insects. The plants and insects were not objects of dirt, but clusters of valuable materials and knowledge, which required research to reveal their meanings. There was electricity, but she never touched the knob to switch it on. Rather, she used her lamp, multi-eyed with cotton wicks and palm oil. As Leku poured more oil into the lamp, she would also put in seeds, uttering strange words only she could understand. The words empowered the lamp and fire, providing more than just light.

Going to Ode Aje to look for Leku was like going to look for the path of a snake on a rock. Leku kept no friends, had no children, and had relatives who revered her but only spoke to her about their diseases or good health. She listened to them, told them what to do, and stopped talking. They thanked her, women kneeling down, men prostrating, both moving on, knowing full well that Leku would not engage in redundant conversations. She must return to her pipe, to inhale the nicotine that gave her limitless energy, to puff out the smoke that would ward off evil spirits. Wandering spirits, we all believed, hated nothing more than the smell of tobacco and would keep their distance, as far as three miles away. The smell provoked them to flight, but also to insulting human beings, not because smoking was a vice, but because humans were a nuisance to the spirits, not leaving them alone to roam the streets and do their damage.

Leku had her confidants, like Pasitor and my cousin Baba Olopa, who owned the Ode Aje residence. She spoke with them once in a while, not usually indulging in long or casual conversations, but on subjects that many people did not know about. I was with her and Pasitor in 1965 when she warned him about the danger of politics and that he should expect a war. I kept jolting my memory in an effort to remember who else Leku had spoken with in previous years and how I might probably track her. I found no answers.

One thing was clear to me: Going back to Akanran to tell Pasitor that I had not seen Leku was out of the question. I would look dumb and stupid. I could not go to Baba Olopa, as he had no idea where I was or that I had left high school. I could not go to Ode Aje, as I knew for sure that Leku would never go there, even if she was sick and dying. My thinking produced no answer, not even a clue.

After walking away from the women with the broomsticks without any destination in mind, I decided to turn back toward Leku's store, to the brooms and their handlers. As I approached the store, two women sprang up from their chairs, again with their dreaded brooms, one of them exclaiming, "*omo were yi ma tun pada*" (the mad boy is back again!). This time, I did not run, as if demonstrating my craziness to my detractors. I walked straight toward them. They were truly provoked; they pounced on me with their brooms, both women at the same time. This time, I did not run. I bowed, as if I admitted guilt; closed my eyes, clenched my teeth, and released my upper back to take the hit. Broomsticks hit painfully, and small pieces can pierce the skin, lodging there for days, causing blisters and later small sores and infections. I overpowered the women with endurance, with stubborn determination not to run, not to cry, not to apologize. If you are being pursued by a masquerade, keep running, we had been told, as the man from heaven will also become tired. Jump into a stream if you see a masquerade, and pray that he follows, so that he drowns, his soaked garments dragging him down to the riverbed. You can then rest on the bank, mocking the dead masquerade who returns to heaven from where he came! A dead man cannot be buried twice.

Other women began to warn the two women to leave me alone, telling them that they risked killing an innocent boy and inviting the greedy police to their doors to take all their money, all their foodstuffs, and ruin their businesses. They were searching for a pin in the ocean; offended by a rat, the hunter was looking for a deer to avenge himself. The two women stopped beating me, realizing that setting a net for an elephant was too big of a task. Then they began to pose the right questions.

"Boy, what are you looking for?" I knew the answer, which was why I had returned to them: Leku.

"Don't you know her house?"

"I do."

"Why not go there?"

"She was not at home."

I could not tell them my reasons for looking for her. I did not even know the nature of my errand. They went back to their stores: If you cannot conquer a man, commit him to the Almighty God who can cast him into hell's fire without asking questions since it is only on earth that we can talk; in heaven all lips are sealed, and judgment is delivered without prosecution.

I sat down in front of Leku's store, in the same spot where I had sat down earlier on. The women left me alone. To my surprise, Leku did not show up all day. As the other traders were packing up their wares, preparing to head home around 5 p.m., before it became too dark, I was very frustrated, disillusioned. I had not had a meal or a drink for over twenty hours. Yet food was the last thing on my mind. My thoughts were not empty, but had a density without focus. It was time to leave again, but I had no idea of my destination. If I stayed till it was dark, I could be mistaken for either a thief or a madman. Leku's store was open, but even Leku herself dared not sleep there. Outside the store, the dream was fearsome; inside, it would not be a dream but a reality. Angry bones of animals, it was said, could turn real with flesh added unto them to create havoc. Even to tell someone that I had slept in Leku's store would turn me into a visitor from heaven or from hell!

Having failed in my aim of looking for Leku, I now faced a second problem: where to stay for the night. I headed east, toward my house at Ode Aje, but not with the intention of sleeping there. It was a familiar path, with friends and classmates along the way, but they would be in boarding school or serving as apprentices in one trade or another. In any case, I had no desire to visit their compounds, where their parents or guardians would ask probing questions. I kept walking.

Coming in the opposite direction was Moses, a former classmate in primary school, in the Ibadan City Council Primary School at Ode Aje that I attended from 1963 to December 1965. Moses was an average student with parents over-eager to send him to secondary school. His dad, a carpenter, belonged to the Christ Apostolic Church, a group of Christians committed to excessive prayer and faith healing. His mom was a food hawker: She would wake up early to prepare rice, beans, and sauce, which she then carried on her head in a big bowl, moving from one place to another to sell to those who flagged her to stop. She was also involved in the church, and both she and her husband forced Moses to follow them to church, not only on Sundays, when they spent hours on end praying to God and Jesus, but on two other evenings a week. Moses hated the church, and was always looking for excuses to escape. His sins were not big enough to require him to devote so many hours to repentance, and his needs were so small that he did not need to beg endlessly for mercy. If his father wanted him to go to school, Moses was not interested; truancy became his best hobby. His parents had no money to put him in a boarding school which would have provided Spartan discipline. As he was a day student, his parents had no way of monitoring his movements. The schoolteachers would report in the beginning, inviting Moses's parents to meetings to tell them how bad he was. As Moses went from bad to worse, the schoolteachers turned to face other business or focus on the better-behaved boys whose good performance they needed to ensure their own promotion.

When I ran into Moses, he was heading home, not from school but from a soccer field. He was sweaty, and the way he carried his school bag did not suggest that he was coming from school. From our immediate eye contact, I knew that he was in trouble: Playing soccer till very late in the evening, without his father's permission, showed a lack of discipline. While soccer was popular, no parent wanted his or her son to become a professional player. In those days, sports brought no money, and they lacked the prestige associated with being a schoolteacher or a clerk, not to talk of being a doctor or lawyer, the two occupations that people had begun to emphasize.

Parents invested in their children in order to reap rewards at a later age when they would have no jobs, or energy to work, or even savings. The ultimate prayer was for parents to *jere omo*, which was to "profit from children." This was the straight language of business, buying wares for £10 at Ibadan, selling them two hours away in Lagos for £25 to make a profit of £15, since overhead and trouble were not calculated into the balance sheet. A son who could not take care of his parents in their old age was a loss, a big loss on the ledger. Soccer had not offered the promise that players could deliver profits—the country had to wait for another twenty years for Muda Lawal, a son of the soil, to emerge and prove them wrong. Moses came before Muda, and he had to suffer the persecution that he deserved for playing soccer, giving bad dreams to his hardworking parents.

Moses instantly devised a scheme to get out of trouble. Bad Moses: He asked me to follow him home to talk to his mother to plead with his dad that he loved soccer more than school. This was like being hit by lightning. His mother would drag me out of her house brandishing a club big enough to kill the strongest man. Even a mother persuaded that sport was the right career path would not dare tell her husband. Both mother and son would be sent packing, two lazy people who wanted to bring a curse down on their family. A bastard would have been discovered, and the mother would be asked to confess who the true father was, as only a bastard would squander resources and have the foolhardiness to state his preference for soccer. The father would regret the day the child was born. A rebellious son should rather protect his status by running away to Lagos or Kano in the north to play soccer, instead of telling his father.

I was blunt in telling Moses that I could not help him but that he should tell his mother that he did not like school because his brains were porous; that for reasons unknown to him, messages that entered through the right ear ran out through the left ear; that when the teacher wrote notes on the blackboard, he was unable to read them; that his head and that of the fish were the same, full of rubbish, useless inedible stuff. As easy as it is, he could not use the bottom of a bottle to write the letter zero on sand. His parents would then have to forget their church and pastors and visit Leku for remedies to solve his problems. However, since Moses was no longer bad but terrible, no examination magic by Leku or any person in the land would work for him. He could then drop out of school and play soccer while I served as the referee to make sure he scored as many goals as possible. Just as a bird is caught by its wings, so could Moses use his tongue to be caught in his inadequacies.

He was happy, very happy, calling me by the nickname they had given me at the age of ten, "Iwin," the "spirit," modified in subsequent years to "Iwin Dudu," the "Black Spirit," which has connotations of power and invisibility. My nicknames provide generational markers: To my primary and secondary school mates, I was an *iwin*; to my higher secondary mates, I was "Bishop," because of my propensity to preach and sermonize; and to my university mates, I became "Igi Iwe" (Tree of Knowledge), as I had the capability to cite sources and page numbers by memory. In the last thirty years, I have been demoted to the ordinariness of TF. When anyone calls me by my name, I immediately regard the person as a stranger, someone whose history and mine have never been connected. No person who is close to me ever calls me by name; at the very least I am called TF, or Chief, or Baba, as the closest refer to me.

When we reached Moses's house, we found that his father was not at home. As soon as his mother saw us, she started to cry, asking her son why he was not like me in secondary school, doing so well, making my parents proud, why he wanted to live a wasted life. Mama Moses did not even know that I did not have a father, and I did not know where my mother was; so I was wondering whom I was making proud. She reminded Moses that she hawked beans and rice all over the streets in order to support him and his other siblings. People of Moses's age, she lamented, would call her as if they were of the same age, calling her "Iya Elewa" to make fun of her, as the Yoruba words for prison and beans are the same. "I am the Iya Elewa all because of you, but you do not care!"

Horrible Moses was indifferent; he must have heard such speeches before. He was indignant, looking like the camel who had endured the long journey across the Sahara Desert from its northern edges to the savanna in the south. Asked to travel further, into the forest, the camel asked where the donkey was and decided to sit down, refusing to talk or get up. Moses's mother asked him to change his clothes before his father returned so that he would not get into more trouble. "Your father is no longer interested in you," said his mom, who added that he had stopped paying his school fees and she was the one doing so. Moses got the point: His dad no longer cared about him, whether he failed at school or not. Perhaps the poor father had been praying for his son, and God had not been listening. Praying to God when this ageless being is asleep is a waste of time. He likely knew that his son was a chronic truant, and, unbeknown to Moses, his father had probably given up on him. Moses began to weep, and his mom and I looked at him in amazement as we did not know why, whether he was crying for joy that he and his father had now gone their separate ways or out of remorse, or for sorrow at putting his mother through pain. I advised his mom to look for charms to enable him to stay in school, and she said that Moses had to tell his dad himself. When I told her that I was not in school, she was confounded, but became relieved when I said that it was only for a few days.

"You must not be like Moses," she advised. Then she asked why I was out of school.

"To look for Leku," I said. She wondered whether this was to obtain some medication for illness or the charm to reinvigorate the brain (*ogun isoye*) that students used to pass their examinations.

"To deliver an errand," I said, but explained that she was not in her store and I did not know where she was. Moses's mom gave us food, beans and grated cassava called *gari*, and asked us to keep quiet and let her do the talking when Moses's father arrived from work. She sensed that I was there for the night, and she did not even ask me any more questions.

When Moses's father arrived, he spoke no word to anyone, not even to his wife, ate his food, and retired to his room. I slept on a mat in the hallway, so soundly that Moses had to wake me up the next morning. His mother was already gone hawking, prior to which she would have spent over three hours preparing the food. Moses's father said his morning prayer, very loudly, as if the God and Jesus that he prayed to had to be yelled at. He left the house as soon as he had said "Amen" to his own prayer; he ate no meal and took no shower. He did not even bother to return the deferential customary greetings that Moses and I offered; he did not ask Moses any questions or even ask how I was faring. He saw Moses as he was leaving the house and shook his head, as if telling him that he was no longer his father or that Moses was a basket case.

I wanted to leave the house, but Sober Moses said that his mother had asked me to wait for her to return. She came back some hours later and told me the good news: She knew someone who knew where Leku was. My life was back on course! God had used Good Moses to help me. I felt like grabbing her and lifting her up in jubilation. She wanted us to leave the house immediately, only the two of us, which made Moses very angry. He was upset: If he was not going to school, why could he not go out, at least to play with us? Moses saw the world as a big playing field. He would now be homebound as his mother asked him to put back all the rice and beans in large pots and slowly warm them up so that they would not spoil. There was no refrigerator, and the method of preservation was to keep heating the food. The buyers knew the difference between the fresh and re-heated foods, and they always complained and either asked for a reduction in price or additional quantities for the same price, as they verbally abused the sellers for offering stale food for sale.

We left the house; she was eager to do so, maybe to get rid of me and return to her hawking, or to assist me and get me back to school as fast as she could, or probably to seek help for Moses. I was unable to understand why Mama Moses was taking me in the direction of Leku's store. Was she at the store? Mama Moses asked me to wait at the store to be collected by someone else. She left. Some two hours later, a boy my age arrived and asked me to follow him, mentioning that Mama Moses had directed him. I did. He led me through a labyrinth of compounds that no modern road could ever pass through, even today, as the houses were connected to one another by narrow footpaths. We spoke little, and I did not know the boy's name. He led me to his mother, who also asked me to sit and told me that we would leave when she received instructions; from whom, I did not know.

Whatever instructions she was expecting came on October 19. I followed her with three other women, and after a long walk, we reached the village of Kusela, which had been deserted as people were talking about an impending war. I knew the village, and I was surprised that we were coming here. We passed by the empty houses and reached the farms. There she was! I could now collect whatever message I had to take from Leku and head back to Akanran which I missed so much. I had not been expecting the delays, and but for Moses, I would have been wearing the same clothes for days. I had left my old clothes in his house and taken his, which he was delighted to give me.

Leku had been at work, perhaps overworked for a person of her age and smallish stature. She was frailer than the last time I had seen her, and she looked tired as well. She could no longer stand fully erect. She was moving more slowly than before, and her words came too slowly. She was at center stage, directing a large number of people to grind various herbs and mix them with other ingredients. These were for medicine, charms, and rituals. The wet ground plants and seeds were the visible components, but the most potent were the words, the incantations she chanted over those items which transformed ordinary leaves to something else. Memorize and repeat what Leku said to those plants, you would not be able to produce the effects that she was able to produce with her own incantations! Hers were the *ogidi ogede*, "concentrated incantations" with potency.

Those incantations, which I heard at different times in various forms, when written down sometimes looked like biblical psalms. The words communicated magical meanings, capable of turning ordinary-looking pouches of leather into power. These pouches were all over the place, in hundreds, ranging from small ones that could hold a few cowries to larger ones that could take more objects. The smaller pouches were put in pockets or sewn on shirts; the bigger ones could be worn around the neck or waist, or tied to the arms. There were no leather workers around, so I figured that the pouches had been brought to this hidden farm.

Leku had left the city to become part of a large team of herbal and charm makers, working together at a secret location. Only those behind closed doors knew what went on inside. She must have left the city days before to come to Kusela. No one could come to the farm without secret codes, without being led there by the gate keeper, a man believed to be capable of seeing the "very inside" of human beings, to know their contents and what they were actually thinking—their intentions and level of wickedness and goodness. The smell in this place was horrible, as if we had been dumped in a toilet with old urine and feces spilling all over the place.

The gathering at Akanran had been of men, women, and children of various occupations, but those at Kusela were mainly herbalists and diviners (babalawo) and their apprentices. They spoke various Yoruba dialects, and they were from all over the land—from Ijebu-Igbo in the south, Owo in the east, Ikare in the north, Ilaro in the west. I did not know what to call them: a diocesan council of eminences or a conclave of priests? They called themselves "Awo Osan," that is, the "cult of daylight," which might mean that there could be an *awo oru* (cult of the night) or an *awo asale/ awo irole* (cult of the evening). Or does *awo osan* refer to the good and *awo oru* refer to the evil? They were working together like a team: The fingers may look different, one short, the other long, and a thumb may look sideways, but all must cooperate to get any work done.

The Yoruba like the babalawo too much, perhaps to such an extreme that, if they fall into the hands of a charlatan, permanent damage could be done. In that long-gone past, the babalawo had a role in selecting a king for them, interpreting the course of life, changing a bad destiny to good, performing midwifery, telling people what to do, and even more so what not to do.

Leku was more of a healer than a diviner. She knew about the power of herbs and dead bones, roots and tree bark, seeds and skins, and all their various limitless combinations needed to treat a host of diseases. She was not a babalawo, but, on October 19 and on the days thereafter, she was among them, directing them on what to grind, and the ingredients to combine. To me, she was like a resource person but to them, a superhuman whose words carried divine weight.

She was so quick to anger, and making a mistake near her was a mistake in itself: Her body language would communicate displeasure, especially her eyes, which would turn wicked. She was a commanding presence, as if even those who divined already knew from their divination trays that Leku was untouchable and could harm them. The apprentices were always terrified, trembling when they moved closer to her, treading carefully, bowing almost to the point of never even seeing her face to take her instructions. As I stood erect observing her, panic-stricken men signaled to me to bend, not to look at her; I would stand, disobedient, rude, untamable, rotten, and raw, as far as they were concerned.

The space was active, with one task or another performed with little communication. People prepared herbal concoctions, half explained as preventive charms; the other half were stuffed in pouches without any explanation. People came to bring plants, corn, beans, powder, and pouches. People left to take with them concoctions and bags of herbs and leather pouches. I did not know where they were coming from, or where they were going. Leku did not talk to me. No one posed questions for anyone to answer. Various tasks were performed, but I did not know who was asking them to perform these tasks or what the end goal was.

I was now an active observer of a complicated knowledge assembly, moving from one babalawo to another—listening, hearing, and looking. I could report what I saw, but the meanings were never clear to me. Both their process and its outcome were vague, appearing disconnected. They divided themselves into groups undertaking different tasks and missions. Some were preparing fortification medicine and rituals, preparing ingredients of wholeness and health that people could take in anticipation of health problems, to prevent a host of diseases, and to cure fatigue and fever.

The herbal concoctions for diseases were made for many purposes. They expected malaria attacks, and they put many herbal liquids in bottles. I was asked to prepare labels, writing *iba* (fever) on pieces of paper, each glued to a bottle with liquefied cassava starch. The bottles were available to anyone for free. Men collected as many as they wanted for their wives and children to drink, whether they had fever or not.

The preparation of the herbal medicine was also dependent on a large number of children and women who kept visiting with baskets of plants on their heads. I did not know where they were coming from, or who was organizing them. They dropped the baskets and were ordered to leave, which they did without questions. Once in a while, a few were asked to stay behind to work with pestles and mortars to pound the herbs to pulp.

I saw the workers combining the plants in various ways, changing them according to the diseases they were intended to cure, but the most common medicines were for dysentery and malaria. The use of the preparations varied: Some were put into caps and hats, and many rags were soaked in herbal preparations. Those on caps and hats were expected to blend with the fabric and then be worn. I did not know what diseases they would cure or how; and they appeared too dirty to me to put on my head or to be good for human consumption.

The hats, caps, and rags were separated and put in sack bags usually used for cocoa beans. Three men at a time were asked to carry the bags dispatched to different villages and towns. The language was stern.

"This is for Egbeda," one babalawo would say, sometimes holding a flywhisk or a walking stick, which he used to point to a man being sent on an errand as if a refusal on his part would have enormous consequences. If no one argued that "the one for Egbeda was sent yesterday," off the three men would go.

I did not know these carriers or those who received the products at the other end. Only the location of the delivery was mentioned, not the names of the recipients. The carriers appeared to me to be ordinary poor-looking farmers, barefoot, or wearing sandals made of discarded tires.

The herbs were prepared in the center of the farm hideout. Food was prepared at the edges by a different set of women who cooked and dished out the food. Corn, and more corn—liquefied as a drink (*koko*), in solid form as cornmeal (*eko*), and cooked or roasted (*agbado*)—was the staple. Beans supplied the protein and fiber. The liquefied corn, *ogi*, was put into large pots of boiling water. The beans were cooked, and some portions were then roasted in large clay pots on high heat. The roasting preserved the beans for days. Those who wanted the beans pre-roasted could take their own portions. I did not know how they organized the supply line, but I saw women bringing corn and beans to the farm; from where I did not know. The women were not chatty, as they were in the city when they traveled together or prepared meals for big events and parties. I found what they were doing at Kusela so repetitive and boring.

I was pressed into service even if my work was neither valuable nor indispensable. Until you invest in something, there will be no interest. I was instructed to put dry herbal preparations into leather pouches of different sizes and hand them over to the men who would close the openings by sewing them shut. It would have been faster to glue them rather than sewing them, I thought, but I kept the idea to myself. At first, my job was fun, as I put a teaspoon of powder into each leather pouch. We then would count the pouches, and a set of three hundred of them would be loaded into a sack. Each sack was then labeled with a symbol written in blue. One bore a crude symbol that looked like the number one. Another sack was labeled with two vertical lines next to each other, but this did not represent either two or eleven. A third sack had two vertical lines, with a further line below them, in between the other two. A fourth bore two vertical lines with two more below them. The symbols looked like incisions.

At first I believed that these symbols represented the number of pouches in one sack filled, as I was telling myself that we had six hundred pouches and then nine hundred. Not at all, as I got to know that the symbols made reference to the contents and not the numbers. The men were not doing the arithmetic as I was, but relating the symbols to the pouches and their contents. I had no clue what was happening, and I decided to stop counting the pouches and the sacks. You should not touch what you cannot see.

The symbols changed as bigger pouches were handed over to us; in these, we had to mix crushed bones with herbal ashes. This set was counted only in twenties and put in cow horns. The opening of each horn was then sealed with black soap to hide and soak the contents. The horns, in odd numbers of three, five, and seven, were then wrapped in a large white sheet. Each white sheet was pre-cut to a similar size, rectangular shaped, but with very rough edges. The sheet was firmly tied and a symbol, only in red, was inscribed with palm oil on each: o—o—1 1—oo. The letter o was not a zero as in a number, but more like a circle. Some of the os were shaded, and some were not. I did not understand the meanings of these symbols, but they were definitely not for accounting, nor were they for the uninitiated.

Leku completely ignored me. After I reminded her for the fourth time that Pasitor had asked me to collect some materials from her, I did not know what else to do. The first time she said, "*mo gbo*" (I heard). To hear is not to accept or to acquiesce. The second time, she waved me off with her left hand, signifying that I should leave her alone; using the left hand was to say that the message and I were not even important to her. The third time, she nodded, telling me that she remembered. The fourth time, she closed her eyes, saying nothing, indirectly asking me to stay by the bank of a river to watch for the moment when the crab would blink. I looked at her for a while, and when she refused to open her eyes, I left to watch the cooks and put stuff into pouches, reminding myself that listening to the thunder's voice will prevent me from being beaten by rainfall.

Work, more work, and more work: work that I did not fully understand or enjoy. No questions must be asked. Same food, every day, several times a day. There was no breakfast, lunch, or dinner—you would just eat the quantity you wanted whenever you felt like it. There was a refuse heap on which to dump trash and to use as a toilet—just bend down when no one was looking and use the water in a dirty kettle to clean up. Walk to the stream if you wanted to shower, but it was the same water you drank. I did not know how long they had been staying in this commune, but I wanted to get out of it. How? I had no authorization to do it on my own, and could only wait either for Leku to dismiss me or for divine intervention to bring Pasitor himself.

On October 23, the order came that they must disband the camp. I heard it as whispers, asking everyone to prepare to leave within twenty-four hours. The women quenched the fires to end their food preparation and asked everyone to take the rations of food they needed. The solidified cornmeal went fast. Roasted beans were put in leaves, caps, pockets, and small bowls. I took neither corn nor beans. I was neither full nor hungry.

Water was poured on the ashes. When the heat cooled off, the remaining ashes were all collected, scooped up with the soil, and then poured inside bags that looked like pillowcases, which in turn were put in baskets that were head-loaded away. Fresh soil was brought from elsewhere to cover the spot and watered; three trees were planted. They grew, as I returned to this site some years later, but are now gone, as with most other trees that have now given way to houses that look poorer than trees. A city once beautified by nature has become one of the ugliest, damaged by men who want to build cheap houses and corrupt officials who allow them to violate regulations to such an extent that you could even build an obstruction to stop the flow of water and extend your living room into the streets.

I was happy that we were about to leave and that Leku would release me. I was filled with excitement. We did not all leave at once, as each person was taking off after whispering to someone else. By the morning of October 24, almost all were gone—men and women, the remaining pouches, pots, and bags. Thirty-three of us were left; I counted all of us including myself, even saying that this was the age at which Jesus died. I wanted to leave but could not do so without Leku's instructions and the message for Pasitor. I was the youngest of us all. Of the remaining number, there were eleven women, fifteen men, six teenagers working as apprentices to babalawo, and myself.

I was not prepared for the confusion that followed. The remaining men, together with their apprentices, and women separated, and both asked me to stay out; that is, I was to be excluded from what appeared to me as a club of men and a club of women. One club moved a little way to the north, the other to the south, and I stayed in the old open kitchen at the center of the site, turning my head to left and right like a lizard restlessly moving its neck. It would have worked better if my two eyes had been located on my cheeks. The men retained their old attire and said things that I could not hear. The women changed their clothes, not at all bothered that they were exposing their nakedness to themselves and me as they did so, all putting on white wrappers and leaving their heads uncovered. They were also talking, but their words were inaudible to me, like those of the men. Their legs, hands, and mouths were moving—I could see the gestures, but could not hear their words.

A man moved in my direction, and then a woman did the same. They stopped close to me. Without any instruction, I moved sideways, some feet away from them. The man and woman remained standing, looking at one another, as if staring, just looking, their heads erect, their necks stiff, their eyes wide open. I was looking at them, but they did not care, as if I counted for nothing. The woman turned away from the man, whose eyes now faced her back. Then another woman walked their way, with a bowl in her hands. She held the bowl as if it must never fall and crash. She delivered the bowl to the other woman, then turned back to join the group of women to the south. The woman who received the bowl turned to face the man, and bent down to put the bowl on the ground. A medium-sized clay bowl, it contained kernels, coins, and some objects unrecognizable to me. The man dipped his hand into his pocket and brought out a small gourd with a crooked neck and head. He bent and poured the liquid from the gourd into the bowl. He told the liquid, as if it could hear the Yoruba language, to wash the contents, invoking the names of gods and goddesses, mentioning Orunmila many times. His speech was incomprehensible to me, and I did not understand the ritual cleansing of the objects. His task done, he lifted the bowl, drank from it, and passed it to the woman, who drank what was left.

As if they had previously rehearsed, both began poetry recitations on Orunmila, the god of divination and wisdom. The woman took a seed from the bowl (I was later told that this was the kernel known as *ikin*), and muttered some words to it. The man took a piece of metal chipped off from a knife and said some inaudible words as well. The man and woman were bonding, not with one another but with some other forces, gods, and goddesses. They picked out some contents in the bowl, their lips moving as if they were talking, but the words did not come out.

The woman knelt down, put the bowl on her head. The man picked up the contents remaining in the bowl, muttering inaudible words, one at a time to each item. The woman stood up. As she walked to rejoin her "club," the other women watching the ceremony shouted, "*Yeye o*," which might mean "great mother" in a sacred space. The man moved about four times in short steps, each step to the left, until he looked straight in the eyes of the other men. He walked toward them, very slowly, taking not a full step but a quarter step. Silence descended upon all. Total silence!

When the man reached his group, they formed a circle, wrapped their hands around each other's shoulders and necks, and bowed down as if there were an object in the middle that attracted their attention. They raised their heads at the same time, looked at one another, raised their fists, and looked up to the faraway sky as if they were to receive a message or collect an object. Did they see something that I did not see when I looked at the sky? In unison, they moved their left legs forward, then stood still, moved their right legs backward, then stood still. They broke away from the circle and began to depart in single file, looking down as if they had to watch out for stumps to prevent them from stumbling. They all disappeared down the forest path, and this was the last time that I would see any of them—except of course if I saw any of them later in life but was not able to recognize them.

I was now the only male left, in what appeared to me as a coordinated exit. I could not have followed the men, as I was not one of them. I could not have left without Leku's permission. When a woman walked toward me, I thought that she wanted to deliver a message from Leku so that I could leave. Rather, she asked me to leave at once. I wondered why, but I obeyed her nevertheless. A few steps and another asked me to stop. "*Omo iya ma ni*" (he was iya's son). *Omo iya* is a term of endearment, as even two totally unrelated people could use it for one another. It could mean mother in a more generic sense, used to structure seniority. When it becomes *awon iya*, the meaning may be cosmic, spiritual, secretive. All the women there were *awon iya*, not women, not mothers, but cosmic beings, without gender. I, as an *omo iya*, was being invited into their company, or so it seemed. It was not even Leku who asked me not to leave, which might mean that she had told others about me or that she had delegated the task to someone else. Or maybe it was that I did not understand the women's actions and activities, their words. I only saw bits and pieces. No one in those years could have seen everything. What I witnessed lacked coherence, and I did not understand how any one piece was connected to any bigger picture.

The women gathered all of their belongings—pieces of cloth, small earthenware containers, herbs, lamps, coins, cowries, and the like. Leku had a shawl, originally cream or white but now brown with dirt, and a bag containing smaller items and probably charms.

There was a bigger basket that needed to be carried, and I was expecting them to ask me to do the carrying, being the youngest. They did not. When the blue wrapper covering the basket was removed, I could see that it contained wooden dolls, the *omolangidi* that carvers made for children as toys. The *omolangidi*, a crude toy that looked like a baby, was the first toy that all children encountered—I had one, and it was good as company, a fellow "baby," good as food, as one could chew it to train growing teeth, and an excellent protest tool, as one could throw it at adults to express anger or displeasure. Only the children of the rich had plastic toys; the majority of others had the *omolangidi*. Maybe the women bought so many of them to give away to their friends with children.

Strange things followed. All the women wrapped their belongings and tied them to their stomachs, adding more cloths to make them bigger, as if they were pregnant! Pregnancies in different sizes from five months to nine!! The one with the biggest stomach actually added a calabash to her belongings. Pregnant women!!! They were not trying to hide their items, which were usually carried on their heads; they were faking pregnancies. They took the dolls, put one each between their breasts and one on their back, as if carrying twins, except that women did not carry their babies in front for fear of tripping and accidentally killing an innocent child. Leku, too, in her seventies, was pregnant!

The pregnant women did not move in the direction of the men, but in exactly the opposite direction. I followed the last woman at the very back of the group, like a dead fish that must follow the stream. They walked slowly, perhaps because they were tired. Or was the load of unborn babies too heavy? Age was certainly not on their side if they wanted to walk fast. As they walked, they were pronouncing everlasting curses, profane words—each pronounced a different curse, but with a chorus "*àṣẹ*" (may it come to pass) to end each.

"They would die." *Ase.*
"They would be denied the favor of witches." *Ase.*
"Evil will befall them." *Ase.*
"Coffins will enter their houses
To load corpses." *Ase.*

The word "they" could not have referred to their husbands or children or their relatives. As angry as one might be, only the most evil would wish death on her relations. Who were "they" and "them"?

As they approached the main streets of the city, they stopped pronouncing the curses and took to singing, praising, praying. They divided the world into two: those to be cursed in the forest, where the spirits and witches would carry the message to the world beyond, and those to be prayed for in the city, where, by chance, an angel of God was visiting and would receive the message on His behalf. Those being prayed for could hear, say "*amin*," and thank them.

Those being cursed were too far away to hear anything, but the trees and animals were the witnesses, and the women had sealed the curses with "*ase.*" Would the curses take effect? Time would tell. A child insulted the huge and majestic *iroko* tree and looked back to see if the tree would immediately fall on him in revenge, forgetting that the *iroko* who heard the insult was just too full of patience. It was this same *iroko* tree who had previously warned the hunters sitting beneath it that they should not let their pride prevent them from running away from danger when wild animals appeared; they should tolerate being laughed at by the hyena rather to confront this big creature, be killed, and be mourned. Well, you could mourn the dead, but as the *iroko* added, you could not recover the meat from inside the stomach of the ruthless carnivore. If the dead man's son appeared, the hyena full of the meat of his father would not budge an inch, not in any panic whatsoever, inviting the sad son to hit a rat who sits on top of his only clay pot. The tolerant tree only wanted to grow bigger, so that when it decided to act, at its own time and its own choosing, it would fall on the child who cursed it, now a man with ambitions, tearing him into hundreds of pieces. As mourners arrived, irrespective of their number, they would not be able to lift or push aside the *iroko* to recover the remnants of the fragments of the corpse.

CHAPTER 3

# Compound of Mysteries

✦ ✦ ✦

I thought the women I was following would each go their own way to their various compounds and families, and that Leku would head to her store where she would give me whatever message was meant for Pasitor. Yet the women kept walking, as if members of a team. The road is always a cheat, collecting tributes and dues from travelers, punishing them with heat and sweat, making their feet turn sore, and drying out their throats. The road is a crooked thief, never a straight mind—a thief that steals time. About half the women, the elderly among them, disappeared, because they could not endure a long walk.

The other half kept moving on and on, praying and singing; people gathered on the sides of the street to look at them and to utter *amin, amin, amin* (amen) at the end of each prayer, as if this was a day when God would answer their prayers. On hearing *amin, amin, amin,* more people rushed out from their homes to see the women and echo their own *amin, amin, amin.* Anything good, worth seeing, must be seen by more than one person. *Amin* must be said three times before God would answer one's prayer. If you stayed too close to your mother and did not say *amin, amin, amin o,* expect a spanking on the part of your body closest to her palms or a knuckle rap right in the center of your head if it was your father hitting you. Prayers had to be carried to God by certain forces, like angels, and your mother, as you were being spanked, would ask you whether you did not know that these praying women were the forces that would take your wishes to the creator. Message carriers gave no notice of their appearance; like these women, they just appeared from nowhere and at unexpected times. Locusts kill one another in a basket: An *amin* kills another *amin*; the louder it was, the faster it traveled to God, leaving behind the *amin* expressed in weak and feeble voices.

It was a really long walk, taking hours. Where the women's energy came from, only they would know. To me, it was tiring. Bad luck and good luck share one thing in common: Both are unable to run with speed. Without any notice, the women stopped singing and praying and started walking quietly. The shouts of *amin* ended, and fewer and fewer people were now observing them. Were they tired? Eventually, they stopped at the small sleepy village of Apete, today a fully built-up part of the city, deforested, heavily congested, and chaotic. There were other women awaiting them, women who had been coming from other villages and towns to converge on the secret location at Apete. As they approached a sprawling compound, they were welcomed with jubilation, singing, and prayer and directed to the backyard, a large expanse of land that could hold hundreds of people. One could see the house from the front, but not the large backyard.

The people in the compound must have been expecting them. The other half that disappeared earlier, including Leku, were already there, apparently arriving by lorry since they would not have been head-carried. The new arrivals were served water in tin cups, then food wrapped in leaves and sauce and tiny pieces of beef in small clay bowls. The people in the compound asked after the women's health. An herbal liquid (*agbo*) was offered, and I joined them in drinking it, although I did not know what it was meant for. It was very bitter, but I had learned to drink this kind of concoction: I would hold my breath and gulp it so fast that the bulk of it would enter my throat without touching my tongue. I drank so much of it that over time bitter leaf became my favorite. My taste buds now revolt against sugar, cake, or anything that is sweet. What I enjoy most must be bitter, and I can convert the most bitter of herbs into tea. Sauce and soup can be bitter, and I enjoy them better than those sweetened with cheese and sugar. Bitterness has its own pleasure that only a few can discover.

This place was in a different world. At Kusela, you sat on the ground if you were tired, slept in the open on a mat, using tree stumps or your folded clothes as pillows. Music was supplied by the sounds of insects, with alarms sounded by mosquitoes rejoicing after sucking your blood. Killing a mosquito was so easy: The pest had consumed much food, and became so bloated that its wings could no longer carry its heavy body.

The mosquitoes at Kusela had had blood supplied in excess, and they would miss us terribly. Parasites did not deserve my sympathy, and I was already thinking that they would die one at a time since the bodies on which they fed had all gone. The mosquito eggs hiding in the belongings, part of which supplied the fat bellies that looked like pregnancies, would hatch at Apete and have access to food. That their ugly parents were dead was my consolation prize.

Apete had many wooden chairs in rotund shapes, as if made for fat bottoms, hollow in the middle and rounded in the base. The chairs were of a size to fit pregnant women. There were many benches, made of bamboo. Mats were abundant, and no one had a need to sleep on the bare floor. The mats were well woven, in attractive colors of brown, red, and blue. The food was an upgrade: corn, beans, bean cake, fried *akara* (made of black-eyed peas), tough beef, goat meat, hens, abundant vegetables, plantains, and fruits. As if I had been starving since birth, I kept eating until my stomach was full and began to ache a little. I was trying to hide the only treasure I had in my belly. I had disliked the beans at Kusela, but the ones at Apete tasted better. I became hooked on beans and adopted them as my favorite food, going against the preference of my generation for rice, which I now seldom eat, and if so, grudgingly.

There were many activities going on in the bedrooms (I could not see inside), within the hallway, inside the two "parlors" (living rooms), on both sides of the compound, and in the backyard. Seeing one meant missing another; listening to one conversation in the parlor meant that you would not know what they were saying in the backyard. I had to focus and choose what was interesting to me, not necessarily what was important to the women. In any case, I was unable to determine the significance of what they were doing, in relation to what was expected, since I did not even know what the future would be. The past was being presented as allegories, the present as proverbs, the future as parables. I did not know these women, I was staying with them by chance, and mainly observing: I could not teach an ostrich how to run, advise the quail on how to fly, or suggest to the dog how to enjoy its bones. I was a stranger.

A long hallway divided the house into two sections, with a row of rooms to the left and another to the right, about twelve small rooms altogether, the first one to the left dedicated to meetings and to receiving visitors. Leku stayed in the one to the right, with a small chair in the extreme left corner, as if to avoid the window and the light coming from it. In the hallway were people pounding herbs in mortars and washing seeds and pebbles in containers with various ingredients. They were not just making decoctions and concoctions of herbs; they were also mixing powders with oil and ointments. The powders comprised ground-up roots, seeds, tree bark, and other things that I did not recognize. They would link the names and assumed properties of plants and seeds to certain actions, for example, using pepper (a hot spice) to make life unbearable for someone; or using the heart-shaped orange tree leaf to cure heart disease. The orange itself can do its own healing: Its skin does something different from its seeds; the combination of skin and seed performs a miracle, while the wet skin could do something different from the dry. The "master plant" was everywhere; I would come to understand that this was what they labeled *awogba arun*, which I was later told is *Petiveria alliacea.*

Whenever the women in the backyard started singing, those in the hallway would abandon what they were doing to join them. If ever there was a chorus, expect a volume that would be heard far away, as Pentecostalists in the city now shout halleluiah louder than the shout of "goal" by spectators, players, and scorer in a soccer game. Should the chorus be repetitive, the earth would turn the roots upside down, and the world would be transformed into a vehicle on wheels.

My eagerness to know and see everything divided my attention. I would go out to see what was going on: New arrivals walked in from east and west bringing food items, plants, and various objects hidden in their containers. Those who walked in empty-handed were carrying words stored in their brains. Some would leave the house on errands, as emissaries carrying messages to other places. I was sent to Leku for a similar venture. The contents of the message were unknown to me; like a wren who never travels to foreign lands, I could not follow those people to know their stories and destinations.

Middle-aged women stood on street corners, watching the movements of people, behaving like meerkats who must look at all sides as they graze. The women were rotated; hyenas do not sleep in the same place. They were probably expecting some enemies, and they paid attention even to small children who were just playing: A small stick can control a herd of cattle. The women did not talk—the grave of the cow resides in its mouth—but they were steadfastly using their eyes to communicate, even watching an innocent person like myself. The bird can see the eggs but not the snare; the fish can see the worm bait but not the hook. They were looking at the snares and hooks, avoiding the eggs and bait. They were wasting their time paying attention to me; a package tied up too well does not lose its contents: I was too firmly fastened to one of them to be a problem.

It is difficult to love a child and not love the mother. Whenever I decided to walk beyond where their eyes could reach, one of them would yell "*omo buruku, pada sehin*" (bad boy, turn back). I would halt, then turn back right away. I did not like their peremptory orders; one does not despise his mother-in-law because she is too short. To keep walking forward was to validate their accusation that I was indeed a bad boy. I had been called a bad boy times without number, a clever trick to control my actions, to use bad words to either cajole or control me. When I turned back, I became a good boy: My feet would tell my head that they wanted to move forward to become a bad boy, but my head told my feet to move back to become a good boy. Fortune does not favor a coward: I moved back only so as to move forward.

I walked toward the backyard by a side alley, a small path that led to a larger one. The entire place was cluttered with discarded items—broken pots and bowls, discarded calabashes, empty tins, leaves, kernels, dead animals, newspapers, rags, and other items. Flies were all over the place—some ran away on seeing me, many stayed behind, greedily drawn to the decaying food and plants. So too were the ants who, when you stepped on their procession, feared for their lives, scattered, and began to run as fast as they could. The vultures fled on seeing me, but they would come back after a minute or two. Useless to humans, they did not need to run; they were not edible, and they must never be killed for sacrifices. Vultures are the best at resolving conflicts among bitter enemies: Regardless of who is right or wrong, vultures do not discriminate in devouring their carcasses after they have fought each other to the death. The living may hate vultures, but these birds are friendly with the dead. If a thief is a man caught red-handed, a vulture caught red-handed eating a carcass is not a thief, cannot become a dog that pays with its own head for stealing, but is a bird carrying out the mandate of its creator. The vulture is not despised because it loves carcasses but because having gained all the valuable protein and having put on muscles and fat from eating us, it is still not edible to us, leaving us to prey on innocent animals who are content to eat grass.

A bad experience is good: Unless I was forced to, I decided never to pass through this side alley again. Refuse, dirt, and bad smells did not seem to disturb my people; from the heaps at the far back of the yard to the side alleys, today they are now stars in the facades of houses and even used to decorate the best streets in Ibadan. Instead of filling your cars with litter, you throw your trash on the streets as you drive along. When you arrive home, the windows are heavily covered with blinds, so that you do not have to see the front yard where the garbage welcomes the guests.

The backyard was full of grace and elegance, a place where the clouds did not cover the moon, where it could thunder without clouds. It is not true that when you put women together they will quarrel; it is not true that two bulls cannot stay together in the same hut; but it is true that women are tigers wearing short dresses carrying calabashes that they give to one another, exchanging valuables with love and affection. The women here were both open and secretive. There were loud exclamations in one corner that I never could understand, the sound of the well in the distance that makes one thirsty; there was scheming in another corner, where the cobwebs set the traps; and valuable lessons in yet another, where you learned to burn the dry wood and keep the ashes. If they all stayed glued in their corners, not moving, amaranth could appear from nowhere, to announce the day of death, a deep pool drying out in a rainy season. Songs punctuated their gentle conversations, one handcuff making noise to warn the other. One person began a song, others joined: The house that catches the fire warns the next to get ready to burn. As the fire burned, it spread to the next person until they were all engulfed, turning the backyard into a concert without spectators. A large space became smaller. I, too, joined them, the child of a crab that had learned the skill of walking sideways.

Their songs were subdued at times, suddenly changing to louder choruses to break the monotony. Songs of empowerment and self-affirmation enabled the women to praise one another; to boast that, though you could catch a fly in their mouths, they were not stupid; that they were not seekers who became he-goats without any decency; and that you did not identify witches by looking for horns on the heads of women. They had enemies, as you have yours and I have mine, but they believed they would overcome them, and their choruses affirmed their faith:

> The hills and mountains look arrogantly up to God
> What can mere hills do to the Almighty
> The one capable of leveling them at will.
> A child does not stand on a viper to wish bad luck to the viper
> You do not stand amidst termites and ants and wish them evil
> Tie all our enemies to trees
> With the ropes that they use to tie us

When a war arrives, we will escape to the land of peace
Our enemies will be left behind to die
The head of the dead does not hide lice
A doll has no intestines
We shall be free of them.

As they sang of seeing the end of their enemies, they wanted their lives to be prolonged:

We have seen the end of death
Surviving countless years the aged moon
Our tasks on earth are too many
Mine requires one hundred and twenty years
Yours cannot be completed in a thousand years
No one can count the sand on the beach
No child can count the number of leaves on a tall tree
Death has ended for us
Disease is over
Sadness is terminated.

What a song! A deadly song! We at Akanran had moved beyond this, caring not about death because we wanted to enjoy life nor about life because we wanted to conquer death. I was on an errand to collect a message because the end of the world was near. Why were the women saying something different, wanting to prolong their lives? If they were afraid, someone needed to tell them that corpses do not testify against themselves, that the enemies they were talking about did not care if they were alive or dead and would gladly sell them into slavery to purchase liquor and beef, enjoy both and laugh, praising their own deeds for their skills in tormenting, terminating, destroying. If the women were not careful, the houses would fall on them, as their enemies were not too far away and would not announce their coming, just as death never announces its time of visitation. Their enemies might not be aware of their location, I thought, but death, as the father-in-law of us all, knew everything. I felt like going back to Akanran, where we were praising death, asking it to choose any of us. Well, these women must not know that I hated that song.

I was possessed by evil thoughts. If these women were afraid of death, why did I not kill them myself? I began to think that they were performing rituals to stop the war. My mind went to the hallway where I watched the preparations being made to combine herbs and incantations to stop diseases and sickness, sorcery, bewitchment, and evil. Anyone seeking death, I assured myself, should be friendly to diseases and witches, not opposed to them. They wanted death to discriminate, to take the men and leave the women, to take the sons and leave the daughters, to unbalance the demography so that there would be more women than men, and each of the surviving men could marry more than ten wives.

These clever women did not allow me to conclude my personal reflections. They interrupted my reflections by changing their songs to curses, asking their enemies to offend the ancestors; to break taboos and thus anger the gods; to invite witches to their bedrooms; to see their days bewitching one another, with good luck on Sunday and bad luck following on Monday; and to see their night disappearing twice before daytime, as one problem followed another before they could solve the first. These songs were powerful, compellingly strong ritual incantations of anger. As they were filled with anger, curses poured out like rain: Should their enemies' affairs be healed by daytime, other problems would follow by night; they would be sick in the middle of the night when the doctors were asleep; the dawn would break into smaller dawns; when they toiled to dig a well, they would not be around to drink from it.

On October 26, the women held two meetings in the backyard; what they spoke about in the rooms, only they knew. About forty of them, calling themselves the *Egbe Apetebi*, gathered for deliberations. I was originally under the impression that these were retailers who had formed a guild to discuss prices and how to send a delegation to the chiefs concerning issues of stalls and taxes. It was on October 26 that I knew that these were not traders but the wives of the babalawo in various cities and villages. I had never seen them before as a "band." Not that I did not know that babalawo do have wives; my father's babalawo, whom I visited several times, had at least three. So, being a babalawo's wife was an occupation of its own? Many of the women were already in the compound; others joined them very early, coming from as far away as Ikare in the far north of Yorubaland. In the evening of October 26, some members of the *Egbe Apetebi* joined in a second meeting, attended by many women. I called them the "Club of Sixteen," since they referred to themselves as *Eerindinlogun*, which in Yoruba means sixteen, but those who attended were more than that in number. They were female diviners who used sixteen cowries as their main device on the divination tray. Leku did not attend either meeting, perhaps because she was not a babalawo's wife and was not a member of the "Club of Sixteen." Nevertheless, the respect for her was apparent, as all knelt down to greet her.

I now understood that these women could not be defined by anatomy, as we all did in school, or by motherhood, as we all did at home, but by the new things that I was seeing and hearing. Leku was an *iya*, but she had no children, so this was not a motherhood label. She was superior to all of us, men and women alike. Leku was a man, as they often referred to her as "Kabiyesi," a title that can be rendered as "Excellency" and is reserved for male kings, or as "Baba Nla," the great father. Still in the same skin, she was a woman to others, but not as an *obinrin* (the Yoruba name for women), but as an *iya*, a superior elder. When men wanted something from her, they would lie down flat on the floor until she gestured to them to stand up. There were women like her, with knowledge and skills that gave them prestige and definitions beyond the association of women with motherhood. Some among the women had the skill to combine herbal knowledge with incantations to make their charms and medicines work, as in the *apetebi*. They were the powerful members of the "Club of Sixteen" who engaged in rituals. Leku knew how to perform rituals, and many could be caught whispering that Leku could kill anyone, but by what means I did not know.

In the meeting of the Club of Sixteen, they used signs and symbols that I did not understand, but that I clearly remember. They were trying to predict through divination; only their clients, not I, could know whether their predictions came to pass. Their signs and symbols were designed to invoke the forces of the cosmos, to attract spiritual energies to themselves so that they would become extra-human. I also thought that they wanted to exclude me from gaining insight into their knowledge. When I repeated what they did and even the incantations that I could write down and read, I saw no changes, no effect. It was like our school dramas where the incantations worked only on stage but not in real life. Why did their actions work and why did mine not do so? Or, as I told myself many times, perhaps theirs did not work either. Their incantations had been frozen in their language, tonality, and pronunciation, as if an adjustment or mispronunciation would prevent the charm or medicine from working.

The *apetebi* wore only a white garment tied around their bodies with the upper part uncovered. They all wore red beads and white *gele* (headgear), and they put red shawls on their right shoulders. These colors must have meant something to them. When their leader spoke, an obese woman whose rapid breath could be heard, they would all say *eleri-ipin a gbo*, that whosoever was controlling destiny and distributing favor and bad luck would affirm their statements. This was, perhaps, in reference to Orunmila, the god who controlled divination and who doubled as the god in charge of wisdom. As far back as the third year of primary school, all the students knew about destiny and Orunmila, how what they would become in the world was pre-determined before they were born. Worried parents wanted to know the fate of their children from the very day of their birth, and they would go to the babalawo or the *apetebi*. Should the news be bad, as in the child growing up to become a thief, a criminal, or a beggar, the parents had to perform sacrifices to alter the child's destiny. Even when the destiny was good, as in the child destined to become a king, the parents had to perform sacrifices to prevent enemies from changing the course of events. Good or bad, the *apetebi* and their husbands would make a living, thanks to Orunmila. Since Orunmila was invisible, clients had to take the words of the *apetebi* as gospel truth.

On this day, the women were not being consulted. They were scheming to put sand in the eyes of their enemies. Their bodies and existence were faraway nations to their enemies who saw them as foreigners, who sent no ambassadors of peace but wicked generals of war. When a child's fingers have been burned, he begins to dread fire: The *apetebi* wanted to confront their enemies but were probably afraid of what lay before them. The *apetebi* were imagining themselves as future orphans; they probably knew that orphans could not care for one another, consumed by sorrow, their resources depleted, powerless. They wanted to cry, borrowing the trick of a child who knows that unless it cries, it will stay wrapped and confined to the back of the mother, suffering. They gathered not to provide counsel, not to engage in romantic fraternity, but to consider their options, commune with their gods and goddesses, and not to behave like children who rejected advice and did a lot of crying as adults. They now needed Orunmila more than he needed them to propagate his name. The *apetebi* joined others in making herbal preparations for which they also needed Orunmila, the god who could empower the efficacy of a charm, a god more powerful than the charm itself.

October 28, nightfall: Whistles were heard, coming from mouths, not instruments. They could not whistle well, and I added my own, much louder, although I had no idea why they were sounding. I knew how to whistle to call attention to myself, call my friends, or imitate birds. The women understood what the whistles meant: Everyone began to gather at the back of the house, with many holding clay lamps to light the place.

The light attracted some insects, and if they made the mistake of getting too close to the clay, they were instantly roasted.

A huge statue of someone, man-like, was placed in the middle of the group. His head was covered with palm oil. The upper part of his body, attached to his large head, was blackened, and the oil was dripping from the head down his torso to the stool that he stood on. The stool had been placed on a large wooden tray, and the oil dripped on to it. On the tray were coins, cowries, and food items. The lifeless head was being treated as if it was alive, receiving food to nourish him, oil to cleanse his body, songs and praises to make him happy. Some women did not even cover their breasts, perhaps to entice him into some kind of sexual fantasy. The women took turns in kneeling before him, as if in fear or just out of reverence. As this man was being honored, without bothering to smile back at those showing him affection or to open his sealed mouth to express gratitude for the kindness being showered on him, he was receiving more oil, more pleading. I believed that Orunmila had now arrived from heaven.

Alas! It was not whom I thought. Once again, these women had made my primary and high school education useless. I was fooled again. The person whose stomach is full may reject bad food. My stomach was empty, and bad food would do. If an orphan lacks the string to cling on to life, he will pay a visit to his dead parents. I must look and learn to survive. Not to play along was to replace water with saliva in the battle of putting an end to a raging fire. The revelation of this strange man was to come through the women.

It was Osanyin! I had previously encountered him in 1965, when a classmate of mine took me to a Baba Olosanyin to obtain a love potion for Sali, another schoolmate infatuated with a girl called Rísí. Then, the Baba Olosanyin spoke to an object hidden behind a curtain that spoke in a strange voice that the Baba Olosanyin interpreted to us. His charm did not work, a failure attributed to inappropriate use on our part.

So here was the man at last. Apologies! The god himself: sitting down dignified, not boiling and curdling. The women might appear bigger than he was, but greater things were sought from him; a positive outcome a thousand times his size was expected. My concentration level was intensified, without any room for fatigue or sleep, the two enemies of progress. I had seen Sango and Ogun, the masquerades, and now, for the first time, I could see the material manifestation of another Yoruba deity. His height was not revealed, his head was not plaited like that of Sango, the always-angry god who revealed a feminine side as his male disciples dressed up like women. The left side of the face was bare; the right bore three horizontal marks. His eyes were wild; his lips were closed. His neck was sturdy enough to hold up his wild chest. In 1965, I thought that Osanyin was living in heaven and the Baba Olosanyin was the only one who could reach him. His voice was distant. Today, he was voiceless, deaf, and probably blind. Did he arrive from heaven thoroughly exhausted?

There were now two of us in the compound, both of whom could look but not talk; a dead observer who was being propitiated and a live one who was not allowed to speak until spoken to. What was Osanyin doing here tonight? I could not ask, but the women again came to my aid. They were appealing to Osanyin to make their herbs work, not to allow the charms to become worthless. They were kneeling down to beg him, like a mighty patron. One woman put some powder in a bowl and asked Osanyin to make her *iyere osun* work well. This was the powder she put on a divination tray, on which she traced some visible symbols with her fingers and then interpreted the meanings to her clients. The celebration, singing, and dancing to appeal to Osanyin produced an excellent result: The women became tired, and all eventually had to sleep.

When I woke up the next morning, Osanyin was gone, traveling all by himself back to where he had come from. I, Omo Iya, as these women called me, retained my position as the only man left standing; Osanyin, the one with the name, a good name that was expected to always bring a good omen, had left to deliver tons of messages and grant wishes and requests. Osanyin's style, full of trickery, was not an act of cowardice but of courage and wisdom. He knew what the women wanted. I was yet to collect my own message. Life is full of hardships; and my journey had opened my eyes to see, to experience, to sleep, and to change, providing the knowledge and adventure that created pain in the heart. Misfortune, as many do believe, can follow ignorance. Knowledge, too, could bring its own misfortune. I did not know what Leku wanted, and I was not allowed to ask Osanyin. I was being slowly cut into pieces while still alive: Having ambition and lacking knowledge has been likened to being a ship on dry land. No matter how long the genealogy is, the story stops when it reaches the last child, the future redeemer who combines hope with fear. If Osanyin could arrive and leave without notice, I, too, could do the same. The god's presence had produced its first blessing: He gave me the idea that I could leave the compound. To me, for Leku to complain about my departure was like leaving a big dog alone but continuing to complain about a small one. A friend of a thief is a thief! I was now a friend of Osanyin—he arrived at night and left at dawn. I made up my mind in the morning that I had retained a rope around my neck for too long, and it was time to untie it. I would wait for many hours, until darkness, allowing the sky to forecast the moment that I would hit the horn of a cow. As I pulled away the hoof and ran, the only thing the women guards could do was to call me a bad boy.

In the very middle of the night on October 29, I had hoped to rely on nature to wake me up before I bolted, but Leku woke me up. Since I always slept in the same place in the hallway, the left-hand corner of the entrance to the backyard, I could easily be located by anyone. No one chose this spot for me. I chose it, so that I could have access to the backyard where many activities were going on and also see whatever was happening in the hallway. When I made up my mind to leave, the corner slot became a wise choice, as I could get out, turn either to the left or right side alley, and refuse to obey the women when they asked me to stop. None had seen my courage among them; they need not see me cross the flooded river to know that I had courage just as wearing shoes to walk in the desert with its cold and heat does not mean that one is brave. I was thinking of being clever, not of being brave, so that I could gain knowledge, not courage. If they were hiding their wisdom from me, I could as well choose the corner to conceal my folly. After all, my stay had not been rewarded; the sweat of the dog is hidden in its hair.

Leku walked me through the hallway and led me to the front of the house. I was confused as to what she was up to. As quiet as she was, she was full of tricks and surprises. She did not know that I had made up my mind to leave. For me to announce my exit or now ask her where she was leading me was to open the mouth of a cobra to see its teeth. Did Leku know my mind, and was she now leading me to the beehive to disturb the nest and release the bees in hundreds to sting me? My mind was instantly clouded. As she walked too slowly, I clenched my teeth and tried to walk like a snail behind her. Both of us were now engaged in an affair without a nose.

When we reached the front of the house, the women who had been keeping vigil outside came forward. When they saw Leku, they dispersed. She crossed the road to the other side. It was dark, and the light from her lamp was not strong. There was probably now a message to give to others, but certainly not a careless one: Her tongue had now arrived to sew things together, although Leku's tongue would never spread beyond her mouth. Leku did not have a yellow mouth, as those with yellow mouths communicate unreliable words, and they must be ignored.

Since she did not greet me or ask how I had endured for so long, how the pinch from the shoe tormented my foot, surely Leku must have been ready to give me a package for Pasitor. But Leku had no package, did not tie any to her wrapper, and the only thing she had on her was the lamp. Where then was the package that I had been waiting for all along? Blood rushed to my veins, but Leku could not see it. Divining cowries were fighting one another: The crisis was so great that the matter could no longer be resolved by the gods. I kept quiet, not aiming at walking about town with my belly, a foolish kind of behavior.

Then came the very low voice with which Leku spoke, asking me to deliver a package of words, not of objects. I must tell Pasitor the following:

1.) The moon and the sun do not hold a meeting; one is not available during the day and the other must work at night;

2.) The cat, the tiger, and the lion are family members; all cherish raw meat; and

3.) In the rivulet of blood, a spoonful collected cannot tell us whose blood it is; in the house of Death, fresh and dry skulls litter the ground for Death to walk over.

Leku then placed her right hand on my head, said some meaningless words and phrases, and concluded that the message was forever sealed in my memory. Indeed, it has been sealed there, word for word.

We crossed the road back to the house; she handed over the lamp to me and asked me to leave immediately. I wanted to leave anyway, but now my departure was official, sanctioned, and the mission, although it had taken many more days than expected, was successful. Patience had now given birth to a baby: success.

When I wanted to move to the left of the house, she asked me to go to the right and told me never to make any left turn unless that was the only option open to me. When I asked how I would avoid a left turn, she said to make a right turn in a circle, and then walk backwards to the left, then turn. I did not understand the reasons behind any of her words or her instruction to avoid left turns.

I had barely walked a quarter of a mile when the lamp went dead, blown out by strong winds. I had no oil to add to the lamp and no matches to ignite the wick. I was now like a hungry traveler on a desolate road without access to food who must decide to die of hunger or eat a rat, a snake, or even a cockroach. This was not a mistake of my own making, a printer's error too late to fix.

It was too dark to go back to the house, too dark to move forward. I must stop immediately: Stubbornness is destructive. I must protect myself: Vultures go after a child, the hawk after the hen. Darkness is a sister and brother to a thief. I was not a thief about to prey in the middle of the night: There was nothing I carried on me to support an accusation of theft against me. But I could be a thief about to steal, a danger to the community, a spoiled baby fond of always excreting on the mother. Whatever I said if I was caught standing there would not be believed, like someone claiming that he told the hare to go and sleep. I must conclude my journey; when a hyena carried a valuable item, only a big fight could dispossess him of it. I was this hyena in the dark.

I blamed myself. It had not occurred to me that the lamp could go out. Everyone in the city, even those who lived in houses with electricity, knew that one had to cup his palms around a lamp to prevent the wind from blowing it out. There was no house without a lamp; at the very least there was a lantern that relied on kerosene. If the master in the main house enjoyed as much electricity as he wanted, it was not always so for his house boy, his driver, his gate man—the poor men and women confined to the "boys' quarters," where the maids and the wretched of the earth lived so as not to disturb the boss, known as the *oga*, and his wife and children. But, if the *oga* wanted to sneak to the "boys' quarters" to have a quick dalliance with the maid, he needed the lantern! The lantern could be dimmed, but the stories of men and their affairs move forward not backward and require no light to narrate them.

My mind was not on the lamp but on the message. I kept reciting the words like a poem, not reciting them to my ears but memorizing them in my heart. Moon and sun? Cat, tiger, and lion? Blood and skull? I had no clue whatsoever. The acts of God, like those of Osanyin, were riddles. I had to think slowly; rashness eats body and soul, both at once. I would repeat an item of Leku's message many times, as if to abandon a repetition was to lose a career.

I sat down on the ground, very uncomfortably, as some pebbles pricked my skin. I felt some pain, but my mind was fixed on the message. If you are roasting locust for snacks, remember not to blink! If you do, all is lost to the heat, and the tiny insects become ashes. These messages were not the familiar riddles that I had solved for years or part of school games, moonlight activities, post-soccer talk. "What is so bold as to walk in front of the king's palace without showing courtesy to the king?" After several attempts, the boy who mentioned "erosion, the walking water following a downpour," gave the right answer and received an ovation.

Dozens of riddles came to me, one after another, and I tried to answer all of them. After a while, due to repetition, one got to know all the answers to the riddles until new ones were borrowed from other cultures. Leku's message was not one of these riddles. What could it be? I had been expecting to collect herbs and objects. Leku had given me words.

It was quiet, as if I was living in a cemetery. I was so fond of talking to people that I became talkative early in life. I could talk to myself if no one was listening. When I sleep, I talk as well. My job is to talk. For the first time, I began to listen, not to people but to the sound of the darkness and the forest. It was then that I noticed that insects and plants were talkative like me, only I did not understand their language. The wind forced the leaves to express themselves as they danced to its music moving soft, slow, and strong. The trees supplied calmness with musical droplets from branches that had collected more than their fair share of previous rain. Vines entangled with trees, and other plants felt uneasy that their hosts were complaining, and they dropped their heads in remorse. Frogs and toads jumped, and their landing produced its own sound, louder than the crawling of millipedes and centipedes. Porcupines were growing new thorns, the older ones being pushed out and protesting with cries as they dropped to the ground, where the worms complained that they hated them. Crickets were rude, but maybe there were some other kinds of insects who were awake and holding a vigil. When the cocks and hens made their loud noises, the day was about to break, which would then force the Muslims to wake up to add their own disturbing noises, louder than those of the animals in the bush. They, too, needed lamps to reach their mosques where, unlike the innocent insects, they had a bundle of confessions to make and sins to atone for.

After a while, I noticed scattered lights in different locations. None were produced by modern electricity. I still could not move, as I was unable to see the footpaths. Dangerous thoughts crept into my mind. What about a snake bite or even scorpions? A hare that was lucky to escape being caught was afraid of noise. The slightest noise put more evil thoughts in me. There was nothing I could do except fight back. But with what? I became one of the women that I had just left behind, solving problems with incantations:

> It cannot be
> No enemy can conquer me
> If the enemy approaches from the front
> I will turn into a viper that stores its venom in front of its tongue

If the enemy appears from the back
I will become a scorpion with venom in its tail
If the enemy appears from the left
I will become a porcupine with needles that pinch
If the enemy appears from the right
I will become bees that sting
If the enemy comes from above
I will become the precipice that kills the mountain climber
If the enemy comes from below
I will turn into a large ocean that drowns the swimmer.

I was emboldened by my own incantation. So, without even the roots and bark, the words could instill courage. I had discovered why they worked. Courage: Choose your own bull in a fight; don't praise the cow until it comes home; stop feeding your dog if it cannot bite the thief; and, if you cannot stop the hyena from damaging your hut, do not build one. Isola, be strong: When your goat acquires scabies, kill it; hide the tail of the sheep so that greedy thieves will not see it and steal it by force; and let your bull be celebrated for its scars. My cognomen always worked well to instill courage, to connect me with Ibadan's political and military strategy of dealing with problems and conflicts not in terms of negotiations but of total defeat of its enemy.

What about a dangerous animal like a tiger on the prowl? I had only seen such animals in two places: in the textbooks and in the zoo located at the University of Ibadan which we visited on public holidays, walking long distances to see the animals. Apete had no tigers, I assured myself. If such animals existed before, we now only read about them in books. Wild game was a delicacy, and those before us had put all those animals in their stomachs, leaving us to enjoy only the stories. The remaining animals took their revenge on us. They began to eat the grass; the grasshoppers sucked the vegetables; the mice consumed the sticks; and the grass that belonged to the goats and cows was only those blades in our bellies. The land was damaged, producing less and less food. The women were bitten by lice, and the men began to look for sticks to kill the last quails. As the land became deforested, men turned to men to continue the fight.

Man became the source of my worry. If you had a choice of one object to fear or be worried about, leave the animals alone as they are predictable. You know that tigers and lions like meat, whether of goat, dog, or man. They are predictable. A man is not: He can appear gentle but be a silent killer; he can be fierce-looking but loving. He can love you in the morning and hate you in the evening. Although I thought I was alone, men could be dangerous, as they might be hiding not far away. A madman could just be some feet away. If he was fully mad, expect a fight; half-mad, he could talk and then fight; and newly mad, he would want you in his company to do things together so that those who saw you would not know the difference between the fool and the wise, the sane and the insane. The mentally ill slept everywhere in the city as their households had rejected them, not wanting to associate themselves with those who could tarnish their reputation and lineage history. Madmen revealed the secret that all was not well in the compound. The mad warned others to be careful, that the lineage could pass on the disease to others. The women among them, suffering from complicated depression and hallucinations, who declared that they were witches who had killed the children of co-wives, their husbands, or even their own children, were stoned to death. I had seen such incidents, and I was appalled that anyone would inflict such pain on others. Witches could be sought to take care of such a woman, I once told a classmate, instead of hitting her with rocks. In primary school, we learned to avoid what would degenerate into rock-throwing, as the consequences could be devastating.

Suppose an angry madman or a witch was not too far away? The thought was frightening. Far worse was the thought, not of the insane, but of the very sane looking for body parts or a full human to make money magic. If someone was very rich and the source of wealth could not be ascertained, the belief was that he had used a human being for money. People did; whether it worked or not was a different matter. Imagination ran wild about how it worked. One was that hidden in the rich man's mansion was the human he used, dead but fully embalmed, kneeling down with a calabash on his head. As the rich man used the necessary words of command, he opened the calabash to find freshly minted money. Many people believed that body parts could be used for powerful charms. I began to imagine myself being sliced into parts, with my kidneys roasted along with herbs for someone to drink or added to egusi soup, drenched in palm oil to eat with pounded yam so that a man could have a long life. My skull would be crushed and pounded, the soft brain mixed with spices to make pepper soup, which a beautiful lady would serve to her rich boyfriend as a love potion. The man would eat it, become a boy, and begin to think like a child crying over the girl who had now become a toy that could not be taken away. My liver would be needed by an ailing chief to cure his fatal cancerous disease. My fingers would be required by a trader who sought a prosperity charm to attract teeming customers and make him wealthy. My tongue would be used to replace that of the deaf man so that he could talk, and they would pluck out my eyes to give them to the governor's mother suffering from blindness. My thoughts about how other parts would be used were suddenly interrupted by human sounds.

I heard faint voices from behind my back, of women talking as they walked in my direction. I could not risk their seeing me, as I would be treated as something else: maybe an *olugbo*, or an *abiku*, or an *oku*. No choice would be considered good to them; all were bad omens. *Oku* (death) converted itself into a human being who walked around with a heavy club, ready to take the next person bound for heaven. Having clubbed many to death during the day, at night he rested in the forest. *Olugbo* was the immortal king of the forest, and *oku* could never kill him; both agreed to share space and live together as rivals. *Olugbo* would occasionally come out of the jungle to look for food, good fresh blood of humans, his main delight. He was not always as thirsty and hungry as *oku*, and he did not have to appear every day. *Abiku* was a child born to die—the child died, but the soul kept wandering in search of the womb of a pregnant woman whose stomach it would enter to come back to the world as a new baby. *Abiku* was just a temporary visitor to the jungle, a tenant to *oku* and *olugbo*. As long as *abiku* did not stay in one spot, his landlords left him alone.

If the women were to suddenly see me at that unholy hour, they would scream, drop whatever they were carrying, and flee in all directions, shouting for help. Like scared birds, they would take to flight and refuse to perch until they became fully exhausted. *E gba mi! eepa!! eeparipa!!!* As they ran, one would imagine *olugbo* running after her; the other would visualize *oku*; and whoever was pregnant or praying for a child would see *abiku*. When they reached a secure place, they would report Isola as three separate elements, figments and fragments of their imaginations. Were any person to doubt their stories, they would pounce on that person as useless, ungodly, anti-progressive, and satanic. Calling truthful people all liars? The women would combine to become vultures to excrete on the doubter. The conversation ended, no longer than the tail of a mole.

I retreated into the bush. As I sensed that the women were coming nearer, I retreated further so that they would not see me. As they approached, carrying their various lamps, I noticed that they were all pregnant, and my mind immediately went back to those pregnant women I had followed to the compound. Their number was increasing, as one lamp represented one person. I was not interested in counting the number of lamps. They were also carrying baskets and sacks, which looked like those in which we put pouches at Kusela.

When the last person had passed by, I waited a little before I moved forward. It was too late to follow them, or to even use their lanterns and lamps to help me see. If I appeared from behind them, I would be no threat to them unless the last woman heard my footsteps. She would look back and scream for help. When a jackal crosses to another place, it hides its tail, pretending to be another animal. If a cow excretes all its dung, it will invite hunger, and lose its weight. Smart quails wait for all hunting sticks to break before appearing.

The day broke. I resumed my journey, passing through the city, seeing familiar places. Lorries were going to the villages, but I had no money to take one. I had to walk well over thirty miles back to Akanran, a route that I knew so well. Fruits were everywhere, and I begged for water. Unless the request was made to a madman, one must not beg for water and be denied. A hawk finds its food through the help of the shepherd. And unless a thief wanted to steal fruits to sell, a hungry person was allowed to help himself to fruits, even corn, along the way. Where the farmer did not want you to pick anything, he would put, in visible display, an *ale*, a charm made of a combination of various innocuous items such as corncobs, snail shells, and red pepper, to indicate that evil would befall you if you stole. *Ale* pricked your conscience, telling you directly that you were a common thief, an unworthy person in the community of people with integrity.

When Pasitor saw me, his face betrayed his joy and relief. He looked like a cow licking its calf. He had probably had no way of searching for me or Leku. He would have expected me back on the day that I left or the next. As I later heard, the school had reported my absence and declared me missing. My mother searched the city in vain, and she was told that I had gone to Mokola, the military barracks where the Nigerian army recruited soldiers to fight in the war against Biafra. Mokola had become a key center: Contractors selling food, raw and cooked, flooded the place; new nightclubs for drinking and prostitution were established; and secondary school students of my age, seeking to experiment with marijuana and loose women, saw Mokola as an attractive place. There were job openings through which you could obtain the money needed for a new lifestyle. As long as you appeared tall or big enough and lied, saying you were eighteen years old, you qualified to become a new recruit. Pasitor did not know whether or not I had ended up at Mokola.

He only assured everyone that I would be back and enjoined them to read Psalm 23 seven times a day. This homework would keep those looking for me busy enough. Pasitor's psalm was like magic for the Christians who saw the Bible as a ritual object with the psalms acquiring the power of incantations. My mother certainly saw the psalms as words with magical power. Muslims wrote quranic passages on slates, and then washed them with water for their clients to drink. There were Christians who treated many biblical passages in the same way, even going to imams to write them in ink on their slates, wash them with water into a bowl, and then take them like herbs to cure whatever ailment was afflicting them.

When the joy of seeing me subsided, Pasitor took me out of the church to the very compound where my journey had begun. I was eager to deliver the message, but Pasitor asked me not to, saying that the message required more than two eyes and ears to receive it. If I was an elephant capable of carrying its load, Pasitor was not big enough to receive it from me. All my rivulets had now become a large river that many wanted to swim in. Pasitor and the others had been waiting for the rain with the big drops. I saw myself as a star, competing with the moon in importance. Leku's words had turned me into a rich boy, a live reed stuck in the mud.

Unlike before, I was allowed to enter the house, where Pasitor joined many other men in a crowded room. Their "chairman," wearing an *agbada* (a large, free-flowing garment), thanked me for assisting them and asked me to deliver the message, telling me neither to add nor subtract, change the order, or forget anything. This was quite easy since I had memorized the strange words and recited them to myself times without number. Whether it was Leku's hand placed on my head or my ability to remember things learned by rote, I delivered the words as they were originally rendered. Line by line; not a word more, not a word less.

Panic struck all the faces. Elephant hunters are mobilized with only one word: unite! They were now united in sorrow as they looked at me, the elephant with the big message. Raised heads were lowered as if someone just died, jaws were widely opened, and flies would have an easy passage all the way to the throat. All eyes stared at me. A messenger has no malice; malice is the one who sent him. The king has excreted in public; you want to run away from the smell, but doing so without permission will bring trouble. Someone has to clean up and collect the feces. My job was done, turning my riches into a mist that evaporated in the twinkle of an eye.

The man who broke the silence added to my confusion with his explanation: "*Iru aroko buruku wo leyi?*" (What kind of bad *aroko* is this?).

*Aroko* was a coded message. As Pasitor later told me, it was a way of communicating in code between two parties. Code words included names of people, animals, food items, and the like. They could be given in combination with objects to express messages of peace, war, reconciliation, and much more. A few among those present who understood the words began to interpret the messages:

1) Many of us would die;
2) The death could not be prevented and would include both the young and old;
3) Enemies would never be reconciled; and
4) Friends would betray one another; trust would be broken.

The mood was gloomy. They had been expecting a message of comfort or a solution to their problem. What they got did not make them happy. The house of a rich man is always beautiful from the outside to strangers who do not know about the strife within. The powerful were inside, as those outside would be thinking, but it was a house of sorrow.

I understood what an *aroko* was, how coded words could be decoded by those who understood. I became fascinated by *aroko* and requested Pasitor to introduce me to those men who explained Leku's message in ways that others accepted. No one had ever mentioned *aroko* to me in school; perhaps the schoolteachers did not know about it either. As I came to understand *aroko*, I realized that objects and words opened a library of meaning. Perhaps Leku had sent an object preceding my words so that the objects were then combined with the words to reach the gloomy conclusion. *Aroko* delivered communications, and replies were offered also in a symbolic manner so that if you sent words and embers of fire to me to indicate trouble and war, I could send a calabash full of water to you to indicate that I had the means to quench your fire; or I could send you additional firewood to say that we should keep fighting. To receive a string of six cowries was being asked to visit the sender; ten in a string meant that this visitation was urgent. If your reply was to send a string of two cowries, you were rejecting the offer of visitation and announcing that you were no longer on good terms. If two were sent to you without prior conversation, you would expect bad news: Your father or mother was probably dead. When other objects were added to those strings of cowries, the contents of the message changed: Add the red tail feather of a parrot to a string of six cowries, and you would be telling the person that he had outstayed his welcome; change the feather to that of a guinea fowl, and the message would change to one of goodwill.

"Baba Chairman," as the head of this gathering was called, adjourned the meeting with a very sad face and in a dejected voice. When someone asked him to make an effort to call a babalawo to make sacrifices, he dismissed him as an ignorant man who did not know that Leku did not talk lightly and knew more than any babalawo in the land. "*Awon aye lo ran an si wa*"; Leku sent them a message she had received from powerful forces that no sacrifices could change. He told everyone to double all their energies, to commission more charms, and to watch out for evil forces.

As Pasitor and I stepped out of the house, pregnant women with baskets on their heads arrived. They were not the women that I had previously seen but another set, all dressed alike. I had now seen three different sets. They unloaded their baskets. All the men in the house came out to receive them. The women explained the contents of each pouch, and the men took one of each.

It was then that I knew what the pouches were meant for. Some were to wear; some were to break open and use the contents to make incisions on heads, chests, and arms; some contained powder to pour into a liquid and drink. Pasitor took samples of all of them and asked me to do the same. I obliged, not just out of curiosity but out of belief. I began to wear the pouches.

As the women were explaining the contents of the pouches, the world of the classroom and the public world began to merge. In school dramas and textbooks, I had heard about how the Yoruba had charms to enable people to disappear, to shorten long distances, to withstand machete cuts and gunfire. On October 29, I saw them firsthand—not their efficacy but their applications. Drama gave way to belief. As the men were collecting the pouches, pregnancies were disappearing, delivering not babies but all sorts of hidden objects such as tortoises, cow horns, feathers, and bottles containing a variety of ingredients including live worms. I had not seen anything like that before, not even in any of the school plays. The women then dropped the wrappers they had used to tie the objects to themselves. All the wrappers were then collected and set on fire. The ashes were collected by Baba Chairman. Pasitor told me that the ashes would be used for medicine.

Two days later, various rules were announced, and responsibilities were assigned to men, women, and teenagers. The land had now eaten the hair, as *aroko* would code the message that no one was happy, that what we were all doing was not right, and that we were experiencing a terrible situation. I could not split the hair. I received my own task. We were told to await orders, from whom I did not know. I was anxious to start and restless, but even Pasitor did not know when we would strike.

There was a big mountain as the screen, to use another *aroko*, between us and them, meaning that we could not see our enemies and know what they were planning, and they could not see us either. The first to climb the mountain would be the first to see the valley, either staying on top, hiding from fear of what he saw, or descending to the valley to fight and conquer, to fight and be defeated, or to fight and retreat, re-climbing the mountain. In a contest between the hare and the plateau, the one would boast that it is swift, and the other would say that it is vast. Whether you won or lost, the other party would still attempt to put the fallen branch back onto the tree, and neither would ever collect their vegetables from the heart, which means that the fight was only suspended and would never be over. The valley could be a deep pool that would swallow you up as soon as your legs were inside it. When you go to war, do not stay at the back, and do not stay in front. If you stay at the back, when enemies attack from the rear, you are the first to die; if you stay in front, when enemies attack from the front, you are the first to die.

I had swallowed a stone, making me as strong as a rock, ready to take risks: If you hit me with an adze, you will injure yourself, and I will damage the blade and the scraper; if I hit you, you are crushed. Throw the arrows and spears, they hit the rock and fall. Shoot, the bullet is wasted, falling to the ground. Box with me, and your hands are injured. Bite me, and your teeth will fall out. I do not need a stick to fight a wild dog; I can use my legs. The man with the red eyes does not frighten me. The stout man is no stronger than the thin one. The stone inside my belly will not be digested.

*Mo ti di omo a gbo "sa," mo sa*
*A gbo "ya," mo ya*
*Mo b'erin ja, mo d'eyin e mu*
*Mo b'efon ja, mo diwo e mu*
*Mo b'ekun ja, mo gba enu e mu*
*Mo leke won.*

I heard "run," I refused to run
I heard "yield," I refused to yield
I held the elephant's tooth to wrestle with it

I held the buffalo's horns to wrestle with it
I held the tiger's jaws to wrestle with it
I won.

I wanted to stay only in front or at the back, not in the middle. Remove the mountain screen so that the man who has swallowed the rock can see.

# CHAPTER 4

# Not Peace but a Sword

✦ ✦ ✦

*Think not that I am come to send peace on earth: I came not to send peace,*
   *but a sword.*
*For I am come to set a man at variance against his father, and the daughter*
   *against her mother, and the daughter in law against her mother in law.*
*And a man's foes shall be they of his own household.*
*He that loveth father or mother more than me is not worthy of me: and he that*
   *loveth son or daughter more than me is not worthy of me.*
*And he that taketh not his cross, and followeth after me, is not worthy of me.*
*He that findeth his life shall lose it: and he that loseth his life for my sake shall*
   *find it.*

(Matthew 10:34–39, King James Version)

Gabriel was feisty and fiery, although not always so: He could be gentle
one moment and combative a moment later; soft-spoken at this hour
and hard-hitting the next. He could smile and frown, only a few seconds
apart. I preferred it when his lips were closed, but, as he loved to laugh
occasionally, his uneven teeth, the two front ones out of proportion to
the rest, revealed an ugliness that sealed lips would hide. Words came
from his mouth much faster than you could write them down, and you
could not follow his logic or train of thought. Amazingly, words could
also refuse to leave his mouth, when, tongue-tied, Gabriel put himself
in a reflective mode or just pretended to be listening to whatever you
were saying. He could never really be a listener, sharing nothing at all
with James the Less, the disciple of Jesus whose voice is hardly heard in

the scriptures. Gabriel shared much more of the Apostle Peter's impetuous, headstrong, and bold manner. Gabriel's words communicated love and hate, peace and anger, loyalty and skepticism. When Gabriel spoke to the elderly, he sounded gentle, tender-hearted. When he spoke to the young, he was harsh, cruel, and impatient. When he spoke about heavenly figures, he was subdued, humble, polite. He was a friend and an enemy: He chose both on his own terms, displaying his temper to his enemies and offering exaggerated promises to his friends.

He could bend his head and talk for a long time, and he could look at you in the face and say just a few words, or utter none. He was short, tall, taller, and tallest, adjusting his height to his messages or intentions. His natural height was about five feet two inches, but this was artificially elongated when he stood on a stool or climbed up to a pulpit. In the pulpit, he was taller than all around him. He became the tallest, which made him proud, really proud, when he went to the *Ori oke*, the hill, and he went there with regularity. *Oke,* a Yoruba word for hill or mountain, was not translated even when Gabriel spoke in bad English about his visitations: "I was at *oke* for three days and three nights," as *oke* had a different meaning to his audience, rather than simply meaning Gabriel was climbing a mountain. When he was ascending, it was with less fanfare, reciting Psalm 121:1 multiple times to all listening ears: "*I lift up my eyes to the hills / where does my help come from?*"

Gabriel had turned the *oke* into a powerful spiritual symbol. I climbed the same hills for the fun of it, my favorite hill being Oke Sapati, from which I could see the entire center of the city. Gabriel and his companions began to change the name of *oke* from Oke Agugu to Oke Samuel, from Oke Agbo to Oke Sinai, from Oke Lalupon to Oke Maria. Changing the names allowed other people's histories in the Bible to migrate to our own land so that our *oke* now became the hill where Moses received his revelation from God, where Jesus wept, where Elijah fought with idolaters, where King Saul committed suicide, or where Moses twice received the Ten Commandments. If *oke* were immoveable, they were no longer so in terms of the mythologies that surrounded them. If you used to look for snails at Oke Agugu, as I did for many years, now you could run into Moses or Elijah there and have a pleasant conversation with them if you had faith in the right quantity.

Gabriel's followers leaked the secret that the prophet was going to fast for three days, or seven, or eleven, always an odd number. The number of days was related to the purpose: If his fast was for the nation, to protect you and me, or to prevent disasters and state collapse, it would last for twenty-one days. For his own renewal, three days should be enough. By the time they mentioned seven days, we knew the fast was to obtain power from the angels or divine guidance from God. If Gabriel needed to fight supernatural battles, cast out demons, kill a witch, or destroy a sorcerer, he had to fast for no less than nine days. To defy the politicians or repel spiritual attacks aimed at destroying him, he had to keep fasting until he received the sign to stop.

As he descended from the *oke*, he would be ringing his bell, a very large one that a boy sometimes carried on his head for the prophet until he needed it. Gabriel would ring the bell multiple times while proclaiming a message, which was revealed to him by no one else but Jesus or the angels who represented him. He would repeat the bell ringing and the revelation. He communed with heavenly bodies; and he affirmed that he saw the angels and Jesus. Thus at Ibadan, Gabriel could now confirm whether or not the masquerades were actually visiting from heaven for, as he told us, *oke* could become a place far removed from this world, an extraterrestrial universe where men cohabited with the archangels Michael and Gabriel, his namesake. He announced fresh dreams and their interpretations. With many more dreams than Joseph, the son of Jacob, or Daniel ever reported or interpreted, Gabriel had news for us, terrible warnings, ominous signs. I climbed the same *oke* that he did, and I saw nothing but wild grass and weeds. I was too unholy to see what he saw.

Gabriel's name was spreading far and wide. My peers and I were already calling him "Buoda Gebu," for Brother Gabriel, and jokingly asking those who offended us to go and see him for medication to cleanse their brains of insanity. If someone yelled at us, we would yell back: "Why not shout louder than Buoda Gebu?" No babalawo in the land was more powerful than Buoda Gebu, who claimed that he could cure leprosy, make the blind see, walk on the dirty Ogunpa River, survive any raging fire, and be with the lion in the same cage at the University of Ibadan without coming to any harm. We all wanted him to play with the lion, always hoping that one of us would actually tell him to lead us there. As one boy asked: "If the lion were to eat him, how could he see God without his flesh?" His flesh, replied another, would be put together by an angel!

Buoda Gebu was confident and arrogant: He proclaimed that no one could fight him, demolish him, destroy him, conquer him, or subdue him. Behind him was the unseen force greater than all other spirits and forces combined: the *olugbala*, that is, the savior. His *olugbala* changed from God to Jesus on one day, and to angels on the other; and at some other times to the biblical kings, notably Saul, David, or Solomon. We knew our gods, but we did not fully rely on them, as they were powerful but fallible. Sango was too quick to anger and Ogun too impatient. Buoda Gebu's *olugbala* had no fault and was reliable at all times.

It turned out that Buoda Gebu could not always rely on his *olugbala*. The story that spread like wildfire was that Buoda Gebu's landlord, a trader from one of those small Ijebu towns, actually conquered and humiliated him. When Buoda Gebu defaulted on his rent, the Ijebu landlord threw him out of his house, a "face-me-I-face-you" type of house with three rooms to the right and three rooms to the left, one common kitchen and a latrine (pit toilet) at the back. You had to line up to use the toilet and kitchen and had to learn to use your bed sheet to cover the door of the makeshift bathroom if you needed a shower. The smart ones competed with the ghosts in the middle of the night to use the bathroom and toilet. When you cooked, if you did not remember to remove your pot and food quickly, a co-tenant could steal from it.

The Ijebu landlord did not allow Buoda Gebu to take anything from his room, including his Bible. His wife and two children, all four of them crowded in a room that could only take a single bed, were thrown out with him, all wearing their only remaining clothes. His wife, who worshipped food next to God, begged the landlord to let her take her freshly made pot of soup with beef with them, but the landlord refused. The ruthless landlord took their possessions to the big market at Dugbe to sell them to those who dealt in second-hand items. As the landlord claimed, the proceeds from the sale did not even cover one-eighth of their outstanding debts. The *olugbala* abandoned Buoda Gebu to his ordeal.

Gabriel went back several times pleading to his landlord to return his Bible, but the Ijebu man refused, asking why his god did not give him the means to pay his rent. Either he was worshiping a fake god, or he was not sincere. His Bible, the Ijebu landlord assured him, already belonged to someone else, a person like him already blessed who could use it for greater blessing. Since the Bible had been touched by a miserable poor man, it could also transfer poverty to the new owner; in that case, he would not hesitate to throw it into a gutter. The gutter was everywhere, in front of all the houses, as there was no hidden sewage pipe. Houses released their dirty water into the streets, from a gutter that passed along their frontage. If you dropped a Bible into it, there was no point in picking it up; it could not be washed clean, as the stench in the gutter was like that of the pit. Both the backs and fronts of the modern houses smelled—feces at the back, urine at the front.

To Buoda Gebu, the Ijebu man was Satan on earth, and Buoda Gebu began to talk badly about him. Words became his weapons, and he put them to violent use. He brought Jesus, angels, and God from *oke* to meet the Ijebu landlord in the valley. Buoda Gebu walked around the city saying that the Ijebu people loved money more than lives. They would perish in heaven as was already foretold: *"What good is it for a man to gain the whole world, yet forfeit his soul?"* The Ibadan people loved this statement and clapped for him as they believed that the Ijebu worshipped mammon. His divinely inspired statement and the Ibadan opinion of the Ijebu converged. If the Ibadan were generous, the Ijebu were thrifty. If the Ibadan could display hospitality, giving you the last pot of soup they had, the Ijebu would starve themselves and, when hungry, put cassava powder in water and drink it to fill their stomachs. If the Ibadan would use the money meant for the school fees of their boys on palm wine mixed with liquor or spend it on their concubines, usually women divorced after short-lived marriages, the Ijebu would use the money to pay the school fees.

Buoda Gebu, in anger, invented a new history and genealogy for the Ijebu. To him, in his moment of zealousness and exuberance, they were not Yoruba, not part of the original group of children of Oduduwa, the ancestor of the Yoruba. One section of the Ijebu came from the Sudan, he said, which was why they were tall and light in complexion like the Arabs. This faction was comprised mainly of Muslims and the anti-Christ, and we were told that they were destined for hell, without any chance of salvation. The other faction came from the sea, just appearing one day from the Atlantic Ocean, some coming as fish and others as crocodiles who became humans. Buoda Gebu's landlord was one of those from the ocean: They had no sympathy for anyone, and their god was money. The Ibadan clapped for Buoda Gebu. The Ijebu could not be Yoruba like themselves, who were originally Oyo people before they migrated to their present home. As the Ibadan boasted, except for their warriors who defeated the Fulani and Hausa Islamic jihadists in the nineteenth century, the war-loving jihadists would have pushed the Ijebu to the ocean, back to where they originally came from anyway, for fishes and whales to devour them. The Ijebu had no "tribal marks" on their faces as the real Yoruba had, with their *pele* and *gonbo*. There were no people among them with a dignified personal cognomen such as Isola, Akanji, and Akanbi, and their girls were never circumcised.

Buoda Gebu was a merciless fighter, using his mouth instead of his fists, confusing prejudice with facts. To hit his landlord further, Buoda

Gebu revealed his love life, that he liked sex a great deal and his two wives were always begging for it. Polygamists never put their wives in the same room. Buoda Gebu told us that his landlord did this, and the talk horrified the Ibadan Alhajis, who put each wife in a separate room, while the Alhajis had their own personal rooms where only the wife whose turn it was could enter. All Ijebu women, to Buoda Gebu, were immoral and sex obsessed, and he reported the noises they made as their useless husband mounted them. He gave the innocent women a name, Gomer, which no Yoruba Christian bore because it carried the badge of prostitution. The Ibadan clapped for him. Criticized for not circumcising their daughters, Ijebu women were presented as loose and immoral, and their propensity for sex was attributed to the lack of circumcision. An Ibadan man could never go home to announce to his parents that he was in love with an Ijebu woman: He would be asked never to marry or to surrender to castration. This is why in many households at Ibadan they say that having an Egba person as a slave is a wasted investment and having an Ijebu woman as a wife is an exercise in futility. If you see a snake and an Ijebu man, they added, kill the man before the snake, as the Ijebu have twice the venom of a viper. The dislike and hatred were mutual: Surely both could not have been members of the same Yoruba race, but researchers are yet to find out which are the impostors.

If the Ijebu landlord had used his power to evict Buoda Gebu, the "evangelist," as he was also called, had used his mouth to rubbish his landlord and his entire tribe. Abusing the Ijebu before the people of Ibadan brought Buoda Gebu nothing but praise. If Buoda Gebu could not get converts by praising Jesus, he could get support by abusing the Ijebu. The support was evident when he went with a crowd to demand his Bible, once again. The landlord was not intimidated. He was adamant and boasted that if God himself appeared on earth, he would not release the Bible and that he had sent it to his hometown of Ijebu-Ere. *Ere* in Ibadan means "mud," creating an opening for Buoda Gebu to pray to God to let his landlord die in mud, for his assets to become mud, and for his offspring to perish in a flood, washed away with the mud. Buoda Gebu was gifted not only at praying but also at cursing, what he called "prayer in reverse." Buoda Gebu prophesied what would happen to the landlord for not releasing the Bible: He said that in years to come, the landlord would die, and his body would never be recovered. The landlord's household should expect attacks from frogs, worms, flies, and hail; one child would become blind; another would die of a tumor. Ijebu-Ere would become the homeland of deadly plague, just because it had a businessman as a son. Sure, as time went on, the Ogunpa River in the city had flooded its banks several times, houses had been destroyed, people had died and been washed away. Was the Ijebu landlord one of them? Both Buoda Gebu and his landlord stretched their hands more than their bones allowed.

The one-man fight between Buoda Gebu and the Ijebu landlord was later to become a one-man fight between Buoda Gebu and the rest of us, we the innocent without houses or land for tenants to lease. We did not provoke the fight or wrong the evangelist. The Prophet Gabriel forced himself on us, on our world, not because we sought him, not because we needed him, not because his received revelations had anything to do with us, but because he chose to meddle in our affairs. Without invitation or notice, he exploded on us. He encroached upon us; he invaded our territory. A long story is difficult to cut short: Until an egg breaks, you think that it is all white!

Gabriel, the evangelist, was known as an Aladura, the label that identified a church, its members, and its movement as the "praying band." If we called our church St. James's or St. Peter's, the Aladura chose all sorts of names, some borrowed and many creative such as the Bride of Christ Church, Mountain of Fire, and Faith Tabernacle. The names grew by leaps and bounds, displaying more and more creativity. Years later, when the Aladura became known as the Pentecostalists, I counted forty-three of those churches on one long street at Ibadan. Yet I was only counting those on the roads, visible from the main streets, and not those behind them. Here and elsewhere, one could come across fascinating names such as Seven Thunders of Jesus Church, High Tension Ministry, Jesus in the Now Global Ministry, Trigger Happy Ministry (motto: always gunning down the devil), Kasabubu Church of God (believing that if one of the conspirators who killed Patrice Lumumba could get a church named after him then you can hope that you will become a saint one day!), Jesus Knows His Children Ministry, Fists of Fury, Laboratory Church of God, The Yoke Must Break Ministry, Run for Your Life Ministry, Jesus Heals Ministry, Face-to-Face Ministry, Angels on Fire Chapel of Peace, Liquid Fire Ministries, Power Pass Power Church of the Mountain Ministry Incorporated, Ministry of the Naked Wire, God Is Real Ministry, Fire Burn Ministries, By Fire by Fire Ministry, Healing Has Begun Ministry, Perfect Christianity Ministry, Spot in the Land of God Church, Elshaddai Shall Not Die Ministry, Guided Missiles Church, Jehovah Sharp Sharp, Strong Hand of God Ministry, Hurricane Miracle Ministry, God in Action Ministries, Healing Tsunami Ministry, Satan in Trouble Ministry, Fire for

Fire Ministry, Holy Fire Overflow Ministries, House of Jehovah's Padawans, Jesus in His Mightiness Global Ministry, Moving Mountain Gospel Church, Fellowship of the Wings, Power Foundation Ministries, Holy Ghost on Fire Ministry, and Accredited Church of God. Whether known as the Aladura in the past or the Pentecostals in the present, they are united by a belief in the power of prayer.

*Adura* means prayer, and those who prayed in their fashion became the "owners of prayer." We prayed silently in my church; they prayed loudly in theirs. As they prayed with intensity, one person could fall into a trance and begin to speak in tongues. The speaker did not know that he or she had been possessed, and only the man of God could interpret whatever was being said, usually warnings to other church members, a prophesy, or requests that must be carried out. The "Holy Spirit" was always present so that a miracle could be performed. There were just too many miracles, and if an Aladura church had none to report in a week, it would begin to decline in membership. In my church, the Anglican Church that traced its history to white missionaries in the nineteenth century, we were supposed to keep our wishes to ourselves and take our requests to God in the inner recesses of our rooms; the Aladura announced theirs for all to hear. We were all sinners, and we confessed privately to God; they must give testimonies for all to hear. Former prostitutes and criminals in the Aladura church must come forward on an appointed day, face the other congregants, and reveal their pasts to them. As they were all depraved sinners, everyone had to take a turn in confessing to one transgression or another. Sin allowed evil to have power; seeking constant forgiveness and repentance cleansed people of their sins, thus driving away evil. Buoda Gebu could place his hands on the head of a former murderer and adulterer, and forgive him or her with an assured finality. Their repentance and confession had washed away their sins. As long as they remained committed to the church, giving it their time and money, their entrance to heaven was assured.

My church told me that I could not know the mind of God or trace His paths; Buoda Gebu was certain that he knew God's mind and the glory that he would collect from Him. When we were sick, we were told to go to the dispensaries or the hospital at Adeoyo. If it was critical and we wanted to prevent death, we were to rush to the University College Hospital, which was then the most modern in the entire country. Not anymore, as whenever the leaders now get sick, they rush off to India and Germany; if they are Muslims, they rush to Dubai and Saudi Arabia, as if the human anatomy and the Quran are related. The Aladura had a list of diseases that they could cure without the sufferer leaving his house or seeing a doctor: blindness, paralysis, barrenness, boils, fever, hemorrhage, leprosy, lunacy, and brain disorders. They also had a long list with all the relevant biblical passages at hand to handle each one. Buoda Gebu predated the rise of HIV/AIDS, denying the whole of humanity the benefit of his curative and restorative powers.

If other Christians wore their Yoruba attire and English shirts and coats, the Aladura wore white gowns, cut in one long flowing piece from shoulders to ankles. The gowns marked them off from others. Most of them wore shoes and sandals, but one sect walked barefoot, claiming to imitate the style of Jesus Christ and his eleven disciples—not twelve, as they did not recognize Judas Iscariot, the traitor. To the Aladura, Judas and Esu (the Yoruba god) represented the ultimate evil. The Aladura members walked together to church, where they also gathered together in worship. I was certain that they were trying to separate themselves from us, creating new "families" of their own. They were using a different language to describe themselves, calling one another "the way" or "the only way," an affirmation that their faith was the only true one. That faith was also a family, as they called themselves brothers and sisters, children of the same father, Baba God. The women shared one "husband," Jesus, also called the "bride" that the unmarried boys should be attracted to and the husband of all widows. Too many metaphors, but their goal was clear: to tell us they were not like us.

That the world would end was an article of faith to the Aladura. They could see all the signs of the end, sometimes in soaring food prices, sometimes in failed politics, but most notably in the ongoing civil war between Yakubu Gowon (the head of Nigeria) and Odumegwu Ojukwu (the head of Biafra), as they sometimes personalized the ethnic struggles with the names of their leaders. The rising number of fake prophets with false messages was another sign of a world about to end. As the number of small churches increased, so too did the number of those who anointed themselves as pastors and prophets, deceiving many by presenting themselves as devout and as servants of God. There were boys like Moses who loved soccer more than school, Isola who dropped out of high school to schmooze with witches and sorcerers, and Kola who ran away from his house to join the army, all adding to the evidence that the end of the world was nigh. Evil politicians and soldiers were in power, with all the good men driven away from public service. This government of men would fail, to be replaced by the government of God.

Buoda Gebu inherited a rich tradition. The Aladura started as spiritual rebels before the First World War or thereabouts, as men seeking their own power realized that unless they left the Catholics, the pope would forever govern them; unless they left the Anglicans, the archbishop in England would always lord it over them. Black power! So they established their own missions, like the Cherubim and Seraphim Society, the Christ Apostolic Church, the African Church, and the like. As the connections between religion and politics became more clearly understood and consolidated, an ordinary carpenter, like Reverend S. B. J. Oshoffa, could become a most powerful figure heading his own church, in his case, the Celestial Church of Christ. A university lecturer like Pastor Enoch Adeboye could become one of the richest men in the world, heading his own Redeemed Christian Church of God. As important as Adeboye is, he may not even be as financially successful as Bishop Oyedepo, who controls a ministry and two universities and moves around in his own jet plane. Black power was wealth and fame, too much of both, and these church leaders acquired them in abundance, demonstrating that God blesses those who worship Him.

In those early years, they called them "independent churches," free but still struggling for survival, like a snake still alive but with its head already cut off. They were free to report to no other power or principality of darkness or light other than themselves. Blacks had been enslaved and colonized, traumatized emotionally and psychologically. As they rebelled or did things differently from others, they became heroes of one thing or the other, freedom writers, freedom fighters. If they hated the white men in retaliation for the whites' domination, adhering to the principle of an eye for an eye as recommended in the Old Testament, they became guerrilla fighters, liberators, and tormentors. The meek among them who had no pen to write or swords to fight turned to the Bible, becoming Holy Ghost warriors. By reading the Bible differently, sometimes as one reads Arabic, from right to left, they started with the book of Revelation, whose words and messages frightened them but should not be ignored. The words in the book of Revelation about the first to seventh trumpets that would follow the various stages of the destruction of the world were not what the Yoruba seeking long life and prosperity in religion wanted to discuss. They rushed through the New Testament, where they discovered Jesus, and then took time to read John 3:16 to get the key to open the door to eternal life. Their real destination was the Old Testament, which had to be read slowly, where Solomon, their favorite king, who sought wisdom instead of wealth, told them that one could marry seven hundred wives and sleep with another three hundred concubines to make up a round figure of one thousand women, a custom that they fully endorsed. There was more for them in the Old Testament than the New: One preached revenge, the other love; one has magic and charms, the other romantic words. The new Bible readers had become truly independent, free of those who had introduced the Bible to them, who had brought the churches to their dark towns and villages without roads and electricity. Although the Bible preached love for all humankind irrespective of race and nationality, they must hate white people first, and those who introduced them to Christ. The church and the colonial masters parted ways, one preaching a gospel of freedom, the other of domination. The colonial officers became the new pharaohs who wanted to throw every new baby boy into the River Nile.

For the Aladura to grow in number and stature, they had to deal with three competitors who became their mortal enemies. Leku, and those like her, were their number-one enemies; they were the pagans who would burn in hell. Buoda Gebu was not seeking their salvation but their destruction. If they surrendered totally by burning the symbols of paganism, and they renounced their philosophy, they could then be baptized. Redemption was possible, but slow and uncertain since, as Buoda Gebu said, their evil spirits were all over the city and could re-enter their bodies at any time, damaging their souls. A body contained more than one demon, like that of Mary Magdalene, who had seven. When you drove out one, others remained behind, and the one that had been driven out actually roamed the streets until it re-entered the body it had previously inhabited or chose another innocent body. Demons, controlled by Satan, possessed people, causing harm, seizure, madness, paralysis, and false power to perform miracles. Buoda Gebu, using the power given to him by Jesus, could cast out demons, but he could not promise salvation to the possessed. Their dead fathers and mothers had also prepared rooms for them in hell—sins and punishments were transferable from a dead generation to the living. The sins committed in the nineteenth century could be punished in the twentieth. Those suffering, agonizing over their failures to do well in life, must ask their dead fathers what their transgressions were.

The basis of Leku's power, divination and herbs (which the Aladura now called juju), must be demolished. Every prayer, every occasion turned against them. But what Buoda Gebu and his people were saying was very different from my reality and experience. Leku and the diviners, we were told, were after them and others, killing their members, killing children all over the town, sucking people's blood in the middle of the night. Leku became a witch and Ogundeji a sorcerer. As I listened to Buoda Gebu, I understood the meaning of Crucifixion—he was putting Leku on a makeshift cross and nailing her to it for no reason. Peaceful people making herbal medicines to prolong people's lives became bloodsuckers. Buoda Gebu must place his hands upon us, but if Leku did the same, she was accused of stealing our memory, converting our brains into juju. Leku ignored Buoda Gebu and those like him, describing them as ignorant people with irrelevant education and useless knowledge. She did not hate Buoda Gebu; rather she told people not to take him too seriously.

The second set of enemies happened to be the other Christians like Pasitor, who were not considered good Christians. All Anglicans, all Baptists, and all Catholics were deceptive Christians, going to church to show off their attire, talk to friends, look at other men's wives, and play politics. Unless they repented, salvation was not awaiting them either. They, too, would burn in hell's fire. Buoda Gebu was disdainful and hurtful with words. My church, where I received Holy Communion and sang in the choir, the beautiful St. Peter's Church, became the cursed house of Satan. Buoda Gebu believed that the church should be converted to a cocoa warehouse because God had departed from it. The land on which the church was built, we were told, was originally an Orisa grove where Ogun, Esu, and others converged. The Anglicans were too lacking in spirituality to know this important fact; and they did not purge the place before they built a church on it. As we met there, the gods and goddesses were holding their dialogues and carnivals at the same time. To Buoda Gebu, all the conflicts and divisions within the church were due to Esu and Ogun in our midst. We were always divided in the church—the pews in the front rows belonged to the rich. When a rich man died, his children took the best lot in the cemetery. Clergymen preaching sermons must be careful not to offend the church's biggest donors.

The Muslims, the third enemies, were next to the pagans, as far as Buoda Gebu was concerned. If Leku was meek, the Alhajis were not. There was mutual resentment between them and the Aladura. The Aladura schools did not generally admit Muslims, and, when they did admit them, they forced them to change their names to biblical ones, from Mudasiru to Emmanuel, such an offensive practice that it tore families apart. A boy could possess two names, Mohammed at home and David at school. The Bible was forced down the throat of Mohammed; when the poor student was about to leave school, he could be asked to say hello to Jezebel when he arrived at home. If a traveling missionary preacher hawked his messages from house to house, he was careful to tread carefully in the compounds of Muslims. To tell the Muslims very early in the morning that Jesus was the son of God was to provoke them to anger, as they held firmly to the belief that God had no son and was begotten by no one. The Muslims separated the Prophet Mohammad from God, and so were also provoked to anger when they were told that Jesus and God were the same. If the Christians believed that Jesus and the "Father" were one, it was not so for Muslims, who did not believe that Christ could forgive anyone's sins. As if to provoke the Christians to anger, Muslims would tell them to their face that no one had died on the cross. Whether you were provoked by words or awakened by messages that you disagreed with, you could make silent comments but fight no one over their beliefs. Our heavens were not the same! We would reincarnate differently: A man could have been a Muslim in a previous world, and now a Christian; when he died, he could be reincarnated as a devotee of Sango.

Innocent holy books were drawn into the war as each side praised its own. The Quran won! The imams, half-time preachers and half-time charm makers, ensured its victory to the extent that the Christians whom Buoda Gebu condemned consulted the imams. When you entered many houses, hovering above your head was a leather pouch containing a piece of paper on which were written some Arabic words. When you undressed a woman thinking that her hips were nice and rounded with beads, you found her wearing *onde*, a belt made of leather soaked in Islamic medicine. When you asked a man to remove his shirt, you found a leather band containing charms. Imams made them. Even members of my church wore them on Sundays to service. The imam turned many of the words of the Prophet into magic: He would write them on a slate in black ink, wash it with water into a cup, and ask the client to drink it. I drank those magical waters too many times. Buoda Gebu used this technique as well, praying into ordinary water, which became "holy water" presented as so potent that it could cure cancer. I drank the holy water as well.

Buoda Gebu and his associates borrowed much from their enemies— church as a building and hymns and prayers from all the other Christians—but they had to modify these to suit their own needs. They had smaller churches, new hymns, and new ways of singing. They borrowed such titles as pastor, reverend, and bishop, some of which they gave to themselves, and others were gained through a promotion ladder. The founder started at the very top as a bishop. They became far more creative than the big missions as they added other titles such as apostle and prophet, which were powerful because these titles implied that they could actually speak to God and bring messages back from Him to members of the congregation. Ordinary members who had old age on their side became elders. If they or their children had money, the church appointed them as chiefs, borrowing older Yoruba titles such as *balogun* (originally a war chief, but a *balogun* in the church could now be a fighter for Christ) or *iyalode*, head of the women. The list of titles was ever increasing as long as influential people joined the congregation. Even military and police titles were borrowed, like captain, to describe a pastor. Whether elders or captains, they were all church workers, and their occupation, *ise Oluwa* (God's labor), was often accompanied by the greeting "*e ku ise Oluwa.*" And of course the general overseer (GO) was a five-star general, or field marshal.

God's labor was different from government labor. Working for God was supposed to bring a smaller monetary reward than working for the government. Government work was easy: Only fools worked methodically and with sweat. The wise ones knew that they must make more money than their salaries either from the government itself or from those who needed the government for one thing or the other; permits to build houses, to own stores, to register cars and businesses, and the like. *Ise Oluwa* was moral, less well rewarded, but when we opened our eyes wide enough, we saw that God's workers wore good shoes and clothes, ate good food, and lived well. Since they were closer to God, He must bless them first, and then remember, but only slowly, the other members of the congregations, because those who labor at the altar must from the altar obtain rewards. God must be patient and slow: If He blessed everybody at once, the churches would become empty. Members must count their blessings, and thank God and pray hard so that future blessings would come.

The Aladura accepted the existence of witches, magic, charms, and the like, but they promised their members that *adura* would chew those things to pieces and send them to blazes. Pasitor referred to the Aladura as *awon oniyeye*, as clowns and comedians. Yet they were not comedians, as they were not being funny or playful. The babalawo asked for palm oil, chickens, and goats for sacrifices; the *oniyeye* said that salvation was free because Jesus died on the cross for you and me. But on Sunday, we must contribute far more money than buying the palm oil and goats that the babalawo demanded of us. And then once a month, we were told to pay a tithe, an amount that it would take ten years for the babalawo to accumulate from our visits. The tithe grew in later years, to be supplemented by "seeds," a euphemism for more cash. To obtain salvation, we must always sow seeds: special offering seed, first fruit seed, redemption seed, thanksgiving seed, harvest seed, pastor's birthday seed, church building seed, evangelism seed, father's day seed, mother's day seed, children's day seed, olive oil seed, and so on. The seeds grew in the gardens of our pastors, gardens in which we were not invited to the harvest. The churches were independent, but they also wanted to incorporate Yoruba culture: the food, the language, the accumulation of many wives and children. Their declared aim was to fight paganism, but their activities showed a desire to dominate the Yoruba people. Yet Pasitor collected herbs from Leku, and the Aladura came to his house to drink the medicine. The children of the Aladura visited Leku to have incisions made on their heads so that they would pass their examinations. Foolish Moses, his dad kept praying at the Christ Apostolic Church without remembering to visit Leku.

The God of the Aladura that Buoda Gebu spoke about and our God shared many things in common. As one or as both, He was supreme, gracious, merciful, immutable, omniscient, omnipresent, holy, omnipotent, patient, good, and sovereign. These were praise names that Buoda Gebu recited. Drawing from the Bible was not enough, however, and he would also turn to Yoruba praise names. God became as mighty as the elephant, and you wondered why God should not be ten times bigger than the elephant. He was a rock, a sea, a jungle, the biggest and the fastest; a long-distance runner who could run without stopping. God also had names unrecognizable to me which Buoda Gebu recited like incantations to provoke an effect: Jehovah-Jireh, Jehova-Nissi, El-Shaddai, Jehovah-Rohi. Sometimes, he became creative by combining languages: Jehova *to ga ju* (the biggest Jehova), Jehova-*ololajulo* (the most eminent), Jehova-*alaye* (the Jehovah who owns the earth). Far more interesting was to give God the same personal cognomens as humans bore, calling him Olorun Akanda, Akanbi, Akanji, as my friends and classmates were called. Like Isola, the cognomen inspired us to be brave and bold. But if God was the bravest and the boldest, why did they have to inspire him?

Gabriel was criticizing and condemning us every morning. He was angry that we allowed the Geesi (Britons) to leave Nigeria. A biblical passage had asked them to wait until the end of the century, but greedy politicians asked them to leave. We were faced with two options: bring back the British or bring back Jesus. The British were angry that we drove them away, and they would not come back. Jesus was forgiving, and we needed him to manage our decadent kingdom. Without Jesus, Buoda Gebu warned us, we were doomed.

You did not have to go to Gabriel's church to hear his words. The Aladura saw Christianity as an item you could market, just as Moses's mother sold beans and rice, going from one street to another. They would not let you complete your sleep before they woke you up around 5 a.m., competing with Muslims who did the same with their first call to prayer. You had to go to sleep early if you wanted to sleep long! The Aladura spoke with the loudest of voices, rang the bells as loudly as their energies could sustain them; walked all around the streets as long as their strength could last. They were not doing a thankless job, for they were preparing their resumé to enter heaven. These were not members of a greedy band of gatekeepers who held the key to the gates of heaven but wanted to lock everyone else out. They wanted some of us to join them, too, and each morning, they told us what to do: Repent, accept Jesus Christ into your life, and note that the kingdom of God was about to be established. This world, which belonged to them and us, was about to come to its final end. To bless us very early in the morning, the Sermon on the Mount, to which Christians gave the baptismal name of Beatitudes, was prominently recited. My mother and some other women preferred to conveniently call the sermon Beatrice, far more convenient to pronounce than Beatitudes. For struggling people who were always in need of one thing or the other, it was comfort to the ears that the kingdom of God belonged to us; the meek, the poor in spirit, the hungry and the thirsty, the persecuted. We were not too happy that we had to die before we got something, but it was a third-prize consolation. The meek had no earth to inherit, and we dismissed this idea. Ogun, the god of iron, favored the swift and aggressive, not the slow and meek. The meek ones were the Hausa who lived in their quarters at Sabo. The thirsty and hungry will be filled? The promise was never fulfilled, as prices of commodities kept increasing. In other lands, as we were told in the church, Jesus turned water into wine when the supply ran low; fish and bread appeared from nowhere, and God sent abundant quails to the Israelites when they lacked meat. If you wanted to see God, have a pure heart, but our hearts were already filled with hatred: The federal forces were already killing the Igbo who wanted their own country, and the Biafrans, too, were killing those of our sons that they were able to grab. If anyone killed Kola, my friend, I wanted to retaliate. Those who showed mercy, the preacher would say after ringing a bell, would receive mercy. Not at the police station. Those cruel people hunted us down. Which mercy? The preachers cleverly omitted the verse, "Blessed are they that mourn for they shall be comforted." They knew that saying this to people very early in the morning was offensive; even if people were mourning, you must allow them to do so in private and not haunt them with bad memories. And no evangelist had the courage to go to neighborhoods quoting Jesus instead of Moses that the man who divorced his wife on any grounds that he chose and married another had committed adultery. There was no need to divorce the woman; she was just relocated to the backroom while the new one lived close to the "parlor."

When the mobile preachers had no miracles to proclaim or treats to offer, they would simply recite the Ten Commandments. No one in the compounds they visited needed any reminder not to steal or kill, and people fired back by saying that the preachers should carry their message to the government secretariat, where all the thieves were, or to Biafra, where both sides were killing each another. Telling anyone not to covet his neighbor's wife was good, not for fear of God but for fear of men who would unite and ask the adulterous man to leave the town. But we coveted the cars, the imported shoes and clothes, the new mansions. Why should we not covet them if their owners collected our taxes, stole from us, and spent our money on themselves? We wanted the items returned to us; or we wanted to set them on fire so that no one had any of them. We boiled in anger when we were told not to give false testimonies. Our enemies were the ones giving such testimonies, depositing marijuana in the compounds and farms of political opponents so that they would be sent to jail. When we paid our taxes, they took the receipts away from us so that we would have to pay again. When we appeared before the judges, the police lied about us. The police took money from us, and we had to see the judges in the evenings to give them money. Asking us to honor our father and mother was a waste of time: They could impose deadly curses on us, that we should not do well, and that when they died and became ancestors, there would be no one to pray for us in heaven, to intercede on our behalf, and to reappear once a year as masquerades.

God and gods! The preachers were making strange statements. We must have only one god. Not so. We had several. We obeyed all of them. We respected them. If a servant of Allah gave me magical water to drink, I drank it. If Buoda Gebu gave me holy water to drink, I accepted it. To prevent a car from crushing me to death, I needed Ogun. If the thunder and lightning were to leave me alone, I needed Sango. I hated smallpox, and I could not disobey Sanponna. Jesus Christ was nice to us, so

I had to worship him. Mohammed did not offend me, and the end of Ramadan brought a good feast. Was Leku not a good woman? No one had only one god at Ibadan, not even Buoda Gebu. Only a few houses were without images of one god or another, what Buoda Gebu called idols. Christians and Muslims visited Leku's store. Those who had twins had them as children, but also as carved wooden images that they venerated as living spirits. Even Moses's mother, the strong Apostolic, had her *ere ibeji* (effigy for twins) in the corner of her room. When an Aladura church was doing well with many members, the talk in the town was that the Prophet had discovered a good babalawo who gave him an effective charm to recruit congregants. When the Prophet became prosperous, people wanted to know who gave him the charm to command people to release the contents of their wallets to him. Christians, even some pastors, visited the babalawo at night. At Adeoyo Hospital, when you were too slow to recover, the nurses and doctors would call your relatives aside to advise them to take you to an herbalist.

Buoda Gebu embarked on his own missionary journey with a big mission: to change the course of history. He understood the ruptures in society and actually told the farmers that they should be angry. He appeared at some villages and came to Akanran on November 1, where I originally saw him as one of the willing spectators. He broke the ongoing monotony and offered a side-show. He looked stocky, as if he could not lift himself up from the ground or jump if asked to. His stomach was twice as large as the rest of his body. If there was a disaster, he would find it difficult to run, and there was no way he could train with his age mates, who were learning to shoot and run in the hidden training location about half a mile away. The white gown he was wearing was transparent, as I could see his underwear and singlet. In his right-hand pocket, he kept handkerchiefs, which he used to wipe off his sweat and the foam from his mouth.

As Ogundele recited the praise of Ogun, Buoda Gebu did the same for Jesus, only with different cognomens: Lion of Judah, Alpha and Omega, Good Shepherd, Light of the World, Friend of Sinners, Messiah, and many more. These were all sweet names, an endless string with powerful meanings to which we all could connect. A god without cognomens was useless anyway.

As he was talking and preaching, he sounded agitated, angry, demanding another solution to the impending crisis. Delivering ourselves up to the fight or from the grips of evil would not work. We were all sinners; our enemies were the Philistines who sent Goliath to us. When David was able to kill Goliath with a sling, it was not because of his strength, but because God wanted it. We had no David, as we were all consumed by evil, the evil of juju, the evil of paganism, the evil of witchcraft.

Esu, our god of the crossroads who cautioned us to be careful, was our Satan, "the father of all lies." We must destroy this Satan in our minds, in his evil representation at the entrance to the village and elsewhere, including the biggest one at Oranyan in the city. He was bold—he mentioned the names of all the Esu representations in the city. Where he got the list from, only his god knew. We were followers of the serpent and the lion, two animals that all sensible people ran away from! We put Lucifer, the devil in another land, on a stool and called him a god. Yes, I remember Osanyin on a stool, but in my church, Lucifer was an alternative name for the devil. Osanyin was totally harmless: He would not even speak back to you, he carried no weapons, and he did not even eat the food placed before him.

Buoda Gebu was asking us to throw away our medicine, charms, and concoctions, none of which, he said, had "power." He asked us not to put our faith in diviners and herbalists, who were agents of darkness; he dismissed incantations as fake, exclaiming that all their claims were lies. He, on the other hand, could cure all diseases, no matter how serious. We must use holy shields, some made of bronze and gold that we could not see, as the angels wielded them on our behalf. He had armor and weapons that were invincible to his enemies: a helmet and coat of mail, a shield and breastplate. His slingshot and small stone could bring down a colonel in the Nigerian army.

The women and their children were the first to leave this makeshift fellowship ground, tapped on their backs by a woman who walked around to ask them to go home. Buoda Gebu did not notice that anyone was leaving. He went from one Bible passage to another, reciting each one several times to repeat his points. The crowd thinned out. He kept talking, citing Jesus who had only twelve people, then eleven, and when he died no more than two. He would prevail. But it was the wrong time to be calling us sinners. As some women were whispering, if they were all sinners, who were the *olori elese* (head sinners), *balogun elese*, and *baale elese*? The women assigned chieftaincy hierarchies to sins. We had desires and virtues like others, but we were harmless sinners, the good people, and our enemies were the harmful sinners, the bad people. We could not buy a scale to measure virtues, but if we had one we would weigh less than our enemies. Buoda Gebu and the Aladura were looking for goodness and perfection; we were seeking rectitude. We did not wake up every morning condemning ourselves as sinners and looking for Buoda Gebu to make our confessions and seek forgiveness. Our minor transgressions were not the cause of our pain. Buoda Gebu had lost his audience.

When his energy was low, he beckoned to his small band to begin singing, songs that reinforced his messages. His members must dance, whether they liked it or not, so that their wailing, as the psalmist said, could turn into rejoicing, to praise God with dancing. In my church, our dancing was rather subdued and genteel. Buoda Gebu's disciples danced as if they were worshipping Ogun and Sango. In a very short time, they began to sweat.

They followed the rhythms in the hymnal in my church, the Anglican, but they changed the lyrics, adding more cultural elements but doing damage to the poetry. Elegance was replaced by explanations; Yoruba notions of the universe overwrote those of the English. Love acquired a different meaning, with less of romance, but more of work. Work to help our fellowmen did not count, and we could not be saved by it. Pasitor had told me that work on behalf of our fellowmen counted a great deal, and was the only key to heaven. Buoda Gebu's disciples were singing that work was no more than the preparation for heaven. Our days on earth were not only short, but they must be fully geared to doing all those things that would grant us entrance into heaven and avoid hell.

Hell punctuated all the speeches and songs of Buoda Gebu. He and his followers would not go there, pronounced as a certainty. But I and others were heading there, unless we joined his team. Muslims were destined for hell. So also were pagans: They were the devils for which eternal fire was originally meant. Christians who were not like him would perish. We were consoled by him: Our enemies, too, were on the list of those who would go to hell—the cheats, the evil tax collectors, the sanitary inspectors, the produce buyers, the politicians, and the liars. At least we were not alone, but the thought of being in the same hell with the state governor was rather unpleasant.

There was no other exit option, there were no other conditions. The grumbling women and men at Akanran had not seen anything compared to a hell in which their bodies would be denied nourishment, their thirst would not be quenched, and their bodies would burn. If something burned, it turned to ashes. But no, in hell the burning people would just keep begging for food, for water to drink, and for water to quench the fire. Buoda Gebu insisted that the fire could never be quenched, not even by all the Yoruba rainmakers combined. No help would come; for they had done on earth enough damage that they would never receive salvation in heaven. This was frightening: Onlookers, fellow inmates of hell, would be gnashing their teeth.

Heaven was the opposite, a paragon of beauty, a fortification that no army could conquer. It was like our world with its own king, God, seated on his throne. If the road to Akanran was rough and bumpy, the road in heaven was wide and straight, actually made of gold. You could not pick up the gold and sell it: All of the thieves were already in hell, and there was no buying and selling. At the center of this extensive place was the throne and palace occupied by God. The much-praised throne of Solomon made of ivory and gold, with six steps and lions standing by the side of each of the armrests, was like a small stool compared to what Buoda Gebu described as God's throne. For someone to sit on this majestic throne he must be as big as Africa. Peace, abundance, and joy were available to all. Land was plentiful, and if a man wished he could live in an area the size of a country all by himself. No slaves, no servants, no market, no services. There was no night or day, no sun, no moon, no stars. The stomach was useless as there was no hunger, no thirst, no gluttony. The body was perfect as no disease could enter it; there was no sickness, no pain. Without worries, there would be no tears. I had heard some of these promises at funeral services, but Buoda Gebu was embellishing them. In my church, we limited ourselves to the end of sin and death, and the end of pain and tears. In Buoda Gebu's eyes, we needed heaven to become masters and kings, to live in opulence and grandeur, to become aristocrats, which our conditions on earth did not make possible. Buoda Gebu spoke not only as if we should head there, but as if we should do so as soon as we could. He was not recommending suicide, but implying that our earth was not only temporary but wasteful. We were living wasted lives, no more, no less!

More drama followed. Buoda Gebu spoke too long; his disciples sang and danced far too long. By the time they finished, the last lorry to take them back to the city had left. The "conductor" had come three times to the fellowship ground to recruit passengers, telling Buoda Gebu to bring his people along so that they could leave. These "lorries" each required a driver and an assistant, called the "conductor," who was an apprentice learning how to drive. Although the driving lessons could actually be completed within seven days, the driver and the businessman who owned the lorry and paid the driver dragged out the training to three years so as to have a source of cheap labor to use. The conductor looked for passengers, advertised the trip, shouting at passersby who might be traveling. At Dugbe, you would hear shouts of "Sango-UI, Sango-UI," telling you the right van to take if you were going to the University of Ibadan. At Akanran, they shouted "Aperin-Elekuro, Aperin-Elekuro" so many times that a conductor could lose his voice. The conductor was expected to take on board more passengers than the lorry could take. As they drove along, they took even more. The driver would apply his brakes suddenly, so as to push all the passengers forward to create more space. If children were occupying seats, the conductor would yell to the adults to take them on their laps, "*e gbe won sese.*" If the adults did not obey quickly, the *kondo* (as he was called) would grab the arm of the child until an adult became so angry that he or she agreed to take up the child. Violence worked; more space was created.

Buoda Gebu ignored the *kondo* who warned him about the lorry's schedule. The work of God was more important. At the last reminder, the *kondo* said, "Evangelist, *iyoku dola,*" to tell him that the lorry would no longer wait for anyone. Buoda Gebu was exercising his power as the director of his church; the *kondo* was also exercising his power as the director of the lorry. In Nigeria, everyone had power. As the lorry moved, if either the driver or *kondo* had a full bladder and wanted to urinate, they would not tell the passengers; they just stopped, urinated at the edge of the bush, and moved on—no apologies needed. The *kondo* carried a short wooden club, known as *soki* (the brake) which he needed to ensure that the lorry would stop when the driver applied his brakes. Whether the brakes worked or not, when the driver signaled to the *kondo* that he wanted to stop, especially on a slope, called "free," the *kondo* must jump out of the lorry to wedge the club in front of one of the tires to ensure that the lorry stopped.

This was power. If the driver made the *kondo* angry, he could refuse to jump out of the fast-moving lorry as it was descending a hill to apply the manual brake. If a passenger made him angry, he could do the same. So the *kondo*, too, had power, the power of his club. I looked at this club many times, and I was always watchful in case the *kondo* decided to hit me with it, or in anticipation that the *kondo* would refuse to use it to stop the lorry. He must always jump out and use the club, for the driver, in wanting to save petrol, would turn off the engine on "free" so that the lorry would run on its own. The steering could lock, the lorry could move in the wrong direction, it could move faster than anticipated, and an accident could happen. I was caught in an accident, in which many were injured, including the *kondo*, who miscalculated so that the tire ran over his arm, crushing it. He lived the rest of his life with one arm gone.

Buoda Gebu miscalculated by ignoring the *kondo*. Perhaps he thought that there were more lorries coming or that the *kondo* was doing his normal recruiting-passengers routine. He did not heed the *kondo's* warning that his lorry was the last one. Perhaps he was just in the habit of not listening to anyone other than God, Jesus, and the angels. The last lorry left. The singing and preaching ended, and they needed to go back to the city. There was no other way than to walk. Yet it was already too dark to do so. Food sellers and hawkers had closed their doors for the day. People had gone into their houses, tents, churches, mosques, and the like. Buoda Gebu not only needed a place to stay, but he had to take care of his followers. A man of God who received revelations, who interpreted dreams, and who saw visions had failed to take into account the simple worldly routine of catching public transport.

I did not know the various tents and compounds that Buoda Gebu went into in search of shelter. We all had left him and his followers soon after they made their last prayer, expectedly long, loud, and repetitive. They needed to do some packing. By the time Buoda Gebu reached the church where I was staying, there was no place for him to sit, let alone sleep. He could see it. He called Pasitor outside by shouting his name. I got up, and Pasitor followed. Buoda Gebu requested a place to stay the night for himself and his followers.

Pasitor asked him to go to the *baale*, the village head. Buoda Gebu said that he was not on talking terms with the *baale*, and that the *baale* had previously asked Buoda Gebu to leave the village and not to preach there. Buoda Gebu refused.

"Is this the right thing to do if the owner of the soil asked you not to step on his soil?" asked Pasitor.

"Not so," Buoda Gebu answered, telling Pasitor that no one owned the land, that everything belonged to God.

"In that case," said Pasitor, "a thief can come to your house and claim it as his own!" Buoda Gebu saw the remark as a curse and prayed that a thief would never come to his house.

Pasitor suggested that Buoda Gebu should try the house of the *Olori olode*, but Buoda Gebu was angry at this suggestion. The *Olori olode* was the head of the hunters' guild, a follower of Ogun, Esu, and other gods. In front of his compound was a mound piled with all sorts of sacrifices: palm oil, food, coins, bananas, and dead fowls. Each morning, the *Olori olode* offered something to this mound, sometimes just two pieces of banana. He was already active in the movement that was building up, and his house was a beehive of activity. It was used for meetings with folk in hunting garb with charms on their bodies. Buoda Gebu said that a man of God must not even go near this house, for it was full of demons and cursed spirits, not to talk of sleeping there. Buoda Gebu called the *Olori olode* a mocker of the Holy Ghost, a wicked instigator of sorrow and strife, a man possessed of more than seven times seven demons that no prophet could cast out, and the chief host of Pharisees and Sadducees. Until the *Olori olode* died, there would be no peace, no end to afflictions and diseases. To stay in the house of this man was to be defiled by demonic powers and participate in debauchery. Were he to even accidentally enter into this devil's house, Buoda Gebu would run out in the nude, as Mark did when soldiers wanted to arrest him in the company of Jesus Christ in the Garden of Gethsemane. Just as Cain and Abel must never meet, so too he would have nothing to do with the *Olori olode*, a man who was doomed. Buoda Gebu referred Pasitor to Deuteronomy 18:10–12. As usual when a church leader made such a reference, someone interrupted by reading out the passages in question:

> *There shall not be found among you any one that maketh his son or his daughter to pass through the fire, or that useth divination, or an observer of times, or an enchanter, or a witch.*
>
> *Or a charmer, or a consulter with familiar spirits, or a wizard, or a necromancer.*
>
> *For all that do these things are an abomination unto the LORD: and because of these abominations the LORD thy God doth drive them out from before thee.*

Buoda Gebu saw the *Olori olode* and everyone associated with him as witches and sorcerers detestable to God; their days were numbered, as they would all perish. Pasitor pretended not to listen to the quotations or the imprecations that followed. When a member of the local church asked Buoda Gebu why he was not as bold as Moses and Daniel to fight the *Olori olode*, Pasitor asked him to stop talking.

"Who else do you know in the village?" Pasitor asked.

Buoda Gebu said, "No one." Pasitor said that he had previously thought Buoda Gebu knew someone and that was why he had chosen Akanran as a preaching ground. Buoda Gebu replied that his message must spread everywhere, to all villages, to all towns, and to all rooms and farms until the last person heard the name of Jesus Christ. He had chosen Akanran and some other villages with the largest concentrations of pagans who needed salvation and redemption. Pasitor commended his choice and congratulated him, expressing his hope that he had succeeded in converting them and removing demons from their bodies. "Yes, certainly," Buoda Gebu answered, and explained that Pasitor would begin to notice the changes in those who had listened to his message and waited for the last prayers. The scales would soon be falling from their eyes. As I was one of the few that stayed to the end of the fellowship meeting, I imagined that I would soon be noticing the changes in myself, although I was neither pagan nor evil.

Buoda Gebu said that he preferred to sleep in the church, a place where he belonged. Pasitor asked him to go inside, either to drive out the people who were already there or to ask for volunteers to yield their own spaces. Buoda Gebu asked Pasitor to announce his presence and request some people to leave. Pasitor told him that he would never give such an instruction; that he, too, was a stranger being generously hosted by others; and that it was un-Christianlike to do such a thing. Terribly agitated, Buoda Gebu dismissed those in the church as pagans—saying that the church was not even a holy place to start with. As he paced up and down, he asked Pasitor how many miracles had been performed by him, and the local pastor, and other church leaders; the number of blind people who had regained their sight; the deaf who could now hear; or the cripples who could walk.

Buoda Gebu had hit Pasitor below the belt. I had never seen Pasitor perform any miracle. I never saw one at Elepo. I did not see any blind man regaining his sight at St. James's Cathedral, the first church my parents attended and the place where I was baptized. No cripple had been made to walk at St. Peter's. There had been talk about the power of the Aladura people and their miracles as far back as 1964, when I was in primary school. The king of the city, Oba Isaac Akinyele, who came to the throne in 1955 and died in 1964, was referred to as a "king-healer," deriving his kingship from tradition and his healing power from the Aladura. The king had struggled for the throne against many competitors. The most powerful city politician of the time, Adegoke Adelabu, who carried the titles of Chief and Honorable before his name, did not support Akinyele. The Honorable, as he was simply called, belonged to the National Council of Nigerian Citizens (NCNC), and the king was sympathetic to a rival party, the Action Group (AG). In the view of members of the AG, the Yoruba should belong to the AG, and the Igbo in the East could cling to the NCNC. In 1967, when the Igbo seceded to form the new country of Biafra, members of the AG felt vindicated in their belief that Nigeria was no more than a geographical expression, a space where one group shared little in common with another, and that each region should have its autonomy and its political party. The AG supported Akinyele in his bid to become king in a series of adroit political gamesmanship moves. Adelabu was defeated, upset, and threatened to remove the king. On March 20, 1958, Adelabu died in a car accident, and the king outlived him. Many began to interpret the king's success as the validation of the power of the Aladura.

The king played up to this interpretation, flaunting his Aladura credentials whenever it was profitable to do so. Various other people claimed to be even greater miracle workers, including the famous Apostle Joseph Ayodele Babalola of Ilesa, and people began to talk of "Olorun Babalola," the prophet that God listened to—the apostle and God, we were told, were always in constant dialogue. Babalola was God on earth—He could pray for anyone to overcome poverty, for the barren to have children, for the sick to be healed. His power was legendary and is even remembered today with a university bearing his name. In Lagos there was Jesu Oyingbo, husband to thirty-four wives and father of thirty children, who credited himself with the ability to walk on water. His sprawling compound at Ikeja, Lagos, became a refugee center for sane and insane, rich and poor, men and women, boys and girls, each seeking a miracle of one kind or another. When the Bible failed Jesu Oyingbo, he was clever enough to seek remedies from notable herbalists in the land. If he could not cure madness, he had the power to inflict it on his doubters. He grew stupendously rich.

Buoda Gebu saw himself as a miracle worker, a healer, a mind reader, and a reader of fortunes. Pasitor could read the Bible, but he could not use its words to move mountains. Buoda Gebu was confident that he could move mountains with his words, that he could command rain to fall if there was a drought. His superior power, as Buoda Gebu told Pasitor, demonstrated who the true Christian was and who was far more qualified than anyone else to claim a bed in the church. The humble Pasitor now had to confront the arrogant Buoda Gebu. Either drawing from the wisdom of a Yoruba elder or from biblical sources, he told Buoda Gebu to follow him inside. A few of us moved to the front, careful not to step on people or trip over them. Without any warning to Buoda Gebu, Pasitor announced to everyone gathered there for the night that the visitor had a message for them.

"*E le e jade!*" "Send him away!" "Out!" "Now!" "Right away!" came from a dozen mouths, all yelling at the same time. If he did not leave, they would throw him out. This was no longer the house of God, but a house of war. A man stood up, telling Buoda Gebu to take his preaching and messages to those who did not mind him and his history. Without any prompting, the man offered an abbreviated history of Buoda Gebu. His father was a former slave, one of the nineteenth-century Ekiti war captives. He was never granted manumission. He did not have the money to marry properly and had to take a wife without a dowry to give him children. One of these poor children of a poor father and a mother who was also of slave origin was Mukaila, now called Buoda Gebu, born a Muslim with an Islamic name. The speaker continued to tell the story with a lot of resentment and many offensive words. Mukaila failed in school. He barely completed his primary education. He was apprenticed to a wood carver, and he failed again, unable to learn the difference between a knife and an adze. His first attempt to carve was to produce an image of a man with one eye and two noses. He was roaming the streets when someone advised him to join an Aladura church where they could pray for him to change his bad destiny. He betrayed the trust of the church, like a Judas, and began to steal its money. Without any training or preparation for a life of ministry, he left the church. The next that people heard was that Mukaila had changed his name, founded a church of his own by renting a small store, and made himself a prophet.

The speaker asked everyone, "Do you know Mukaila the thief?"

"No, no, no!" was the answer. If a child is not properly trained at home, he will receive tough lessons outside. His words were now like stones, thrown to hit, never to be retrieved.

He then pointed to Buoda Gebu: "That is him, Mukaila, son of two slaves, a useless Muslim, and a thief, standing before you as a prophet." Buoda Gebu was stunned, short of words, all thumbs. He stood still as a statue. He was totally deflated.

His followers who were outside heard the noise and the story, since the man who told it spoke at the top of his voice. Some curious souls wanted to enter the church to find out what was happening to their leader and others, to stop the storyteller from continuing with his history lesson. The entrance and the pathways between the benches were too small for them. People in the middle and the back rows of the church called out that Buoda Gebu's followers must not be allowed to enter. All hell broke loose. When two men tried to force themselves in, they were grabbed, overpowered, and thrown out. One fell, hitting his nose on the pavement. When he saw blood flowing from his nose, he cried out loud for all to hear: "Blood, blood, blood, take me to the hospital!" But there was no Samson among Buoda Gebu's disciples.

There was no hospital at Akanran. In each election campaign since 1952, politicians had promised the village a hospital, or at the very least a dispensary, electricity, pipe-borne water, and a school. There were many promises. Nothing came of them. What the people saw were tax collectors, and police officers who arrested tax defaulters. As in Elepo, people were afflicted with guinea worm, and they nursed their painful sores for a long time. When their illness became serious, they were taken to the city, to the Adeoyo Hospital, where they waited a long time to collect prescriptions and medication. Some never came back—they were dead and buried within their compounds in the city. Those who came back became so heavily indebted that they used their cocoa trees and land to raise loans from sharks, money lenders who lent at over 100 percent profit, or from produce buyers who took advantage of the poor indebted people to buy cheaply. Poverty was on the rise, and any serious illness meant that a contract with poverty was signed for life. Combining anger with hunger produced a time bomb that should never be detonated.

"The hospital that your father built," came as a speedy response to the man with the bloodied nose. This was an insult, abusing the father of an adult who was probably already married.

"Shame on your mother," was the response from another of Buoda Gebu's members, cursing the mother of the person who abused another person's father.

From the verbal quarrel came an exchange of blows at the entrance of the church, as men began to yell and hit one another, tearing one another's clothes into pieces. Peacemakers rushed to stop the fight, shouting, "In the house of God, in the house of God." Buoda Gebu recovered from his shock and silence and began to speak loudly, saying that Esu ("Satan") was now among them, and he would cast out the demons. He was being persecuted like Jesus Christ, turning his work of God into that of grief, tormenting his heaven-bound followers with scorn. They would rise again, overcoming their tormentors, the "ungodly serpents" who thought they could stop Nehemiah from rebuilding the walls of Jerusalem. We were too ignorant, like devilish "roaring lions," not to know that we could be consumed by drought and famine, leprosy and poverty. Pasitor hurriedly went outside, and his order for all to disengage was promptly obeyed, although profanities continued to be uttered on both sides.

I enjoyed the fight, and I was not happy that it ended so quickly. I hoped that the fight that was being prepared for would be larger and longer, and many would tear their clothes to shreds to reveal their nudity; that some would fall and would not be able to rise again, and blood would be everywhere. I rejoiced internally that more pleasure awaited me. This was a happy moment for me.

Ashes of embers can burn; a snake cut into two pieces can still spit its venom. Someone shouted Mukaila, instead of Gabriel, calling him the Satan in the church, the Satan who came to destroy Akanran, the Satan who sowed discord among members. He was asked to leave the church immediately. He was indignant, saying that all the agents of darkness could not move him an inch; he was a mountain that thousands of axes could not chip away at, an immoveable rock blessed with the blood of Jesus. Buoda Gebu was putting men and God to the test. The response was swift: He was surrounded by people who held him up, lifted him into mid-air—one holding his left arm, another his right arm, two holding his left leg, about three holding his right. One held his head. He was carried like a corpse and thrown out of the church. He crashed to the ground, hurting his back. His followers surrounded him. When he was asked to stand up, he could not.

He was carried a short distance away from the church to a spot where he and his followers stayed in the open overnight. They were lucky that the weather was friendly. I joined them for a little while, listening to their conversations. Either they were too tired to notice my presence or they did not care, speaking their minds in anger. When the dust settled, the humiliated Buoda Gebu began to compare what had happened to him to the way Moses escaped with the Israelites from Egypt, the way an angel unchained Peter, who had been tied to two soldiers, before King Herod could kill him. Buoda Gebu called himself by another name; not Mukaila but Lot, who was able to escape from Sodom and Gomorrah, two cities destroyed by God. Akanran was the new Sodom and Gomorrah; by his next visit, God would have destroyed the place for insulting the "shepherd," throwing rocks at a bird who wanted to spread his wings over his brood. He praised his followers, calling them "the salt of the earth" who would not only inherit the kingdom on earth but also that of heaven.

Buoda Gebu was not done with his Bible reading, as he asked one of his followers to use a lantern to enable him to read aloud Mathew 5:11: *Blessed are ye, when men shall revile you, and persecute you, and shall say all manner of evil against you falsely for my sake.* He described his followers as giants working for God. They had not suffered that much; they should remind themselves of Job, whose friends told lies against him, who lost his animals, whose servants were killed, and whose wife always nagged him. He abused Pasitor and the other church leaders for their failure to tame their "pagan Christians" into becoming like little children needing to experience God's kingdom. Buoda Gebu said that the severest judgment of God was not for *Olori olode* but for Pasitor. They did not have a church, but an *Ile Esu* (house of Satan) which, as he predicted to his members, would go up in flames; its members would be visited by hardships, and their elders would be struck down. Akanran had become the Babylon and Samaria of Nigeria. Balls of fire would arrive, destroying the church, all the houses of evil, and the farmlands. When Buoda Gebu called those at Akanran dogs, a part of me felt like rushing back to the church to tell them what he had said, but I knew what the consequences would be: They would descend upon Buoda Gebu and his followers, starting a physical fight that would end in serious injuries. To call someone a dog was to say that he was a prostitute, unreliable, evil, even deserving of death.

They were too tired to hold a vigil with prayers and songs. I left. They became quiet and slept until the sound of the first lorry that entered Akanran put all of them back on the alert. They had no food or water; they could not brush their teeth or wash their faces to refresh themselves. They did not even wait for the Kondo to make his commercial noise, "Akanran-Aperin-Elekuro," before they all drifted quietly into the lorry. As the lorry drove off, my mind went to the metaphor of the narrow and broad roads that I had heard many times: one road leading to destruction, the other to success. When I went in search of Leku, I took the narrow road; when Buoda Gebu was in search of us, he took the broad road. Did he not know that the broad road that led to us did not lead to life but to destruction?

As soon as Buoda Gebu and his disciples left the village, Pasitor, who had been quiet all morning, randomly opened his Bible and asked me to read aloud Psalm 8:3–4:

> *When I consider your heavens*
> *the work of your fingers*
> *the moon and the stars*
> *which you have set in place,*
> *what is man that you are mindful of him*
> *and the son of man that you care for him?*

If King David was credited with composing this poem in praise of stars and their constellations, Pasitor saw in the words a way to ridicule Buoda Gebu, who had been cut down to size, whose ego had been deflated, and whose message had won no hearts and minds. Pasitor described Buoda Gebu as a fake evangelist, a false witness who had come to Akanran to observe and report them to the government—a spy, an agent of darkness, one bent on sowing discord among brothers and sisters. Pasitor gave Buoda Gebu other names: Hitler who tried hard to exterminate the

Jews; Herod who was looking for all the male infants to kill so that Jesus would not remain alive; then Jezebel who tried to kill Elijah; and Jacob who tried to deny his brother his birthright. Pasitor accused Buoda Gebu of speaking as if he were around when God laid the earth's foundation and would still be around when He terminated the planet. Buoda Gebu needed soap to wash out his mouth for talking as if he were Christ.

"I can do this, I can do that, forgetting that Jesus is the only vine, truth, and way," Pasitor said in an angry tone, like someone jealous of the power of his opponent.

Buoda Gebu was a man of confused faith without deeds, an impersonator who called himself an angel of light when he was actually an agent of darkness. I agreed with Pasitor that his name should have been Jacob, as I knew a Jacob in later years, an incompetent college teacher who behaved exactly like Buoda Gebu, a devious arrogant fraud whose fake demeanor disguised the mediocrity of his mind, a man whose skin color matched that of his mind. Permanently conniving, dangerous lessons imbibed in childhood from his father, his head, since the head can be duplicated in Yoruba belief, would be that of Buoda Gebu. If God changed Jacob's name to Israel, this other Jacob should become Esau. Jacob, proclaiming himself as religious, could use my internal organs to make magic to repair his damaged brains, his demented ego, and his unfulfilled ambition. Pasitor accused Buoda Gebu of stealing from God, of being a prophet who could claim that a man was capable of bearing a child by himself. He was declared a fraud whose mission was to deceive people, to use the Bible to seek his own honor, to work for God to make money, and to destroy the good name of innocent people. When he reached the city, Pasitor continued, his swift feet would run to the politicians and soldiers to collect money for his services. Buoda Gebu was a man of God with a proud face and a lying tongue, with a heart full of wicked devices. Anyone who did not admit to his sins was destined for hell, so concluded Pasitor, who said that there was no saint who was as clean as Buoda Gebu presented himself to be.

Pasitor asked: "Did Adam not disobey God, did King David not commit murder, did Peter not deny Jesus?" I am sure of one thing: Buoda Gebu regarded Akanran as such a cursed place that leveling it was justified by God and killing the pagans was not a matter of shedding innocent blood, but of preparing mankind for greater glories.

My attention was diverted by beautiful roosters enjoying their early-morning routine near the church, pecking the soil for insects to chew. I had sympathy for them, and began to think that we, as humans, were like them in their painful journeys. What is the end of a rooster? How could it survive?

> There is no escape for the rooster:
> The hawks are hovering above, looking for birds to eat;
> The fox is hiding in the bushes, looking for food to eat;
> The owner of the rooster is thinking of making a pot of soup with a
>     hen to devour pounded yam;
> Put in a cage, termites and ants find an easy prey;
> Released to roam, the fox and hawks rejoice;
> There is no escape for the rooster.

I stopped listening to Pasitor. Only God knows who is devout and sincere. As I was fiddling with the Bible, I accidentally opened the Book of Jeremiah, and my eyes caught 12:5:

> *If you have raced with men on foot*
> *and they have worn you out*
> *how can you compare with horses?*

Pasitor and Buoda Gebu were two different men of God. Pasitor spoke like Prophet Amos, talking about social justice, helping the poor, and leaving God to decide the fate of sinners. At Akanran and until the time of his death, he was a one-liner person, drawing from biblical passages showing that one person must care for another: "Be honest with one another," "Pray for one another," "Care for one another," "Be kind to one another." If you complained about someone at Akanran, after listening to your long talk, Pasitor would respond with just one sentence: "Forgive one another." Buoda Gebu, to me, was talking like Prophet Isaiah: We would all be destroyed because we were sinners, but the faithful like him would be spared. I had read the Bible too many times to understand either of them. Pasitor and Gebu had worn me out, but the anguish and sorrow of those that I saw and spoke with every day had prepared my legs to race with horses.

> *"Lord, save me!"*
>
>                                         [Matthew 14:30]

CHAPTER 5

# Sworn to Secrecy

✦ ✦ ✦

Pregnancy precedes birth. As part of the lead-up to the war, the distribution of roles and responsibilities was secretly guided. Only a few people knew the chain of command, from the main head to the junior officers, down to the rank and file. Thanks to Pasitor and the numerous tasks assigned to me, I knew about a quarter of what was going on. I participated in many activities, observed quite a lot, and I later filled in some gaps with haphazard post-war discussions and note sharing with many people, usually as we ran into each other and moved off to street corners to reminisce. Still, no one could know it all.

No one saw it all. The eyes could not see a mile away; when the ears hear words said at a great distance, the mouth of another person has served as the courier. When you say that a ruler knows it all, human agents are the secret behind his omniscience. Walls have ears, but they depend on gossip mills. Two blind people do not describe a big baobab tree or a mighty elephant in the same way; their submissions are based on how they perceive different parts. One can be describing the base and another the stem of the tree, or one sees the tail of the elephant and another observes the trunk. Whenever I asked Pasitor a question relating to things that were unclear to me, his answer was always the same: "The eyes cannot see the bottom of anything; the contents of the intestines are hidden, only the pit latrine can describe a few items dropped into it." The bottom is always too deep, far beneath the earth's surface. As you go near the edge, as if to fetch water from a deep well, you look inside and see darkness, your eyes become blurred, and for fear of falling into the water, you retreat. I never saw the bottom of the pool, only the surface, full of mud and quicksand. The smile of a dog and the deeds of God, done rather slowly, are hard to understand.

By 1969, the public face of our movement had become Tafa Adeoye and about twenty others who came to prominence in the process of negotiations with the government. Tafa, a lean-looking Muslim from the village of Adeoye and the Elekuro ward of Ibadan, was a farmer. While he was unable to read or write in Yoruba or English, his memory was impressive. He did not like party politics, and he was only reluctantly forced into political activism. His farmland was not substantial, and his income was too meager for him to live a decent life. He did not start in the capacity of a leader, but he emerged as a series of circumstances propelled him into power, and his choice was also to avoid revealing those leaders who had engaged in face-to-face gun battles with the police and council officials. By the time the public fully knew about Adeoye, many structures had been reorganized and some institutions redefined. Many of us were surprised that he was being called a chief. If the public knew him as Chief Adeoye, we called him Sebotimo, the equivalent of asking someone to cut his coat according to his size, to live modestly, to be frugal. Sebotimo was a poor farmer, so emaciated at one time that a strong wind could blow him away. Sebotimo was a decent human being. Chief Adeoye had a different lifestyle, with a car parked in front of a two-story building. The two men were the same, only at different times.

At the helm of affairs, before Tafa became known by all and sundry, was a man whose real identity not many knew, and which, if they did know it, must never be whispered to anyone. It was an act of betrayal to mention his name or direct any stranger to his abode. I knew him, but to this date the silence is yet unbroken, at least to the best of my knowledge. As with many aspects of the rebellion which were sealed with oaths and promises, no one has ever come forward to make revelations. On my part, I locked the door of the secret and swallowed the key.

The leader's title changed many times, from *Olori* to *Asiwaju*, from *Alaga* to *Balogun*, then to *Oba*, and later *Kakanfo*, and much later on to Chairman. Each title translated as a head or leader, but carried different meanings: *Olori* s a generic reference to the head of an organization, the one who listens to suggestions and advice and announces collective decisions when asked to do so. *Asiwaju* is the *primus inter pares*, a member of the committee of leaders of which he is the *Olori*. *Oba* is the title of a king, invested with spiritual and secular force and power. *Kakanfo* is the field commander—the grand marshal and the man of war—the one who calls the shots in battle. These titles assumed that we were forming a republic or a state within a state with a structure of governance. No. We could not break away from Nigeria or the Western State, and this was never our intention. Or it could be that the status of our leader had to be that of an *oba* of a major city. Or, it could be mocking the real kings whose title we adopted, because not all of them supported us. Since we had our own *oba*, why did we need those who based their claims on royalty and traditions?

When the war began, the leader had to change his garb, becoming pregnant with pouches or becoming fearsome, ruthless-looking if he wore his full war regalia. Even in a relaxed mood, he would wear a war vest, full of charms: pouches, medicated cowries, rings, pins, and small metal objects soaked in herbs. He slept in the war vest. He attended all meetings with it on, putting an *agbada* on top of it that made him almost double his normal size. Thus, the title changed to that of a fighter, a war leader, a generalissimo. The *Olori* became the *Kakanfo*, not because there was a ladder for career mobility, but rather an evolving naming system and a dramatic changing persona. The *Olori* or *Oba* could exhibit a gentle demeanor, smiling at all and sundry, respectful to cultivate affection. The *Kakanfo* could not—the lion in the midst of men who would not be served with goat dishes but platters with the heads of men and palm wine in containers freshly made from human skulls.

Given the changes in titles and the concealment of the identity of the leader, the state government and its security apparatus were confused, unsure of who was who, who was in power over people, or who was coordinating activities, not knowing who the supreme commander was, unsure whether the *Balogun* and the *Kakanfo* were two persons or one and the *Olori* a third person. When the possibility of peace arose and the government sent its delegation or the state governor addressed angry mobs, we sometimes put forward fake leaders—sometimes a half-educated person who could speak some English (called "broken English"), who was asked to disguise himself as a poor farmer, and who could give rehearsed responses on behalf of those who took no instructions from him. Knowing that the police would track down that person's address, he was asked to go to his house in the city or to stay in a secret location far away from his real abode. While they were in his house, the police were on a wild goose chase, confusing the man's visitors with activists.

Our leader had many lieutenants, various military and civil commanders who were accountable to their own organizations and not to the constituted authorities of the villages, towns, and cities. They too could be confused as to the overall leaders, not knowing that they were reporting to someone else or taking their commands from a powerful council. The most powerful ones among them gave instructions to disobey the real authorities. The lieutenant at Ogbomoso was so headstrong that his orders must be obeyed. When our leader was known as the *Olori*, the lieutenants in other towns were known by the same title as well, with a hierarchy that started with *Otun Olori* (second-in-command), then the *Osi Olori* (third in command), to denote some kind of seniority and ranking. The *Otun Olori* was a sort of divisional head and had his own chain of command and various other officers. All saw themselves as warriors presiding over divisions and battalions. The titles and officers confused the government and the media, and many reports in the newspapers at the time were dead wrong.

The names of villages and towns were given to these divisions and battalions, and they were divided into four areas: Egbe Ibadan *ati agbegbe re* (Ibadan and its outlying villages), Egbe Egba, Egbe Ijebu, and Egbe Ogbomoso. *Egbe* is a Yoruba word for an organization or club, but there was no legal structure in terms of registered membership; these groups were more like movements with no membership fee. Each had its own leadership structure, and they never coordinated very well at any particular time. Not wanting to be discovered by the police and state intelligence forces, they always operated underground. The belief was that an agent could always be planted among the members and betray them. In order to avoid a mass arrest or a mass extermination, of which they were afraid, the location of meetings and their agendas were never written down and were kept secret. In disseminating messages, they used women and boys like me, which enabled me to understand the shifting structures and leadership.

As if to add to the confusion, each town had its own movements, grounded on issues that we all worried about but adding their own peculiar ones, usually controversies over chieftaincy titles and land. Each sent delegates to Ibadan, which emerged as the headquarters. Some movements did not even feel obligated to report to the central command, and there was nothing anyone could do to compel them. I was not part of any of these structures in the various towns other than the one in the headquarters, and I did not have any insider's knowledge of their prewar or post-war actions. I knew that they adopted their own titles, an imitation of age-old ones, thus creating parallel sets of titles within the city. *Seriki* and *balogun*, denoting the ultimate power, became fairly common, and it was not uncommon to hear references to *Seriki* Ogbomoso or *Balogun* Ijebu Remo, two titles that had nothing to do with the official ones that already existed in both places but with those claimed by members of the movements. Once accorded those titles, the men enjoyed the respect associated with them and the right to issue instructions to their followers—as well as to impose sanctions. They also fought among themselves in later months, as the government began to bribe the leaders with money in order to destroy the movements. As they fought, splinter organizations emerged with still other titles, some elevating their status with a superior title such as that of *Onikoyi* (Generalissimo) and telling government officials that all others were under them.

Although, in practice, coordination broke down on many occasions, the various groups agreed to a set of principles on how to organize their military actions. Indeed, I was one of those who wrote this down for some groups whose members could not read or write but sought a device to remind themselves and avoid trouble. They emphasized the rule of obedience: The generals in each town must be obeyed. All the generals formed a conclave and a council, and they could issue joint instructions. There would be no unified army, but rather fragmented armies under different flags. Support would be rendered to each when it called for help. Strategies would be coordinated. Only members of the movement could be soldiers. There must be no open invitation for anyone to join. Loyal members recruited other loyal members.

Though the military wing was the most visible, there were several other organizations and units within the overall movement. There were many cooperative societies, formed long before the rebellion began. They had links to the government and to various traders. The leadership of these societies was not usually trusted. The Egbe Ilosiwaju ("progressives"), made up of reform-minded people, was formed to talk about reforms to the government and the public. It put forward ideas on modernity and modernization: the need for roads, electricity, and pipe-borne drinking water and the establishment of more schools, adult education centers, and much more. Their statements, to me, were not very different from what politicians looking for votes typically said, only they were expressing the wishes of the people and giving voice to the legitimate needs of society. There was nothing to dispute about what they said. The progressives were more talkers than militants, and they tended to imitate the style of the politicians who managed city councils: The owl borrows all its bad omens from what people say. The population was already fed up with listening to promises and proposals: A house does not require nine dogs to bark before it can be protected. The wise procrastinators could be confused with the foolish politicians.

Various organizations created a semblance of government. The Egbe Oloja (traders) were charged with supplying raw food at rates that generated little profit to show that they could work with compassion. The traders supplied beef, beans, corn, and vegetables. Women organized themselves into labor gangs and made all sorts of food that could stay well-preserved over time after being dehydrated. Beef was never fried but grilled in its own juice with spices. As you tore it into pieces with your teeth, the pieces appeared like threads instead of chunks. You had to chew each thread for a long time, breaking it apart in your mouth, releasing delicious juice and spices. Bean powder and corn powder were mixed to provide a nutritional balance of carbohydrates and protein, and the combination was further mixed with pepper, salt, crayfish, and spices and then slowly roasted. Similarly, cooked beans were roasted. All these good foods have disappeared from the current menu of society, no longer made at all or desired, perhaps because there are now refrigerators or perhaps because a new generation has lost the knowledge of how to prepare them. Today, everything is fried, and even the rich and educated eat fried rice with fried chicken; fried fish and fried plantains, and chips are treated as delicacies; and fried meat, put atop oil-soaked melon soup for consumption with heavy, starchy foods such as pounded yam, is another favorite food. The rise of diabetes and obesity should be expected in the current dispensation. A previous generation was wiser, much wiser, to have fed on grains, vegetables, fruits, and roasted food.

The Egbe Onimo, a club of learners, was designed to emphasize the values of Western education, provide literacy lessons, and emphasize the importance of history and memory. Stories of the past were told by those who claimed a knowledge of it and had the stature to narrate history. Knowledge seekers like me gathered an abundance of data from chanters who were always praising one god or goddess or another, one warrior or another, and from women performing their poems and panegyrics. Singing and chanting presented histories in exaggerated formats such as eulogies of those adjudged to be extraordinary and devastating critiques of those deemed to be bad. I was allowed to ask questions when narrators and chanters took a break. "Young lad, the person who seeks directions does not miss the road," would precede a long answer.

The Egbe Onimo had volunteers ready to narrate stories, usually of politics and wars; the politics that brought us to the present situation in the country and the wars of the nineteenth century to inspire greatness. Those were always fascinating stories told with embellishments. If children were in the audience, digressions into tortoise stories would be offered to them. The tortoise is the principal animal in Yoruba moral stories, replaced by the spider when Yoruba became enslaved in the Caribbean, and revealing characteristics similar in many ways to those of the Coyote among the indigenous populations of North America. "All problems, all evils, all misdeeds, start and end with this crooked animal," always preceded narratives about the amazing tortoise. Even his broken shell, the dilapidated house that he lives in, is said to have been caused by his misdeeds. We were told by narrators that the habit of the tortoise of always hiding his head inside his shell is to avoid shame and guilt, to avoid seeing the many people whom he has deeply hurt and offended. Humanity has been delivered from his scheme to destroy us. As the story goes, the tortoise wanted to collect all the wisdom in the world, so that he would be the repository of it all. He was very successful in collecting wisdom, using thousands of tricks and stratagems. The dilemma was where he would hide himself and his bagful of wisdom. The tortoise eventually chose the tallest tree and decided to climb it in order to hide the bag, so that the world would become disorderly and come to an end. He put all the wisdom in a bag, tied it to his neck to hang on his chest where he could watch it carefully. As the tortoise was climbing a tree, it would fall down. After many trials, climbing and falling, a snail that was observing him went to tell him the source of his problem: When you want to climb a tree, you put your luggage on your back, as I have done with my shell! The tortoise was very angry, that as simple as that knowledge was, he did not know it, and he couldn't figure it out. It dawned on him that he had failed to collect all the wisdom, since the inconsequential snail still had some left. His failure saddened him, and he returned to the world to redistribute the wisdom to its owners. Dejected and sorrowful, he withdrew into the forest, lakes, rivers, and sea, hiding in places where no one would remind him of his woes and follies. I love tortoise stories, and I have mastered the art of telling them.

The narrator was careful not to let the tortoise story destroy his main theme. Thus, the narrator would choose a fictional story of political greed and its consequences or of valor and courage and their positive outcome. The tortoise replaced a man in explaining the instigators of conflicts: greed, fights over land, competition over women, betrayal, unpaid loans, disagreements over profit sharing, and endless struggles over kingship, thrones, and chieftaincy titles.

The tortoise, the substitute for man, was a cheat who could exploit, betray, disappoint, and even destroy. The tortoise was a pathological liar, a thief, and a fraud. Give the tortoise a laborer to work on his farm, the laborer would be put to work for twenty-four hours with only small amounts of food and water. Loan the tortoise money, he would not repay it. Swear an oath with the tortoise, he would not keep to it. When the tortoise had land to sell, he would sell it to five or more people at the same time. The aggrieved persons would approach the tortoise for settlement, to talk things over. The talk would break down, leading to strife. The tortoise was unruffled by a fight. His head, limbs, and hands would be hidden in his shell. In conflict or war, he could move the shell to a hole, to cohabitate with a crab. The angry man who had lost money had to move from a small conflict to a big war, creating a force big enough to eliminate the tortoise together with the crab. He drowned the crab hole with poison, and started a fire on the path to the riverbank. The war was over, the angry man was satisfied. On reaching his house, the first person he saw waiting for him in his living room was the tortoise! As the man looked dejected and bewildered, the tortoise mocked him, saying that one should be able to kill his brother to get to the throne, commit fraud to become rich, attach no importance to contracts, fight wars to make captives to be converted into slaves, commit adultery with a woman and leak it to the husband.

Seek no friends, warned the tortoise, for the world was about chaos and war. The tortoise sat on the man's best chair, confidently and with poise, and told him a few truths: Beauty and money make a fool of the smart. A captive began to cry when he was sold as a slave, lamenting his fate and cursing the seller; the buyer began to grumble and to cry that he had bought a sick slave; and the seller was angry and started to cry that he had gotten so little, not even enough to buy a gun to raid for another slave. Let this war be over, the tortoise pleaded, enjoying both his own conversation and his saliva. The hyena that eats meat does not excrete blood; it can run to catch its prey, but it does not run for its own life. Life is tough, admonished the tortoise.

The tortoise asked: "What do you do if a snake enters into your mouth and runs to the throat?"

He gave two options: "Do you use force to take out the snake when you know it will break into two, or do you give it time to continue its journey into your stomach?"

"Take heart," the tortoise spoke the last sentence before reaching for the door, "and never behave like a hungry man who can wait for hours for his food to cook but cannot wait for it to cool."

Stories of wars were always eagerly awaited, as the narrator spoke as if he lived during the nineteenth century. Wars must be avoided, as they destroyed cities like Owu and Ijaye that were razed to the ground and no longer exist on the map. In a war with its element of surprise, a village could go to bed in peace to be awoken in the middle of the night by noises of stampeding and invasion. Panic and anguish followed, along with pain, arrests, and even deaths. When the villagers were fast asleep, the enemies crept in and set their houses on fire, preventing their men from reaching for their clubs, machetes, and guns. To avoid being roasted in the raging fire or killed by the smoke, they all rushed out, naked and half-naked. Men and women of virtue lost their respect and dignity, the breasts of maidens were revealed, and boys who were still uncircumcised were exposed. The jubilant victors had no mercy as they displayed their trophies. The men were the first to be thoroughly humiliated. The noisy ones would be beaten, with whip lashes on their backs as they were compelled to lie down flat. The so-called warriors among them would get a machete bite, enough to release streams of blood to scare the cowards and the women. Then they took the married women before the eyes of their husbands to a makeshift room created by men holding wrappers and bed sheets to cover the rape that was going on inside but allowing the loud noises of protest to be heard all over the village. The big prize: The beautiful maidens who had been preserving their virginity were deflowered in public, an act that permanently destroyed their chances of ever getting good husbands and inscribed scars of shame on their bodies. The bees that sleep outside have now shown that they are more important than the flies that sleep inside.

A few victims were lucky, based on their crafts and occupations: drummers, trumpeters, blacksmiths, leatherworkers, and griots who recorded and recited histories. These were spared from bullets. They were protected by customs dating to an ancient time that no one remembered. Perhaps reproducing those creative talents was difficult and entailed long processes. Perhaps they were more useful as captives than dead, so that their skills and talents could be carried elsewhere. To escape being killed, we were told with relish, such specialists must come forward with concrete evidence. If you were a masquerade, you were expected to sound like one with a voice and message coming from heaven; if you were a trumpeter, you had to blow your instrument loudly and produce familiar tunes with expertise; if you were a smith, you must carry the embers of fire. A griot should be able to spontaneously recite poems praising the courage of his tormentors. If they all passed the proficiency test, they were marched away to perform and work for the evil king now forced on them as their new master.

Emotional trauma spread to all the vanquished, so severe that the men pleaded with death to take them away to a land without an address. Death was better than shame and pain, but they had no instruments with which to commit suicide. Perhaps one could forcefully hit his head on the ground, but one can flee from worms and still end up in the mouth of a snake. One or two failed to hit the ground hard enough to break the skull and release its full contents, and these contents would then be fed to dogs to prevent the full body from leaving the world in peace. The women who thought that their teeth were instruments of defense regretted using them—the bitten enemy got angrier and used stones to knock out the teeth. Do not attempt to kill a lion if you are not prepared for war.

The women, men, and children were herded together and bound with chains, then marched slowly to the town of the victorious where the king and his chiefs thanked their soldiers and praised them to the high heavens. The king and chiefs were eager for their share of the spoils, giving their warriors meager portions. The women were converted into wives, both those previously married and the maidens, and they all began their new journeys as domestics and reproducers of children, tomorrow's laborers. They became ants that had to work slowly by using their saliva to make the anthill. After the hard work, the hungry man looking for protein demolishes the anthill in search of the hidden queen. The enslaved, perpetually struggling like ants, carried their bitterness for so long that the citizens were afraid to allow them any power, so that they would not be able to avenge their defeat and humiliation, and settle the old score. The citizens would not allow the ants to produce a queen. The citizens must all sleep with one eye closed and the other open: The slaves were looking for the right time to fight back, and the slave masters were watching for the time when they would have to save their own necks.

The narrator never presented his own people as the defeated. As the narrator was always an Ibadan man, his stories carried some legitimacy and truth. The Ibadan spent the greater part of the nineteenth century fighting wars. It is true that they never lost any, but there were a few stalemates, especially in the last and longest war, which lasted from 1877 to 1893. The success stories of the nineteenth century retain their boasting rights up to today, to the extent that all families are now descendants of great warriors.

There was an irony to the story that escaped our energetic narrator.

We gathered to listen to him because the government was not good to us, treating us shabbily, defaulting on its promises, showing wickedness to all and sundry. When the narrator boasted about how the enemies were defeated and enslaved, was he not describing the government of the past that was now being imitated by the government of the present? A viper can sting a boa. In the past, too, the slaves rebelled, the colonies sought independence, the Ibadan empire collapsed. Life became a vicious cycle: Those who tormented people in years gone by were being tormented today. Erosion is difficult to prevent with manure; a wise person finds it hard to save a country in decay.

There was a public face to the rebellion-in-the-making. There were widespread complaints about taxation, corruption, official abuse, and ceaseless harassment of poor farmers and urban dwellers. Although only a few believed that the complaints, protests, and delegations to high-ranking officials would solve any problems, the movement used them as a diversionary tactic. The government did not know the preparations that were under way, and treated the complaints as if they were the only option left to the poor. Fake leaders were stationed in the city to write and send petitions to the government secretariat. Political parties, scheming to get back to power when the military eventually left, were vigorously courting the fake leaders. Among the fakes, some used their position to make money, a few began to convert it to privilege and assure the government that all was well. The rest of the fake leaders were men eager to know the real story, men who wanted to throw a spear and catch its end.

They could not. The fake leaders were outsiders, nests of snakes inhabiting the same hole. Caution: The powerless moth can put out your candle and throw you into darkness. The insiders were those who had at various levels sworn oaths of secrecy, participated in drills, and taken crash courses in fighting. They had access to the powerful charms being distributed and others that they commissioned on their own. The insiders had the trust of the upper echelons of the secret leadership, and they were not expected to dig a hole for one another since they did not know who would fall into it. Vigilance: In running away from a scorpion, you can step on a viper.

To attain a high level of efficiency and outsmart the authorities, it was necessary to create a cult and to use cult leaders to mobilize non–cult members to fight the government. The deep, pervasive anger in the entire southwest and other parts of the country made the second task much easier. There were thousands of angry people who were available to participate in a rebellion. They had to be prepared and then instructed as to what to do, or to follow whenever they were called upon. However, to involve outsiders in planning and complicated details would be to risk failure. The government would know, and the lives of innocent men and women put at risk. The military government had acquired the power, by military decree, to arrest and jail anyone it accused of being an enemy without any rights to the judicial process. The anger directed at Buoda Gebu revealed the danger that Pasitor sensed: Not only would there be those opposed to a rebellion on various grounds, but also there would be those who would betray the loyal ones and lead them to their executioners. There were the fake leaders in the city who hobnobbed with both the government officials and thugs. Attention seekers with some access to money from government officials and politicians, they could use free money to buy people, engaging in a grand deception that they could represent good and evil at the same time. The eagle claims to be a relative of the birds, but its best food is another bird.

The genuine leaders at Akanran and other politicized locations knew that they not only had to create alliances and solidarity based on political messaging but also had to find the means to generate trust, prevent penetration by saboteurs, and secure unshaken commitment. The totality of what they did amounted to the formation of a type of cult, a secret military-cum-political organization. Pasitor was a key member of this fraternity, deeply devoted to its core ideas and philosophy. So too was his grandson, Isola, my humble self, who carried his bags and ran his critical errands while adding to the mission, putting his nose in other things, and his ears to the ground. Isola's eyes and those of the owl became the same. I will never reveal those matters on which curses were imposed, immortal curses that have not been lifted. If you do not believe in curses, there is nothing I can do about it. Pass it off as how the minds of primitive people work, and spend your time re-reading works by Margaret Mead, with a glass of undiluted mead. At least, you believe that your government, whether you live in communist Cuba or capitalist America, routinely destroys records while labeling others as secret and confidential, the modern equivalent of a curse. Yours is not primitive!

The idea of the *oke* (hill) on which Buoda Gebu believed he could commune with the angels was the starting point in building a commitment to our noble cause. To be an insider at Akanran, you must swear by the Okebadan, a hill that symbolizes the god and goddess of the city, a hill that was celebrated and venerated each year, to affirm loyalty. Buoda Gebu had to choose a different *oke*, as Okebadan was already avoided by the Aladura, who saw it as the abode of paganism and the home of deadly evil spirits. To the Aladura, the real power of that Okebadan was the "evil spirits"! Angel Gabriel would not have anything to do with it. Since all those at Akanran believed that both evil and spirits existed, then both could be invoked by Christians and Muslims alike for or against something. And since the "pagans" among them worshipped the "evil spirits," they did not have to be convinced of the power of Okebadan. Thus, neither Jesus and nor the Prophet Mohammad had the power to deliver as much as this uniter: Okebadan and all the spirits locked in it. In Akanran and other centers that grew as the movement expanded, swearing upon Okebadan or its equivalents became one of the apparatuses of identification. If we had used the Bible, the Muslims would have objected, and similarly, if we had used the Quran, the Christians would not have been happy. Both Christians and Muslims recognized Okebadan.

An *oke*, defined in its most powerful religious essence as monotheistic by Buoda Gebu and pantheistic by us, the rebels, controlled people's minds. We knew that the hill could not move to bring them down. What was behind our belief was the force of the hill itself, its creatures living within it that could destroy anyone. To Buoda Gebu, there were no such creatures, but the idea that its very top was distant from the valley and close to God. Atop the hill, Buoda Gebu was far away from the machinations of men, protected by closeness to the angels. The Yoruba God lives in the sky, just on top of those hills. If you could actually get the longest ladder, you could keep climbing until you reach Him. Buoda Gebu was using the *oke* to reach the angels and God, to convert his solitude into meditation, to deny himself with fasting so that as he suffered more, salvation would come.

Salvation would always come with the Okebadan; otherwise it would have been leveled or ignored. For not only were the spirits in it very powerful, but the *oke* itself was a woman with multiple breasts that could feed hundreds with her ever-flowing milk. The very top where Buoda Gebu stood, the top pointed to heaven and on which angels could land, was the place where masculine patriarchal power resided. The multi-breasted woman inhabiting the cave there exuded feminine power, but she also had the potent force of a mortal curse: Betraying the woman with many breasts meant the inability to procreate and, for those who already had children, the death of each in turn, all buried by their parents. Swearing to Okebadan meant, "I am in, we are one."

To get in was the first stage. You had to be counted upon to carry out instructions, to manifest courage, to signal to others that you could die for a cause; and others had to signal to you that you would not die in vain. Okebadan could get you in, but it was not enough as a signal. There must be coordination and trust. A fellowship based on the revival of indigenous principles and beliefs supplied both the ideas and the principles to be followed. One must be civic-minded and community-oriented at the same time. What is a game for the cat is life and death for the mouse.

Ogun was dreaded, no doubt, but men dreaded one another more than they probably did the gods, or so it seemed to me with the creation of yet a further secret group, an inner caucus cemented by elaborate oaths and swearing ceremonies. An Ogboni secret society emerged among us. As Pasitor told me, the leaders of the Egba farmers—located in villages and the city of Abeokuta to the south of Ibadan—who joined the rebellion insisted that without such a secret conclave they should be counted out of the rebellion. Leadership had to be cemented in signals, symbols, signs, and codes. Freemasons had existed before now, notably among the educated, and the farmers would never have been invited into their fold. The Ogboni had existed long before as well, mentioned at least as far back as the nineteenth century, in part allowing powerful men to control politics. In its revival, it was to consolidate leadership, to prevent the infiltration of those who could not be trusted, to ensure that members spoke with one voice and that they were bonded on the basis of one philosophy. Their meetings were held in secret; their conversations were held close to their chests. The older Ogboni conclaves, with members known to the public, based their prestige and power on secrecy and intimidation. The conclave associated with the rebellion did not have a public face, and its members did not display public insignia. Indeed, even their wives and children did not know that they were members. They did not seek to entice new members, and they were not connected with elaborate political and social networks that sought to obtain access to government contracts. They simply wanted to organize a successful rebellion and dissolve thereafter. It was more or less a trust mechanism. Lacking connections to state power and bureaucracy, and without members that were well connected in the world of business and politics, its members were primarily focused on rebellion and what to get out of it, not for themselves, but for millions of the dispossessed. The Ogboni allowed them to create the talking points for whispers, and to use whisperings to relay messages among key members. Its esoteric nature ensured that statements emanating from it garnered tremendous respect and immediately connected with a political agenda that was already in place. I was part of the message relay team in countless instances, on one occasion taking a message from Ibadan to Ijebu-Igbo, walking the twenty-eight miles each way to do so.

The leaders were in hiding, and their bonding was secret not out of fear but to enable them to develop effective clandestine strategies to deal with ruthless power, manipulative authorities, and constipated military officers. They met in hidden locations, avoiding the houses of leaders and prominent men. They established rules of secrecy, using codes to send messages to one another. Symbols revealed their ideas and inter-actions, especially their peculiar use of the left arm and palm in their handshake, an act considered rude by the majority of the populace. The Yoruba have a problem with the left hand and fingers—you cannot use them to eat, to take items from others, or to shake hands as a greeting. Thus, the Ogboni members turned that which was considered rude into a signifier. And they greeted one another as women greeted, by sinking halfway into a kneeling position, borrowing from women's established habits to create masculine symbolism. The members of the Reformed Ogboni Fraternity, composed mainly of Western-educated Christians, adopted the Bible as a symbol. The new Ogboni, predominantly plebe-ians, had no need for a written book. Rather, they based their creed on a triangle inserted in the letter *O* of the alphabet, denoting eternity. The triangle is inverted, making its base appear like a plateau on which you could place an object. Made of wood, it was used to swear the sacred oath of commitment to the rebellion, to promise to go to prison and to choose to die rather than to reveal the name of a fellow member to the police or the authorities, and to keep silent on various matters forever. The initiation was pretty simple: Initiates were to avoid heavy drinking and had to make affirmations that they were progressive. Millions of people were angry with the government. Pockets of resistance had opened up. Organizations spread like weeds, but they were disunited. The Ogboni united them extremely efficiently and far outside the knowledge base of the government and its security apparatus. What was previously a series of ragtag associations and movements now had a center, with leaders speaking to one another.

The language of Pasitor was becoming hybrid, drawing from his Bible but also from Yoruba words of divination. I think he needed this duality for his multiple roles, for the benevolence that his heart was releasing, and perhaps for the malevolence engraved in his mind. Trips to and from the conclave involved reciting one *ifa* divination verse or another, and I had no clue where and when he acquired a knowledge of these. Some of the recitations asserted the definitively positive outcome of the struggle: "Our future is as safe and solid as the roof," assured Orunmila. They would encounter problems and end with riches, prosperity, and happiness. Their enemies would triumph only when stones oozed out blood, and sea sand could be counted. This was not Christianity mixed with fetishism or the expression of words from the mouths of idols. Pasitor was imitating the philosophers of change, using words of divination to reflect on the rebels' secret mission, making the hidden agenda more intelligible, affirming that they were not anti-social but social, not anarchists but political activists. And they were also religious. Those divided by religions and religious denominations, Okebadan and Ogboni, had been all united. Pasitor was seeking wisdom for himself and his grandson, telling him about the existence of magic and the power of words. The initiations and rituals were to convert many from their individualism to membership in a formidable social movement. Social change was possible; Pasitor was convinced about this, and I took it as an article of faith. Struggles were inevitable, and some had to be violent. If their price involved death, those who wanted to kill the rebels also had a right to be thrown into coffins. I mean real coffins and not coffins as a metaphor.

The parameters of my life were being shaped by Pasitor and all these undertakings and actions. I was excited, in spite of the occasional depression that I noticed in Pasitor. Sometimes he spoke as if it had become difficult for anyone to be happy, but I would always say that I was happy. A sweet life does not require sugar to coat it. When Pasitor complained that the country's independence in 1960 had not brought freedom, I disregarded this, as what I saw around me was freedom. I was free! We agreed on one thing: The rich and the poor were living separate lives. Many walked, a few rode in fancy cars. Flowing gowns were worn by some men, rags by others. Some used perfume, powder, and deodorants; some exuded a foul odor. Pasitor wanted to level the playing field. Sure, I could work for this. I wanted to fight for this. He had heartache, daily, constant during his waking hours. The bigger the head, the bigger the headache; mine was smaller than his. He wanted us to go ahead with the rebellion, but he did not want to see bloodshed. I wanted to see bloodshed and coffins. Pasitor refused to touch guns and clubs; I touched them. He took all the charms but kept his Bible to his chest; I took and used all of the charms as directed and read the Bible only involuntarily and with indifference.

The civil and military leaders of the movement were united further by the rites of Ogun. The god of iron was the only one able to bring the leaders and the masses together. The masses did not know what was going

on inside the conclave. The military side involved planners and war leaders, but they were powerless without the foot soldiers, without those who
would simply join on the spur of the moment. Ogun inspired these foot
soldiers as well as the leaders: The instruments they wielded affirmed
Ogun's might and role. The belief in Ogun inspired acts of courage.
Ogun gave them the courage to challenge the authority of chiefs, kings,
politicians, and soldiers. They did not need to operate underground—
Ogun's courage was enough for them to operate above ground and
question the values of the government, the orthodoxy of leadership,
and the wisdom of policies. The masses could not be arrested; they were
in the millions. No prison space was wide enough to hold them. The
leadership could be arrested and jailed, and they needed Ogun, too, to
create invisibility, to turn themselves into a dangerous cult that had to
be feared. Ogun gave them the zealotry that was needed. Ogun was not
supplying spiritual growth to members—many were actually Muslims or
Christians—but emotional strength. Salvation and earthly work should
not be confused. Rebellion was work, a notion based on the worth of
self, the conscience of justice, the relevance of virtue. Fair play must be
central to politics; equality must underpin the very process of the distribution of the public resources collected from the public.

Ogun had now inspired a movement from the discussion of god to
the discussion of man. Pasitor was a man of God, but Ogun converted
him to a man of the people. To talk about Ogun was to serve men, to
put value and philosophy at the very center of life. Be it through the
Ogboni, Okebadan, or Ogun, the recalling of the religious forces and
the use of religious symbolism were able to build a political network,
to use spiritual forces to build commitments, and to arrange rituals of
initiation to gather together a movement. The state was already being
questioned, its managers distrusted. If you do not like the clouds, you
cannot like the rain that follows. The mysteries behind our actions and
activities were not to make us into mystics or free ourselves of sins, but to
free ourselves of our fellowmen. What Buoda Gebu saw as paganism was
a source of strength. Self-improvement was the core value, grounded in
spiritual cleansing. The outcome was to obtain not treasures or thrones,
but justice, fair play, and respect.

Mythologies are powerful. The movement had succeeded in restoring the power of past traditions, of Ogun, of Okebadan, and of secret
societies. The philosophies that Buoda Gebu was questioning and that
educated folks were rejecting became much stronger to serve a purpose

connected with modern politics and the social conflicts it gave birth to. The government and educated citizens were later to wonder why poor illiterates could command so much attention and why thousands would obey their commands. They missed the point: Support for a cause was powerful, and obsession with the leadership was grounded in a belief system. The secret initiations into the Ogboni provided the esoteric mysteries needed to overcome miseries. The discipline of the leadership contrasted with the greed and wantonness of shameless political leaders and military officers. Hooray for cultists!

Unrecited and unscripted, a set of commandments emerged from the various practices grounded in the engagements with the secret world and the open world of religious affirmation. You could hear one man mentioning a commandment, and another man saying the next. There was no order to them. There were not ten of them. "Be loyal to fellow men." I understood this to mean not all men and women but only those with whom you were bonding. Loyalty was about trust, and it could not have been given to those who had betrayed us. Cockroaches and anthills do not form a union.

Indeed, the entire premise of the association and the impending war was that the *aye* ("world") was tough, and that human beings were not trustworthy; that those entrusted with money were crooks; and that those with power misused it. *Omo araye*—humans—are difficult to trust. *Omo araye le!* Anyone who has never heard this phrase must be a stranger who has never met a Yoruba or does not understand a word of Yoruba. The *le* that ends the phrase means that something is tough, hard, difficult, unbending, unpredictable, dangerous, destructive, calamitous, cunning, wicked, and devious. Choose one of the *le*, you are dead. The exclamation mark after *le* means that as you say it, you must shake your head, adjust your seat, move your legs, and fidget. Although as a movement, we were a part of the world as humans, we had become a microcosm of it. The world itself (*aye*) was compared to the ocean, expansive, without an end or a beginning. The Yoruba who saw the ocean (*okun*) knew that it was limitless since their eyes could never have seen the end of it, and they could not swim from one end of it to another. The *aye* and *okun* were so powerful that they could not be subdued. The *okun* contained whales, snakes, and sharks; the *aye* held similar destructive elements including sorcerers and witches. Humans could become the *aye*, and, by inference, *okun*. As a small part of a whole, we were enjoined to trust only ourselves. Our small world must be different in the way we defined citizenship and dialogue based on truth, comradeship, sharing, and love. Love was not interpreted in any decadent form, more as a notion of responsibility than a notion of feeling.

"Be strong!" This sounded like a motto, understandable because of the unpredictable nature of our future. To be strong was to be prepared in both military and religious terms, to develop acts of fortitude and temperance, and to assume that the flame in the stomachs of enemies could not roast beef. If you would not partake of a feast, do not praise its aroma. If you are shy, do not attempt to have a fight with a brave man. If a coward throws a spear and it reaches its target, doing the right amount of damage, he becomes a hero. Do not be a fool who, like water, follows where it is led without checking the consequences. If you need a horse, avoid the swift; choose the tamed.

"Be just!" This had a moral tone, combining the actions and behaviors of humans with the fear of supernatural forces. There would be a day of judgment, and all the wicked would burn in hell. But the *ika* (the wicked ones), members of the families of scorpions and snakes, would not begin their punishment in hell, but rather in this world where they would suffer in pain, losing their children and other family members and being unable to overcome diseases. Worries would burn their hearts, and sores would burn their fingers. One must also be able to read a situation clearly, to know when to walk leisurely; when summoned, to run or mount a horse, racing to reach the destination before the enemy; and when caught, never to rat on others. The world is crooked, and only the just could make it straight.

In a community, dialogue must be grounded on respect. Tongues reveal what hearts hide. Harsh words could be used on enemies, but not on insiders unless we wanted to become the handsome man with a stinking mouth. Food should be given to the needy. Only a few had excess money, but the commonality in poverty did not exclude the few successful farmers and their access to land. Those who were affluent were celebrated for their hard work and values and not for cheating others. Humanism and moralism combined to produce a worldview, not grounded in any specific religion or in intellectual rationalism, but in the experience of the time. The intentions were clear: In order to be a strong member of the community, one must be progressive, politically active, and secretive.

Today, as the entire society has degenerated into a cultural morass, many of these commandments would sound hollow. "Thou must steal and flaunt the loot" is what people now subscribe to and mouth loudly.

People no longer do what is just but what they desire. Service to the self has replaced service to the nation; loyalty to money counts far more than loyalty to God; family members are no longer relations but tenants living under the same roof; and fellowship is about transient alliances formed to seek fortune rather than to promote good virtues and values. The good leaders are all dead; the living ones are dangerous snakes with legs and wings; and their followers have taken ratting on others to the level of an art. Truth is getting leaner and leaner, and it may soon perish.

Spiritual and magical preparations were an integral part of the military. They cannot be separated from the behavior of warriors, the preparation for wars, or military actions. As arrows were being prepared, so too must the poison to put on arrowheads be prepared. Yoruba arrows and spears were not thrown over long distances but only to be aimed at someone that you saw: What did the killing was not the metal but the poison. As knives were being sharpened, the knife-wielder must also take precautions to ward off any force that might cause him injury from his knife or other knives. If you want to use a knife on someone, he, too, had a knife to use on you. It was not the knife that would kill you but the poison that touched your blood. Close encounters were the expected strategies of war. Attacks would not come from the air with bombs. Teargas to disperse fighters and crowds was the only chemical weapon that the police had. Liquid medication was prepared against teargas, and would be used to immediately wash the eyes. Guns would be used on both sides, but you would have to see the person that you wanted to shoot, the person who wanted to kill you. This would be face-to-face warfare. The religious and the military must be well combined so that we could see the enemies, as we hoped, but the enemies would not see us, as we believed. Lacking resources, modern guns, vehicles, we were vulnerable to the police and the army, but possessing charms and magic, we were invincible against our foes. A horse can take you to a war, but it won't fight your fight.

We were to attack first. Were we to be attacked first and pushed onto the defensive, we would be routed, as hundreds would hurriedly retreat to the bush and take to footpaths in their flight to other villages and back to the city. The collapse of the central force, in such a circumstance, would destroy the movement. If the leaders joined them in a retreat, their reputation would be in tatters, the faith in charms would be destroyed, and Ogun, the mighty god of iron, would be humiliated. The emphasis was on a surprise attack from us in which we would suddenly descend on the city. For the surprise to occur, it had to be coordinated by the Ogboni, bringing again to the fore the agency of the religious forces added to that of warfare. The surprise would be such as to lead to larger operations that could not be controlled by the police. We would have to take positions that would be difficult for the army to seize without killing hundreds of civilians, mainly women and children, just standing in front of their houses. We would not make the mistake of allowing the police and army to meet us on the edge of town, but in dense areas of bush. Were we to be routed, merging with the civilian population would be a backup option, and we were all told to use the cover of darkness to relocate to our bases. In addition, there must be stealth attacks and killings of state officials and policemen. If possible, no one must be caught, but if caught, one must endure the consequent pain and not reveal the identity of others.

To become able to endure pain, it was necessary to make physical preparations. I practiced the art of flogging, already associated with the annual masquerade festival in the city. During this festival, to be a follower of a masquerade, notably the biggest of them all, the *Alapansanpa*, you needed to carry whips, freshly cut from the bush. You learned to beat your opponent, usually from the waist down. It was considered cruel to beat him in the face and upper chest. Legs and backs, however, were fair game. It was fun but painful. In the endurance practice in the war camps, all parts of the body were included, even the eyes. In the masquerade festival, you could wear cloths and rags to minimize the pain. In the endurance practice, no protection was used since the enemy would undress you. Flogging was more painful than a gunshot. If you cried, not only did you lose masculinity and attract ridicule, you would now get more beatings that could send you into a prolonged illness. The trick? Never cry, no matter the intensity of the pain. You could also run, but you must run so fast that you could not be caught. Running was considered an act of bravery, not cowardice. It was not easy to run since the practice periods included the setting up of a ring of people to prevent any escape. To overcome this, you needed to use force to push over a person to break the ring. And you should expect fast runners to pursue you. If you were to climb a tree, it was not considered an act of cowardice, and the fight was considered over, as it was grossly unethical not to leave you alone at that point. A man who had converted himself into a monkey needed a banana! Death was inevitable, but it could be prevented for now by resting on a tree branch. A poor life, some believed, was better than a good death with lavish celebrations.

To ensure that one did not talk when caught, Ogboni, Ogun, and Okebadan were needed to seal mouths, to prevent disclosure. Courage did not derive from drugs, as the state alleged when it saw the youth in action. No one was under the influence of any spell or drug that made men fight or young boys turn into thugs. There was no leader that preached martyrdom, and we were not fighting for rewards, as Buoda Gebu was preaching.

We had no fortifications, no caves to hide in, and no castle for the leaders to run to. The bush was the place of protection; there were huts too far away for any police forces to visit. The labyrinths of footpaths led to hundreds of villages and cities. I could walk to Ijebu Igbo, Ijebu Ode, Ibadan, Oyo, Ogbomoso, or other places. Modern roads were far less reliable as escape routes, as they were too open and well traveled.

We wanted a fight. It was time to provoke one. On November 3, an intense series of war activities began. Over a hundred emissaries were dispatched to many villages and towns with an *aroko* and a simple statement, "*enu ko, ojo ko*" (there is unanimity, date is set). Women prepared extra food and were told to leave for the city or the farm huts away from the villages. Movements were not rushed. Those who were accompanied by small children and elderly people were asked to stay behind until they were told to move. The same instruction was given to the elderly men who refused to relocate to the city.

Active men repeated some oaths, using the machete to swear in the name of Ogun never to betray one another. This took hours. The leaders, with titles, collectively calling themselves *eso* (field officers), affirmed their allegiance to their commander. They carried clubs, guns, and a war staff. They used the war staff for their oath. The fighting troops were separated into divisions. Another oath-taking ritual ensued, bonding the boys and men with a specific commander. I joined one division. Songs of courage were used for entertainment, and those who were afraid of being injured or killed were asked to leave for the city. No one did. There was great excitement, and no one wanted to reveal his cowardice or fear. Everyone was also clever enough to realize that to leave was to be monitored. A wise person could use the cover of darkness to hide and run, but to openly indicate withdrawal was to invite considerable danger to oneself.

We were all instructed to get our arms and ammunition ready. No one would forget the charms—many were already incised on the body; people had been drinking concoctions; almost all were wearing at least one leather pouch. The guns had been rubbed with magical oil. The war bags contained knives, amulets, dried food, nuts, and all sorts of items. The tips of swords, machetes, and knives were soaked in poison. All those carrying these weapons were warned that the tips should not touch their bodies, as they would die. Even small children who would stay home were carrying sticks, and some were carrying rubber slings used to hunt birds and chase away lizards.

No one must raid any store, take food from any street vendor, harass any passerby, or taunt any innocent person. The expedition would take no booty: It was a free service. This was a contrast with the wars of old, which booty, especially captives, served to motivate many to join. Successful warriors expected labor and land, palm wine and palm oil, and women that would not attract dowries. While people went to war in the past out of loyalty to a higher cause and patriotism, they also saw it as a route to fame and wealth. Even the ongoing war between Nigeria and Biafra was generating cash for officers, contractors, and politicians who saw the dead bodies as nothing more than the carcasses of the ignorant. The wise ones in the civil war never died, as the leaders fled in the last plane and the last vehicles, with the luggage sections full of currency of different types in different denominations. Heroes became fugitives. One fled away to the far west outside of Nigeria, enjoying it so much that he forgot to write his memoirs. Another started with secular statements and ended with biblical ones. And the most atrocious of them all later became a head of state, not once, but twice, becoming power drunk in the process, and counting not just money in excess but also wives and bad manners. When the general was bored, ignoring the records of the brutality of the war, he invited his son's wife to his bedroom for sex.

A rearguard army was created, not to go to the city but to act as a buffer between the city and the villages, to protect the villages, and to send signals back and forth. If a village were attacked by the police, the members of this rearguard were to rush to the farm huts and relocate the women and the children. Rather than calling members of the rearguard army *jagunjagun* (warriors), they simply called them *olode* (hunters). Indeed, many were indeed hunters in everyday life, having gained experience in the use of guns and an understanding of jungles and how to create pathways in the bush, how to move at night, how to disguise themselves, and how to hunt animals. They provided a very valuable service, as they were the ones who welcomed soldiers coming back to the village and would direct them to places where they could eat. They had clothes ready for them, to enable them to change from combatants to civilians, as part of an effort at disguise. They were good at communication, able to use words of comfort, to sing praise, and to extol virtues.

The overall commander of the operation appeared around noon on

November 3, wearing a mask made of different fabrics, raffia, and cowries. Unless you knew him before, you could not recognize him. No part of his body was visible, not even his fingers. This was smart: *omo araye le!* Not to be confused with a masquerade, he wore a war jacket and war sandals, but his feet were covered with blue stockings. He was all charms, as one of his poetic lines reminded everyone: "*gbogbo ara kiki oogun!*" (fully loaded with charms!). Yes, it was not an exaggeration. There were charms in his intestines and organs, that he must have been consuming for weeks. You could not see those unless you were capable of finding dirt inside an egg. Each morning, he drank new doses. The external charms were all visible, and there was no need to try to count them, as his war garb had run out of space. No one would ever follow a commander who could not disappear into thin air, repel gunshots, get a deep machete cut and close the space in an instant, hit the ground for it to open up and swallow him, or conjure a whirlwind and disappear into the sky. No one would: The dog allows the hyena to pass before barking. Who wanted to follow a commander who could not use a flywhisk to command the enemies to fall asleep? No one would: A dog will dare not lick the nose of the leopard.

There were women working around the clock inside his compound monitoring the magic that sustained him. One woman would be constantly putting palm oil in his lamp so that the wick would keep burning. As long as the lamp was lit, the commander was safe. Another woman had to be speaking with witches to placate them; for if they got angry, our commander would be in trouble. We must be lucky enough that the witches did not demand fresh blood; otherwise, once in a while, one of us would go missing. It would not have been me, since Leku had diluted my blood with liquid so bitter that witches would not drink it. The only way, as those who knew the witches confessed to others, to prevent witches from sucking your blood was to make it less tasty and sweet. Mine had become worse than the taste of bitter leaves, and it smelled like rotten fish, so bad, as I was assured, that witches could smell it ten miles away.

The commander held the war staff, the symbol of his leadership and of war. He promised to be just and firm. He invoked Ogun and bowed a few times to the earth. In his full regalia, he was already transformed and transposed: human; yes, but manifesting the attributes of war gods. He was a mystifying figure before us: the mouse that could bite a spear; the rat that is bold enough to attend the birthday party of a cat; the hen that played with a wolf; the horse that would not run away from ants; the goat that kissed a leopard; the louse that removed the underwear of the proud woman; the donkey that refused to enter into the hyena's stomach. Mighty one! Sting like a bee! Who dares take meat from the mouth of a lion? A cow cannot urinate in the presence of a lion. I salute!

He paced left and right, forward and backward, with impressive gestures of aggression. He would stagger as if he wanted to stumble or fall, like a drunken man walking on a sidewalk, but he would be erect a second later. Charm, it is said, possesses the possessed superciliously. His eyes were red, not unusual, sometimes from excessive nicotine and other chemicals or the power of possession itself. The force in him was such that he could not prostrate to anyone—the standard way to greet an elder—not even to a king. The belief, strongly expressed, was that if he did so, the person so greeted would die. The rock!

No one hits an albino.
The favor of *orisa*
Respect.
No one hits a cripple
The favor of *orisa*
Respect
No one ties the hunchback with a rope
The favor of *orisa*
Respect!
Do not try to catch a leopard by its tail.
When you visit our leopard, leave your goats at home.
He was so thirsty that he drank the river dry.
Generalissimo! The sun that does not get tired;
The moon that carries the night with it.

He gave instructions: The food in your bags belonged to everyone. Yes, if you refused to share food with friends, you would end up enjoying it with mice. The medicine belonged to all of us; share with the sick. True, sickness and hunger come and go; it is reputation that stays. When someone was shot, change his clothes and take his body to the appointed place; you must never talk if arrested; if beaten, never cry; if arrested and tortured in a cell, do not talk or cry. Correct, bad company will break anyone, and unity is strength. You must never take food from people's farms or from sellers. If you run out of food, endure hunger. There must be no thought of women. Everyone understood that sex ruined the charms, and even menstruating women could disempower their efficacy with the mere smell of blood. He did not speak loudly or even with the intention to impress: No one could have perfumed his mouth to release sweet talk. He did not raise his voice. An *akigbe* (communicator) repeated everything he said in a much louder voice. The message was then carried by word of mouth from one person to another, as in a relay. A type of musical emerged in my ears, with lyrics that appeared structured and repetitive but lacked a chorus.

Baskets of kola nuts were placed before him, and three women pronounced some incantations. The kola nuts were broken and passed round for each to eat. I ate half and kept half, thinking that I could show part of it to someone later on. I always felt the urge to talk about the activities, the part that I was allowed to talk about, and I put small pieces of evidence in my own bag. Then another set of bitter kola (*orogbo*), which symbolized old age, was passed around for us to take one each. As you took each item, you prayed for yourself and others: The sun never dies, Isola will not die; the moon never gets sick, Isola will always be healthy. *Ase* (so shall it be). The rain does not know how smoke gets out of a house. *Ase.* The enemies will run inside a flooded river, stabbed by invisible thorns, and their earthen pots will collide with river stones. *Ase.* Prayers are tricky: You must have your own unless you want to fail. You must direct one to a force above you, a force that could protect or kill you. You must express a wish. But there is an aspect you must not forget: sending negative forces to your enemies. When you do this, the words become curses: My enemies will remember to buy the spears when the war is over. *Ase.*

The collective prayer was different as many did not hear its contents, but only shouted *ase* when they heard others saying it, so that the multiple *ase* rolled on after the end of each prayer. The *ase* filled the air, bringing good, sweet noise that generated sweat and aromas. Satan was conquered. *Aseee.* The enemies defeated. *Aseee.* If you visit the lion in his abode, you will return. *Aseee.* This war enterprise was more difficult than going to Mecca and Medina. The reference to Mecca and Medina was directed at Muslims, who saw the pilgrimage as the most difficult of all their enterprises: You had to raise the money or walk all the way. You would have to fly in a plane for the first and last time in your life, and you might crash. On getting to Saudi Arabia, you could fall sick and die. In the rush to throw the stone at Satan, you may be hit by one. Your return from Mecca was always greeted with joy and a lavish party. Many more prayers followed, and *aseee* ended each one.

Ogun rituals came at the end of the proceedings. This time around, there was no dog or blood. The Ogun ritual without blood signaled that warriors would move within days. The Ogun ritual with blood would now come at the end, to mark the end of the war. I have never understood the reasons for the decisions on when to give Ogun his dog and blood, other than that he was already full with the previous pre-war sacrifice and would not need food until much later. The ritual was tagged Ogun Ajobo (collective offering), and it was fast and simple. The food items presented were the common ones: kola nuts, snails, palm oil, palm wine, and roasted beans. The overall commander left, using his flywhisk to bid us farewell. A wise person speaks once! He was not interested in proclaiming his wisdom in deciding on a case, but displaying his heroism in winning a war.

On November 4, the order came for us to march out in eleven directions. Mount either from the left or the right, you would reach a saddle. At each exit was stationed a woman who represented Ogun, carrying a sword. Each warrior had to cross over a machete, another Ogun object. The woman was giving a blessing, and the crossing was a reminder of the consequences of betrayal. The woman gave us an instruction: "If someone is shot and fallen, say, 'the dead salutes you, brave man,' and move on." The last person in the line would take care of him as previously instructed. This was doubly coded: The one who was shot was either still breathing or dead; you did not know, but you were telling him that you were dead before him, and, if you were not dead, he should derive comfort from the promise that you would also die and join him. It was both strategic and clever: strategic in its intention to keep the war plans intact and clever in eulogizing both the fallen and the active. No one must look back, which meant you could see only those ahead of you and did not know anything about who came behind. Other than to relay instructions in whispers, no one must talk. It was now too late for anyone to change his mind. Too late.

My team took a detour to join a group of others coming from Ijebu Remo, and we waited at the village of Idi Ayunre (southeast of the city) to await further instructions. Food came in abundance, good food, hot, delicious. This was supplied by women and children. Most of us had no idea who organized them, who bought the food, or who paid for it. We just ate. The women were known as *aya ogun* (women of war). None wore any war uniform except for the usual Yoruba dress, a wrapper with *buba* (a shirt). They were carrying no weapons and looked totally innocent. A stream supplied drinking water, fetched in buckets by volunteers. Or you could go there on your own and drink from a bowl or by joining your two palms together to make a cup. Emissaries came and left, delivering messages to our unit commander, known to us as "No Worries."

Mr. No Worries was about five feet ten, broad chested, probably in his early forties because his father had told him that he was born during the Great Depression when everything was scarce, which would be around 1929 or 1930. In those years, imports were in short supply and expensive so that there was not even enough salt to put in the food cooked for his naming ceremony. His father was unable to buy new clothes for his mother to wear at the party. However, he had sufficient money to pay a competent circumciser who made the "tribal marks" on his face—heavy, scarified lines on both sides, of depth and width that no amount of beard could ever cover. The situation improved in later years, and his father put him to work on his farm. He became a farmer himself, got married, and had seven children by two women. Things were still very hard for him. To augment his sources of protein, he learned to hunt game, and in becoming a hunter, he learned to use guns. To survive, he borrowed money to set up his wives as small traders—one selling fruits, the other kerosene. The proceeds and profits were not enough to pay back the loans he had been obliged to take out. His fortunes plummeted. He was stressed out; blaming his wives for adding to his problems. The wives were angry with him as well; one refused to cook for him, and the other imposed a sex ban. He was always short of money, not always able to provide a "house allowance" to feed his family. The minimum expected of a man was *owo obe* (soup money) for his wife to buy meat, tomatoes, and pepper to make sauce to go with the roots and tubers that the husband could bring from the farms, the products of his labor. Without an *owo obe*, a wife was free to leave. No Worries was lucky: His two wives continued to endure, listening to his talk of expectations of change and the benefits that would come with it.

No Worries got his name from his response to conversation, questions, and queries. He ended his statements with "no worries." If you asked him a question, like "What do we do next?" his answer would be "No worries, you know later, no worries."

Or, "How is the food?"

"No worries, you will eat another meal tomorrow, the stomach does not show appreciation, no gratitude, no worries!"

"Would you ever build a house in the city?"

"No worries, those who built houses in yesteryear are dead, gone!"

No Worries became not just a name but a philosophy: Life is transient; the world and everything therein will perish; if you swim too long in the ocean, you will drown; if you keep walking, your legs will crumble; do not leave your eyes open all the time as you will become blind by overusing them.

No Worries fascinated me. I approached him, offering to teach him how to read and write. No Worries asked: "To read what and to write to whom?"

"At least you could read newspapers," I said.

He shrugged it off: "No worries, it is all about lies." Whenever he looked at the newspapers, the photographs of the governor, which he could see since they did not have to be read, annoyed him.

"Must his photograph appear every day, no worries, to always remind us what he looks like?"

"You could read books and other stuff," I pleaded.

"What about the knowledge in my head, no worries, that is already too much?"

"Knowledge has no end," I countered.

"It does, no worries, when you know what is beyond the clouds but you cannot reach them."

He moved away from me. I, too, let go, and I never brought up the subject again: If there is no willing mouth to kiss, you go for the cheeks.

No Worries was always alert, changing conversations, putting his legs to use to walk all over the place, to talk to people, to inspect boundaries, to check the works of spies on the lookout for state agents. His eyes were big, and I even joked that they were as big as those of a cow. He put them to good use. While others looked around, he was interested in looking at the sky. No Worries believed that the movements of birds and changes in clouds were signals not just of rain but also of human activities and movements in other places. He knew when birds were in a panic and where they were flying from and to. Before he ate, he looked at the sky, as if to receive a signal to skip his meal. Sometimes he would.

He was a man of antithesis in the way he combined his words and phrases: A huge goat, even if as big as an elephant, must not appear before a lion; if the tiger is a barber, the cat will not pay a visit to him to cut his hair; when the tiger moves casually, it is not borne out of coward- ice, but patience; when the cat lies low, he is not tired, just waiting for the rat to make the first move; when the grass cutter walks slowly, it is because the dog is not around; no trader would be so bold as to take the masks and garment of the masquerade to sell; a greedy thief would not steal the king's crown for an auction; let the dog drape itself with fire, let the tiger wear the toga of thunder, and let the cat be naked, all are carnivores. These and other statements were about the differences between cowardice and bravery, opportunities and failures, action and inaction. If you thought that the termites were making you miserable in your house, you should try living in a cave, no worries. If you did so, you would meet the snake there, no worries. If the world was tough, heaven was tougher, with all the good angels stoking the fire of hell so that bad people would burn; no worries, the good angels could rejoice at the charred bodies of sinners while God watched without saying anything, no worries.

Mr. No Worries could become a therapist but not a soothing one: "What will happen to your property in case you die tomorrow?" He would not allow you to answer: "No worries, you wasted your time acquiring them." In the olden days, he reminded his obedient followers, people had to take care of the assets of those at the war front. If they returned to meet their houses in disarray, they just killed more people. In the present day, the people left at home would be praying that the warriors did not return from Biafra or from our own war so that they could inherit whatever soldiers had. He asked his listeners to consider the better option of not returning, as there would be no property awaiting them. Thieves were now everywhere, enemies in the compounds, foes in the rooms, fire on the roofs, and the floors already flooded. If anyone knew the things they had and where they were keeping them, those who were dishonest would go after them. Those who took loans from the warriors were already full of prayers that they should be killed during the war. Some men, while we were at Idi Ayunre, were already eyeing our favorite wives. In the past, it had been a criminal offense to do that, to even contemplate it, a betrayal of a fellow soldier and of Ogun himself. Death could follow. To be fair to newlyweds, they were excused from going to war in the nineteenth century, lest they died without enjoying their brides.

No Worries reasoned that the government was not the only problem. Individuals, too, were enemies. The government, no matter how bad, could not die. In his political philosophy, states and governments had a permanence to them. Nigeria had nowhere to go. Its government could be dissolved; those who managed it might lose power; there could be secessions, like the ongoing one, but Nigeria, to Mr. No Worries, had no legs and could not move. Presidents were like kings: Some brought rain, some brought famine. We only had those who brought famine and wars, rulers with hearts full of evil, stomachs full of bile, and deceptive mouths as sweet as honey. They mopped up the money; their wives controlled prices and goods, making it difficult for us to afford soap to clean our bodies in the morning, to buy good shirts and shoes to wear to work. He had many children, No Worries confessed, but he wondered what else he could have had in abundance other than them: "Could it have been cars and cows, no worries?"

Sometimes, No Worries spoke in metaphors. He began a storyline with the statement, "You spread your grain to dry." Hens arrived to peck the grain, to feed and grow fat at your expense. You saw a fox that wanted to kill a hen, to have a free meal. You looked left, a snake was crawling by, moving swiftly toward your baby on the floor, confusing your baby with a frog that it needed for a meal. You needed your hen to make a pot of soup to consume with your pounded yam—its flesh, meat, and even bone marrow. You did not want to lose your grain, the source of your livelihood and food. Your baby was the most important. You could not run after the snake and the fox at the same time. You opted to save your baby; the fox killed your hen. You lost something. The government would always make you angry and make you lose something: your meager income, your savings, your land. As bad as the government was, there were individuals who ran it, and there were family members in every house who worked for it and manifested its greed.

It was not all about work or philosophy. Mr. No Worries and his lieutenants must always engage in boasting about military prowess as part of motivating all of us, providing assurances, demonstrating valor, and enjoying games. It was all fun. Taking turns, each boasted of his accomplishments in previous fights with individuals, powerful animals in the jungles, wild dogs. They hit the ground with their heavy wooden clubs, saluting the clubs for their work in crushing skulls and bones. They praised guns and gunpowder, the spirit of war. Ogun (war) was a masculine figure, huge, tall, broad, the one who controlled the forest and jungles, the savanna, and the desert. Meet Ogun with ten sons, you would be left with one. The mention of his name threw you off balance, forcing you to flee half-naked, forgetting that you had a house with wives and property. Everybody was on the run. As the dust settled, the rich became poor; the poor became rich; cowards survived; the strong were dead. They sang, and we all joined in the dancing, mouthing choruses:

War is worthy;
It brings fame;
A source of honor.
Cowards, leave
Go sell weeds and dung.

More songs! Many described the crimes of the traitors, called *olote*, who included soldiers, politicians, kings, and prominent chiefs. As each name was mentioned, we would all add a chorus of "*olote*" or "*omo olote*," clapping and hitting objects with rocks. In war and in work, pride is acquired when others see what you do: It was more honorable to keep singing and dancing than to sit down doing nothing; restless roaming was more desirable than constant napping.

"*Ki lo dè?*" (Why?) a singer would ask. And others would say "Why, why, why?" beginning a terrific game of songs.

Is it not an irony that water, the natural habitat of a fish, is also what humans use to boil the fish to death in the kitchen?

"*Olote*," everyone would shout aloud, making water the enemy of the fish.

Why would someone be angry and dump salt into water and natron into sand?

"*Olote*." Only the enemy of salt and natron can do so.

Why would the lion pursue a cat?

"*Olote*," an animal that does not respect its size and grace running after something smaller than its own offspring; the rich coveting the possessions of the poor.

Why would the powerful pursue the powerless? Today, their upper lips will despise their lower lips. In the next world, the powerful will be reincarnated as car tires, punished by the car; then repossessed by the shoemaker and turned into slippers ground into the dust by the feet.

"*Olote*."

Why would you say that you do not know the thieves among us? A fool keeps secret what is public information.

"*Olote*."

Another would change the subject. Snacks would go round, usually *ipekere* (plantain chips) and *robo* (baked melon which looks like seeds). These and others had been prepared well ahead of time and wrapped in various leaves, air tight for preservation. Hunger and guns do not live in the same house, they are two brutal enemies. Stomachs hate pain: The snacks prevented belly anguish and supplied the energy needed for vigorous action.

Everyone acquired the generic name of *omo ogun* (warrior) and was greeted accordingly: "*Ooku, omo ogun*" (Hello, brave one). Real names were unknown, except to your relations. Even then, members of the same family were divided into different regiments. If you did not know a person's name, you called him an *awe*, simply meaning "mister." Only males were *awe*. If the person was much older and needed to be respected, to use *awe* was rude, very rude, and you simply said "Abogunloko"— "the great one who meets the war in the forest"—a wonderful name signifying that the man was battle ready, not one who would run away on seeing a fight. He was going to his farm to work, with just a simple instrument. You laid an ambush for him. Instead of running and retreating, he confronted you head on with your superior weapons, beating you so ruthlessly that you ran for your life. Whenever you called a man "Abogunloko," he became elated, inspired, and good.

I had my own name, Iwin (spirit), which became modified over the years—first to Iwin Dudu (the black spirit) and then to Ifa Iwin Dudu (the divining black spirit). Whenever someone called me by any of the three names, I instantly knew the moment in time, with stories and memories rushing back at me at the speed of light. No one in that movement called me Toyin, not even Pasitor. They did not even know me by that name, but a good number knew me as Isola. To call me Toyin is to be outside of my life. Toyin has sounded strange to my ears ever since those days, sometimes serving notice that I should withdraw into my shell to protect myself from the danger that the stranger poses, the cultural divide, the social gap, the intellectual distancing. Toyin is strange to me, except on the covers of books.

Toyin is decodable; Iwin is not. In popular imagination, Iwin is non-human, a persona without a fixed address. He lives in an extraterrestrial space, today as wind, tomorrow as a physical embodiment. Do not search for him in your Bible, as Iwin does not exist there as your Satan or devil, or the demon you have to cast out. Your biblical demon-spirit cannot be trusted; it is evil, a liar, useless, disobedient, insolent, hasty, faithless, the being who prayed without cleansing itself from its sins. You cannot swear by Satan's name, whose thought is an egg that breaks. Our own Iwin is different. No one knows whether he was once a being who died and refused to leave the world or a dead man who was reincarnated as something else. Iwin could have connections to death: He died. Then, as he was being interred and people were weeping at the graveside, he fooled them with his physical body just lying down while his soul disappeared. The soul roamed the universe, deciding what to do next. It could choose to enter into the womb of an innocent pregnant woman, forcing out the baby that was already there, committing a murder to begin a strange career. Or it could simply keep roaming the world, traveling between heaven and earth. You might run into him in the forest, jungle, or marketplace, always in the dark. Iwin will terrify you. He may choose to live in the banana tree that is right behind your house, wreaking havoc on the days of your joy.

Caution! Do not always be afraid of Iwin. One or two Iwin may be message bearers, good ones, their messages calmly expressed. An Iwin might direct you to witches, to the storehouse of wisdom, to locations where fortunes await you, to hidden treasures in the desert. No two descriptions of an Iwin ever agreed even if two of you saw the same one. The Iwin could be a short man today and a long man tomorrow. He could be a woman or a man. He could be clean today, well shaven and good looking, and tomorrow so dirty, with mucus in his nose, a purulent discharge from his eyes, and pus draining from various parts of his head.

Iwin is here to stay. He cannot be killed. He cannot fall sick. He cannot die twice. He was not your bone that you could cut off at the joint. He could be made angry by tobacco smoke, the only way to make him avoid you. He would avoid you then, but not without heaping insults on you, telling you how bad human beings are, and promising to come back since you could not keep smoking forever. But to kill him was out of the question: Stone him, he bounces back; shoot at him, he turns into a rock; club him, you will feel the pain. Iwin could not be crushed. What you cannot do anything to change, you have to endure.

The living Iwin in me forgot that the real ones avoided humans and lived far away. I was in the midst of humans, interacting with them. I ran out of luck on November 8, changing the course of my participation and, probably, my history. A dane gun was on the floor. Not mine: I never had one, as Pasitor had insisted that I must not carry one or be given one. I had only those things needed to protect myself and run: a knife, a half-size machete, rocks to throw, and a small wooden club. Everybody in my age bracket was prevented from carrying guns. It was what the elders agreed on. We had our own roles, very useful roles, as spies, running errands, carrying secret messages, delivering *aroko*. We must never shoot, although we had the usual repellants to ward off gunshots. Our best job was actually to run, to run so fast in warning others about the opposing forces, to warn them to retreat, to carry messages from one post to another. Adults were not expected to run, a most undignified thing to do. Not even for exercise! An army needed spies and errand boys to succeed, boys who could run without attracting attention to others. Boys were expected to run, even for no reason, but not men. I was fit for the job. Indeed, perfect. I was tough, able to swallow a knife if necessary. I could not imagine myself like a pot that burns itself in cooking the water it does not drink and the food it does not consume.

I looked at the gun again. I had seen guns so many times that I could not remember the number. I had seen shooting being practiced. I had followed hunters on small hunting expeditions. Everyone in every village compound had seen guns. On entering his compound, the owner would put his gun in the corner of his room, sometimes in the corridor. He would have removed the gunpowder so that even if any person pulled the trigger, nothing would happen. The quantity of powder varied with the target: small for bush rats and sparrows, more for antelopes, and perhaps much more was needed in a war between men. I had played with guns before when their owners were not watching or not at home or occupied with other duties.

In mid-afternoon on November 8, I picked up this gun. I stood up. I aimed at a tree. I pulled the trigger. A loud noise was released: *o tun ku.* So loud that the entire battalion was thrown into panic. The gall bladder has spoiled the meat! The sound became troubling news for the ears. Each warrior reached for his gun thinking that someone had shot at him. Mr. No Worries sprang into action, taken by surprise. He issued the commands in place, moving soldiers to cover all four corners of the camp. Then came the revelation: It was Iwin who had pulled the trigger. Iwin's knife, meant to cut bones and sticks, broke in cutting the liver. Iwin cut the veins, and blood did not come out of them. The pregnancy that he carried was all gas.

In anger that could lead to murder, Mr. No Worries asked that my hands be tied with a rope to my back, like a noose on the neck of a goat being led to the slaughter house. Using the tight rope on me was like cutting lungs with a sword; I was no more than the blade of an axe that could not cut a stone. No Worries kicked me as many times as he could within his power or his mercy: A finger may smell rotten, but it is not cut off and thrown into the trash. No Worries had to do his job: Respect is a very fragile bottle, and he would not allow his to break. I had made a mistake, but I was not the enemy. Believing that one finger could not catch a fly, he asked four people to march the goat back to the headquarters. Only united cotton fibers can hold down the strong lion. One hand cannot hold the camel by the belly.

Either because my escorts were kind or because they wondered what people would say, they untied the rope and just held my hand to prevent any possible escape. This act of kindness marched the nickname of their leader, "Who Know Tomorrow," a taciturn character. I did not know how he came about his name, but this was what they called him, using "know" instead of "knows," a name signifying that the problems of today do not mean there will be problems tomorrow. I remembered the rules: Never talk, never cry, so that weakness will be mistaken for strength. My heart wept, but it was hidden from view. I endured: It is smarter to kiss the leg that you could not break! The feet should take a person to where his heart is, but mine was walking far away from it. The gun and No Worries had blocked my road and heart. Boys of my age left behind were frightened to death, which was probably the message that No Worries wanted to send to them. Their faces showed it, but their tongues remained in the shade and their bodies in the sun. Grief may follow upon the heels of small pleasure. Iwin had come and gone. Regret and the tail are not leaders, but followers. Truth and praise travel too slowly.

Is this the end of my mission? When speed comes to an end, the distance remains. Well, I now have the time to tell you what the fight was all about. I appreciate your patience thus far. This is the least I can do to recover from my humiliation and disgrace. You have been fast asleep; it is now time to dream. My stomach is ready to vomit both the food it failed to digest and my mouth the words it hates the most. The blind man loves to speak about a past when he had two eyes, not that he forgets that even if he tells it all, his heart will remain empty.

CHAPTER 6

# Cocoa Politics

✦ ✦ ✦

We lived in the world of cocoa. The green trees that produce in their trunks the oval pods containing beanlike seeds were an integral part of my personal history as well as of our history as a nation and people. Nicknamed *igi-owo* (cash tree), these trees determined our existence and livelihood: prosperity and poverty, hope and fear. We gave the same name, cocoa, to the trees, the beans, and the pods. We wanted the beans and needed to cultivate and cherish the trees: If you love a woman, always remember to love the daughter as well. When cocoa was pregnant, the child it produced was a good one, behaving like a good woman who produces pleasant kids. Cocoa was our cash machine, the source of our credit, the cow that gave the milk and the beef. Our two universities were built with the proceeds from cocoa, as well as our secretariat buildings, roads, hospitals, and schools. We even had Cocoa House, the tallest building in the country, located in the very heart of the city and surrounded by other buildings built with cocoa money.

If some cities and towns had electricity and pipe-borne water, someone at the secretariat had the power to use cocoa money to make it possible. Where there were no hospitals, schools, or electricity, as at Elepo and Akanran, someone at the secretariat determined that there was not enough money from cocoa to reward them with those facilities. Such facilities would reach them but only on one condition: They should produce more cocoa. If you planted yams, expect no roads. If you wanted roads, plant cocoa. You cannot plant wheat and expect barley.

Cocoa farmers sold the products of thousands of farms and villages to a legion of produce buyers. The farmers were usually paid below the world market price: Merchants and companies made more profit than the farmers, and the government collected customs duties from the big firms that shipped the beans abroad. It also used the agency of marketing boards to fix the selling price of cocoa and to collect the difference between its worth in Nigeria and its true value on the international market. As if not enough money had been made on the backs of the farmers, they were then taxed to supply more revenue to run the government. Without cocoa, there would be no sustainable government, not to talk of sustainable development.

I knew the tree, the pod, and the seed. I knew many of the farms where the trees grew, the paths along which the pods and seeds were carried on heads from the farms to the villages, and the grounds where the wet seeds were sundried. At Elepo, I had stayed in the sun and its heat for hours driving away animals who wanted to eat the cocoa seeds as they were being dried on mats and cement floors—both the seeds and those preventing the animals from feeding on them were sundried and overtanned. It seems so simple to describe it yet much harder to experience it: I suffered from dehydration, and I might have to manage with little or no food for long hours, to say nothing of being deprived of play. The goat and sheep played complementary tricks. The sheep stayed gentle in one corner, pretending to be full and contented. The goat was overeager, expecting you to pursue him with a whip, until you tripped or became worn out. As you pursued the goat in anger, you looked back to see the sheep enjoying a free meal. The hens could not eat cocoa, but they derived joy from using their legs to scatter the seeds so that they could look for insects. As if to torment you, they would turn the place into a toilet, forcing you to immediately remove their mess, like their unpaid cleaners; for if you allowed it to dry, produce buyers could downgrade your cocoa from Grade A to Grade B, claiming that your basket was full of dung. Meanwhile, the goat knew that you would lose the battle of the pursuit, that you would get tired and doze off, allowing him a good, free meal. When it was full, it would thank you by coming near you, walking leisurely, and looking at you straight in the eyes. I would smile, and the goat would change its demeanor, as if to express gratitude.

Times without number, I followed Pasitor to his cocoa farms to weed, to apply the pesticide known as Gamalin 20, to harvest, to break open the pods to release the milky seeds, and to work on food crops. It was a grueling ten-hour schedule, from the very early morning, once we could see, to the late evening until it got too dark. We had to carry green vegetables, plantains, yams, and cocoyams back to the village for dinner. During the cocoa harvesting season, we had to carry the fresh juicy seeds back to the village. When they were placed in baskets on top of plantain leaves, the juice dropped all over the carrier's body. I could lick the fresh beans, and very tasty they were, as many as I wanted, but they were not to be thrown away but put back into the basket with the rest. The seed was bitter, and there was no point chewing on it. We did not know what those who bought the beans from us did with them. Our goats and sheep loved them as food but not our people. No one that I knew drank cocoa powder or ate chocolate. They knew about tea, which you could buy at the side of the street from the Hausa traders who carried large hot kettles and sold the tea in small cups. The tea was sweet, as so much sugar was mixed with it that one was probably drinking more colored sweet hot water than tea itself. Buying the tea and, occasionally, sugarcane from the Hausa traders was one way of enlivening a boring day. But not cocoa powder, chocolate, or coffee: Even the Hausa did not know about those.

*Igi-owo* offered not only cocoa beans but also aspirations and desires. The trees that produced the beans offered the path to prosperity and far more influence and prestige than the kolanut-bearing trees that preceded them. Kolanuts were reliable products, growing in the forest region and traded far and wide to the savanna and desert where they were chewed for their caffeine. Kolanuts became one of the objects used for sacrifices, as gifts to visitors, as a part of rituals, and as a major symbolic item with which to pray for good luck. Cocoa beans never had that status; they were never connected with rituals and never used in naming, marriage, or funeral ceremonies. The beans were just too much more valuable for outsiders than for insiders to waste them on local consumption. Both cocoa- and kolanut-bearing trees were very popular, but cocoa trees brought in more money. We just had to dig up the earth, tickle it with a hoe to plant seeds and seedlings, look for food to eat for a few years, and laugh each year as we plucked the rich harvests. Once cocoa trees began to produce, after a long wait of at least seven years before the first harvest, each was handled like a fragile baby, treated with respect bordering on worship. You could now swear using cocoa trees, just as you called upon Ogun. You could now use the trees to boast about your worth. You now had the perfect excuse to fight over land instead of seeking peaceful mediation, as had been the traditional practice for hundreds of years before the tree's arrival.

The land on which cocoa grew particularly well became so valuable that siblings would fight over it as an inheritance. If in the past the fight had been over clothes, horses, or younger wives, it was all now about the land that was excellent for cocoa cultivation. As two siblings fought, either of them could claim the cocoa land and sell it to an interested third party, a stranger, thereby generating more conflicts, with two parties increased to three. The buyer, in a panic that the person who had sold him the land and trees had not been the rightful owner, could sell it to another. From three parties, the number had grown to four and could be further increased so that by the time the matter got to arbitration, eleven people might be competing over the same land and trees, each with what appeared to be a credible argument to justify ownership.

The arguments needed a history to back them up, the myths of origins dating back to times on which no one could put a date, to the time when one ancestor was the first to acquire the land by conquest or settlement, describing how this ancestor had been transferring it from one generation to another. If one person provided a genealogy through the male line, a rival could provide another story through the female line. The third person could tell the history of a gift to his family in the nineteenth century. Another could say that the grandfather fell in love with a beautiful woman and in appreciation of her unflinching love gave it to her as a gift, and the woman gave it to her son who passed it on to her grandson. Another contender could base his claim on an unpaid debt with the land as collateral. Each story would sound so credible that the contenders had to resort to a second approach: bribing the judges. The judges would collect bribes from all of them so that one bribe neutralized another: each giving the same number of bottles of gin and goats, roasted delicious wild game, notably the one known as "grasscutters," and some cash.

Since the judges were unreliable, a new line of attack was opened: resort to juju. You started with a threat: "If you do not yield the land to me, your wives and children will die one at a time." Lo and behold, one might die, and all the rest would warn the man not to risk losing more lives because of land. Then the real "juju" itself must show up: in part to destroy rivals and in part to ensure that ill health would weaken a contender so badly that he would not have the ability to fight. Visible evidence of powerful juju would be installed to warn off the competitors. Since juju was always in the mind, its efficacy was not in doubt. A thorn has to be removed with a thorn: If you could not counter juju with juju, it was better to yield the cocoa land and relocate to the city to scrounge for food. Juju, whether it worked or not, would torment your mind—you

Ibadan in the 1960s—the two-level buildings and corrugated iron roofs were made possible by earnings from cocoa. Ministry of Information, Ibadan.

appreciate peace when peace becomes disturbed. As juju disturbed your mind, the land would no longer seem important, and you would begin to withdraw. The juju of the other person had worked: Water does not get dirty on its own without a reason!

Cocoa was our major line of credit. The land, the trees, the seeds, and even the crops that were yet to grow were all valuable as collateral in raising loans. The trees could be pawned to buy textiles, the land could be pawned to raise credit to build a house, and the seeds could be sold in advance to pay for social celebrations. To have land with many cocoa trees was to have access to the source of bride wealth, to marry more wives, and to multiply the numbers of people in your household. You could plant a tree today and spend the money that you would make years later. As with all credit mechanisms, you were postponing the evil day.

As many people remembered, cocoa and *oyinbo* (white folks) arrived at about the same time. Both looked different from my people: One looked brownish, and the other pinkish. Cocoa, to get us the money, must travel out of our land, going to where the *oyinbo* came from. On reaching there, cocoa and *oyinbo* were united, with cocoa ultimately ending its journey in the stomachs of the *oyinbo* people. Just as we liked yam so much, especially with palm oil poured over it, so did these *oyinbo* people like cocoa, and, as we were told, added sugar to make it more delicious. There were two graves to be dug: the graves of those who were fighting for the trees and seeds; and then the graves of those who drank cocoa powder and consumed the chocolate and sugar in excess. The two graves were separated by the Atlantic Ocean, the great divide, but their histories were united by cocoa, how the trees got to us, and how the seeds left us.

I heard the stories of *oyinbo* and cocoa in 1968 in fragments, in fractions of fragments, and even as small word particles, one unrelated to another: one quarter of the story from Yúnúsà the farmer; another quarter from Wàhábì the tenant-farmer; one eighth from Iya Adinni the produce buyer; and one tenth from Baba L'Egba the village head. But never a whole story. It is only historians in universities who tell full stories, with one endnote on page one and two footnotes on page two. The "full story" is then divided into chapters, one following another. Iya Adinni had no full story that could be divided into chapters. "What sort of question is that?" was her response if you asked a question. One stick, she would say, does not burn; it can only smoke, which is to say that no one person can know or do it all. And that, indeed, is the underlying theory of true history.

While not associating absolute time and date with their tales and narratives—histories, memories, reflections, refractions—the farmers piled one historical era on top of another, and it may take your understanding of a later era to make sense of the previous one. The year 1940 did not have to follow 1939, and 1970 could come well before 1895. I now know the historical timeline as academic historians have studied it, but this was not my world in 1968. Neither is the format of the university historian and his chapterizations doing justice to what happened; the university historian validates himself by speaking to outsiders and guild members, many times having neither value nor use for other people's lives but working for the elongation of his resume to pay for his car and his mortgage. What a pity, "o pity pity," as the farmers were fond of saying, adding an *h* after the *p*, to sound like "phity" and always ending with "I phity you, you phity me, we are all phity." Let us bury the scholars and their footnotes and endnotes in the libraries and follow the farmers where they lead us. One quarter from Yunusa, and one quarter from Wahabi, no whole story, as there was no such order in the way the words reached me.

Cocoa began its childhood years as *igi titun aramanda*—"the new tree of wonders." Wonders and magic are relations: The first makes you open your mouth wide, and the second feeds your eyes, not allowing you to close them. The effects alter your thought processes, making you frightened and bewildered. As you calm down, you gaze around to regain coolness. A tree that conjures magic and wonder both at the same time! Those who brought the trees were strangers who came from other lands to live among us. They came from other lands with the baby trees and seeds, putting them in pots, hiding them in their pockets and luggage, boasting about how they would seek means to make money other than planting yams and cocoyams. They called the strangers all sorts of names: Oyinbo dudu (black white men), Ara Saro (folks from Sierra Leone), Baba L'Eko (the Lagosians), and many more. Some had just nicknames: Padi Alako (the majestic Catholic), Eligansa (elegant man), and Faripo (super sartorial). These were all men who arrived among us when the new tree arrived with its wonders.

Waiting for *igi titun aramanda* to grow and yield its crops, these new men worked leisurely at other things, looking at yams, "the king of crops," with scorn and contempt. Cocoa was not food like corn or yam that you could boil, roast, and eat, with or without companions. Our farm products now had two names: the food that would feed our stomachs and the cash crops, the cocoa, that would bring money to fill our pockets. Cocoa, the crop that brought cash, could give us better food—not our own food, but the food from *ilu oyinbo* (the land of white men), like tea, milk, and bread. Baba L'Eko preferred to stay in Lagos, looking for new farmlands far away from the big merchants. Faripo went to Abeokuta to boast about his trees. Padi Alako braved Ibadan to do the same thing. *Igi titun aramanda* began to travel around, spreading its stories. Baba L'Egba said that this was long before *Ogun tulu* (the flu epidemic of 1914) and *Ogun Etila* (the Second World War). He was correct; it was before the First World War. This is enough information.

Those who brought this cash tree were full of surprises, the wonders that came with their secret. The strangers were able to speak another language, not Yoruba, but English—not "full English" but "half-English." The "full English" was reserved for the *oyinbo* and those who went to their schools and stayed until the right standard, like Standard IV, although Standards V and VI would complete the process. Those who worked for the *oyinbo* or dropped out of their schools were good with "half-English." As the *oyinbo* needed cooks and servants, messengers and carriers, they needed those subjects who could use "half-English" so that when they said "go," the subjects would not mistake this for "come." Anyone who could use "half-English" should no longer be behaving like an ape. All such a person needed in a sentence were the action words: shoot, kill, run, lift, jump, sit, stand, laugh, cry. Action words came in a commanding tone: obey first, complain later. Those who lived in Lagos, working for the railways and government, could use "half-English." As more and more people began to use it, they changed the name of "half-English" to pidgin, which sounds much nicer. Their relations to the west of Lagos sometimes called it Krio, the name of a group in Sierra Leone, claiming kinship with a large number of enslaved people during the transatlantic slave trade. The Krio were related to Faripo, as he was said to be talking about his brothers and sisters in Liberia and Sierra Leone.

Be it "half-English," Krio, creole, or pidgin, it means the same thing: the combination of English with Yoruba, with its own grammatical rules, style, and flavor. If you were speaking with a person who understood more Yoruba than English, then you would use more Yoruba; if the person understood more English than Yoruba, then you would use less Yoruba. You would add gestures to put your points across, and raise your voice if displeased. To use half-English was to impress and dazzle men and women with new knowledge, to show power over those who could not even pronounce one word in English.

Cocoa came with half-English, a wonder that would become, in the vocabulary of half-English, "wonderfulment," as joy becomes "joyfulness," since wonder and joy have stomachs that had to be filled, as in "bellefull" when the stomach is filled with food. Cocoa could turn an "inusurate" or "illusireate" (a noneducated illiterate) into a literate person. The conversion would come with a new look: a hairstyle with a "pattern," a trim line on one side of the head to create a visible design, and a shirt, a tie, and a coat. The really successful would even move about in three-piece suits, made from woolen fabrics designed for colder climates. "Real wool": They had to impress upon you that the fabric was genuine, made from the best sheep in Scotland. Could it be second hand? Who knows? A famous story, said to have been confirmed by the first cousin of Iya Adinni, was that the suits originally belonged to dead *oyinbo* people. The suits were collected from mortuaries and shipped abroad. "*Aso oku!*" the cloth of the dead, became one of the fascinating labels describing the elegant suits made of wool.

True or not, those who came in contact with these men and their cloths of the dead said that they smelled like the he-goat, the dreadful *obuko* smell. The smell defines the he-goat from a distance. Even after the goat is slaughtered, cleaned, and cooked, the smell remains. After eating it, with anything, you must not belch, as the gas from your mouth would smell like that of the he-goat; and you must not fart, as the smell would reveal your presence and put you to shame. After the he-goat was cooked, your house and clothes would smell for three days. The men in suits sprayed *obuko* cologne whenever they wore their British-made jackets. Who knows? The smells could be those of the preservatives available in abundance at mortuaries! The men in suits looked good in photographs, and many photographs were taken as evidence of success; the new men looking Victorian with a hat, sitting cross-legged, what became known as *kroslege*, a new posture of modernity. Photos do not smell, and those who described the half-English as he-goats might be indeed be jealous, and should learn to *kroslege*. They also had to learn to *lege,* which was a new way of walking in style to let everyone know that you were not from the village or farm. Both to *kroslege* and to *lege*, one needed some cash. Those who wanted to be like the half-English should look for cocoa. To use the half-English language, cocoa could make one's eyes see "better better"—one "better" was inadequate to describe the "goodlucky" (not "good luck," as lucky in half-English is more powerful than luck!) of this "wonderment," which was meant to end in full "wonderfulment."

More wonders! Cocoa came with a book, the very first book that people saw and touched. Volunteers even read the book to a number of people. The signs and symbols were different from those of *ifa*, the elaborate Yoruba divination system. They knew how to stare at *opon ifa* (the divination tray), but this one had too many trays, and you could keep opening and counting until you were tired. The book offered the longest catalogue of the most powerful charms, medicines, and incantations. In this book were passages that could bring good luck and conquer evil, and love potions enabling a husband to marry two or more wives who would show docility and gratitude, even if he showed no affection. Like the *opon ifa*, you could place your hands on the book to discover the future, or to receive counseling or guidance.

There was some sadness and a big disappointment. A chapter was missing from the version of the book that reached my people, incidentally the most important chapter, which contains the key needed to open the door of treasures, to discover all the remedies of long life, good health, and happiness. As the story goes, the chapter was stolen by an *oyinbo* man who used it to create the good things of life for his own people and to attain the power to subdue the rest of us. The source of *oyinbo*'s power could be found in this missing chapter. To discover the missing chapter was to automatically become wealthy and famous, just as fast as using a human being for money magic. Using the missing chapter was much better than the money magic: No murder was committed. Complicated and secretive rituals were not necessary. No room in a house was under lock and key with no one allowed to enter it just because a speechless human being was carrying a calabash on the head to mint fresh currency notes when visited in the middle of the night; there was no gossip all over the city to damage the rich man's name, and the money would not come with the drawback of a short life, which prevented the abundantly rich from enjoying their lives to the full.

This book was the Bible, and Pasitor was always angry if the preceding name of Holy was not included. "It is not the Bible," he would yell, "but 'The Holy Bible'!" It was the only book that most people had and the only reason some wanted to be able to read at all. Cocoa came with the Holy Bible. Christianity was one thing, as those who read the Holy Bible came to become Christians who were different from those who did not read it. But this great book could do more: It contained passages that could make the trees grow faster, make them produce higher yields, and avoid damaging insects; that could attract better prices for cocoa, and overcome enemies who wanted to steal the owner's crops, trees, and even land. It is a book full of powerful magic and charms; you just have to know the right verses to consult.

You could not mention the Holy Bible without being told about the missing chapter. As soon as I had ears to listen, it was the first thing I heard after reading the Lord's Prayer. The love of God was also needed to obtain His assistance in locating this missing chapter:

Our fathers who live in heaven
We need you
Remember us
Before your kingdom comes.
Show us the way:
Give us the Book of Success
Lead us to the source
For you know where you hide it
So that we are delivered from pains and sorrow
For now and ever more. Amen.

I memorized this at the age of ten. Let God give me the missing book and keep the glory to Himself. I did not know who composed this prayer, but schoolchildren wrote it down on pieces of paper for circulation. You would hope to find it before an examination or when you needed to avoid the wrath of angry teachers and parents. This is the truth! Just as I believed in the Book of Success, the missing chapter, others believed in it too, but the problem was that it could belong only to one person. This was a lesson in greed—you were living in a community, but you wanted to be the first to discover this chapter, as it would catapult you to the glory of God and you would inherit the earth and all therein, from east to west, south to north. You would be above all kings and much closer to the angels. And we begged not one father in heaven, but many of them, as one would beg many gods, instead of one, to seek favors. The chapter would also enable us to do well in all examinations, avoid punishments, and get away with minor transgressions. Since we had offended no one, we need not seek forgiveness for our sins. Those who were feeding us could pray to God for their daily bread, not us. We were not eating bread anyway, but *ogi* and *amala* with or without meat.

Recited over and over again, and recalled many times thereafter, the prayer did not work. Maybe I did not shout it loudly enough, did not fast before I prayed, or did not kneel down in the middle of the night surrounded by twenty candles as the Aladura would do whenever they wanted a big favor from the Almighty. Being too casual with Jah was not always the best way to go. Only the clever hunter can get a deer; the man who can wait gets the woman. I did not find the chapter, and it has yet to be found by anyone in our part of the world. The search for the missing chapter, we were told, would entail going to Israel, the land where it was originally created. Jesus Christ dictated it, ironically to Judas Iscariot, his most reliable treasurer. Jesus loved and trusted Iscariot so much that he confided in him how to succeed on earth and in heaven. The fight and the fallout between the two were not divinely ordained: Judas knew the secrets needed to perform all miracles, and Jesus was angry that his right-hand man could betray him.

No! Someone would reply: The chapter was no longer in Israel, as it had already been stolen from there and later taken to India. No wonder: Indians have the highest number of magicians and talismans, and their fame had spread to Nigeria. There were reputable Indian talismans at Gbagi market, hiding the magical rings behind textile stores, and some were already famous for supplying the magic to big-time women to make profits from their "buy and sell" businesses. One of these women had used an Indian *tali* to prevent her husband from marrying a second wife.

No! The chapter had already left India, stolen by the Lebanese, who misplaced it in Beirut, where it was discovered by an Ethiopian who fled to

Addis Ababa. The knowledge of our geography was now being enriched, even at an early age, as one must locate all these places on a map to trace the path of the missing chapter. Luck was not on the side of the Ethiopian man as officials of the Emperor Haile Selassie impounded it and gave it to the great king. The emperor only read the first page, and he became no longer a human being but the rich king of kings, the number-one Rastafarian whom Bob Marley worshipped, with or without the *ganja*. We had to make do with the Bible that we had without its most important chapter. I have no idea why a later generation gave up on the search; perhaps because in the late 1950s, the country had discovered the most powerful *tali*: free oil from the Niger Delta. But surely they still need this missing chapter to enable them to put the oil revenues to better use.

There was yet another "wonderfulment": Cocoa came with money— "cash," as it was popularly known. *Owo tutu*—"cool money." Not the *owo gbona*—"hot money" that thieves and robbers made by depriving others of their possessions or the money that Alhaji Girigiri of Alafara made after using his first son for money magic. This "cool cash" drove away the cowries, the older money that the Yoruba had used for many years, although they neither manufactured nor invented it. Cowrie collectors, now impoverished, had to give them away for free to make the *sekere* (strings of cowries woven round a calabash gourd to produce musical sounds), to make toys, and for use as ingredients for sacrifices and charms. As the *oyinbo* dealt a fatal blow to the cowries, they brought in coins and paper money, also known as *owo*. Coins were as good as cowries, and those blessed by the Holy Bible and cocoa would have more banknotes than coins. Whosoever had notes had more coins anyway, becoming an *olowo* (rich man). People wanted an abundance of both the notes and the coins, as they could never have enough. If you could count the money you had, you were not yet there. It was when it became uncountable that you became elevated to the level of a god, the *igbakeji Olorun*, that is, the representative of God on earth. Your cognomen could be transformed by cocoa and cash from one word to a fine verse: "After God, the next person is the rich man." This would not require any additional chorus for praise singers and drummers to do their work, adding more lines:

Climb us like a horse:
Ride us like a camel;
Use us like a donkey.

If more cash came, the rich began to think that their kingdom had come, and one or two began to boast that:

God is great
But the rich man is not small either
The very rich man, who has what God lacks
The rich man has ten wives; God has none
The rich man has fifty children, God has none.
The rich man has five concubines, God has none!

The *sekere* adds the sound needed for the rich to dance to these lines, in a very slow bodily movement, as if the rich were drunk and must avoid falling down. Let us give glory and gratitude to cocoa! Cocoa had now replaced the war booty collected by the warlords of the nineteenth century, when the best access to wealth and power was through warfare. In those days of wars, no one wanted to be a farmer, but a warrior. With cocoa, you wanted to be a large-scale farmer if possible. The new war of the cocoa era was to claim lands and turn others into laborers for you so that you could make money. Do not ask how much the rich had, as no one was counting in the millions, billions, and trillions, as Nigerians now do, carrying tons and tons of cash in Chinese bags nicknamed "Ghana must go!" Cocoa and oil money were not the same, and had to be counted differently—the cocoa money in hundreds and a few thousands. When an ant sees the water in a coconut shell, it looks like the Atlantic Ocean; when successful cocoa farmers earned their money, they regarded themselves as wealthy.

The poor surrendered to the rich, voluntarily, willingly. They even agreed to become exploited tenants on cocoa farms. The rich man now carried a bag full of whips, although he had neither oxen nor goats but only poor fellowmen to use and control. As the poor sang his praise, he left the donkey alone to bear the load. The poor looked at him, just as they looked at a fool, with hatred, but they masked this with a pleasant smile. Perhaps the poor thought that those who refused to obey and go along could never become commanders.

Everybody remembered the time they first saw *igi aramanda*. In 1968, some boasted that they had seen it first when they were just babies; some said that they were born with it in the same year; some said that it preceded their birth. Everyone remembered. None was telling a lie, even if you said you saw cocoa on the very day of your birth. One way of recounting memory in depth was well understood, as if one was telling of a moment when the eyes were located on the knees. As they told their different stories, cocoa and other events were united like friends and families: Cocoa and the use of "half-English" were united like bones and meat; cocoa and the book were united in land sites; and cocoa and money were united like mother and child. Akanran was full of stories of *igi aramanda*, personal stories of what people knew about cocoa and what it did for them, and what it failed to do for them. I enjoyed all these stories from members of different generations, each relishing the story of how cocoa presented a glorious beginning.

By the time many of the story narrators were born in villages and towns, the *igi aramanda* that they saw had become *igi-owo*. The story of cocoa in the morning was different from its story in the evening. Cocoa enabled them to generate a living and to become *olaju*, civilized people who could use cash to purchase objects of modernity—radios, wristwatches, shoes, fine clothes, and corrugated iron sheets to cover their mud houses. They began to see the ebb and flow of life politics on the basis of what cocoa could do and what it could not do. When cocoa fetched good prices, people celebrated the anniversary of the deaths of their fathers who had died ten years earlier—an excuse to call a party, slaughter a few goats, and feed people with local delicacies. A man could foment troubles with his first wife so that he could use the opportunity to marry a second. He could aspire to have one house in the city and another in the village. Everybody wanted more from *igi-owo*. Individuals wanted more, and the government wanted more. Cocoa: the savior of individuals, the hope of the poor, the shield of the powerless, the dream of the living, and the backbone of the government. Then came a preacher with the message of a new day, a new beginning, when cocoa would create a paradise on earth.

Cocoa should do good for all of the poor. It must do good for them. Cocoa could be compelled to do good. Its doing good must be a mission, rescuing the bulk of the money it produced from the hands of *ijoba ika* (the wicked government) and putting it into those of *awon eniyan onin-urere* (the kind-hearted people). Cocoa was not doing enough good for the poor because the *ijoba ika* took the profit from it and spent it in England. If all the profits from cocoa could be spent in our land, the people were told during *Ogun Etila*—the name for the Second World War, with Hitler's name stamped on it—there would be no single poor person in the land; all the roads would be paved with gold; everybody would have a job; indeed, many could even just sleep, and they would be fine. Why would the *oyinbo* not vomit their hatred of us? Talk circulated everywhere that if cocoa money were spent on the cocoa producers themselves, the world would become as good as the heavenly paradise. What they were waiting for, shortly before I came into the world, was just one good man, a kind-hearted one who would stop the *oyinbo* from spending the profits in England. A mother may laugh before pregnancy, but she will have to cry before delivery. We would laugh first and cry later.

Enter the reformer, a man who received the code name of Ojugo (the bespectacled). He was called Ojugo in discussions that linked his name to the struggles of 1968, and also as one of those who would eventually be involved in its resolution after things had spun out of control. Not that half the people in 1968 liked Ojugo, but this did not matter for now. Ojugo, the reformer, wanted to link the cocoa pods with politics, the farms with progress. By the time the farmers saw him and listened to his ideas, he himself had left the village for the city, moving from possession of a minimal set of clothes, short of wearing rags, to possession of one of the largest wardrobes of any Yoruba man; from poverty to riches; from believing in Ogun and Sango to believing in Jesus Christ; from a polygamous setting to a monogamous one; and from a bare face to one always covered with a pair of glasses, which gave him the nickname of "Ojugo"—a face covered with glasses. His eyeglasses were not his mask, as you could still see his full face and figure, and he could see you. His real name was Obafemi Awolowo, but those at Akanran always called him Ojugo, and those in the public called him Awo. If Oduduwa created the Yoruba, Ojugo promised to create the food to feed them.

Ojugo fell short of being deified, although he was canonized. There was just one reason why Ojugo did not become a god: It did not occur to him to ask his people to make him one. Awolowo, his surname, had a cultic origin, as in *awo* (secrecy) and *babalawo* (possessor of secrets). As a master political strategist, he was a cultist of extraordinary competence, using the mythology of political fraternity as a source of power. Forming a cabal, his cult members were fiercely loyal to him, in both life and death. This was precisely what Sango, the fiery god, accomplished, using his ability to spout fire and water from his mouth to ravage farms, burn and roast his enemies, or destroy villages and towns with a deluge of unstoppable rainfall, thunderstorms, and erosion. If Ojugo had asked members of his fraternity to make him a god, they would not have declined, for he was both clever and ambitious. They already had many images of him in clay, wood, metal, and paint. They already had the stools on which to place the symbols. They had money to buy palm oil, cocks, and corn to use as objects of sacrifice. Their man, like Sango, could appear angry

Nicknamed Ojugo, Chief Obafemi Awolowo was a preeminent politician, first premier of the Western Region in the 1950s, then chairman of the Federal Executive Council in 1968 and 1969. Photograph taken in 1956. Ministry of Information, Ibadan.

and defiant, the cool water that disturbs the hot, the wind that blows away flour and powder. Or he could have asked to become their second Ogun.

After all, he was a pathfinder. If Ogun had used his skills to clear paths in the forest and jungles so that humans had roads to reach their game and farms, Ojugo raised money to board a ship to cross the Atlantic Ocean to receive Western education from *ilu oba*—the land of the kings, not the Alafin of Oyo, once our greatest king, but England, where a woman known as the Queen was their monarch. He did not receive an education in the skills to build roads, cure diseases, or teach, but to argue for and against, to defend the guilty and innocent, and to gain entry into government houses. It was the right set of skills for the time, as his people had to argue first before they could build roads and bridges. Ojugo was among those who argued that the *oyinbo* should go back to their own land, and he was also among those who defended the *omowe* (the educated) in collecting power from the *oyinbo*, who did not return power to their original rightful owners, the *oba* of this town and that. *Oyinbo* and his *omowe* enemies always talked before they acted—and their talking produced verbal warfare and physical destruction.

Ojugo became part of the story, for it was he who, for both good and bad reasons, told the people what cocoa could do for millions of them if they were willing to do things differently. They must agree to stop sharing profits with the *oyinbo*, thereby giving Ojugo the power to control revenues and re-channel funds to the localities where cocoa grew and where it was traded. Ojugo needed both the people and the cocoa they produced. Our pain was caused by those preventing us from using our cocoa money, the sore we had to touch many times because it hurt. We began to wish evil on the *oyinbo* and to treat them like the guest you put in the corner of a house because of your resentment. We used to go to the forest for sticks to cook with, not aiming for the perfect sticks, as one was bent, the other crooked, and the next had multiple curves. Our hands were full, but now we were told that we could search for perfect sticks and would not come back home empty-handed. This was very charming indeed.

"Life more abundant!" Ojugo pronounced. When you see cocoa, smile, as fortune is about to smile back at you, he assured his followers, who numbered in the millions. They began to believe that the multiple wives and multitudes of children that cocoa had given them would no longer need to worry too much about their future. With Ojugo in command, there would be schools to educate them and jobs awaiting them in government offices, too many to fill. Pay £1 a year in tax and get £30 back in benefits. With our river now flowing, we did not need the small streams or the drips of water.

With Ojugo, cocoa was a miracle of change; cocoa farmers were the miracle workers; the roads and schools that cocoa would build were testimonies to the miracle. If you needed gold jewelry, you must look for cocoa. *Igi-owo* became the *igi ominira* (tree of freedom): freedom from the *oyinbo* and the land they came from; freedom from poverty; freedom from want; freedom from disease. I was born into the moment of *igi ominira*: The hospital where I was born was made possible by it; the free elementary education that I attended was the product of that time. When I went to march to celebrate the Queen at the Liberty Stadium, we were reminded that it was the largest stadium in West Africa, made possible by *igi ominira*. Cocoa was beginning to deliver on its promises, a god whom we worshipped and who showered us with kindness and benefits.

In the years preceding the conflicts and violence of 1968, cocoa's name had changed to *igi ijongbon* (the tree of troubles) and *igi ote* (the tree of intrigue). The rewards of freedom were not equally distributed, as cocoa was giving wealth to some and poverty to others. Cocoa showed its real face, that of *wahala*, a loan word of Hausa provenance that means "trouble," "obstacles," and "tension." An individual could be afflicted with *wahala*, just as an entire nation, too, could experience it. Cocoa divided the rich from the poor, a *wahala*. There were those with education and those without, another *wahala*. Buoda Gebu and Leku had to live in the same place, with Buoda Gebu assuring his disciples that they were going to heaven and Leku to hell, the *wahala* of afterlife. The *wahala* was now round the clock: In the night, cocoa sent out sorcerers and witches who roamed around in search of blood to suck; during the day, cocoa sent out devious men disguised as good ones, sometimes as clerks and police officers, or even as chiefs and commissioners, or as council officials or cooperative officers.

Cocoa revealed its dark side in the 1950s: It could promise you some money and actually take it all back. The trees would grow, give you crops to sell, and you were fine, very fine. You began to plan on the money not just for next year, but for the years ahead. You passed among the trees, and you began to dream of wealth in later years; you began to think of new loans, even dream of new wives. Then cocoa came with its tricks, as Ibadan farmers saw in the 1950s in what they called the sickness of "swollen shoots," which meant the trees refused to produce the crops that could be sold. By the time the diseases were cured, the land was no longer good—the new trees refused to grow as the farmers had hoped. Those who had money looked for land elsewhere; those without were stuck in thick mud, raising their hands to heaven with open palms, begging God to assist them. As cocoa failed, confident people began to call themselves *eru Anabi* (the slaves of Allah) and *mekunnu* (the poor).

Cocoa had penetrated everywhere. Cocoa was the core of the government: no cocoa, no government. Cocoa could survive without the government; but the government could not survive without cocoa. The new money from oil, discovered in the faraway Niger Delta, was just coming in trickles in the late 1960s and being used to buy weapons and ammunition to kill both Nigerians and Biafrans. Oil, which has been the main source of revenue since the 1970s, came with bloodshed, neither of which has ever been disconnected from the other ever since. The second chapter in the marriage of oil and blood is that of corruption, to which cocoa also contributed, but as a widow's mite compared to what later occurred with oil with all their imperial majesties stealing as much as uncontrollable greed would allow them. In our days, when cocoa was king, politicians and bureaucrats received their salaries from cocoa revenues. Corrupt politicians and state officials stole from the cocoa revenues. Cars and buildings were made possible by the sale of cocoa to other countries in exchange for imports.

For the government to work and for the politicians to have a large enough cut to take, cocoa and those who produced it must be tamed. In arranging the power hierarchies, you can put those who produced cocoa at the very bottom and those who managed the revenues at the very top. In the middle were the intermediaries, salaried state workers who lived in the cities and managed the people in the villages. Many of these intermediaries were stationed at the secretariat; they were the *sekiteri* (secretaries), with agreeable offices in what they called the Ministry of Agriculture. Cocoa would never be found in this ministry as a product but only in files, with officers wearing ties using "full English" to discuss cocoa and other crops. Policies were discussed without those in the villages and farms in attendance: They were too dirty to enter those buildings and too ignorant to have opinions.

Were the *sekiteri* and their *mesenja* (messengers) discussing serious matters on cocoa or just gossiping about the Akanran people? Surely, they were gossiping for the most part because of what they later told us in public: They described us as indolent, uneducated, unresponsive to change, and insensitive to their need for generating revenues. The tongue of an enemy can kill faster than a gun. Whenever there was a revenue shortage, we were anti-government. Our laziness, we were constantly reminded, would ultimately bring down the government. Did we not see the bees and termites, how they worked hard to build their nice homes and make a living for themselves? We did. How could villagers miss the termites and bees, our neighbors? We got it: We were the termites and bees who should be working hard in order for them to live well. The queen mother and the honey were delicious for city dwellers.

The work habit of those men at the secretariat was different from ours at Akanran, and they were different in terms of what they did with cocoa money. They were not like those bees and termites they wanted us to emulate but more like the big crocodiles in the water and the lion in the forest sitting in the shade. After the men at the secretariat had talked for two hours in the morning, they would take a break to drink tea and eat biscuits, read newspapers, and relax. They were taking their second meal of the day at the same time that we were taking our first bite at Akanran—roasted yams in a farm hut. I was always eager by that time to have my first meal of the day. When we arrived early to the farm, we rekindled the fire from the previous day. We never allowed the fire to die completely, as it meant starting all over again. We dipped the yam into the hot ashes and put out more firewood to have something ready to roast corn and grill small game, which the snares might have caught if we were lucky. The tea and biscuits became one of the reasons we wanted to do well in school, and the roasted yams became the thing to leave behind. Children of the civilized would sometimes hide biscuits in their pockets to give to those like me, but they would reject the pieces of roasted yam that I took out of my pocket and offered in exchange. I just ate both. No tea.

Tea break over, the men needed to discuss the urgent matters of the day, and only one matter was always urgent: the numbers needed to win the football pool bet that must be submitted and paid for by Saturday morning to await the result on Sunday. The numbers were known as "bankers," that is, assured, certain. They were the "bankers" revealed by dreams and prophecy, by witches and sorcerers, conjurers who could change nights into days, days into nights, men into women. They were talking about the results of soccer matches in the faraway United Kingdom, matches played in stadiums that they had never visited, but their fortunes in Nigeria were tied to the draws, the away and home victories or losses. Credit is due here: They knew the names of all the teams and players, no matter how many. They even knew the names of the fathers and mothers of soccer players and their horoscopes. They studied the profiles and results of games from previous years, made informed bets on those that would end in draws by looking at photographs of soccer players, the weather, and the statements of British politicians. Horoscope calculations could yield numbers: If a player was born in December and the game was in December, try to manipulate figure 12, but since a match could not end in a 12–12 draw, begin to think of 1–1, 2–2 as your first permutation. But there was also 0–0, if none made 1–1, but why not add some figures to 1 and 2, to make it 3–3? I joined in this game of permutations at some point in 1969 but quickly discovered that Sunday would bring not salvation or redemption, but only the gnashing of teeth.

As men spoke about the "bankers," they circulated stories about people who had won the previous week, the missed opportunity of those who lost by just one wrong number. This week, they would win! Now, they had to talk about what the winners of the upcoming results would do with their money. All openly declared their ambitions. The short man would buy more clothes and shoes at the main market in Gbagi. With excess cash in his pocket, he would not haggle or bargain. If the Kora, the name for all Lebanese merchants, even if some were Indians, asked £4 for a piece of fabric, he would just pay it and leave. He would then walk back to the store so that the Kora would think he had changed his mind, not knowing that he wanted to buy another set for Sikira, his would-be wife, to make the "& co," when men and women dressed the same way, as in wearing a uniform.

The long man already had enough clothes and would spend his own windfall on buying a plot of land. He was tired of living on family land and in a compound where everybody would "poke nose" into his affairs. He wanted to live far away. My father did the same, leaving our compound at Ojagbo to build his house far away at Agbokojo, among Ijebu people and other strangers. As people gained new sources of money, they began to leave family compounds to build their own houses, starting with one-story buildings. As they acquired more money, they would add another story on the top, neither seeking permission from the authorities nor checking whether the foundations could withstand the addition. What the salary of the long man could not do, the lottery would deliver. Amin Jesu. Imagine! Greedy people dragging the holy name of Jesus into gambling matters.

The hefty man would dream of using his own winnings to host a party. He had not been happy that he could not put on an elaborate funeral for his mother who had passed away seven years earlier. He felt as if he had betrayed his mother. As her only son who left the farm to get a job at the secretariat, he was expected by everyone to have a large feast with the funeral instead of just dumping the woman into the grave and failing to provide tables full of food and cold beer and cool music to entertain his guests. Until he had money to reclaim his honor, his life would not be the same. He was single, not because he wanted to remain so, but he did not want to owe society a second party or to hold the marriage feast before the funeral party. This was his week to win money, and he had better spend more of his salary on the football pools this time around.

The lean man, always looking as if food had never entered his stomach, fantasized about traveling abroad with his own money. He was always carrying his passport in his left pocket, the pool numbers in the right. Through correspondence with a pen pal with whom he exchanged monthly letters, he already had a friend and a place to stay in Glasgow. He would fly to London and then take a train. He was able to recount all the train stops between London and Glasgow, and he knew the station at which he had to exit the train. His friend would be waiting to welcome him with open arms. Six months later, he would marry a white woman and raise seven children, all with names of the apostles. He would visit Nigeria every three years. One pool win, and he would buy his air ticket, and off he would go to the land of fortunes where money grows on trees. Moving from one win to another, his life would end in peace and tranquility.

They had all spent the money they were yet to make. Every week, they had a dream; they repeated their dreams each week. They needed the money from betting, as the profits made possible by cocoa were not enough for them to realize their ambitions. We needed money at Akanran for the necessities of life, just asking for less taxes and more money for our product. Men who gambled needed money for new houses, cars, clothes, and shoes. Their children had to go to good schools. A man needed more than one wife to display success. Each week as they gambled, they gave our cocoa money to the Lebanese and Indians who controlled the football pool trade. The Lebanese and Indians gave a cut to the English and pocketed the rest. The majority of them would lose on Sunday, a common story, but they would rekindle hope on Monday morning.

Out of the multitude of stories of pool winners, one winner could neither be found nor identified by the players. When you asked for the big winner at Ibadan, the one whose name every gambler mentioned who won close to "thousands upon thousand pounds," they would tell you that he was now living in Lagos in a big mansion. Were you to go to Lagos to look for him, you would hear from the football pool gamblers there that the richest man at Ibadan made his money from pool betting. If you rushed back to Ibadan to look for the man, you would be told that he had relocated to the northern city of Kaduna, as too many poor people who wanted his assistance were disturbing him. All these rich men existed only in the imagination, and their specific addresses and locations were always alleged to be secret. I knew the houses of those who supposedly used human organs for money, but not what should have been the easier ones to find, the houses of those who made money from gambling. Why in the world would Yoruba men think that they could grow rich through the Lebanese and Indians?

The discussions on betting, away and home games, draws and winners, dreams and aspirations, could be draining. The men had become hungry by noon. As only a few drank coffee, there was no need to take a coffee break or look for cafés for lunch. There were no cafés anyway: Those arrived forty years later, places people actually drank no coffee but used computers for 419 scams. From a café at Ibadan, you could receive an email in Austin announcing that you would receive $50 million left for you in a will after paying $2 million as processing fees. Fools fall for it, for their frontier in Austin no longer has oil to extract, Angolan slaves to put to work, or Mexicans to clean the streets. The Nigerian 419 is the new frontier.

The secretariat men drank tea, of course, but this was mere hot water that could not fill their stomachs. After one visit to the toilet, their stomachs were back to empty. More tea, more visits to the toilet. When the stomach was angry, there was only one sacrifice: food from the *buka*, the "bukataria" stores made of makeshift sheds in unoccupied land around the secretariat, behind buildings or by the roadside. Planning in the city has never been about beauty but about convenience. The elegant buildings needed *buka* companions to make things look normal: that is, in chaos. The wood used for scaffolding and decking was converted to good use to create *bukas* everywhere. It was not necessary to have public toilets, an undue burden on resources, but it was acceptable to allow citizens to turn all the available spaces into toilets. Even the governor could stop his car and pee by the roadside. The women and their domestics cooked at the back of the *bukas*, releasing smoke into the environment, but no one cared about this; it was the aroma that mattered. The aroma was actually used for judging the best time to go. As the aromas reached the offices, it was time to stop talking about soccer games and gambling and the numbers they needed. Off to the *bukas*!

The customers arrived in twos and threes, and would find benches on which to sit inside the *buka*. You could go to the back to see the food and check on your meat preferences, even to flirt with the cooks or the serving women. The gentlemen looked at the boiling pots of soup, with the red palm oil floating on top. They salivated, and you could see it in the movements of their tongues and eyes, their eagerness to demolish the starch, just as the viper attacks the frog. The not-so-gentle ones, the ugly men who knew no shame, looked at other things and all of a sudden might tap the buttocks of a cook who would respond in anger one day and with a smile the next.

"Give me two pounded yam, one cow leg, one cow skin, one tripe, and one meat." This person wanted to eat well and had the money for what they called the "assorted" option.

Another would raise his voice: "Jemila, I want *amala* with *gbegiri* and two pieces of liver." This must be an Ibadan man ordering the favorite food of the city.

"Answer me now now, Iya Kamoru; I requested food one hour ago, *eba* and okra; are you ignoring me because I do not want to eat meat today?" This must be a lowly paid staff member of the Ministry of Agriculture whose salary was not enough to add protein to his meal. Not to buy meat would lead to jokes: "Old man, you must be broke." No, he was not—he had been consuming so much meat in the last seven days that when it was all added up it was bigger than a whole goat minus the horns.

"You wanted to say a cow, not a goat," someone would reply in a jiffy. He would keep quiet. Why not try the liver of the tortoise or the intestine of the mosquito or the horns of the snail, someone might say, just to keep the mockery going. When the *eba* without meat arrived, the man would look only at his food, finish his meal, and rush out before anyone remembered the absence of meat.

It was not always the case that the man without meat was ill paid. Maybe he had overspent on the pool and was waiting for the results. Maybe he had to pay a hire purchase installment on his motorcycle or social attire. Maybe he had many wives and children. The messengers had more children and wives than the administrative officers—the latter had power and status in the office, the former in the compounds. Whether a messenger or an officer, by the middle of the month, with two weeks to go to the next paycheck, many would have run out of money. Payday and the two days that followed were always the best: Everybody ordered meat and would add beer to the order. Days later, they dropped the beer and drank water. By the middle of the month they began to reduce the number of pieces of meat. Some few days from payday, they even gave up the *eba* and *amala* and began to look for a Tapa woman. The Tapa were all over the city, immigrants from the Borgu region to the far north of the Yoruba. The real name for them is Nupe—only God knows what they called us, but it would not be Yoruba, if only because they would want to treat others as they had been treated. The Tapa were good at roasting corn and peanuts, and they knew how to sell them in the most minute amounts. "I want more nuts than corn," from the one with more coins than the one who ordered more corn than nuts. Both would fill up their stomachs with water. They called it "clean water" as it was from the pipes. The secretariat had metal pipes that brought water from a dam, much better than the water collected from the streams that we had to drink.

Lunch over, they remembered work; more files to be read. Work in the ministry was about reading files or holding meetings. An easy job, at least much easier than at Akanran, where people worked on the farms in heat and humidity. But many of them were already tired after their heavy lunch. Pounded yam and *eba* have an excellent way of shutting down the body, asking the person at least to take a rest. I use both to induce sleep; even now, five minutes after I have devoured pounded yam, the loud noise from my snoring fills the room. They did not want to rest: They wanted to work, but the relevant files were missing. Maybe they had mistakenly sent them to the Ministry of Finance. Well, there was always tomorrow, and it was better to work on those files when the head was "very cool" from a night's sleep. One man took his bag, and off he went; another took his bag and followed. They were supposed to close at 5 p.m. but by 3 p.m. half of them had already left for the day. Several files would be left open on the tables to give the impression that they were still around. The others who remained behind spent their time complaining about one thing or another.

These "ministry men," as they were called, were never happy with us: To them, we were too lazy and unproductive. We did not work hard enough to produce the vast amounts of cocoa they needed. We were cheats as the cocoa that we supplied sometimes contained small rocks, animal dung, and dirt. We needed to be instructed about the value of work, the methods of work, the ethics of using time, and the ethos of spending. The ministry men must send us materials to read, but, since many of us could neither read nor write, they would send us people who would read them to us and give us instructions to ensure that we obeyed. Some farmers asked questions: Why send those materials in the first place if you knew that we could not read them? At first, they said we did not follow the contents because they were written in English. So, these ministry men were dumb. Unbelievable! Then, they spent money to translate their pamphlets from English to Yoruba. We got a second copy of the same materials. The photographs were similar but not the words. The ministry men forgot that those who could not read English could also not read Yoruba. So they sent their men to read the materials to us in Yoruba. People listened. After the ministry men left, the women would be the first to talk: "Do these men have jobs to do? What do they know about the paths of the snake in the bush?" A man could answer: "They are just around for relaxation." Sure, that was it, as they demanded free food and drink, good palm wine and pounded yam with good bush meat.

We needed to cooperate with the ministry men, collaborate with the government, and coordinate with ourselves. Cooperation was the keyword, and people pronounced the word in various ways: "kofurate," "kopulate," "koferation." In order to cooperate, we must never fight with the government but always support the government of the day. God appointed the government over us. We must form cooperative societies. Many of us joined cooperative societies named after villages, neighborhoods, and aspirations, as in "Egbe Owode" (money has arrived) and "Egbe Alalubarika" (the society of the blessed), or even named for a wish, as in "Madojutimi" (do not put me to shame). Some societies appeared as unions of farmers, again with various names, to discuss cooperation between themselves and cooperation between our unions and the ministry men. The better cooperatives were in the city, and the government used those to teach us how to manage our lives in the villages.

These cooperatives had more half-educated members than those of the villages. The produce buyers, ten times richer than the farmers, joined together, adopting names that portrayed themselves as successful and happy. Produce buyers and farmers lived in two different worlds: Produce buyers had better clothes, ate better food, and had closer connections with the ministry men. Politicians, too, joined cooperatives. You have to understand what this meant if you ever saw a politician who was a member: The accounts of the cooperatives would always be in trouble— when money was not missing, there would be no records of those keeping the money, and when money was missing, there would be no treasurer in attendance to confirm it.

There were bigger cooperatives, some much bigger than our villages. The biggest was the Cooperative Department, an arm of the Ministry of Agriculture. Do I need to remind you of the heavy work schedule of these men who worked harder than bees and termites? The honey they produced was the Cooperative College, where their sons obtained certificates in Cooperative Studies that were said to qualify them to supervise all the cooperative societies of the farmers. Whenever the Cooperative officers attended the meetings of farmers to discuss with them how to organize, they must be well fed and entertained and given cash to enable them to travel back home in safety. Cooperative officers got paid in the city, in their ministry, and they received their allowances and emoluments in the villages from the poor farmers whose lives they promised to elevate. The allowances must be paid if the farmers wanted government recognition, which qualified them to sell their cocoa to approved buying agents and to receive subsidized pesticides and promises of government loans to expand their acreages.

The small cooperative societies must deposit their collections in the Cooperative Bank, so that all cooperatives were linked, with the smaller ones feeding the bigger ones. The politicians and produce buyers who opened voluntary accounts were those privileged to take loans from the Cooperative Bank. It was the same with the Agricultural Credit Corporation, which, we were told, was created for us. The majority of small farmers could not obtain loans from them. Those with the privilege had the collateral, the farmers had not. What were non-farmers doing with credit from an Agriculture Credit Corporation? What about the farmers' valuable land and cocoa trees that the ministry men had spoken about? No, those were not good enough for collateral. All of a sudden, when a farmer applied for a small loan, the land that produced the cocoa that built the Ministry of Agriculture and the Cooperative Bank was no longer valuable. "You know," the bank officer would lecture the farmer, "the land could die, it may not be yours by this time next year," or "You do not have papers that the land is yours," or "The land has no cash value."

The poor farmer looked terribly puzzled by what he had just heard. He remembered the days shortly before his father's death, in the presence of all his father's wives, when the land was transferred to him. Was the word of his father, now the ancestor to whom he made an annual sacrifice of goat and chicken, not enough? Beads of sweat covered his face, as his hope for access to capital to improve on his cocoa farm and set up his youngest wife as a small trader was now dashed. He had been hoping that his wife would be selling food and palm wine in front of the house so that he could augment his income, and also so that he could allow the woman to send her children to school. When expenses were to be incurred, the children belonged to the woman; when gifts came from the children, the man suddenly became the king. He wondered why the ministry men told him that the land had no cash value when its product, cocoa, was being used to send the bank officers' children to school and to pay for the building that now served as the ministry men's office.

Very cleverly, the Cooperative Bank destroyed the age-old method of saving and raising loans, the *esusu*, so well established that it crossed the Atlantic Ocean with the slaves who introduced it to Jamaica, Cuba, and Brazil. Such a charmingly simple and friendly arrangement: You formed a club with those in your community to contribute money and collect your savings in rotation. What you put in was what you got. *Esusu* instilled the discipline of saving, since you must pay as agreed to without fail, as well as invest, since others must see the good things that you had done with the money. When you began laying the foundation of your house, *esusu* made it possible; when you roofed it, it was your *esusu* collection that gave you the bulk of the money. *Esusu* allowed you to have enough money to marry a wife and send your son to grammar school. You must respect others in the community because personal interdependence was crucial. You could not collect money and run away. The Cooperative Bank was for the others, and it was very successful in collecting small amounts of money and giving them out in bigger sums to the privileged and well connected. As the big men defaulted, they brought the Cooperative Bank to its knees until it eventually crashed and collapsed some twenty years after it was opened. My own money, put there in the 1970s, went with it—not up in smoke, as it was not a case of fire, but into the private pockets of rogues, some dead (their souls remain restless) and some living, parading as dignified chiefs riding in fancy cars.

Whether the ministry men visited the villages or the villagers visited the Cooperative Bank, they talked down to us. One day, I felt like a maggot, the next a fly. The life of the fly was very short, and you must learn to avoid the lamp. I carried cocoa on my head thinking that I was a good citizen serving Pasitor and the community. No matter how hard we tried, we were cast in a dead past. When the government needed new products, like tobacco, we were praised for adopting new practices and ideas that would bring us closer to our fortunes. We worked hard, as a group, as individuals, as struggling villagers, but the new practices swelled no pockets with cash. We began to disconnect work from success. Work, I was told many times, did not translate to success. I was called an *akura* to my face many times, an insult that meant that I was an impotent man who could not spend his time in private rooms with women and could focus only on work. An *akura*, lacking any passion for women or hobbies, worked around the clock. Bad news: The more he worked, the poorer he became, and the farmers began to compare him with the Hausa in Sabo (the ward where those from the North lived), who walked around the city fetching and selling water and firewood but wore rags. Work, some began to sing, had no correlation with wealth: The man with two legs walked about without any means of livelihood, while the cripple who sat on the same spot was able to amass wealth.

Maybe the ministry men would bring some luck to us—maybe good luck and not bad luck. In the hope that the new ideas from the agents in charge of change from the secretariat would work, like magic, not a few became risk takers. They actually took loans from moneylenders to buy new clothes and shoes, not realizing that the creditors would later pounce on them with vehemence. Itinerant moneylenders flooded the villages, diverting profits from trade and produce buying to money lending while charging exorbitant interests. Known as *sogundogoji* (convert twenty to forty), they ruined not a few farmers who just could not repay the principal no matter how hard they tried. The charging of interest of well over 100 percent, so that you took a loan of £5 to pay £12, sent many to their untimely destruction, death, or relocation. Villagers were now on the lookout for tax collectors and creditors, and they had to set up monitoring posts to spot them and flee to hideouts on the farms where mosquitoes awaited. Some had to go on the run, ending in faraway Kano, where they were lost forever.

The ministry men had good allies in the moneylenders, and both treated the legions of poor farmers as mentally retarded, only able to eat, drink palm wine, and associate with their fellow dirty folk. We needed help, the money lenders and ministry men would say, but we hated ourselves so much that we rejected what they offered. Our *esusu* was only made up of folk and friends who could do less for us, they warned. *Esusu* was not enough, we were told, as it was inadequate to gather resources to bring about any significant progress. So they asked us to form cooperatives. We did. They collected our small monies and stole them. Trust broke down. We stayed with them for a while, in clusters of cooperatives, if only to avoid their wrath. We lacked the means to withstand them. They threatened not to buy our products unless we were members of one cooperative society or another. Whenever we were broke, we would accept the terms of the *sogundogoji*, not because we were fools, but because we had reached the end of the earth. We could not do anything right. If we did our work and remained quiet, we were seen as stupid. If we did our work and spoke up, we were too aggressive. If we supported political candidates, we were being used; if we did not support the politicians, we would be victimized. If we spoke a few sentences, we were harsh. If we spoke not a single sentence, we were docile. Speak, you were arrogant; keep quiet, you were dumb.

We contracted our tongues to others who spoke for us in public. We understood; we let them talk. Maybe those who listened attached importance to the words of chameleons with nine faces. We did not. Whenever we spoke for ourselves, with vague references to what to expect if our demands were ignored, we were met with a barrage of criticisms: We were disrespectful; we spoke too much; we acted prematurely; our plans were too old, ill conceived, too far removed from the modern age. So, let them speak for us. They even spoke about how bad water gave us guinea-worms, as if they drank bad water and had guinea-worms, and they wanted the government to give them money to tell us not to drink guinea-worm-infested water. Did we not know that the water gave us guinea-worms? City landlords proclaimed themselves as farmers who knew our interests. We did not know most of them; we knew only those among them who had cocoa lands and used many of us as tenants. We were told that they wrote about us in the newspapers that we could not read, talking about how they wanted to champion our interests. They claimed credit for our struggles; they spoke as if they were in pain, as if they felt the pain of others. These were handsome men who forgot that baldness creeps in slowly, followed by wrinkles and then collapsing legs, forgetting that they would become ugly before they died.

We began to notice that they were writing us out of history. Nigeria was created without us. They sent the British away without our efforts—their Western education made it possible, and all we did was to clap for them, shouting "messiah" at the top of our voices. They were able to form political parties, but we were too poor and illiterate to form our own associations. We only followed them as idiots, zombies, and cannon fodder. When those with Western education fought the British to grant us independence to become a new country called Nigeria, we were not to be found.

*Awa ode*. We the fools. We accepted the slogan, their motto. We fully understood the game; for it was no more than a game of power designed to tap into cocoa revenues. The nation was the playing field and we the people, the ball that you kicked around until you put us into the net. The goal was the score that made your pockets full. Take a break, rest, enjoy the victory. Yes, we had neither money nor access to power. Yes, we had too many uneducated people among us. Yes, we could suffer from divisions caused by our allegiances to different leaders and religions, but we understood the politics, the goal of politics, and the behavior of soldiers and politicians. We understood the young military officers who took over power in 1966. We saw the governor as too young to be a governor and saw that the basis of his power was not in rationality but in the guards who surrounded him. His office and residence were military fortresses. The man on horseback, he saw himself in the color of gold, displaying vanity and pride, overrating his manhood. They wanted us to follow and support him, but we understood the lies. When the politicians recited the list of promises, we called it an *alo*: stories, tales, fables. Whenever the farmers were gathering to listen to a politician, they mocked him by saying *alalo de*. "Here comes the fable man." When they looked at him face-to-face, they would smile; when they turned their back, they would lift their noses up to indicate that he was telling stories. When the promises piled up, they added a second name, *alala de*. "Here comes the dreamer." Fables and dreams were close, both existing in the realm of disbelief.

When a politician gave us money, we said it was just a token from the revenues stolen from us, for where else could he have gotten the money? We disliked the *oyinbo* because they hated us, only keeping to the law of Moses that if you get slapped on the right side of the face, you should yield the left side to be slapped too. We thought that if we sent away the *oyinbo*, we would at least know the homes and addresses of the new leaders, Yoruba like us. We even knew and could talk to their relatives. And anyone with an *oriki*, a cognomen like my Isola, could be spoken to in words that would cool down his anger and generate calmness so that he could say what was on his mind. Call the madman a bridegroom so you can have a conversation and then be granted passage. So we followed them when they asked for independence and for our support. We followed evil, and we reaped evil. Some of these, our own men, were funny; many of them sold butter when it was hot and salt when it was raining, and some among them could remove house posts and mainframe to use as firewood to roast meat.

We were on our own, hanging in there, hoping that as we kept moving, we would not reach the wall to be pushed back into retreat. No one represented us at the secretariat. The shame was that some claimed to represent us, calling themselves honorable councilors—Honorable for Ibadan, Honorable for Ogbomoso, Honorable for Abeokuta—all "honorables" moving about in flowing gowns and in newly acquired cars, baboons who looked exactly like humans. Honorable Nonsense! These were men who would take cats to graze in the savanna and feed a lion with grass. They rode their tongues like an angry horse, racing with fury to crash in a pit, and buying troubles with their legs. The military boys, who dropped out of high school when these honorables were still struggling to complete their education, came with their whips and guns to send away the honorables and their luggage from their offices and houses to the bush. The farmers called the coup a "cough," like tuberculosis, although the last two letters of *gh* sounded like a long *ph.* In jest, they spoke about the "cough" that brought an honorable to hide in the village, that sent another to disguise himself as a Fulani cattle herder with his white kaftan and straw hat marching slowly with his six cows. Some borrowed their wives' clothes and dressed like women, putting oranges on their chest to make fake breasts. Misfortune befell the health and wealth of a few of them, and they disappeared from circulation. Those who survived grew into monsters in later years, able to steal drums and play them in public without caring whether anyone shouted at them "thief, thief, thief."

Behind the backs of the ministry men and the *sogundogoji*, we began to talk in whispers and to form our own associations, united by our dignity in poverty. We began to see money as no more than a "messenger" to be used to run errands. *Eniyan*—the human—should not be the errand boy of money; money was a slave, not a person. The source of our strength and dignity was not *owo*, money or wealth, but poverty. There was no point in continuing to look for an object that we could not find. It was an elusive object, a *kadara* (one that was glued to you as your destiny), *alejo* (the visitor that appeared and took off before you were able to spell his name), and *asitani* (the biblical Satan that misled and cast spells). Rather than looking for *owo*, we would look for *asiribo*. *Asiri* meant a secret: As long as you were able to cover up your secrets, you were just fine. We were fine. The hunger of the body nourished the souls: The fragility of the body strengthened the mind, the collapsing legs empowered the brains, and the deadening silence supplied calmness. We were beginning to summon up courage, realizing that hundreds of flies could not lift the cover of a pot, that pigs do not eat men.

The mottoes on the lorries that conveyed us from the city to the village reflected our mood far more accurately. "Trust no one" was written on the left side of one truck. Correct. We began to meet in secret and to keep secrets: A thoughtful person does not reveal his hiding place. The politicians and ministry men were not our friends or allies. As we were avoiding their falsehoods, we were befriending the truth. We had nothing to learn from them. The moneylenders despised us: We were beneath them in dignity. They did not want to assist us but to destroy us. We were not at the same level with the morally deprived. The new soldiers were also not our friends. A bad person does not provide good advice. They promised peace but brought war, the poor cooks who spoiled themselves and the porridge. They lied like the politicians and robbed us of our sons and brothers who were now in a place called Biafra to fight a civil war that we had no hand in causing.

The landlords among us, with big cocoa farms, did not speak for us either. We were the fools who gave them the source of wisdom. The landlords preferred the wisdom of their enemies rather than the love of fools. Bald headed, their other beautiful parts gone, but not their mouths that remained brave and their tongues still full of growth. They were farmers like us, but they no longer touched hoes and cutlasses. Their stomachs were actually too big for them to bend down, but their restless fingers could still reach the anus. A farmer had no big stomach. A blacksmith who made the hoes and cutlasses, like the farmers who used them, lost so many calories in his work that consuming an entire mortar of pounded yam would still not make his stomach grow. So, when you saw a farmer with a big stomach, he was more like a businessman who put others to work, the supervisor who was always consuming while others were working. You saw it in the neck, as his would be twice the size of that of his laborer. Produce buyers claimed to represent us, but what they cared about was how to buy cocoa cheaply from us and sell it at higher prices for huge profits. We worked for them. Vultures do not fly over dead bodies without reason. They gave us fake smiles when they wanted to buy our cocoa. We were the hot porridge: Blow air into it to cool it off, then swallow it to destroy it. We would not learn from them, but from ourselves; to accumulate wisdom and power, learn from your allies. We must part ways with the ministry men, produce buyers, and moneylenders and create other means to build bigger fences that make good neighbors.

Over the radio, we were given a generic name: *mekunnu*, the poor. In the newspapers, we were called the masses. We were the poor masses, having the number but lacking the voice. There was a dividing wall between us and them, the non-masses, the non-poor. In bridging this divide, interlocutors and intermediaries were used. We did not choose them, they were chosen by fellow members of their group of non-masses. So the non-masses came to us to "listen" to us, to take back the talking points to members of their class. Nothing happened. Nothing could have happened. We got the blame since we were presented as docile, village cocks that do not know not to crow in the city. We were politically inactive, so they said. What a statement! After we supported the two political parties, the AG of Ojugo and the NCNC of his arch-rival and enemy, the Igbo man from Biafra whom we called Kikiwe ("all books"; his real name was Nnamdi Azikiwe, but he was given his popular name

Nicknamed Kikiwe, Dr. Nnamdi Azikiwe was a preeminent politician, first
president of the independent country of Nigeria, and Biafra's spokesman in
1968–69. Photograph taken in 1960. Ministry of Information, Ibadan.

for using big words in the English language). We believed in those two
parties until they stopped believing in us. The party leaders had their
interests, as clear to us as looking at a photograph: They wanted to line
their pockets with cocoa money. Once in a while, our leaders from the
village or cooperative would be asked to visit the secretariat to meet one
*oga* (boss) or another. They did. They even met *oga patapata*, the very
boss at the top, next to God himself, a man called the *gomina* (governor).
We did not know what was true or false from what they told us; we must
be patient. Development was like a snake that crawls, and it was only very
slowly crawling to our villages, one village at a time. Even today, half a
century later, the snake is yet to crawl as far to reach Akanran.

No one could save us other than ourselves. We started to write letters to express our grievances and demands. We called them petitions, observations, appeals, and prayers. They all made it to the secretariat. They were not read, and we received no replies. Those who received them had to file them, which was why they were paid. They had to spend time to discover the right person to read a file. We spoke to one chief or another, appealed to all the kings in the land, the First Class, the Second Class, and even the Third Class kings; nothing happened. These chiefs ate our food, but no sooner had we left than they went to the toilet to throw up. The letters sent to the secretariat were written in "half-English," not correct English, but clear enough to understand. The words to the chiefs and kings were in Yoruba, correct and clear, very respectful. We called them "our fathers" who lived on earth; nothing happened. They thanked us, which is different from showing love. Our prostrations and profuse declarations of loyalty did little, just as three thousand camels could not purchase the blessings of the prophet. It was time to appeal to our fathers who lived in heaven, wise men who visited you with hatred if you tried to fool them. We were the half blind who never lost hope of seeing. Our hen with chicks must stop perching on the branch of a tall tree if it wants to protect its children.

Action Group (AG): This was the name of a political party that the military proscribed in 1966, that had been founded by Ojugo. We had become members of a "group" (not the proscribed AG), but now needed "action." The bee has honey on its tongue, but it can sting with its tail. We had nothing to do with Ojugo's party; the AG and NCNC only made us laugh because they wanted to count the number of our missing teeth. We were not a political party, but we had become a social movement, no longer the cowards who got beaten without doing any wrong. You can blame those who push you down, but the blame for being unable to get up is yours. Many now wanted to get up. Groups emerged all over the place with different names. Each group comprised poor people coming together as farmers, barbers, traders, tailors, or craftsmen. The farmers in the villages and the poor in the city began to talk, no longer needing the ministry men, resentful of *sogundogoji* and distrustful of politicians and soldiers. Liberation had finally arrived; action had to follow. Woes come within days; happiness in years. We now had the groups in place, and what was needed was the action—action that would speak louder than words. The action must be now, today, for there is no tomorrow. Tomorrow had already chosen to become the parents of the poor. If you want to spend your night in peace, let your neighbors, too, live in peace:

The robed masquerade is ready to dance;
A heavy rain is about to fall;
The man with only one piece of cloth is ready to watch.
A masquerade must never dance in the rain;
The rain cannot change its mind;
The man with one cloth cannot afford to get wet.

Isola was there, not even missing the cockroaches as they gave birth, the butterflies as they dated each other, the frogs as they mated in the shrubs. Isola, the big actor in a big event, needed to get home before he could report what he had seen. Is he home yet?

# CHAPTER 7

# Locust Invasions

✦ ✦ ✦

Ogun was called into action because locusts had invaded the land, devouring all the plants and animals. They brought some strange insects with them that consumed all the water. The locusts and the strange creatures stopped the rains and blocked all the sources of irrigation so that no new planting was possible. Humans were being beaten and made helpless. All the people abandoned their jobs, trying to flee, but the insects kept pursuing them. The farmers had had their last harvest. They now hurriedly had to begin to prepare their own corpses and coffins. They had come to accept their fate: Everybody would soon die, wood had to be cut for the carpenters to make thousands of coffins, and hundreds of mourners had a heavy schedule ahead of them in a season of funerals. Since the deaths of all were inevitable, they had to think about how to bury the last person who himself was responsible for burying the person who died before him. The scheme was that the last person would commit suicide on the day he buried the last corpse but would do so very quickly, within minutes of burying the last corpse, and he too could fall into the last grave. Indeed, the last person's suicide must take place at the very edge of the grave so that he would collapse into it. The last bodies would decay: The vultures would take their share, and debris would cover the rest. Rain would fall to wash the soil over the remnants and carcasses. Thousands of years later, the bodies would become hydrocarbons producing oil that would provide revenues for another generation.

This was my understanding of politics and society in 1968. I had unsuccessfully sketched the scheme I have presented above into a possible performance since I was continually drawn to the mingled reality and dream of that very moment. The locusts and strange insects did not come from a distant land but from within. The deadly insects were not only vegetarians but also blood-loving cannibals who could turn into vampires at any time of their choosing.

The performance started with a poem entitled "Song of Freedom," but it was no more than a disguised representation of politics. For immediately following it was the narration of a crisis set in the animal world, which is a way of speaking about people. The elephant was tricked into agreeing to become the king of the jungle. A delegation, led by the tortoise, went to announce it to him. "You are the best and the strongest," the tortoise started his nomination speech with a grand deception. Then followed a long story designed to show how the elephant was more powerful than the current king of the jungle, Akiti, the man-hunter who had scared all of them into submission; who had more power than the lion, tiger, and wolf; and who roamed the jungle in whichever way he liked. The elephant was told that he was the only one who could defeat Akiti, the one whose body was too big for Akiti's club to crush or for his gun to kill. Akiti, a powerful wrestler, would not even have a place to grab on the elephant's body. To reassure the elephant, the tortoise told him that the animals had taken away all of the power of Akiti, a man who could turn into a serpent in one moment and a fly in another. The elephant was calm, and as the tortoise ended with his eulogy, he made the elephant appear ten times wiser than the lion. It was the elephant that they wanted as their new king.

The elephant was flattered; seeing himself as the best, the most competent, and the most honorable, he accepted the honor. A date was fixed to place the crown on his head. A site was chosen. His enemies, led by the tortoise, dug the biggest hole in the land, with a breadth and depth that could contain three elephants. They put an attractive carpet over the hole. A beautiful fence surrounded it. Then came the décor: charming flowers and enticing shrubs. On the date that had been set, in a festive mood, all the animals went to the elephant's house, one holding the beautiful crown. They sang a beautiful refrain: "We are set to enthrone the elephant as king, rejoice!" The jubilant animal was excited. He agreed to follow them to the decorated site where he would be enthroned. The elephant did not notice that he was walking behind most of the other animals: It is the camel in front that pulls the caravan, but it is the one right at the back that gets all the beating. He saw the beautiful site and was full of joy. Seeing his throne in the middle, he walked straight to it. Down into the hole he fell. Severely injured and unable to climb out, he looked up to see all the other animals at the edge of the hole mocking him, singing a derisive song. At nightfall, all the other animals left. The elephant died slowly: of hunger, of pain, and of insect bites. As he reflected on his fate, he wondered why he had fallen for deceit and flattery.

We were the elephants who had fallen into the big hole. Cocoa and the politicians tricked us, making us believe that we could use one foot to create a footpath. The commodity traders and sweet-talkers led us into believing that a throne awaited us. We were being led into perdition and downfall. The politicians of the 1950s and 1960s were wolves in human skin, the parents and grandparents of the present ones who are far worse than anyone could ever imagine. They spoke so much about development and progress every day, friendly foes who sugarcoated everything. Ibadan would soon be London; Akanran would be like a suburb of Paris. Even the market women, ever so clever and careful, did not see the fake teeth protruding from stiff lips and consequently fell into the hole dug for the elephant. I am related to several people who were tricked into falling into the same hole and died in it. I will tell you about only a few of my relations, all known to me in flesh and blood, all related in one way or another to my mother.

Monsurat, who lived at Beere selling palm oil and was known to us as Monsurat Elepo, believed in Honorable Adegoke Adelabu, the preeminent politician of the 1950s who was made a federal minister and worked hard to become the premier of the Western Region, although death ended that destiny. For Monsurat Elepo, Adelabu would fix her life even if he could not fix the city council. Monsurat Elepo began to dream and scheme that her first daughter would marry this politician who already had six wives, and she would become the in-law of a great and wealthy man. "We are set to enthrone the elephant as king, rejoice!" Selling small tins of palm oil was a commitment to a life of poverty. With her daughter as Mrs. Honorable Chief, wife of the Honorable Himself, Monsurat Elepo would give the rest of her palm oil to her sister and begin to live on gifts from the Honorable and his seventh wife. There was nothing that she did not attempt in the effort to make her dream come true, short of picking up her daughter and dumping her in the Honorable's house. As the story got to my mother, and then to me, she even slept with the Honorable's friends in order to lobby them to ask the great politician to marry her daughter. As the politicians acquired money and fame, they began to have some kind of negative influence on values, and Monsurat Elepo ruined herself in the pursuit of a desire. Today, the politicians, especially the state governors, behave like emperors far more powerful than Julius Caesar of ancient Rome. To be a girlfriend to a Nigerian governor, not to talk of being his parlor wife (aka "first lady"), is to have so much money as to banish poverty from her lineage for a thousand years to come. Monsurat Elepo failed and fell into a hole, with her daughter ultimately ending up as a woman of easy virtue.

Sali Onigi was selling *igi*, firewood. We at Ibadan did not stick to the same last name for all of a man's children as English people do, so that you can go to their phonebook and see many people bearing the name Smith. At Ibadan, a man with the first name of Kamoru and the last name of Yeosa, the neighborhood where he was born, could have six children with six different last names. Each would have his name and cognomen, but Kamoru was the one who knew he was the father of them all. As the children grew up, their second names could just refer to their occupations or their personal traits. So, Sali, Kamoru's son, became known as Onigi, named after the product that he was selling. His sister, Sufi Eleja, was dealing in *eja*, fish, and this became her last name as well. Then and now, you could find many last names linked with occupations, such as Maikeli Tisa (Michael the teacher), Joonu Telo (John the tailor), and Baba Olopa (elder policeman). Some names may just be qualifiers. If you call many women *iya* or *mama* (mom) and many men *baba*, then, to identify particular individuals, you have to look for an additional name that is more specific. Thus at Ibadan, you could hear such names as Mama UI, Baba University, Iya London, and Baba Chicago, all linking the people with the place where they lived. Or they could be connected to their occupations, as in Iya Elewure (the woman who keeps a herd of goats) or Baba Birikila (the bricklayer). This limitless creativity in names and labels continues today and supplies a different set of identities from the ones we have inherited from the British.

Sali Onigi was always complaining to Sufi Eleja that he would never make it in life, as no one could ever make ends meet selling firewood. He was right, as I assisted him a few times to move his pieces of wood hurriedly inside the house when rain threatened. Sufi Eleja said that her fate was the same, no better than that of their sister, Musili Alagbado, who survived by selling roasted corn (*agbado*) on the roadside. Not that their father, Kamoru, had better luck either. Hail providence! There came a series of fortuitous events.

Ojugo's party, the Action Group, collapsed in 1962. While the AG remained in existence, others were created, with the most formidable

**General Yakubu Gowon, Nigeria's head of state. Photograph taken in 1970. Ministry of Information, Ibadan.**

one, the Nigerian National Democratic Party (NNDP), led by Ojugo's former right-hand man, Chief S. L. Akintola, whom we called Bamu because his face was beautified by the most elaborate scarification. With a most colorful tattoo in bold, heavy lines, many saw Bamu as handsome. He was a profoundly gifted orator, his command of English and Yoruba legendary. Right or wrong, he had a way with words that attracted you to listen to him. And people loved to listen to him. Why Awolowo and Akintola fought need not delay us here, only to say that when two elephants fight, it is the grass that suffers. As they fought, the people took sides; some gained and others lost. Even during our own rebellion, Ojugo and

Nicknamed Bamu, Chief Samuel Ladoke Akintola was a preeminent
politician, second Premier of the Western Region; he was assassinated in
a military coup in January 1966. Photograph taken in 1958. Ministry of
Information, Ibadan.

his supporters originally thought we were being influenced by loyalists to
Kikiwe and Bamu. They got it wrong.

As Bamu built his own party, he recognized the fault lines in Ojugo's approach. Ojugo had talked about the collective spending of
cocoa money. All well and good. Akintola, too, promised all the good
things of life. Some people believed him while others doubted him.
Bamu did not dispute what Ojugo said about progress, but he added
that individuals, too, must be able to keep in their pockets some of
the cocoa money collected by the government if they were connected
with him and his party. Two former friends became foes for life until

Bamu died in a violent military coup in January 1966. So extreme and bitter was their hatred for one another that Bamu was part of the conspiracy that sent Ojugo to prison in 1963, and Ojugo was glad that Bamu came to a violent end, as he was shot by coup plotters in his residence in January 1966. Ojugo even called for turning Bamu's house into a museum to show others how violently they would end if they betrayed Ojugo.

Their supporters have remained divided ever since, and when one university was named after Ojugo (formerly the University of Ife), the supporters of Bamu did not rest until they had changed the name of another university to Ladoke Akintola University of Technology (formerly the Oyo State University). The two will never speak to one another even in the next world. They remind me of the tortoise and the crab, who were mortal enemies. It had not always been so as the tortoise and the crab started as friends. But then a small fight arose. They began to fight with words, and later with blows. They fought themselves to a stalemate, and both agreed that their strengths were equal, based on their shells. They began to boast that one could not destroy the other, even saying that no other being could destroy them, as their shells were the strongest armor ever created. One day, a young boy looking for toys saw the crab and picked it up, and then he saw the tortoise and picked it up as well. The boy changed his mind: He now wanted both to play with and to eat. He boiled up the tortoise and was delighted that he could use the shell as an ornament. Then he stewed the crab and served it in his new ornament. Ojugo and Bamu were like the crab and the tortoise, one an ornament and the other the food served in it, and both gone, mortal enemies, forever irreconcilable.

To undercut Ojugo, Bamu began to appeal to Sufi Eleja, Musili Alagbado, and Sali Onigi. If they would become members of his political party, they would be able to obtain some of the cocoa money through the back door. There were jobs to do for the parties, as thugs, cheerleaders, and hangers-on. Sali Onigi saw a new career for himself. He could be a party thug. On his first assignment, instead of selling his firewood, he used the pieces of wood as clubs against the thugs of the other party. He came home to boast that he had injured well over twenty people. He was paid over a thousand times more than his firewood trade had paid him. He saw his shoulders growing, and he even thought that they could raise themselves to the same height as his head. He left his job, dreaming of wealth. "We are set to enthrone the elephant as king, rejoice!" He lost his path to reason:

When ancient lore drums
"We are set to enthrone the elephant as king, rejoice!"
Only the wise take the liberty to dance.
The friendship dance
Away from fiendish foes
"We are set to enthrone the elephant as king, rejoice!"

In 1964, Sali Onigi went on a mission, as one of the thugs of one party who were sent to challenge the thugs of the other side. As usual, a free-for-all ensued. The novice forgot the adage of his people that it is better to run away from danger and be mocked than to face danger and be killed. He was hit by a beer bottle, and then came a knife through his chest. He was hurriedly carried back home, where he died. I attended his short funeral ceremony after Sali became yet another elephant that fell into a hole.

His sister, Sufi Eleja, who heard all the boasts that Sali Onigi had made about his association with members of Bamu's party, began to think of how she could give her brother a decent burial and then report the matter to the police. She tried calling on others in the compound to assist her: After all, the strength of the soldier ants is in their number. No one answered, as no one wanted to be associated with a thug. She was advised to see a party baron, and one was located, a powerful politician who controlled a municipal council. After waiting for many hours in his reception area, she was eventually invited into the "inner chambers" to see the politician. Sufi Eleja started by crying. The politician was unmoved. Then she said she needed to talk about funeral arrangements and how to report the matter of her brother's death to the police. The politician and council boss was angry: "Am I the one who killed your brother?" Sufi Eleja said that her brother worked for them. "No, not for us; he was a mere thug, a dog; he died the way dogs should die." This was a blow. So, her brother had been telling her lies all this time, telling her stories of the meetings they had held and how they would share more power and money. He had even told his sister he could see Bamu any time that he wanted.

As Sufi Eleja wanted to leave, the politician told her she was good-looking and asked whether they could be friends, an indirect way of asking for sex. Men and women were never friends in those days at Ibadan unless something was going on in private bedrooms. Before she could respond, the man gave her two options: "By force, which you will not enjoy, or by consent, which you will enjoy and which can give you a job at the council."

Masquerades have I seen
My gaze pierced screens
Of visages wrapped in colorful camouflage
Ah, ha! Ah, ha!
Treacherous entities wear daggers
They carry death under nets and masking ensembles
Dare I dance?
In the company of these masquerades?

Only the goddesses could know what was going on in Sufi's head. She was not even allowed to answer before the politician called a party thug to take her to his room. Up to today, we know they had sex, as they later did many times over, but no one knew whether it was initially by consent or by force.

Sufi Eleja, like her brother, began to boast about her connections in the council. She was given a contract as a food vendor, for six months in the first instance. From selling fish, she was now selling food to "the government." Her wardrobe changed. She began to use other people's hands to beat her chest. She chose to determine the depth of a river with both legs. "We are set to enthrone the elephant as king, rejoice!" Having realized what one contact could do, she began to date some other men, all associated with political parties. Men began to come and go, men with such funny names as Talontan (who are you deceiving?), and Ari-kuyeri (he sees death and runs!). Pasitor and others warned her, but she refused to stop. When I said, "Anti [Auntie], listen to what they say," she insulted me and asked who had invited me into her affairs. She dipped into her bra, which women used not only to hold their breasts but also as a wallet, to bring out some coins as a gift, but I refused to take them. Pasitor was proud of me for rejecting the money:

The gods I thank
For great insights.

Then she disappeared for days. All the search parties that went out failed to locate her. An announcement came over the radio of the discovery of a headless body at Igbo Agala (a forest reserve). When we went there with her father, whom many of us called Baba Kamoru, we found it was her body. We all cried. But there was a problem with recovering the body: We did not want to identify her, for the police would come after us, and those who had committed the murder would panic and kill more people. Everyone knew what had happened. This was a ritual murder. One of her men friends needed some body parts, perhaps for money, or perhaps to ritualize his power so that his enemies would be afraid of him. Irrespective of the reason, Sufi Eleja was gone the way of her brother:

> If sleek politicians seek our heads on a platter
> There is a brutal dangerous chief
> Lurking in my shadows
> Eager with daggers drawn
> To sever them from my member
> Brutal chief, the man with seven wallets
> Justification is never far from his lips.

I have been telling you about members of just one family, those related to me. But what about other stories that I heard, of those that I knew, even if they were not blood relations? What about the story of Alani Kapenta (carpenter), who left his job to work for the council as a tax collector, a formerly decent human being converted into a ruthless brutalizer?

> A calculating tax collector
> Slippery as an eel
> Never found a friendlier foe
> Never found on a path of justice
> Master of double sense
> Spoilt by untold privileges
> Eager to lure, to roam
> To raze and to erase.

I heard about Suraju Onimoto (driver), who left his good job as a taxi driver to become a driver to a rich man who happened to be a man of the underworld dealing in stolen goods. Here was a monkey who held the branch of a tree with one hand for too long and fell into a big ditch. Suraju Onimoto was the one caught as a thief while the police released his boss. He was sentenced to seventeen years in prison:

> The one whose Ori ("destiny") has deserted him
> My Ori, do not desert me
> When serpentine f(r)iends bare their fangs!
> When eyes engorged with hatred and envy
> Emit consuming fire

My Ori, I beseech you
Direct my feet away
Far from calamitous manholes
Lest I become the proverbial elephant
Lured to its peril
By the crafty tortoise

Enough! I saw and heard too many things:

My eyes have indeed seen a spectacle
The spectacle of the big masquerade
With entrees served by smaller masquerades and dancers
Wondrous performers
Disarming their audience
With dexterous steps.

The locusts mentioned earlier were the government of the day and the members of the political class that ran it. The threesome was the military, the politicians, and the city officials. Sand was already flowing out of their hourglasses, but their power remained dangerous. With all their fingers infected with leprosy, anything they touched became contagious. Their members sent Sali Onigi and Sufi Eleja to their early graves, both cut down in the prime of their lives. Their lifestyle led Monsurat Elepo to the temptation that destroyed her. The threesome knew you: You confided in them, you trusted them, but they would betray you. They were the worst: enemies who traded information about us, some of which was true, such as our poverty, but also some that was alleged to be true, such as our ability to pay more taxes and levies. Some among the threesome did not know us, but they hated us. They could cause devastation to fall on us and claim to sympathize with us at the same time. They were wicked, and they knew how to use the machinery of government to do evil.

The arrival of a new Nigeria, which ultimately led to a systemic collapse some three decades later, occurred in January 1966 with the first military coup. By the people in my city and the majority of the Yoruba, the coup was welcomed with jubilation. I did not hesitate to join others in carrying leaves, parading from one area to another, in a sign of happiness and peace. The newspapers of the period revealed statements of jubilation. They were not happy in the north because people believed that the Igbo in the east had killed all their leaders, from Prime Minister Tafawa Bale-

**Bamu at the height of his power, acquiring the traditional war title of *Are Ona Kakanfo* to affirm his superior traditional authority over Ojuugo. Ministry of Information, Ibadan.**

wa to the far more powerful premier of the huge northern region, the *sardauna* of Sokoto, Alhaji Ahmadu Bello, and many other big men. The north was thrown into mourning, and its leaders wanted revenge. They got it, with another coup in July 1966. More revenge followed: The Igbo were killed in the north by the thousands, and those who survived fled back home to Eastern Nigeria to prepare for a further cycle of revenge.

The welcome given to the military was short-lived. Young, inexperienced, and deeply imbued with the politics of "tribalism," their capacity for mischief was greater than their capacity to govern. The Nigerian Football Association introduced "tribe" into everything they did, even the selection of players. Many blamed favoritism for the choice of players, the majority of whom came from clubs based in Lagos. The "tribal this" and "tribal that" led to talk of conflicts and secession. The military moved the nation into a civil war that lasted from 1967 to 1970. Nigerians and Biafrans were killing one another in the eastern part of the country. The locusts that invaded that area produced more children, who fled in our direction. We also needed to engage in conflicts and shed blood. We had already found our destiny with Ogun.

The locusts found cocoa highly edible. They must eat all of it. Locusts transformed themselves into the Western State government headed by a military man, whom we called Irunmu (the one with the moustache), but whose real name was Brigadier Robert Adeyinka Adebayo. Irunmu, unknown to us in 1968, would have a long and successful career in politics, first as a military man, and later on as a civilian. The more you cursed him, the fatter he grew. Many of the military boys did well in politics, making a great deal of money as military leaders and then using small parts of the loot to acquire influence in political parties and buy their way into power in order to repeat the exercise of making money from the government and using it to buy government. The government became the chicken that lays golden eggs and then hatches them to produce beautiful babies.

The regional government needed money from cocoa to finance local government, remit a percentage to the federal level, and also pay for the war. Irunmu was accountable to his boss in Lagos, General Yakubu Gowon, who needed money from whatever sources he could get it from. Other requirements were on the table as well, including the requirement for politicians and administrators to steal some money. Nigeria had not started to see the gains from oil by then, although revenues were beginning to accrue, but they were used largely to purchase the weapons needed to kill both Nigerians and Biafrans. The way to make money for the regional government was through the established colonial source: the exploitation of the farmers who must sell cocoa. They had only one revenue source: the proceeds of taxation.

In April 1968, the Western State government decided to increase tax rates affecting the farmers and the urban poor. For jobless adults, the payment demanded increased from £1 17s 6d to £3. For those with the lowest-paid jobs, who had previously paid £3, the new rate would be £6.

**Nicknamed Irunmu, Brigadier Robert Adeyinka Adebayo was the second military governor of the Western state. Photograph taken in 1967. Ministry of Information, Ibadan.**

Those who were considered very poor and whose overall annual income was less than £50 should expect to pay close to £4. Do not divide £50 into twelve calendar months as no farmer made money that way. Farmers could go for one-third of the year making nothing. Crops have their own minds, refusing to sprout when expected. Harvests were unpredictable: God might bless a farmer this year and forget about him the next. Whether people were poor or a step above being poor, they had to pay a sum close to £1 as a contribution to the State Development Fund and another sum close to £1 to the National Reconstruction Fund/Scheme.

Irunmu disturbed hundreds of beehives, and thousands of angry bees began to look for him so as to sting and kill him. The announcement stunned millions of farmers, craftsmen, and members of the urban poor. Almost immediately, the farmers in various parts of the state demonstrated their opposition to it. They organized into various associations to send delegations to the government, kings, and chiefs. This was the beginning of many highly organized farmers' unions, such as the Egbe Mekunnu Taku (Association of Angry and Adamant Poor) and the Agbekoya (Farmers Reject Suffering). While other organizations were created, the public thought of them all as the Agbekoya, as it was the most prominent and the best organized. I was an Agbekoya boy.

They wanted more of our cocoa! As Irunmu outlined in various speeches, there were two million taxable adults in the Western State. Of this number, about eight hundred thousand were paying tax. The government must force more people to pay and increase the amount being paid by the 40 percent who were obedient. The obedient must suffer. The government would set up assessment committees that would have the power to impose higher tax rates on a number of people. This meant counting cocoa trees—not the pods, not their productivity—to impose arbitrary rates. Millions of people saw the stratagem to destroy them. They were even threatened with the creation of "tax nominal rolls," interpreted by the illiterate farmers as lists of names with imposed amounts.

Everybody had a point. The federal government needed money to prosecute the civil war and had limited money to assist the states. The states had financial needs and could not support the councils. The councils needed to increase their revenues. Taxes went up by 63 percent. The poorest of individuals must now look for £8 a year to sustain the government. If the government was looking for more money, it was targeting the wrong people. The very economic conditions of the country, which were blamed on the civil war, had also diminished the opportunities available to generate a respectable income. In 1968, harvests were not as good as the farmers had hoped, blamed in many places on excessive rains. It was not even as if essential services were being maintained in the villages to impress the farmers.

One did not require Western or Islamic education to understand our own point. Farm incomes were diminishing, not because the people were not productive but because the soil was already becoming more and more degraded with intensive use. The monkey toils and sweats, but the hair on its back hides the pain and the flow. I had been noticing the shrinking sizes of crops and the unpredictable harvests. Incentives were diminishing, making it far more lucrative to become a laborer or messenger in the secretariat than a farmer at Akanran. Laborers were beginning to make three times more money than farmers. The laborers and messengers paid less in taxes than cocoa farmers. Cocoa had already yielded so much profit for the government by way of export duties, sales, and manipulated prices. It was common knowledge that farmers were flocking to the houses of politicians and powerful civil servants to look for jobs as laborers, messengers, gardeners, and in any other low-level government work because they provided regular monthly incomes. The laborers were even talking of a "pension," the money you collect after you retire, when you can go back to your farm. As the farmers were told, these pensions were paid for as long as you lived, even when you were terribly ill or hit by any misfortune. Some were even warning their family members and children not to announce their death so that they could keep collecting the money. City officials, too, profited from the laborers, creating a long list of ghost workers. The officials then asked friends and family members to come up every month to give their thumbprints for small fees so that the officials could then collect and pocket their salaries. The reports of ten laborers and ten messengers working for one arm of a local government that you now read in the archives might be fake, as there could be just one laborer and one messenger, with the boss pocketing the wages of others.

Almost immediately, enemies appeared in cities, in villages, on road-sides, and in markets. These were the tax assessors. If you wanted to pay the minimum tax, you must bribe them. If you were religious and not a bribe giver, you must expect persecution. The tax assessors became the thunderbolts that strike with storms. When you saw them, you should try to run. If you could not run, you should prevent them from knowing the number of your wives, children, and pots and pans in the kitchen, not to talk of your land and trees. If they learned anything, you were set for destruction. Their brothers were the tax collectors, thugs in official uni-forms working for the local government administrations, called coun-cils. These thugs even went inside mosques to ask for tax receipts and arrest those who did not have them—Caesar pursuing mammon into the very house of God! When the councils needed more collectors, they recruited unemployed people, paying them out of what they were able to collect. If they saw money on you, your tax would increase from £3 to £6, but you would get a receipt for £3. They could even take everything you had in your pocket and go after your rings and necklace if they were of any value. They behaved as both police and judges. If you did not pay, they could tie your two hands behind your back with a rope and disgrace

you before your children and your wives. Your manhood was gone. Time
without number, tax defaulters were asked to sit on pebbles in the heat
and open their eyes to look into a raging sun.

Terrible men followed the tax collectors, their coworkers, but going
by the name of *akoda* (court messengers). They wore khaki shirts and
knickers and carried batons. They had the power of arrest, dragging you
before a low-quality judge who would visit you with punishment. *Akodas*
had more power than was written in any law book. They were not governed by codes of conduct, but by corruption and excess. Millions of
farmers were cheated. Their tormentors were called *akodas* because they
shouted the word "Order!" at the court or in the palaces whenever a
court was in session and people were becoming rowdy.

The majority of villages had nothing to show for their years of tax
payments. The unpaved roads that linked them to the cities were created to allow them to move to the farms to produce, and to move cocoa
and raw food from farmlands to the cities. Nothing more. The roads did
not require maintenance. There were no facilities. There was a small
modern church, like the one that Pasitor managed at Elepo, and next
to it was an ugly building divided into six small rooms that served as
the elementary school. Six teachers and one headmaster, or six teachers
with one doubling as the headmaster, were there to oversee it. That was
it. No electricity, no health clinic. No formal jobs. No benefits accrued
to them for paying taxes and supplying cocoa. And we were also being
forced by the local governments to pay for facilities to be provided in
the future: schools, motor parks, market stalls, night guards to monitor
council buildings, dispensaries, and new roads.

There were other monies to be paid in the form of market levies,
parking fees for lorries in garages, water rates, electricity rates, education
rates, and local development rates. To find money to finance the war, the
national reconstruction fund and development program asked for donations. While the scheme and program were presented as voluntary, this
became a mandatory levy in some cities, as in Ede and Osogbo, which
created a great deal of resentment. At Ibadan, a Compulsory Savings
Deposit of ten shillings was expected of all adults, along with a minimum
contribution of £1/10/0 to the Development Fund to pay for the war.

Water rates had to be paid, but people did not object to them if pipe-
borne water was supplied to their village or ward. However, demanding
such a levy from villages without such a water supply was an act of injustice. Pipes did not even reach the place to justify any collection. The
people relied on streams to clean, wash, and drink. They collected rain-

water when possible, and children rushed into the rain to shower, and for many days thereafter they had to wash their bodies in the streams. Where pipes were laid in the city, public water taps were erected, but they provided water only erratically, and only in the morning. We would wake up in the morning around 5 a.m., walking fast with our containers to form a long line. At Ode Aje with just two public pumps, you would find containers already in line in the middle of the night, as if some witches also needed water to clean the blood from their mouths. By 6:20 a.m., the quantity of water began to drop and people knew that it was about to run out. Fights would break out, with adults pushing children away, men pushing women aside, and bigger buckets smashing smaller ones. Humans and buckets would clash, producing harsh sounds until a bucket was able to sit firmly under the tap. Even then, its owner must use all his or her strength to hold it down. As the water dropped into the bucket, you would see a smile of relief all over the face of the lucky one. We carried the buckets full of water on our heads to our houses to be poured into a huge clay pot from which all and sundry took water to drink. It would be time to rush to school but not to the shower. If water was scarce, why was the payment of a water rate necessary? And if there was no water at all, why impose a levy?

The insistence of the government on collecting taxes led to complaints, pleas, petitions, and finally rebellion. People began to count the taxes as four that were new: the compulsory savings scheme, the water rate, the development rate, and the increased taxation. Women now had to pay as well, in a new tax imposed on those making above £100. Ultimately, the rebellion exposed all the flaws in both traditional and modern governance; the ruthless ambitions of bureaucrats, politicians, and soldiers; the underbelly of politics; the failure of development efforts; and the attempts by the poor to link their poverty with politics. It was no longer God, gods, and goddesses that made people poor, as the ideology of fate had engrained into their thinking, it was now our fellowmen. Prices of imports were on the increase, caused by the government's collecting more in sales tax and customs levies and by traders who wanted higher profits. These collectors of taxes and profits were not gods but fellow men.

The farmers did not set out to fight and lose their lives. The months of September and October 1968 saw many peaceful efforts to pressure the government to reconsider. The farmers began by following the established patterns of political behavior: They sent delegations to the chiefs and city managers to complain. They wrote petitions to the government. Although the majority could neither read nor write, their unions employed the services of public letter writers (often called *leta-raita*") to compose their messages. These letters were many, but they were saying the same thing, which was all too obvious: The rates were rather excessive. They wanted to pay but had no means to do so. They understood the need for taxes, they assured the government. Everyone did, and they certainly knew that taxation was the revenue basis of the state. The Yoruba had been paying taxes and tributes for centuries. Their kings collected tributes, market dues, tolls, gifts. The judges were used to collecting gifts before they announced their decisions, which might favor the person with the longest hand. However, for people to pay, they must have incomes. The complainants claimed that the cocoa harvests in 1968 were so bad that their sources of income had been downgraded. A poor man who went to an herbalist for a sacrifice could not be asked to bring a goat instead of a chicken.

The months of August and September were dominated by appeals to the government to reduce the flat rate of tax. The government ignored them all. Council officials were full of insults, calling farmers stupid illiterates who knew nothing about progress. They were hurling foul language at them, forgetting that throwing words is like throwing rocks— once thrown, they cannot be retrieved. Tax evaders, when arrested, were treated as common criminals and threatened with being taken to court and convicted. The policeman would remind you that he and the judge both worked for the government. The government radio and newspapers joined in ridiculing the poor. The newspapers were not so much of a problem since many had no access to them, but this was not so with the radio. The agents of propaganda and Irunmu were indulging in "slips of the tongue," using words so damaging that no one could forget them.

Allegations and charges were made, calling our leaders rabble rousers, and their followers useless thugs. To Buoda Gebu and those of like mind, our leaders were pagans and occultists, worse than Satans who should be cast into hell's fire. Those who conspired with evil must be condemned and executed. The Ogboni must be quashed, and their symbols, presented as some kind of Holy Grail, must be found and destroyed. Aspersions were cast on men and women who set out to do good. Open-minded people were presented as closed-minded. The very tolerance that had made them endure suffering for years was presented as intolerance. Buoda Gebu had a point: Those who could fall back on juju power could not be "solid Christians" like himself. Christianity had to be qualified—there were solid, devout, godly, sincere, and true Christians, as just identifying a person as "Christian" meant very little. Buoda Gebu was also correct in one respect: There were more Muslims than Christians leading the rebellion in all of the Oyo-Ogbomoso-Ilorin divisions. Not only were they Muslims, they were also "illiterates" who could not read or write either English or Yoruba. The hunters who supplied war strategies were largely hybrid—half Muslim, half followers of Ogun.

The farmers and their leaders had no friends to turn to. These were men without influence, without even the money to survive for a week. They lacked the resources to manipulate the media or to purchase any influence. As poor as Pasitor was, he was far ahead of the majority of them. As low as my educational qualification was, I was the star, actually a superstar, sometimes called *akowe* (the lettered one). It was Pasitor and my *akowe* credentials that fully inserted me into the movement, as well as my own deep commitment.

We were surrounded by enemies; all the powerful forces were fully ranged against us. The traditional authorities had allied with the government to say that the tax assessment would never be changed. "Pay your taxes" was the only instruction that came from the mouths of chiefs and kings who did not want to offend the government. Some said it loudly and repeatedly to gain attention. Some said it in low tones to indicate they were only carrying out a mandate. But they all supported the "tax drive," and whenever Irunmu was with any king or chief, that king would insist that all must pay tax and abide by the law. The ranks of the ex-politicians were divided. Those who wanted to benefit from the military regimes and war-related contracts did not care much about the tax grievances. And those who cared about these grievances wanted to use the farmers for their own political gain. They even used the old division between the AG led by Ojugo and the NCNC led by Kikiwe in their effort to understand us. Ojugo thought that we belonged to the party of his archrival and enemy, Kikiwe, a man who changed his mind like the weather to support any party that would control federal power. So, it came to be said that the poor farmers were the ones causing the trouble; the rich farmers stayed in the city and were telling the government to deal with us with all ruthlessness. The children of the rich farmers were in the city schools and were looking for progress while we were anti-progress. Well, by the second week in October, the struggling farmers and their anti-tax collaborators had come to one conclusion: What the petitions and pleas could not achieve, guns and machetes would deliver. There were no sane men in the land who could take up the cudgel on our behalf. The war of words must now give way to the war of bullets. The saliva that comes from the mouths of men and the guns that men carry produce different results. Your back must be bent to allow anyone to ride on it.

It is time to go after the locusts, to drench them in water so that their wings wither; to collect them in the thousands, roast them, and use them as snacks. We had now reached the end of pleading. The impending war acquired a nickname: *ogun oye*, the "Harmattan War." The weather changes in November and December, becoming slightly cold—not winter cold, thanks to the wind that travels all the way from North Africa, passing through the Sahara Desert, where it gathers loads of dust to drop on the savanna and takes some cold to the south.

Unknown to the government, the preparations were already under way in October in secret locations. Irunmu was behaving like a chicken who keeps cackling too loud and does not hear the coming of the hawk. His officers who had sown thorns should not expect to reap flowers. As previously narrated, the sacrifice to Ogun had now been performed; the charms had been prepared and more were being made; military units had been formed; and unit leaders had emerged in various parts of the Western State. Powerful cultic men and women had been drafted. The protection of women and children had been put in place. New manufacturers emerged in various villages, making new iron products, setting up mobile smithies where old machetes and spears were restored. The people expected that they would find no markets in which to buy new ones, or that the roads to the city market at Ibadan would be closed to prevent the acquisition of new weapons. I saw various private collections of spears, swords, shields, knives, catapults, machetes, and clubs. Everyone had knives. Many had catapults, commonly available for hunting birds and scaring away pets and other animals from stealing raw food items placed in the open. The only investment involved in a catapult were the small rocks that had to be collected. As small as a catapult is, the idea was that anyone with the advantage of time to put the rock in the small leather holder, pull the string, and hit the desired object would incapacitate even the strongest adult. A rock landing on a person's forehead was capable of doing major damage.

Added to this list of weapons were the most important ones: dane guns. I had yet to see the largest collections of dane guns. Before then, one would see a hunter in the village carrying one. In the households of hunters, one would see one or two guns standing in the corners of rooms. One could see the hunter pounding the pellets in a mortar placed outside the compound. Sometimes, the hunters would grind the pellets into fine powder. During their celebrations of Ogun, the hunters would bring out their guns and assemble in groups of about ten to sing. In November 1968, all the guns were out, the rusty and the new. About four to five feet long, the dane gun was carried on the shoulder in such a way that it looked taller than the man. Its handle leaned forward; its mouth leaned backward so that if accidentally triggered, it would kill something in the sky. Weapons were ritualized and soaked in charms. The arrows and spears were poisoned with a combination of local herbs. Those with poisoned arrows and spears warned their children and relatives not to go near them.

Our leaders had mobilized a large fighting force, put at *egberun lonà egberun* (one thousand times one thousand), a way of saying a very large number but without knowing the actual number. The strategy was to amass a number sufficient to overwhelm the government police forces and the contingents of mobile police and army that would also be put into service. The leaders also wanted a fighting force that could overwhelm the city, should it happen that the government decided to rent a crowd to fight on its behalf. The idea was to present our fighting force as saviors and not as terrorists. If we were perceived as saviors, we would be welcomed, and the government and its police and army would be humiliated. Should we be perceived as terrorists, which we deemed unlikely, the people would be afraid and take shelter in their homes, thereby allowing us to control the streets. We wanted to control the streets anyway, and whether we were received as heroes or terrorists, the same effect would be produced.

The decentralized force was also being organized into commands under various war chiefs and thousands of common soldiers. They spoke the language of bravery, but confirmation of bravery was still in question. Obedience and discipline were not the values in dispute. What made it very easy to establish a command structure was the strategy, used very successfully, of merely enlarging the guild of hunters that was already in place and using the Ogboni to bring the leaders together. Long before 1968, Yoruba hunters had derived pleasure in forming a guild that enabled them to present a common voice, display their craft, entertain themselves, and lead in the worship of Ogun. Now in 1968, their idea and presence were becoming the most important feature in the military front of the movement. The hunters made many of the fighting rules, dividing themselves into the youth section (*omo ode*) and the experienced section (*agba ode*), each with different functions.

As part of the war preparations, motivational speeches were common-place. We knew the truth: that we did not want a war. We did everything to prevent it. It was the last option after we had been driven to the wall. We had no king who wanted to profit from war, as the kings of old did when they wanted more tribute from their subjects and control of the trade routes. We did not even have a political system built on violence as the state did. Neither could we overthrow the government. It was common knowledge that we could complain and fight but that we could not replace the government and move into the secretariat. We did not even like our own king, the Olubadan, that much. While we listened to him, we knew he would always be on the side of the government, even when he disagreed with the *gomina* (governor).

At the end of October, we were instructed to make our big move after the seventh sign. The seven signs might come within twenty-one days, one sign every three days. They might come within fourteen days, one every two days. It could be one sign per day. Or all the signs might come in a single day. When the seventh sign revealed itself, everybody must move in the directions instructed by the men in red. "Follow only the men in red," was a very clear instruction that no one could misunderstand. The problem for me in the beginning was that I never knew any of the men who would be in red. The majority of us did not know. The list of all the signs was not announced either, but everybody would be told with the approach of each sign, and everyone would know what the seventh sign would be. Anticipation filled the air. It was like the expectation of death: No human knows the period and the time when the end will come— even those who want to commit suicide might not have anticipated it ten years earlier. The restless men wanted all the signs within one day, and some even wished that all the signs would come within seven minutes. As we awaited the signs, preparations were made to acquire more weapons. The acquisition was decentralized, as there was no single place to pro-cure weapons or store them. The most accessible weapons were the iron implements of old which were either restored or made new.

The first sign arrived on October 28, 1968, and was known as the *ode merin de* (the appearance of four strange hunters). All the villages were told about a day before that at a time they would not know, four hunt-ers would appear from the road leading back to the farms of a certain village. One would dress like a woman but wear a man's cap; the sec-ond would dress like a man but have plaited hair and earrings; the third would be dressed all in red and carry a machete painted red; and the fourth would carry a covered calabash containing an unknown object.

They would appear and disappear, and the village that saw them must announce it to all. The *ode merin* is a preface to war, a glorification of war, of Ogun, the fighters and their military prowess. Since no one knew where the four came from and where they were headed, it most likely had been used as a morale booster. Sudden and strange appearances were part of the mythology used to build awe, surprise, and courage. The men must appear and disappear, making the sight of them both mythical and mysterious. Messages could be confusing, as in dreams, and required interpretation. Just one village seeing the hunters? Yes, but not everyone in the village would see them. Maybe one person would do so, and this would trigger off opinions, descriptions, and more questions. Who was in front? Who was tall? Did they talk to you? Did you offer them a drink? If you said no, it would become, "Well, you missed the opportunity to receive the blessings of a lifetime."

The second sign was in the form of another visitation by *awon iya*, which means women with the power of witchcraft and sorcery, with all the forms of supernatural power. The women arrived on October 29. Whether it was good or bad witchcraft, the Yoruba were terrified of the idea of witchcraft. The bad witches were believed to be everywhere, many living in households where they killed their husbands, co-wives, and little children. Allegations of witchcraft were a sufficient reason for divorce. A woman who lost her children might believe her mother-in-law or other women in the compound to be responsible. Except for the elderly, only a few people were known for certain to have died of natural causes. Even someone killed in a car accident might have been "pushed" onto the road by the overpowering force of evil hands, or witches could have closed the person's eyes so that he or she would not see an oncoming vehicle. The *awon iyá* were the "good witches," not seeking our allegiance but offering assurances that we would triumph over our enemies. These were the "white witches" who offered protection.

The third sign was a sudden change in the moon, in either its appearance or the object that the moon portrayed. If it changed in shape, cloud covering, location, or the object that it portrayed, then we had received heavenly blessings. The moon, it was believed, communicated messages. During election campaigns, Ojugo had appeared in the moon, even with his cap on. Someone would ask everyone to look into the moon, and the longer you looked, the more the possibility that Ojugo was actually there. If you said you saw no one, your coach would ask you to look very closely, to see the lines representing his face, another representing his glasses, and another his cap. You were left with two options: to agree that you saw Ojugo in the moon or that your eyesight was poor. Or you could see a flying meteor, in full flame, held back from crashing down to the earth. The schedule of the moon was used to signal the commencement of Islamic fasting. They could say it was for thirty days, but the moon could cut the period short by a day or two if it changed its schedule. It would not prolong it to thirty-one days, as someone far away might see a different moon and announce to others what he had seen. It took only one person to see something in the moon that no one else saw. Someone with astrologic eyes, or extra-sensory power, that is. As this person told others, within hours, one mouth carried the news to other mouths, and everyone began to see the same thing or to say, "*won ti ri i*," that is, they had seen something.

What they saw was a long sword in the moon, the Ida Ajasegun, the "Sword of Victory." This was on October 30. This looked to me like something Buoda Gebu would claim to see. The "Sword of Victory" was associated with Christianity. But a sign was a sign, as long as it was extraordinary. Someone saw what looked like a sword, and someone else slapped a label on it, and someone else interpreted it. This is how it worked. You had a dream and you reported it when you woke up, saying that you saw two rams fighting so bitterly that they killed one another. As with the one seeing the sword in the moon, you were the one who slept and dreamed and reported the dream. Someone else would interpret it: "Thank God, you killed your enemy in that dream; you were the ram who survived!" While another person could say: "Rush to the diviner for sacrifices or to Buoda Gebu to collect holy water, as an enemy is working hard to destroy you." You began to act on what the fight by the two rams meant, and you might have either regained or lost control of your life.

The fourth sign, we were told, would be visitors appearing in villages, saying they had missed their way or they had no place to stay for the night, or they would walk around and leave. We had already seen Buoda Gebu coming to Akanran uninvited. Villages saw many such visitors, perhaps state agents looking for information, perhaps members of the security service looking for rabble rousers, perhaps plainclothes policemen. So this fourth sign was quickly disposed of.

The fifth sign was a sudden rise in the number of insects, notably mosquitoes, bugs, termites, and others. Some villages reported by October 31 that they had seen many, some even saying that a few of them came in different colors. What had insects to do with us? Animals and insects do have a connection with us: For example, the Dogon of Mali look at the footsteps of the fox to foretell the future. You can send termites to the house of your enemy to eat the wood and bring it down. Various interpretations were given to this sign, as one person told me that the insects represented the faces of enemies coming from the jungle and departing to places unknown, as if they were crushed. Signs do not lend themselves to rational interpretation.

The sixth sign would be the sighting of three cattle egrets flying at the same time. Well, you could see this every day at Ilorin and further north where these birds followed herdsmen, assisting them in getting rid of the parasites that disturb the cattle. They would fly to Ibadan in certain seasons looking for streams to quench their thirst. Over time, they became part of the folklore, the content of prayers: As no one can change the whiteness of the egret, so too can no human force overpower you. If you pour palm oil on the egret, it will not stick, and the egret will become whiter. The egret is free and safe, never to be hunted for food. Humans are so friendly with it that they give it a pleasant name: "the bird that belongs to the house," that is lovable and friendly. Ducks and hens are homely, too, but the affection given to them is because of their delicious bone marrow that you must save for the last, after using your teeth to inflict pain on the flesh. Cattle egrets have never been tamed or domesticated, just left alone. They have been treated as loyal birds, even with their own set of loyalty songs. The egret symbolizes peace, which might mean that we were fighting for peace. Because of their whiteness, they are presumed to signify purity.

The last sign arrived on November 4. Men would appear at night in major villages carrying burning firewood. They would then instruct the *omo ogun* (soldiers) to move. It was time to move. Verbal warfare would now escalate to aggression and violence. November would energize anti-government nationalism. The harmattan wind would bring the war in December. My excitement was intense on the appearance of the seventh sign, and I was ready to spring into action.

A full-scale rebellion would now commence. There was a holy trinity to our methods: Know the enemy, study its strength, and plan its defeat. The military government, council officials, bureaucrats, pro-government chiefs, and kings were the enemies. We could not attack one and leave the others. We expected reprisals, but the counter to these would be to inflict greater damage still, that is, to intensify the level of violence. We would no longer initiate any dialogue, but unleash a reign of terror, strike fear into the minds of officials, and overpower council workers with our might, weapons, and charms. We would not run when pursued, but instead risk as many lives as possible. Including mine! I was not afraid, just waiting to hear the sound of the first gunshot.

# CHAPTER 8

# The Harmattan War

✦ ✦ ✦

*Oke mefa la o san*
*Bi ko gba kumo*
*Yo gbori bibe*

We will pay only £1.10s
If we don't use cudgels to attain our wish
We will cut off heads.
[War song]

We started with those who should have been our staunchest allies: chiefs and kings. The instruction was to move in the thousands to the palace of the king of Ibadan, known as the Olubadan, to let him know that he was no longer representing our interests. The crowd was huge and well armed, shouting war songs. The village heads, called *baale* or *mogaji*, whom the Olubadan appointed over the villages, were sacked, violently removed, and driven out of hundreds of villages. It is hard to chew very well with a rotten tooth in the mouth. This cut off the traditional sources of control and stopped the collection of land rents and tribute. It was as if tenants could now become landlords, and no one had the authority to go to the villages to ask them to pay. The tenants were happy, and they understood that their gains and newfound freedom had to be protected. This was a serious blow to the power of traditional authorities which was based on the control of land and rent collection. These would now have to calculate their interests, whether it would be in their interest to support us and get back their power or to support the government and lose one of their key sources of revenue.

All the *baale* fled the villages, and the movement appointed new ones of our own choosing. For many years, the kings, chiefs, party chieftains, and wealthy farmers had conspired to appoint *baale* for the villages. These *baale* were not unlike the "warrant chiefs" appointed by the British to administer the Igbo during the colonial period, men who had no commitment to the people they administered. Lacking roots in the villages and with commitments to those who appointed them, the *baale* we had now removed were no more than party agents appointed to do the bidding of those who put them there. Irrespective of your case, you knew the decision before it was announced: Landlords, moneylenders, and chiefs were always right; the government was never wrong. The traditional *baale* of the indigenous system did not receive salaries; the *baale* we had now removed were collecting monthly stipends, which meant that they must support the collection of taxes. With their removal, unpaid village heads were appointed, known as *baale agbe* (heads of farmers) instead of heads of villages. The new heads were poor, and their source of income was their farms. They were subordinated to the leaders of the movement.

Then we hit at the root of grassroots corruption. Word went around to prevent the sole administrators who managed the councils from getting to their offices in the villages. Their cars must be burned should they try to get there. These sole administrators had been handpicked by Irunmu to replace politicians previously installed after fraudulent elections. Although the sole administrators administered the local governments, they were not accountable to the people. These were powerful figures who respected the chiefs and kings, as both were engaged in sharing out money, but did not respect those whom they were supposed to represent. A farmer could not just walk into a council office to see a sole administrator—that is, if the administrator had actually shown up for work. In any case, these administrators had no abode in the villages but just drove back and forth from the city to the village. To them, the village was the venue for drinking good palm wine and getting fresh organic food to take back home. Once the sole administrators were sacked, the local government had reached the first stage of collapse.

A tight grip was maintained on commercial vehicles on the city-village routes. They would be forced to report any people unknown to them that they transported and dropped off at the villages. Without the permission of the new *baale*, they must not carry council officials. This was a deft move as many of these officials had no other way of getting to work, and, if they disguised themselves in order to get to work, there was no way they would get back home; thus they would be playing with their lives as no one in the village would accept them as tenants. As we heard, they began to lie that they had gone to work while actually staying at home. "Who wanted to die?" they would ask.

The new *baale*, chosen to replace the previous corrupt ones, were given specific instructions on many issues. A wise *baale* knew not to disobey, not because he could be removed but because he could be killed. The *baale* was not accountable to the government, meaning that the power of the state no longer extended to the villages. The *baale* must know everyone who lived in his village, and a register of visitors to all households must be kept. Indeed, heads of households must report all visiting guests to the *baale*. This was to prevent the infiltration of intelligence operatives. Known as the CIDs (as they were members of Criminal Investigation Departments), these security operatives were known for their ability to fabricate incriminating stories and to plant evidence to justify arrests and incrimination. In earlier years, they had been used by political opponents to plant marijuana in enemies' cars and houses; later, they prepared the way for the police to appear from nowhere to arrest an "offender" whom the judge would throw in jail.

We carried out our own census of all the villages involved in the rebellion, keeping records of all households and the number of their occupants, broken down by sex and age. This was more than likely the most accurate headcount ever conducted in Nigerian history and demonstrated that a headcount was actually possible. All the villages and towns where we had members and our own *baale* in power were instructed to appoint guards, known as *masunmasun* (never sleep), who watched all the entrances to the village and kept their eyes open for strange movements. In villages like Akanran, where the census activities were intense, the census was dead accurate: No stranger was allowed to enter, and men and women used codes to identify each other. If you called anyone by his or her real name, it was a clear signal that you were an outsider.

The *baale* had security duties to perform. Along the stretches of the conflict zones, as one village and farm led to another, they must ensure there was food if fighters were stranded. They must hide and protect the sick, those on the run, and the exhausted. They must report unusual movements. Names of birds and animals were converted into signals and into *aroko* to spread messages. These names were changed as soon as numerous people understood them. The police acquired such names as leopard, tiger, and hawk. Council officers were labeled as fox, vulture, bedbug, and cockroach.

At last, Irunmu noticed the farmers; it no longer mattered to him

A small contingent on the way to a battle, ca. 1969. Ministry of Information, Ibadan.

whether we were being manipulated by his enemies, as he had previously claimed on several occasions. He had hitherto refused to read any petition, grant an audience to our delegations, or listen to any complaints. It is difficult to wake up a man pretending to be asleep. His government was now in trouble: He must now dig a well as his house was burning. Early in November, he was looking for dialogue, but he had no means of contacting the right people. He went through the older channels of kings, chiefs, and politicians, cajoling and bribing them to create a backdoor channel to dialogue. Irunmu virtually compelled two noted Ibadan politicians, Chief Mojeed Agbaje and Adeoye Adisa (his commissioner for Home Affairs), previously accused of instigating us, to lead him to the villages. He wanted to undertake a tour of the villages, as was announced on the radio. He softened his tone and began to frown less and less. We did not believe him: A set of white teeth, we knew, does not mean that the heart is pure. He even set the date of November 15 to see as many villages as possible, a cat hiding its claws underneath its paws to cultivate the friendship of a rat.

Irunmu had miscalculated—no one was afraid of the governor, his uniform, or his army. How could he activate a successful dialogue and with whom? He tried, and he failed. He failed woefully. We had become two goats with locked horns struggling to drink water from one bucket. There were no leaders mandated to speak with him. In some villages, there were no roads to take him there, as the roads had been made impassable. He even tried to take a helicopter to the village of Olode, the headquarters of the Ibadan South District Council, where he was allowed to land just to embarrass himself. He was allowed to speak, but the response was that they were ready to fight and he should buy more bullets. As his helicopter took off, there were shouts of "*ole, ole, ole*" (thief, thief, thief), and war songs followed for an hour. In one other place, farmers refused to listen to his speech. At Akanran, he was drowned out by angry voices, and no one listened to his lessons on the necessity of taxation. His dog, never satisfied with its supper, was still eating garbage. By early morning on November 16, the central command had instructed all villages not to welcome Irunmu, and, if he should come with the assistance of an army, everyone should withdraw to the farmsteads.

Irunmu was being called *omode lasan lasan* (an ordinary useless boy). Many resented the way he was talking to them, as if they were recruits in his battalion. They cast themselves as the peaceful ones and the governor as the aggressor. War and violence could originate with words, provocative words that could lead to the exchange of blows, even the use of weapons. If the people thought they were being treated as fools, then they believed they could fight back with words and guns. Those who were blaming them for the path of violence were confused about one point: When Irunmu was using offensive and threatening words on radio and television, not many knew the way the people felt, the shame they bore, the ignominy they had endured. When they reacted to those words, after they had been pushed to the wall, using language that Irunmu understood, everybody began to take them seriously. When the pot was boiling the yam, everything was quiet; it was when the pestle began to pound the yam that noise broke out and the neighbors knew the food to be served for dinner. The people were the pot, doing its work in quiet dignity; Irunmu was the pestle, the rascal hitting the poor mortar, creating the noise that diverted the world's attention to the innocent ones. When Irunmu taunted them, they were faceless; when they chose revenge, they became known. Fighting words with words was not enough.

When someone pushes you, you must push the person back, as in the law of Hammurabi: an eye for an eye. Irunmu had pushed my people. Irunmu elbowed us, and we elbowed him back. Encounters could produce altercations and then escalate to a fist exchange between two people. Then a third person joined, then a fourth. More actions, wrestling, sounds of anguish, expressions of pain. The fifth and sixth people joined. Blows hit harder. Teeth fell to the ground, blood dripped into the eyes. Cries for help arose. Many more joined. The village was now up in arms, everyone. The mustard seed had fully grown to become a tree.

The governor received a clear message and realized the futility of all talk. As if we anticipated betrayal, we had no one whom the governor could even bribe or influence. The established way of resolving protests in Nigeria has always been to isolate the leadership from the rank and file by calling them to explain the "government's position," giving them money, usually in cash, and promising them a contract or an appointment. Such an approach had worked too many times, and it still does even today. Those in government always think that a protest cannot last more than three days, and members of the public distrust political activists because they can be purchased for a price. The path to change, perhaps even to revolution, has been aborted too many times just because corruption works. In this model, "You cannot die for Nigeria" becomes the slogan. In private, less committed friends and relations reminded the activists that the purpose of life is survival. Opportunity comes but once—if the government offers you money, take it. Government money belongs to all of us, and this is your only chance to take part of what belongs to you. If you asked, "What about the mission and the followers?" The answer: "God's time is the best . . . this is your own time . . . my brother, take the money." Even your wife would remember to call you *dalu*, as the word "darling" was pronounced by the farmers to mock monogamists.

A thief can be lucky for many days, even months, carting away stolen goods; however, one day, he will run out of luck and be caught. Irunmu had been caught! There was no one to give money to, to sweet-talk into some kind of deal. The city-based politicians were distrusted since we knew they were manipulative. They deceived the government into believing they had influence and could talk us out of rebellion. We had already anticipated their deceit. And the leadership of the movement knew there would be fifth columnists, which was why it adopted its organizational approach.

Anti-tax protesters in the city acquired a uniform, clothing themselves in palm leaves, the attire of Ogun, to differentiate themselves from the rest of society. I was addicted to the radio, listening to the news several times over each day. The newspapers, especially the *Nigerian Tribune*, a private newspaper owned by Ojugo, were selling like hotcakes. Word of mouth was spreading faster than a bush fire. When the king of my city, the Olubadan, issued a press statement on November 24, repeated several times on the radio, we were all amused. He issued a "stern warning," as the news reported, to all rural dwellers and agitators not to come near his palace to protest against taxation. Oba Salawu Aminu instantly became a subject of ridicule. Unless he had accepted heavy gifts from the governor, people wondered why he would make such a silly statement. He was right to have reminded the rural people that he was not the one who assessed them and that the palace was not the venue where the assessment was carried out. We all knew he was not the government, but he was party to the decision to raise the tax, and he collected his own share at the end of each month.

As if his words could not threaten anyone, about a thousand rebels descended on his palace on November 25; I was one of them. To further tell the king that his image was already tarnished, the protesters said they were all from just one village, Olojuoro. If they were all from just one village, this meant that many more would visit him from other villages. He understood the reference to "one village" as a sign of trouble that he would never be able to handle. Clad in palm leaves, we told him we could only pay seven shillings as tax. He was stunned, caught by surprise, and visibly shaken.

"Seven shillings!" he exclaimed with his mouth wide open.

With heavily armed policemen at his side, he said we now wanted the government not only to go broke but to collapse. The four previous delegations before us, he reminded us in a very cautious tone, sought a smaller reduction. The protesters yelled back, asking where he wanted them to get the money to pay when the king knew their cocoa trees were dead. He was too old to realize he was being insulted by his "subjects," men who had previously treated him with respect and deference. The old man began to seek counsel among the octogenarians who were with him. Maybe it was his own idea, or maybe a piece of advice handed over to him, but he told us to go to the governor's mansion as he himself had lost control. In the days that followed, the Olubadan vacated his residence and went to stay in one hideout after another. But we were able to track him.

Various calls for peace, for the angry farmers and poor to settle their differences (as if they had created them), went unheeded. All the districts around Ibadan were becoming strong centers of rebellion. On November 25, an employee of the Western State Ministry of Works and Transport who, certainly out of carelessness, forgot to remove his uniform, was mobbed at Iyana-Ofa, a village northeast of Ibadan. His right arm was cut off with the instruction that he should take it to Irunmu to show what the protesters would do to anyone who asked them to pay taxes. Fear gripped the civil servants as news spread that they would be beheaded if caught. They began to deny that they worked for the government.

Also on November 25, 1968, tax protesters attacked the king of Isara in the Ijebu province, Oba Samuel Akinsanya. Leaving his crown and symbols of power behind, the king fled. The mob set fire to his Mercedes-Benz car, his palace, and his library. The objects of power and modernity went up in flames. Then the rebels marched on the houses of all the pro-government chiefs in other smaller towns and burned them down. The traditional authority had not only lost respect, it was on the verge of collapse. Dignified men were called dirty names, labeled as thieves. By the time the news reached Ibadan, the seat of government, a great deal of damage had been done. By the next day, the army and police had rushed to Isara to secure the troubled city, but the protesters had made their point. Four delegates from there came to report the full incident, as they were mandated to do. They actually wanted to kill the king, as they said, but he was lucky to have escaped, although not without sustaining injuries. The king had been too vocal in his support of tax increases. The police used maximum power, injuring a large number of people. There was an exchange of gunfire, and our side retreated as far as they could. Up until today, no one has been able to determine the number that died.

On Tuesday, November 26, in a highly coordinated onslaught, we marched in thousands to attack various places in the city of Ibadan, especially Mapo Hall, the stronghold of city politics, the location of the major council. This attack had taken ten days to plan, with the mobilization of close to ten thousand foot soldiers. The full details will never be known, as key decisions were taken by just a few of the most senior leaders. While the Akanran movement, as well as hundreds of villages relating to it in the struggles, was known as the Agbekoya, there were others with their own different names, although all of us were known to the public by the same name of Agbekoya. But they all agreed to coordinate their efforts. War planners divided the city into four entrances, avoiding the major roads. Some of these leaders became prominent rebels—men such as Dairo Alata, Alimi Sunmonu, and Lajire Boade (all from villages in Ibadan South). From the Akanran axis came Tafa Adeoye (Fada village), Yesufu Omiyale (Olorunda village), Folarin Idowu (Abigina village), and Layiwola Akanran. From Ibadan West came even tougher men such as

**Assembly of warriors, ca. 1969. Ministry of Information, Ibadan.**

Oladimeji, Alimi Lajumoke, Lasisi Iyanda, and Lasisi Ajanpako. Without knowing what was to be done, thousands of us were moved to villages closer to the city in the vicinities of the major entrances. The movement to the outskirts of the city took almost three days and entailed the provision of food and water for thousands of people. It was not possible to convey our army in lorries, and this had never been the strategy at any time. We walked, and the distance and hours needed to cover it had to be calculated into the strategy. If we wanted to fight in the morning, we had to leave the villages and move closer to the targets during the night. The police and the army moved faster in trucks and followed a different approach altogether. That the security apparatus of a state government would not know about the movement of thousands of people close to the edges of its capital shows their high level of incompetence. Perhaps the police could be defended as being strangers to the area—the farmer-soldiers were operating in familiar territory.

At 6:30 a.m. we were ordered to move to the city, and by 7 a.m. we were within it. War songs followed, their chorus repeating that the taxes should be no more than seven shillings. To obtain sympathy, thousands of us added palm fronds to our uniforms, a sign to tell the women that we were peaceful and fighting a just cause. Shops and stalls along our routes quickly shut down, perhaps fearing that they might be looted by thugs. Three hours later, the main targets had been taken over, especially the palace of the Olubadan and the Central Police Station. The contingent that went to the Iyaganku police station met with superior firepower and retreated to join others in easier locations. By 11 a.m. Mapo Hall, the most powerful seat of municipal government in the state, had been subdued by a force of over five thousand, too many for the police force to deal with. The place was sacked, officials were injured, and some of the offices were damaged. This was a brilliant move, although the cost was high in human lives and injuries. Clashes were intense. The oldest market in the city, Ojaba, was thrown into a panic, as traders abandoned their wares and fled for safety. Thieves took over, stealing clothes, food items, and even goats.

Irunmu mobilized the police and army to fight back. They sent teargas and live bullets into the crowd. The teargas suffocated not a few. Thugs attacked the army from behind with stones and broken bottles. The army opened fired on the rebels and on innocent bystanders. As thousands in the crowd were forced to disperse, some were crushed to death. We lost over a hundred men, although only twelve, whose corpses could not be carried away, were reported by the media the next day. Scores were injured so severely that they died soon thereafter, either in the hospital or in their private homes. In the days ahead, corpses were found in various parts of the city, some inside gutters. Nine dead bodies were reported unclaimed in the public mortuary. The police arrested many who were unable to run fast enough or who were just bystanders mistaken for rebels. They claimed to have arrested eleven, but we could not account for over fifty men. To avoid being arrested at the hospital, many who suffered from gunshots were carried to private homes, where they were treated with herbal remedies and older ways of removing bullets from the body.

In Sagamu, sixty-nine kilometers away from Ibadan, a powerful group of protesters took over the streets, carrying placards that called for massive tax reductions. All the major roads were blocked. Villagers around Sagamu sacked council officials, and at Iperu, ten miles away, a tax clerk almost lost his life. A few houses were burned. The army and the police, using teargas and the threat to kill, forced the crowd to disperse. Arrests followed; as usual in such post-battle sweeps, innocent people were caught in the police net. Numbers were announced over the radio to frighten the cowards away from joining the brave.

The entire region was shaken. Where they were not organizing to fight, many communities were refusing to fill in assessment forms or to pay their taxes. The talk about unfair taxation became talk of an unfair government. Talk of an unfair government became talk of a "greedy government," which collected money without providing necessary services. Irunmu hurriedly arranged a major evening broadcast on state radio and television blaming the rebellion on misguided farmers instigated by "unscrupulous" politicians who wanted his government to collapse. It was not about taxes or standards of living; we were being used and misled in order to destabilize the government. His budget was already formulated, and he needed the money to deliver services. The ongoing civil war, he added, was creating its own economic problems, and we must suffer its repercussions. If we wanted public services, it was our responsibility to pay for them. He could review the compulsory war levy (not the tax) for the lower-income group after he had spoken with his boss in Lagos. He spoke tough, threatening that the full force of the police and army would be used against "demonstrators."

Members of the public were divided in their opinions, as expressed on radio and in newspapers, some blaming us, some blaming the government, and some blaming the police and army for the excessive use of force. There was a growing fear that market women might join us, and this would certainly paralyze the economy. Irunmu was now being advised to set up a committee of inquiry. Meanwhile, on December 23, he imposed a dusk-to-dawn curfew on Ibadan, Oyo, Isara, and Ede—four main areas in which our men and ideas had had a considerable impact—banning everyone from leaving their houses between 6 p.m. and 7 a.m. Only the police and army could be on the streets. Unfortunately for him, the police and the army could not get to the villages, and we were not night operators. Irunmu allowed the police to give special permits to his friends and associates to enjoy the roads at night, including, as gossip spread, for visits to their mistresses in hidden locations. To convey that we were not bothered about his curfew, we asked people in certain parts of the city to stay outside their compounds and houses and not to cancel their nightly events. When they sought vigilante protection, it was offered.

The aura of state power was broken. The government had lost its grip on millions of people. For days afterward, people were afraid, shops were closed, city council and court officials stayed away from work. The curfew hoax became an effective propaganda instrument, sending people into panic by using the gossip mill to spread misleading information that they must be indoors by 2 p.m. If the state government could not defend Mapo Hall, more than half its power was gone. As our army marched away on November 26 in many directions, the belief was that a quick dialogue would follow, tax rates would be severely cut, the governor would apologize, and we would declare victory and fold our tents. It was not to be.

Thinking that the government would yield to our request but needed a channel through which to reach a consensus, the leadership divided itself into two: the invisible and the visible. The invisible leaders were the most important, following the agreed-upon structure and the instructions that their identities must not be revealed. The public knew the visible ones, but tight control was imposed on them as well. I knew three well, both in private and public spaces: I lived with one for about nine days, and I wrote dictated notes for the other as he could neither read nor write. The third I knew through meetings and delivering errands.

One was called Ageku-Ejo, a man believed to be so powerful that even if the government trailed him, they could not know his destination; if they thought they had cornered him, they would find no one there. His people would say "*Ageku-Ejo ti n soro bi agbon*"—the decapitated viper that inflicts mayhem like the venomous wasp! The widespread belief was that he had a charm known as *isuju*, which allowed him to be standing before you, although you would not see him. He could speak with you, but you would not see his physical body. *Isuju* allows a man to become thin air. No force can arrest and capture someone with *isuju*. Before you could make your move, he would lose his physicality. And when he becomes air, you had better run, as he has the strength to hold your neck and strangle you to death. So potent was *isuju* that the herbalists and diviners in the land agreed to make it only for distinguished hunters and warriors, to avoid its being abused by thieves and armed robbers.

Ageku-Ejo had connections with a large number of hunters, and within a few hours, he could mobilize hundreds of them. Ageku-Ejo believed in the power of violence and was always opposed to dialogue. Whenever he was forced to accept a meeting, he would make elaborate preparations for war, asking over a thousand hunters to stay not too far away. If he did not appear within a specified time, they must not wait to find out why but march on the venue of the meeting and begin to shoot at random. "A snake cut in half," the translation of his name, was appropriate to his behavior, as the half still with the head retains the venom, and whosoever the teeth grabs goes to heaven with the snake. Ageku-Ejo struck fear into the *baale*. He created his own separate force, accountable to him, even giving his men their own titles, such as *olori* (head) and *jagun* (commander), titles that were often confused with those used in the movement as a whole.

The second, and the most famous, was the lean-looking Tafa Adeoye, later a public hero, and the darling of the press. He was completely trusted for most of 1968 and 1969, but he lost his reputation by 1970. What was said of him moved into the realm of legend, and I will present it as such. Tafa had *isuju* and much more. He was a real *gbetugbetu* man, a person who could command you to do whatever he liked: If he said, "Keep dancing and singing like a mad man," you automatically did it. If Tafa told a policeman, "Bend down and shit, and eat the shit," he would do so within an instant. If he told a soldier, "Point the gun at yourself and pull the trigger," you would hear the sound of the gunshot and see the dead soldier fall to the floor. No one, including Irunmu, could mess with Tafa. If Tafa appeared in battle, he could move toward the direction of the firing. As you showered him with bullets, these would fall on the ground, diverted by his *ajabo* charm, made for him by a most powerful Igbomina medicine man. Should you want to invite Tafa to a meeting, you should just tell him the time and venue. Lock all the main entrances and doors. Leave a vacant chair. A second before the meeting commenced, Tafa would be on the seat. This was possible because of *egbe*. When the meeting was over, before you could shake his hands, *egbe* had taken him to his next meeting. Tafa had his *egbe* made at an unknown location close to the lagoon side of Okitipupa. The charm maker had never been found, after he made the charm using components including items that mysteriously dropped from the sky. Everyone wanted Tafa's *egbe*, but the maker was either dead or had gone elsewhere.

Myths about Tafa were now competing with those of Ogun, Sango, and Esu combined. I heard all of them, and I have reported here just a few. However, he was actually an astute war manager, with very strict rules. He and the invisible leaders created ground rules. When our soldiers were marching back to a village, the *baale* had to make sacrifices to welcome them. The soldiers muttered words, and they entered the village without looking back. The key element in that sacrifice, as Tafa insisted, was to prevent internal divisions. The leaders were constantly swearing not to betray one another. At one time, they swore by the soil collected from the burial site of Honorable Adegoke Adelabu, the first Ibadan superstar political leader and council manager. Adelabu had become a celebrity since his death, celebrated with annual lectures, two of which I have been privileged to give. People used his gravesite as a swearing spot.

War staff was issued to warriors with leadership qualities. For the southeast, Tafa obtained the authority to issue and collect war staffs. To have control over the use of staffs and over promotion recognized the authority of the upper echelons of the movement, and those privy to political calculations and war strategy.

Tafa and others, aside from having powerful charms, were actually very bright and strategically astute. As soon as police personnel and their vehicles were sighted, code and signal already set in place would be activated so that, within a few hours, the entire region would know. There were no telephones, but there were legs, legs that ran as fast as telephone cables, and a chain of mouths. Thus, if the police were scheming a surprise, there was already a strategy in place to sabotage them. The *baale* must not welcome council officials or anyone associated with the government. They could not give the police water to drink, to say nothing of food. To do so was to be accused of betrayal, the equivalent of treason. You could not even speak to those who were associated with the government, much less answer any of their questions. To be seen standing with a government official or police officer without authorization was a punishable offense, as it had been stated that you could be beheaded. Well, if you did not like your head standing on your neck, you could try it. No one, at the end of the day, was actually beheaded, but you could hear mothers, holding their heads and warning their sons not to lose theirs, not to bring sorrow in the daytime to humiliate them. Midnight sorrow was preferable since you could hurriedly bury the head and the body in makeshift graves. Heads are delicacies in the pot, but not those of humans.

The third person of note with whom I interacted was Abinuwaye— one who left heaven in anger to live in this world. He was a most impressive personality whose appearance was always preceded by praise songs:

*E maa sa te le won*
*E maa le won lo nso*
*Won ti mere sa*
*Eyi ti ko sa*
*Kumo lori e.*


Pursue them
Run after them
They are on the run
If he stops running
Clobber his head.

He would acknowledge the song with his flywhisk. Then the drumming and singing became faster. He stayed still in one spot, turning his head to left and right, as if observing everyone. The faster song presented him as the main chief-commander-in-waiting:

> There were more than a million soldiers
> And another million policemen
> He killed all of them
> becoming the king
> No one is superior to Abinuwaye
> Whenever he hears the sounds of war
> His joy knows no limits
> "War is nasty," the mother said
> Abinuwaye replied, in laughter, "This is why I like it!"
> "War kills"
> He rejoiced: "This is why I want to go!"

Abinuwaye exceeded all in symbolism. He used animal skins to make his jackets. Whenever he was wearing the jacket said to be made of tiger skin (it resembled leopard skin to me), you would need to be very cautious of the number of sentences you uttered to him. Quick tempered, he could fell you with one blow if you said something he didn't like. His cap was long, bent sideways or backwards, reaching back to his neck. You could see that he was not just covering his head but hiding something in a reachable container. Perhaps the cap was a container for first-aid items needed in an emergency, like pre-incantation powders. Terrifying but not bizarre, his aide carried the skull of a dead man. It was the second time that I had seen one. The Ololu, the anti-female masquerade in the city, had a mask made out of a human skull. Women were not allowed to see the Ololu in his annual performance. As thousands of followers shouted "Ololuooo" or "Ololuuu," women rushed indoors in a hurry and did not peep out. The skull I saw during this performance was part of the mask, held together by pieces of cloth. The skull that accompanied Abinuwaye was grafted to a wooden staff and held by an aide wearing a blue uniform.

The government had decided not to hold meetings with us. Irunmu and his officials were talking to the kings and chiefs and city politicians. We were dumbfounded: How could they not understand? Had someone leaked our decision to stop the war if the tax rates were reduced? Anger spread: The government had collected wood containing insects, which the lizards would follow; its dog had lost its sense of smell, ready to die; its monkey was climbing higher and higher, exposing its dirty buttocks; its dog had put a bone in its mouth and still wanted to bark. Tens of thousands became more resolute in their anti-government stand: The bullet that kills an elephant is not as big as its toe. The officials were like animals that eat thorns but do not have the stomach to digest them. Council agents were deaf to the sound of the thunder and would now be soaked in rain.

We held more meetings to rethink and update our strategies. You cannot dance all night with just one tune. The widespread belief, based not on any verifiable data but on sheer suspicion, was that city-based politicians and chiefs had advised Irunmu to ignore us. City politicians were men who could call a cow a "brother" because they wanted to eat beef. They could send a houseboy to buy salt in the market and ask the rainmaker to follow him. They could grind hot pepper just because they wanted to punish the nose and eyes. Many politicians were suspected of complicity with the government, with names flying around. Whether it was true or not, all contacts with politicians supportive of the government had to be cut off. There were a handful of politicians outside of government with deep roots in village politics. We needed to create an alliance with them, as they could mobilize other forces in support of the rebellion. One such figure was based in the city, and on a few Sundays, delegates were sent to speak with him. This politician engaged in a risky triangulation: on Sunday with us, on Monday with a council official, and on Wednesday with the media. He seemed to be enjoying the limelight, but we were never fooled. Not even once. We had greater plans; when a rat mocks the dog, it stays close to its hole.

Those who are surrounded by enemies must sleep with one eye open. If the government would not change its position, we had to change ours. December saw an escalation in the conflict. If the previous strategy was simply to prevent council officials from reporting for work, the new one was to frighten them so much that there would be no councils at all. If any staff member had the courage to report for work, he was so badly beaten that he ended up in the hospital. Unfortunately, three were killed. Council officials disappeared, going into hiding to seek one day of peace in a year of stress, that one day becoming the equivalent of hundreds of days in paradise. No one in the land could save the council officials—Irunmu and his forces had become a team of lions led by a pig, much weaker than our own team of pigs led by a lion. Council offices in many places entered on a long process of decay, overgrown with weeds, and many did not reopen until two years later.

A dead antelope was less angry with the hunter who shot him but more angry with the dog that exposed his hideout and drove him away to where the shot could hit him. The end of the council offices brought about the end of taxation in the villages. No tax estimator could visit dangerous places. There were no more tax collectors where there were rebels. If you are ready to burn down your house, your enemy will make a match available to you: No longer just being asked to reduce taxes, the government was now without any revenue in the villages. Officials were still collecting tax in the towns and cities, waiting for farmers to dare leave their villages. They could carry out tax raids in the cities, focusing on urban workers, but not in volatile villages.

Rebellion had become widespread by December 1968, with intense activity in such places as Ede, Egba villages, Ibadan city and villages, Ijebu-Igbo, Isara, and Oyo. Our official name had become "troublemakers," which could have served as the title of this chapter, only that it would be more appropriate as a title for the government and its officials, as they were the instigators of the crisis, the pot calling the kettle black.

No man can be in two places at once. I participated in only the events of Ibadan, but I listened to all the other reports, as each unit must always come to the coordination center within twenty-four hours of any operation. If the media sometimes portrayed the rebellion as made up of members of one political party or another or as being manipulated by one politician or another, they got it all wrong. Local issues existed, as each unit understood those realities, but the collective objectives were the same. On December 15 at Ijebu Igbo, thousands took the palace by surprise, fully armed. They set the king's car and his convoy of motorcycles on fire. They damaged the palace and shot at will. Luckily for the king, he managed to escape. Anti-riot policemen did their notorious job of dispersing the crowd after pumping teargas into their eyes. About ten were arrested.

At Ede, the war arrived on December 19. The sole administrator for Osun-Central Division stoked the fires by requesting a meeting with the farmers on December 19 in order to explain to them why they must pay tax. They agreed to meet with him, setting up a trap. Instead of a small delegation of a dozen hand-picked farmers meeting at the palace of the king, the Timi of Ede, the farmers had mobilized a contingent of almost two thousand. Unknown to the sole administrator, a strategic plan had been worked out earlier in November to handle such a meeting. Where we wanted to fake cooperation, we sent fake leaders with known address-es whose agreements were nonbinding and who had no one to report to but themselves. Where the farmers represented themselves, as in the case of Ede on December 19, the plan was fixed: Allow the "ministry man" to talk, disagree with him, treat him with disrespect, and request him to leave and deliver the message to his boss. This was a strategy of maximum insult to a constituted authority. Cutting a sole administra-tor down to size in the presence of a king and in the king's palace was not just questioning power but showing the irrelevance of power itself. Power had lost its ability to tax, to coerce, and to arrest. Power had been unmasked, and its bearer disgraced in public. The sole administrator would have to make up excuses at the secretariat and figure out the way to save face.

Violence was expected. The sole administrator could attend the meeting with the police, heavily guarded. If he allowed the farmers to abuse him and walked away with his armed men, they could all disperse in peace. If he got angry and threatened the use of force, they would ask him to go ahead. If the police moved toward them, they would not run but advance. Those in the frontline hid their weapons, with *buba* (loose shirts) over their war gear. Those at the rear, fully armed, were hiding. The guns were at the rear, clubs and knives in the middle, charms in the frontline. Those at the front would retreat to allow those in the middle to charge. When the police fired teargas to disperse the crowd, they would be ruthlessly attacked before the gas took its effect on the eyes.

The sole administrator did not show up. After they had waited for hours and had been treated disrespectfully by the enemy, their anger had to be manifested. The government had told them they did not count, and a spy among them had probably leaked their preparations. In any case, the Ede contingent had been instructed not to bring the war to an end, and this was an opportunity they could not miss. Rather than dispersing, thousands of armed farmers descended on the city to inflict destruction on the houses of tax collectors, tax officials, and their sympa-thizers, all of whose addresses had been compiled beforehand. With the power of the local government already destroyed, the Tìmì took over. Lacking the means to stop the violence, he called on the army and the police. They did what they knew best: They harassed and arrested the innocent. Eleven farmers were arrested and marched to jail.

The Tìmì had lost credibility. On December 23, he was greeted by war as armed protesters stormed his palace demanding the release of those arrested. The Timi again called on the police, who brought more men and teargas. There would be no Christmas or New Year's celebration in peace. A few days later at Oyo, anti-tax protesters inflicted enormous damage in various parts of the city, leaving five dead and scores wounded. A prominent chief who was supporting the government lost his life, and a police constable was kidnapped, but later released out of sympathy for his wife and children.

Outbreaks occurred in numerous places; small battles here, skirmishes there; disturbances in a market; and panic in a motor park, in Ibadan city, Ibadan Division, Isara, Ijebu-Igbo, Oyo, and Ede. At Isara, six people were killed by the police in a fresh outbreak on December 22 during a rapid exchange of gunfire. On the same day, three died at Ede. Back at Ibadan, on December 20, villages along the Ibadan-Lagos road, most especially at Idi-Ayunre, attacked council chiefs who tried to show up for work. Akanran and Ijebu-Igbo established a connection, and all the villages along that route came under the control of "rebels," driving away anyone associated with the government, council, chiefs, and kings. Women were evacuated from those places. A customary court judge who was passing through was recognized, taken out of his car, and thoroughly beaten. So also was a council officer who was identified and so badly beaten that they broke his thigh.

The government was frightened. It released figures announcing that in the span of three weeks, twenty people had been killed and fifty injured. This was false, very false. In December alone, our list of the dead was over a hundred, the injured approaching five hundred, and the missing over a hundred. On December 22, the governor announced a cut in water rates, thinking that this would assuage the anger of millions of people. This impressed no one. Even if water rates were reduced to one cent, most villages would still not pay. Pay for water that we collected free from the stream? Even Irunmu's people, in his hinterland big town of Iyin Ekiti, far away from his office at Ibadan, had no such privileged access to good water, although they refused to join us, as they were proud of their son in power. In defiance of the governor, small skirmishes occurred, and the front was extended to Abeokuta; twenty people were arrested in Abeokuta for harassing tax officials. On December 23, Irunmu called a meeting of the so-called Leaders of Thought. We were all glued to the radio, thinking they would say something positive. No, Irunmu was full of scorn for the "troublemakers," threatening hail and thunder. He would reeducate us about our civic responsibilities and punish those misleading us. One by one, people were turning off the radio, calling Irunmu and all his "leaders of thought" birds of the same feather flocking together. Let the rich befriend the rich, and let us the poor people stay together. We called the rich the agents of darkness, and we represented light and progress. Day and night never meet, and we vowed never to listen to whatever the other side said.

Whether I saw them or not, and whether I took part with them or not, many units shared much in common, reflecting the instructions put in place as well as the anticipated outcomes. Let me speak to three issues of importance: the role of thugs, especially what we thought about them, as well as whether they helped or harmed the movement; the men who were dead or missing; and the role of charms—how we should understand the belief in them, and how important they might have been in comparison to the war plan.

In all the battles in November and those that followed, thugs were drawn into the invasion—not because we invited them but because we provided action and jobs for them. Ibadan had always had its thugs, incidentally created by the politicians who funded them. Then and now, political parties rely on thugs to harass opponents, to intimidate the followers of a different political party, and to protect their patrons from attacks by other thugs. Thugs were used to plant evidence, notably hemp and weapons, in the houses of political opponents so the police could arrest them; to recover unpaid debts; and/or to send tenants who refused to pay rent out of their houses in the middle of the night. Before any election campaign, politicians would buy guns and other weapons to arm the thugs. When the elections were over, the politicians were afraid the thugs would turn on them as they did in a few cases.

Some former thugs were delighted to join us in order to turn on those leaders who had abandoned them. Party-affiliated thugs were unreliable; they changed their allegiance on the basis of the highest-paying bidders, not on the basis of commitment. They wanted revenge, not change. Grievances drove them, not gratitude. Many wanted to join us as "insiders," but we wanted them to stay in the cities. Thugs were not much interested in farming and cocoa; they were too lazy for jobs with such little reward. They survived well in the cities. Ejo (snake) was a well-known thug, prominent in the early 1960s in a political party dominated by Bamu. When Bamu was gunned down by coup plotters in January 1966, Ejo became jobless. In 1968, when our own troubles started, Ejo joined the Egbe Mekunnu Taku, where he recruited other thugs, most notably a daredevil known as Akeke (scorpion), also known as Buoda Akeke. If you were younger than Akeke, you had better put

Buoda (brother) before his name; otherwise he would grab your head and shake it until you threw up. When Buoda Akeke was angry with you, he could ignite a wrap of marijuana, shove it into your mouth, and make you inhale it until you lost consciousness. As you inhaled, he would hit you on the head with his fists.

Both Ejo and Buoda Akeke wreaked havoc, especially whenever Ibadan was invaded. They had their own large following, recruited and sustained by booty gathered in all the "wars." No police on foot could do anything to Ejo and Buoda Akeke, and any cunning policeman showered them with deference so he could return in peace to his wife. Any invasion of the city led to their "pillaging" markets, taking yams and chickens, and raiding "beer parlors" for free beer, cold or hot. Ejo and his boys could carry a steaming pot of soup from "Iya Alamala" (a food seller). They were above the law, but they served useful functions—just because your son is bad does not entitle you to shoot him!

However, it was more rewarding and lucrative for the thugs to turn on innocent citizens, which they did by damaging their cars, robbing them of their valuables, killing some, raping others, and flogging the lucky ones. They did not need to cover their faces or paint parts of their bodies to become anonymous. They were anonymous in a country where many could simply melt into the general population or relocate to another city. The big ones had patrons who protected them. The clever ones who were part of a syndicate had a boss who shared the loot with the police. Syndicates were anti-social criminal gangs, operating as secret societies. Members could be hired and paid to assassinate business rivals. Thugs were delinquents and wasteful: They drank and played when they had money. Beer and women were great pastimes, and marijuana was the snack of choice. When they were broke, no job was too small for them, from harassing small street traders to carrying out armed robberies. The small ones worked in disorganized teams, and they were easy to identify. The big-time ones were generally affiliated with a well-oiled underground crime network, and much more difficult to identify.

Protests, rebellions, and wars were always events of interest and fascination for thugs. They joined. If the protest was peaceful, organizers must ensure that thugs did not turn their activities into violence. If the protest was not peaceful, thugs would escalate the violence. Formidable rogue groups, thugs converted protests into profit: They would attack stores and harass their owners so as to take whatever they wanted. Angry with society, they would take their revenge by beating the innocent. Alienated from the government, they would seize the opportunity to beat any police officers and officials they could lay their hands upon. Emboldened that they were part of the public, they defined themselves by their bravado, machete wielding, and drug use. While peaceful protesters were motivated by idealism, thugs did not act in the name of God or honor. Like the Agbekoya, they not only resented the authorities, but they became lawless. Unlike the Agbekoya, lawlessness for the thugs must bring rewards and war booty, enraging the public and state by revealing the ugliness of chaos. And they must leave evidence of their activities: the destruction of stores and buildings. The thugs were useful; the government used their involvement to paint us all as criminals, to justify shooting innocent people, and to question the honor of the worthy. The noble desires of the Agbekoya and the nefarious activities of the thugs converged to overwhelm the power of the state.

Death came to people. Merciful God took them all, whether they died of gunshots, cholera, tuberculosis, or incarceration in crowded prison cells. What killed them was one thing: the evil government. Who made it possible was another: the merciful God who could do and undo, who allowed the toad to walk freely before a greedy chef, who allowed the successful to walk gracefully before the jealous. We could not admit to the power of the government. This would be giving them too much credit. When a person died, in both war and non-war situations, all his possessions, food, money, and charms must be removed and passed on to his family.

To lessen the demoralization of the living, a small group of professional mourners was set up. They knew how to break the news, how to start the mourning, initiate a cry, and then stop it to discuss funeral rites. The corpse must never be taken to his compound until the announcement was made and the mourning commenced. Everything must be fast, within a day, as the body would begin to decompose and smell. No hospital, no mortuary. Indeed, in most cases, the corpse had already been carried closer to his compound. As soon as the first stage of mourning was done the corpse arrived. The professional mourners were able to conduct the rites, prayers, and rituals. Full respect was offered. If the dead was of adult age with children, they asked for drumming and singing, turning the mourning into a celebration of a successful life. Where death had been preceded by sickness or serious injury, the person concerned might have left instructions on what should be done. Most probably, he would have been carried home before his last breath. It was not so complicated, as there was no need to go to a formal mortuary, to register the death with the government. People had the right to bury within their compounds, at the front or back of their houses, or by their land in the city or village.

Sometimes the dead were buried not too far away from where they died. Young men in their twenties and those without children did not have to be carried home. Their families were informed by mourners, who also carried along with them signs of the dead: their clothes, caps, and other memorable objects. In some instances, they cut the nails of the corpse and shaved his hair, and these were collected and put in his bag or cap and returned to his compound as his parting memorabilia. Representatives of the family would then follow the mourners to see the grave, where they would cry one more time before they dispersed. For those with children and those considered adults, social events must be held, but at a much later date. Many were held after 1970 with entertainment for guests.

People were lost, and not all their bodies were ever accounted for. The police were very careless about record keeping, and it was not always clear who was in their custody and where. They brutalized and killed many people and threw their corpses into the jungle to cover their own excesses. The fact that fake names might be used by those who had been arrested made it difficult for their families to trace them. Another major problem arose when sickness forced people to the hospital, where they died. If their bodies were left uncollected in the mortuaries, a mass burial of the unidentified would be conducted. There were many unconfirmed rumors about people who were said to have fled to Lagos, Ghana, and northern Nigeria and never came back. A few were attracted to join the army, thinking that the movement had trained them in combat. Those who betrayed the movement in 1969 were promised jobs as messengers, gardeners, and laborers by the government. They, too, disappeared.

Only the dead could be mourned. Those who were lost had to be forgotten over time. After the panic and the immediate frantic search, families began to lose hope. Death was preferable to being lost. The former brought finality, the latter misery and false hope. Beliefs circulated that the missing might have been sighted, appearing to family members like ghosts and then disappearing. A myriad of stories and beliefs had currency throughout the city, all deriving from the need for people to reconcile themselves to their loss. Families were told that their missing members had been seen in the marketplace. Since it had always been an established belief that the dead might appear as ghosts, the missing could do the same. One must never mourn the lost, as a person could have planned his own disappearance. Two charms many people sought in 1968 were called *pasiparo* (replacement) and *idanda* (reincarnation). Several people made both charms, which included the making of incisions on the chest, over forty-eight incisions on the skull, running from the front to the back, and drinking some concoctions from a skull, described as that of a man who had died in his late nineties and donated his skull to the herbalist. The recipe for the concoction included worms and banana trees: Cut either, and it reproduced. Fell a banana tree, and another one would sprout. Magic is about similarity: If you have a headache, pour hot water on your head. The man becomes like the banana whose mother may die, but whose baby remains.

There was much talk of *ogun* or juju (charms). The successes of the rebellion, it was believed, were made possible by charms. Charms represent a belief system, and one cannot prove or disprove this belief with evidence of efficacy. You see what happens when a charm works, and when one fails to work, you say it is due to a badly executed charm. I can explain how *pasiparo* or *idanda* was supposed to work. Upon death, many will go to the land of the dead, but a few may refuse. Both charms enabled a person to stop at the gates of heaven and then turn back, roaming between the two worlds, earth and heaven, and deciding once in a while to visit the world in human flesh. On such visitations, someone who recognized the dead would see him and report to others. The dead man might choose to visit a new town, where he would be seen walking all alone and talking to himself. For the charms to work, when the user died, he must be presumed to be missing and not dead; his death must never have been announced, and no one must have cried. In the most potent form of *pasiparo*, you could be beheaded, you could be shot, but you had the ability to swap a dying head for a living one ("replacement"). A fast deal: Before the bullet could reach you, you simply proclaimed "Exchange!" And so it was done: You were dead, but your head was gone with its breathing soul, replaced by that of another person who died in your place. When a person was cut into two pieces, an "*eso*" incantation could make him whole. Should you lift a machete to hit him, he could stop you before you landed it by invoking the magical phrase "*Agbero nikun n gbowo*," and you would no longer be able to move your hand. Someone who was cut could use the *abedi* charm to heal the wounds within a second without leaving any visible scars.

One or two commanders from Iwo, north of Ibadan, were called *lagewu* because they had war vests that could withstand bullets and rocks. One inherited it from his great grandfather. The other had a new one made of iron, called *apata* (the huge rock). When he wore the vest, the commander's movement was slow, but his ability to lead and issue instructions was great. He certainly acquired terrifying power that added credence to his boasting that no police force or army in the land could overpower him.

Those who emphasized charms, however correctly, ignored one thing: strategy. There was a war plan. There were dos and don'ts that were revised as the situation changed. Fighting must never be extended into the night as there was no way to see. To enforce this, it was said that some charms needed to rest in the evening or that the maintenance of potency required dialogue with unseen forces. Learning from previous mistakes, retreats were now to be conducted in what would appear a disorganized manner to make it difficult for the pursuers to trace the fleeing warriors back to their base. In the earlier plans, retreats were coordinated under various unit leaders. In all encounters that involved the city, people were told to change into civilian garments and to divide into smaller units—that is, we could move to the city in hundreds, but must move back to base in trickles.

Various instruments of violence were accessible. The most basic were rocks of different sizes. They came in handy when the police fired tear-gas, as you could throw a few rocks before temporary blindness set in. The catapult, which was easy to make, was a device to make the rock travel faster and hit harder. Depending on the force exerted in pulling the string and where the rock hit the body, it could create major damage. Many used a piece of cloth to make a catapult, folding a rock in the cloth and swinging it several times before releasing it. Many carried knives, machetes, and clubs. Many even revived older forms of machetes and swords from the past, copying their design and technique.

By mid-December 1968, we had succeeded. There was peace in the villages: no more tax raids, no more police, no more tax collection, and no more councils. As it turned out, we did not miss the councils or the government. If you can stay hungry, you can conquer greed; if you undermine need, you conquer want! The government was not spending the tax money on the villages anyway. Council offices were spaces of humiliation—if a farmer was dragged there, he should expect to be insulted. He could be kept waiting on a bench for hours on end. All services required the payment of some form of bribe or gift. To obtain a birth certificate for your child, if someone told you it was necessary to obtain one, you paid for the certificate and gave yams and palm oil on top. Each council had a police station. They policed nothing except looking for ways to create false charges to enable them to arrest people and put them in jail so their family members would have to pay a bribe to obtain their release. The police even wanted free food, free palm wine, and free lodging. We had no criminals or thieves; the police themselves were the criminals. Councils said they wanted to improve our sanitation, but they did not provide good drinking water or mosquito nets. However, their sanitary inspectors could arrest you for wearing dirty clothes. Women could not carry their products to the market unless they paid dues for using makeshift sheds.

This could not be the end of the war, however. On our side, we still had serious issues. Trust had broken down between the government and ourselves. We lost many men, especially on November 26 at Mapo, when the police and army chose to fire randomly. Taxes were still being collected in the villages we did not control, nor had the taxes been reduced. Some were calling for the abolition of taxation altogether. We had over a hundred men in prison, including those arrested at Ibadan, Ede, Isara, Ijebu-Igbo, and Oyo.

The elite needed the villages for land and labor. They could not just drive away all the farmers, as the land would become useless. Nor could they take over the land, as there would be no laborers. Some politicians mobilized the electorate on the basis of village identities. Those at Ibadan, like Agbaje, built their political fortunes on identification with "sons of the soil," that is, using a familiar city identity to create a political platform. Such politicians were operating all over the region, pursuing their own ambitions by claiming to represent their own people. The farmers were thus essential to the maintenance of political ambitions. These politicians could not afford to completely alienate us, as they were aiming to control the councils and make money through them. They needed the councils back. The overthrown *baale* wanted the villages back in order to recover their power. City landlords who relied on farms to supply food to their tables and to make money from selling cocoa needed to regain control of the villages.

I can never know what all the vested interest groups were telling Irunmu. They needed him and us. Therefore, they needed him to "conquer" us so that they could have us back. They had no police or army of their own to use against us. Some spoke tough, asking Irunmu to behave like a dutiful soldier, forgetting that if you throw a stone in a rage, you miss your target. We knew these interest groups, and had compiled a list of them in case revenge was necessary, as it was in one or two cases. A hen that loves to preen itself should not swallow the needle. There were politicians in Lagos who wanted "federal power," and they, too, sided with the government. Even Ojugo, with his socialist credentials, was now speaking for the government in his new role as a finance minister and chairman of the Federal Executive Council. If we paid our taxes, Ojugo assured us, we would see enormous benefits. To save the life of the king of the area he himself came from, he rushed there on November 28 to mediate between the king and his angry people. As if he were the governor of the state, Ojugo promised the Isara people new roads and hospitals. Ojugo's suggestion that some of our members should apologize to the king became the subject of mockery. "He should do so on our behalf!" was the statement passed around, and he should prostrate full flat and put dust on his head. The man who had almost become a hero was already tarnishing his image.

There were some who sneaked into the camps and villages in the middle of the night to speak to our members. They called it giving "encouragement." Do night robbers encourage the house owner? These were crooks who wanted to swim in shallow waters and hide their backs. We knew they were deceitful, double dealers who would also sneak into the secretariat. It is better to sleep and suffer in the corner of a house than to share the bed with a hostile partner. The chiefs and kings were no different. They had to support Irunmu and his government. On top of their salaries they received occasional bribes and largesse. Irunmu always fed his pigs before slaughter, believing he would get good pork by so doing. It was pork, but not good pork. Irunmu was trusting clever men who kept telling him that the hippopotamus is a handsome animal. The kings and chiefs were preaching peace, but they did not want to pay for it: Peace is never cheap. They could not preach to us; what the radio called an "appeal" always ended with this chief or that king having been assured by Irunmu that we would be fine. Irunmu assured the kings that the "rioters" who had burned some of their palaces would receive no mercy, and he would maintain law and order at any cost. Listening to these people was like trying to buy parts of a goat from a leopard.

Lawyers were trying to reach out, sending us signals. Some called themselves "socialist lawyers," that is, radicals or communists. They stayed in comfortable offices reading Lenin's works bought on street corners. "Workers of the World, Unite!"—but not the dreariest workers in city offices or those on the farms dwelling with rats and cockroaches. The nicer ones among them, with some university people, wrote kind, sympathetic words in the newspapers but did not forget to drink their cold beer in the evenings. University students were told to mobilize to teach us the necessity of taxation—the source of the revenues the government needed to assist us. This was a gross insult, associating what they called "illiteracy" with ignorance. The British who governed Nigeria had said the same, and now the children of farmers were repeating the message.

The non-communist lawyers wanted money or else payment in foodstuffs and wild game, most especially the grasscutters that go well with pounded yam. They wanted to sell sand as salt but did not want to be paid in stones. We opted for three non-communist lawyers who were paid in foodstuffs but with the understanding that they would later get our votes. Unknown to them, the military had their own hidden agenda; their plan was never to leave power, and these lawyers schemed in vain. Who was left? God and us.

If we could do without government, the government could not do without us. We supplied cocoa and cash. Both were diminishing, undermining the economic basis of power. Tax evasion became so popular that over 70 percent refused to pay. Officials began to publicly complain of this loss in revenues. From December 1967 to January 1968, the Ibadan City Council collected about £60,000; between the end of December 1968 and January 1969, it could only collect £194. If you paid and the rebels found out, you became an enemy. In the city of Ogbomoso, the movement there decided that anyone who paid was as bad as the collector. Disaster was looming. There would be nothing to steal: The council member with four wives would not be able to explain the sudden change in upkeep allowance and might not show up to his mistress's apartment; the other with six boys in grammar school would not be able to pay their school fees. Tax collectors and tax assessors would now have to beg for food—they had no way of being paid if they were not bringing in money. And they had not been basing their expenses just on their salaries; also gone now was their power to harass the innocent.

On Saturday, December 28, 1968, in response to the growing concerns of the "good citizens," the virtual collapse of night businesses (notably nightclubs and "pepper-soup" joints), and the desire to show Lagos that Irunmu was in control, the government lifted the dusk-to-dawn curfew. We were told to be of good behavior, to respect Irunmu and his government, and to be sympathetic to their efforts to capture Ojukwu, the leader of Biafra. All these were funny words: Ojukwu was not our problem; it was Irunmu and the other officers who were using us to fight their wars. The government would also set up an inquiry, to sit in private, to look into the causes of the "disturbances." Those who know the cause of their illness have no need to consult the oracle. Irunmu needed an oracle if he was still thinking in terms of "law and order." We were long past that stage. We did not regard ourselves as disturbing the peace but as looking for peace. Irunmu and we had become two goats with locked horns that cannot drink from the same bucket. In frustration, and perhaps in desperation, the police ordered us on December 27 to surrender all our arms—everything that could be described as dangerous weapons—to the nearest police station within forty-eight hours. This was like seeing a comedian at work, only there was no audience to laugh. We had no respect for them: We had shut down all the police stations in the villages. We had even modernized our arsenals by capturing police weapons as their previous owners fled. The police were so afraid of us that they had no way of enforcing the instruction they themselves had issued; indeed, when they heard about our movements, their instinct was to run!

As if to ignore the police order, the people in the Egba-Obafemi group of villages began to harass the police, and on December 29, they ambushed a combined team of army and police who wanted to enter the villages. A shootout followed, leading to over thirty deaths; only one of the dead was a soldier, and the others were farmers. Indiscriminate arrests followed, with close to three thousand "agitators" lodged in various cells and barracks. Dane guns were confiscated, and the police announced that they had collected almost a thousand. To close the year, thousands marched to the palace of the *Alake*, the king at Abeokuta, indicating that peace was not possible. Their statements revealed the myriad of corrupt practices existing, for example, asking pregnant women to pay two shillings to avoid sanitary inspection, and every village to pay a quarterly bribe of £3 to avoid the visitation of sanitary inspectors.

There was no way that the government could keep feeding the thousands of people in cells or maintain peace; thus, by January 3, 1969, all the prisoners were all released. The celebrations usually held to mark the arrival of a new year had to be called off in many towns and villages. Rumors were rife at Ibadan that we would attack the city early in the new year—stories that delighted us very much. A lie that circulated, alleging that we would no longer be supplying food to the city, scared thousands of people and became the subject of a newspaper headline. In fact, we had thought about doing this, but such a strategy would ruin millions of farmers who would withdraw their support from the rebellion. Without food to put in the bellies, the hands could not hold weapons: Trees learn to dance to the tunes of the wind.

The state government sought to impose itself on us, a cockroach that does not need to dress well to live in a palace, an insect that enjoys a free lodging in one's clothes and bites its host. Control through dialogue would no longer work: Irunmu wanted to pick rocks from the bottom of the river, and he must be ready to get wet, if not drown. Other than in terms of access to better guns, our fighting forces were actually more powerful than those of the government. Strategy-wise, we could outsmart them. We lacked resources, sometimes so desperately that an adult had to rely on charity to be able to eat. When I was with Pasitor, meals were assured; when I was not, I had to beg for food. What we had in abundance was faith: that the commitment to our own truth and cause would eventually prevail. We would fight on: A tortoise can never make any progress until it sticks out its neck. You cannot be looking for honey and avoid the painful stings of honeybees.

CHAPTER 9

# Rebel Gangs

✦ ✦ ✦

*Ifa o wa eyele*
*Ifa o wa akuko*
*Atari alaseju ni ifa n wa*

Ifa does not want a pigeon
Ifa does not need a cockerel
It is the scalp of the mischievous that Ifa seeks.

We lived in a land of anger and blood. There was war in the East, with the fiery-looking, heavily bearded, cigar-smoking, red-eyed Colonel Odumegwu Ojukwu in charge of his army. From what began as Biafra, which encompassed what used to be called the Eastern Region, stretching from its boundaries with the North, where Ojukwu's arch-enemies lived, to the Atlantic Ocean in the South, the secessionist republic had been reduced to Igboland, a landlocked enclave with nowhere to run other than to Cameroon to the east. In the North, the people were claiming to live in peace, but they had driven out all the Igbo. The Yoruba in the North were afraid. Jubilant northerners carried sharpened knives in their pockets, looking for throats to slit. In the West, the Wild Wild West, as it was then called and is now fondly remembered, age-old social stratification, the maintenance of the power and status of the chiefs, along with the dependence on cocoa, had caused irreconcilable divisions that had now led to conflicts and wars. Things were falling apart, and they had been doing so for ten years. Kola, my childhood friend, was now on the war front on the side of the federal forces, and Basil, with whom I had started elementary school at St. James's Cathedral, Oke Bola, was fighting on the side of Biafra. I missed them both, and I cried each time I remembered them, assuming they were already dead. This was the age of face-to-face communication, before the age of cell phones or the Internet. I would later look for both of them in circumstances too grueling to delay us here. And what about me? I had become an integral part of the Agbekoya movement, serving in its intellectual wing, in the courier outfit, in the rear to organize supplies, and in the attack units. Ifa, the god of divination from whom I took my surname, had now lost his gentle way of asking you for a sparrow and cock to appeal to the gods. He now wanted human skulls for sacrifice, but to decapitate the head and remove the skulls, you had to kill first. Ifa was now fully aligned with Ogun, seeking blood to drink. Ifa, thy wish must be obeyed in the North, East, and West.

The government turned to the highly educated men and their pens to find out what happened and why, both the direct and indirect causes of our anger and war. It did not turn to us since we knew nothing. It could have consulted us, through the backdoor channels of imams, priests, Ogun worshippers, or even some kings and chiefs. It decided to find out what had happened in private hearings but still allowed things to be reported in the media. In mid-January 1969, it created a commission, named the Justice Ayoola Commission of Inquiry, to probe what it called the tax riots in parts of the Western State. The governor chose a high court judge, Olu Ayoola, with the investigative power to find out the causes of the rebellion—causes that we had already known before the very first battle. The government called it a "tax probe," as if we were the tax collectors. It chose a judge as if the matter required arbitration. The label Ayoola Commission betrayed the emphasis on the commission's official orientation. And the additional label, "The West Tax Riot Commission," revealed the emphasis on tax collection and not the deeper social issues and the failure of development. The government wanted to know what the police and army were doing to bring the situation under control. Was the government expecting more dead bodies? It wanted the commission to make recommendations on how to avoid future troubles. We had told them the solutions times without number. As the movements had splintered into uncontrollable groups, it would not work if the commission just went to Akanran or Ijebu-Remo. The commission had to visit several major fronts and hot spots: Ibadan, Ede, Oyo, Ijebu-Ode, Ile-Ife, Ilesa, Ado-Ekiti, Akure, Owo, and Ondo. It would collect facts, not looking for accused persons or accusers, only determining what had happened.

The commission invited the members of the public to its formal sittings, which began at Ibadan on January 22, 1969. They should appear before the commission and say whatever was on their minds. Nonmembers of the movement must now speak together with those spending our cocoa money to talk about cocoa producers. To us, the joke was that even tax collectors appeared before the commission. The government loved them anyway. Witnesses were told not to speak with bitterness, but what we heard was bitter. The rebellion, the public was warned, must not generate divisive debates and conclusions that would create further problems. What the commission wanted was peace, and those appearing before it must testify about what caused the absence of peace.

The commission began its work in ways we found amusing. The very first group to appear happened to include the very people we hated the most: council officials. The information reported back to us by the observers whom we had planted in all the places where the commission sat was very upsetting. Pasitor and I attended the first two days, and he then decided it was not worth it. The first presentation to the commission was by the former sole administrator for the six district council areas in the Ibadan Division. He asked the commission to go no further, as he knew why we had launched our war: An Ibadan chief and lawyer, by the name of Chief A. M. F. Agbaje, was behind it all. I knew Chief Agbaje very well. I knew the compound of his great father, Chief Salami Agbaje, who had built one of the most imposing mansions in the city. With its incredible floor plan and elevations, Agbaje's mansion became a tourist attraction. His son, also a famous politician, was ambitious. He might have been bitter that the military did not consider him for a position in 1966. The ex–sole administrator mentioned the names of other chiefs. I knew all of them. These were city-based farmers who were interested in exploiting rural farmers, who hired tenants from non-Yoruba areas and put them to work on their cocoa farms. The Agbaje family's wealth was realized from money lending and produce buying, occupations that became part of what we resented. Agbaje and his cohort were among those we detested. So our enemy was now the one instigating us to action. Nothing could be more ridiculous.

This same Chief Agbaje had come to the precinct of Akanran in late 1968 to plead with us. I was there, seeing him standing by Irunmu and pretending to speak the Ibadan dialect with the correct accent. I heard him clearly, when he took the mobile microphone from Irunmu, whose Oyo-Yoruba language was not fluent: Agbaje was telling us not to use violence and to accept our fate in life. The Olubadan was also there, and they all proclaimed the love they had for us and the need for peace to reign. Fake love. Chief Agbaje was also at the hearing on one of the days when Pasitor and I were there. He came to demonstrate his support and loyalty to the government, from which he needed positions and contracts, not to support rioting farmers. When the sole administrator was asked for evidence against Agbaje, he said he had been informed by the local leaders in the councils, whom he himself had selected. Two secretaries in district councils also told him of Agbaje and other politicians going around the villages to tell us not to pay taxes or levies. So the accuser had selected his own people as his witnesses, first to make an allegation and then to provide "evidence" to support it.

Trust in the commission was gone within the first two days. The first set of people to appear before the commission came to mislead, saying we would have eagerly paid our taxes if things had been explained to us, that there were not enough police constables in the villages, and that we were hooligans being manipulated by former politicians. Even the chiefs lied, saying that we preferred them as tax collectors, and we would have willingly paid to the local heads appointed by them. Government officials were speaking with government officials, trying to blame politicians who were outside the government for the activities of the frustrated poor. Another officer of the state spoke about how he personally knew the representatives of farmers from whom to obtain information, and he was told of the activities of discredited politicians.

These people quoted their own agents; the information they heard was from the ministry men they were trying to plant in the villages or from discredited council officials. On the second day of testimony, another council official, talking very loudly, spoke about how he saw politicians going from one village to another inciting the farmers, and how he asked us to trust him by complaining through him, so our words would get to the "government quarters." We were not part of the government but outside of government; all that was part of the government was the cocoa we produced—not us.

The ministry men came up with a second reason to explain our anger. We wanted to pay tax, one submitted, with a very calm demeanor and aura of respectability, but what we did not want to pay was the contribution to the war efforts. In the attempt to raise money to finance the war, the government had set up the National Reconstruction and Development Savings Scheme, commonly known as the "war loan." It was easier to encourage government employees to make contributions than to encourage the poor farmers.

Pasitor reported angrily to those who had sent him as a spy to observe the work of the commission. As he told our leader, the *asiwaju*, witnesses were not blaming the assessors and collectors for their evil malpractices. He was angry that they were associating us with banned political parties, as if we were boys and toys. He reported back that the commission was not concerned with the financial status of millions of people but with what the government could extract from our pockets. Pasitor added all the asides he had heard from those who thought he was one of the ignorant, stupid farmers—that the products from the farms were bad, diluted with dung and rocks, and that we had put the name of the country to shame in the international markets. He was really enraged when his church superior, the Right Reverend S. O. Odutola, Anglican Bishop of Ibadan, blamed the agitation on the work of the devil. "*Bisobu ti yo*" was his refrain, telling all that Odutola's stomach was too full, he was suffering from indigestion that was slowing down his thinking processes. Many were alarmed when Pasitor told them there was no plan to reduce the tax rate, as if he were already writing the final report of the commission.

The second day after the commission began its work, Irunmu went public to make it clear that certain things would never be negotiated. He summoned all the "boss men" of the "ministry men," known as permanent secretaries, administrators who had reached the pinnacle of their career and could now grow fat—both in their stomachs and in their bank accounts. These "boss men" had university educations, and Irunmu did not; they spoke better English than Irunmu, and a few were older. But they were afraid of him. He sometimes dressed for the office with a short gun hidden somewhere in his apparel. Not that he would shoot the permanent secretaries, but he could fire any of them on the spot, and no court in the land could overturn that decision. He told all the "boss men" to ensure that more people paid their taxes. Indeed, he would be appointing more experienced men to head local government councils in order to improve what he called "field administration." The title of "sole administrator" would be changed to "inspector." Rather than administering the villages and farms, these inspectors must begin to inspect them. The troublesome divisions, such as those in Ibadan, Egba, and Osun, must have senior inspectors capable of taming recalcitrant people.

When the commission visited other cities, the blame game was repeated: Local politicians instigated the crises. In one instance, in the case of Ede, the council administrator expanded the list to include Oba Adetoyese Laoye, the Timi of Ede. The Timi had imposed an additional tax burden of his own in 1968 by collecting a levy, presented as voluntary, on thousands of his citizens, allegedly to pay the legal fees incurred in fighting the case over the boundary dispute between Ede and its neighboring city of Osogbo. The Tìmì could not deny this charge, as the central coordinating unit of the Agbekoya had written to him in mid-November 1968 to stop the collection, citing the reduction in harvests in cocoa and other products in his area because of the damage caused by excessive rainfall.

Another party to blame was the best friend of the politicians: the press. Even Irunmu blamed journalists for adding to the problem. They should suppress the news of the war. Irunmu insisted that the press was part of the government, and it should only carry the government's news, events, and views. Irunmu was saying what we already believed: The press was part of the government. We collected the papers we read to the farmers who relayed the information to others in Yoruba. The papers gave little support to us, instead calling for the use of force, more deadly force, the force that the "Kill and Go" police could deliver. We should be shot on sight. We were a nuisance preventing the federal forces from quashing Ojukwu and his defecting Biafrans, diverting resources away from that bearded monster in order to deal with us. The press called for collective punishment to send many of us to prison with long-term sentences. We had never planned to deal with the media, and it was better to ignore them. Dealing with journalists, it was reckoned, would lead to betrayal; our tracks could be traced through unreliable contacts. We did not have the resources to match the government in the use of bribes to journalists. The government owned all the radio and television stations and the leading newspapers. The one or two independent papers were always too careful not to get into trouble with those in power. We gave up on the media—let those journalists speak with the ministry men to entertain Irunmu and his boss in Lagos.

On February 12, 1969, the unit at Ogbomoso launched a series of surprise attacks, launching a wave of violence. Many people were injured, and at least three were killed. The rebels partially destroyed the palace, the offices of the Ogbomoso District Council, the town planning authority, and several private buildings. A senior tax assessor was targeted, leading to the destruction of his car and the buildings belonging to him and his wife. The police and army were rushed there. As usual, arrests were made in the days that followed. The rebels were quick to regroup. There were incidents in Ife in the same month, as well as a major outbreak of violence in the Lalupon district of Ibadan, leading to the arrest of seventy-three men.

Perhaps noting the damage done at Ogbomoso, testimonies before the Ayoola Commission, as reported on the radio and in the print media, began to attribute blame to council officials for their corrupt practices and to appeal to the government to pay better prices for cocoa and offer more incentives to farmers in order to develop agriculture and reward producers. Where government could flex its muscles, it did, charging people in various towns with "unlawful assembly," arson, and related crimes and remanding hundreds in custody with or without trial.

The incident jolted the Ayoola Commission and the state government, and it revealed the duplicity that characterized the relationship between the local government and the state, and between the king and the governor. When the commission visited Ogbomoso, it had even been advised not to hold hearings. It had been told that Ogbomoso was a peaceful place—that all the farmers and their unions were supportive of the government and eager to pay their taxes. This was the danger of having the wrong people speaking for us. No one had to ask the council members and the so-called representatives of farmers to make this kind of statement. They were "half-educated" fake farmers who were collecting money from the government, assuring the government of their power to prevent riots. They had even added that taxes were being collected, when the only evidence they had was payment from urban workers. The commission sat and received fake evidence and fake promises. The radio and television reporters were wondering what had happened and why the commission had been deceived. We knew what had happened: No member of the movement appeared before the commission. Indeed, those who appeared and promised that everything was calm, including the Oba, were marked as targets. The February 22 outbreak was not spontaneous, as claimed, but planned to discredit the fake representatives and the government that listened to them. It was a huge success.

Millions of farmers and urban poor were restless and angry. They were very surprised that council workers were still going about insisting that taxes and levies would be collected, yet thousands of innocent people were constantly being harassed to pay. Millions expected that the government would suspend the collection of taxes and levies while the Ayoola Commission was doing its work. Since it did not suspend the collection, a rumor spread that the government was using the commission to buy time until the Nigerian civil war ended, at which point the government would be able to divert thousands of soldiers to the villages to kill the farmers. Everywhere, people began to say that they must prepare more intensely to fight the soldiers with better weapons or lose their lives. No one could not admit he was afraid, as this would be cowardly.

The commission did its work, with the poor taking a temporary break here and there to rush back to their farms and crafts before their poverty level reached the point of death. The break also enabled me to read a lot of books, mainly textbooks. In early April 1969, the report was submitted to the Executive Council of the Western State Government. Among the key items recommended were that taxes should continue to be collected by local governments and that those who had suffered losses in the various riots should be compensated. To obtain money for this compensation, the government would have to impose new levies on people; however, since it was clear that this would provoke more troubles, the idea was dropped.

Irunmu, the military governor, was already boasting, before he even read the commission's report, that peace had returned. In the course of reviewing the report and making decisions, the government promised to reduce the tax rate, which was concrete enough. So, less cocoa money would go from the pockets of the poor to the government. But what about spending the tax that was collected? Irunmu did what the politicians before him had done many times: He made promises of welfare services. New bridges, schools, markets, and roads would be constructed. Irunmu forgot we had been listening to the same list for many years. He needed our money, what he called "personal taxes," to improve our lives. Promises were made that the Marketing Board would release a substantial sum of money to develop rural roads and that the farmers would receive better prices for their cocoa. When would this be?

A new agency, the Public Complaint Commission, would be created to allow people to complain. Citizens would have a place to which to send letters to voice their feelings. As far as the farmers were concerned, there were supposedly channels already in place to express those feelings, especially to the kings and chiefs who were paid to be their representatives. But such feelings had been expressed for years: The powerful and the ministry men had listened to them but had done nothing about their complaints. In May, the government arranged a meeting with some representatives of farmers' unions. We heard about it on the radio, as well as the so-called agreement that farmers were ready to pay taxes. The government and city politicians conspired to set up the meeting, but they were probably fooling themselves. Since we had no way of issuing a release through the print media or radio, a group comprising over a thousand people descended on the palace of the Olubadan to say there was no truth to the government's announcement and that the tax should be no more than ten shillings.

If the government believed that its response and decisions on the Ayoola Commission would bring an end to the trouble, it was to be disappointed within weeks. We believed that we had been taken for a ride by the government, the produce buyers, and the politicians. The commission did not recommend reducing the tax rates, did not recommend abolishing the levies, nor did it ask corrupt members of the local government to leave us alone. The commission noted the poverty in the rural areas but made no recommendations to solve the problems, only pleading with the government to do something about it. The poor had expected this and had been poking fun at Ayoola as just one of the rich men who was trying to talk about the poor. We should be provided with financial aid, Ayoola said in a casual manner, but this had been said many times before him. Farmers had requested such aid from the Cooperative Bank without success and from the cooperative societies without luck. What they had tried to get before and had not received, Ayoola could not give. And when farmers heard over the radio that he also recommended the establishment of industries in the villages, they came to the conclusion that Ayoola was some kind of comedian.

To us, the critical questions, our daily staple, were the same. Why must we pay taxes? The government's answer was not convincing, and we could see with our own eyes how our money was being stolen. If the government loved us, as it claimed, why did the district councils hate us so much? If we must pay, why not collect the money in the most convenient way when people could afford to pay? Why not exempt the very poor in society? Why must human beings be hounded like dogs? Why arrest adults on the streets, in marketplaces, and in garages to humiliate them for their inability to pay or, even if they had paid, for not carrying their receipts with them? If a person had no money with which to pay, why send him to jail? A jail was dehumanizing, turning a humble citizen into an *elewon* (prisoner). *Ewon* is to put someone in chains, like putting a rope around the neck of a goat and tying it to a pole. To be stamped with the label of an *elewon* is to destroy an adult's manhood, to put him to shame, and to make him ineligible for marriage. It is to tarnish the essence of his human personality. Should a person who had been sick for months, unable to farm, sell his products, or engage in any profitable trade, be forced to pay? When they were thus forced, poor farmers took loans from *sogundogoji* (moneylenders), whereby the principal and heavy interest rate to the lender made £3 in debt become £10. Tax collectors and moneylenders swooped down upon many people who were struggling to make a living.

Word spread announcing the decisions reached by the conclaves: Taxes must not be paid, levies must not be paid, council offices must be attacked, tax collectors must be attacked, policemen must be attacked, and there must be no cooperation with the government. There was no evidence of community development, as was expected. The people would still have to pool their own resources to build and run their grammar schools, and they would have to maintain their unpaved roads on their own. The talk by the government about calling on the well-to-do to contribute to community funds was read as deceit. Council members and tax collectors saw Ayoola's report as an act of vindication, affirming that they must continue to collect taxes and that their methods were fair and good.

All secret meetings must continue, although there were military decrees in place banning such meetings. We were back at ground zero. Ojugo was about to be discredited. The revered reformer had been co-opted by the state government to move from one city to another to urge people to pay their taxes. When he lost his son in a car accident in 1963, the people were full of sympathy for him, and they blamed his political opponents. When he was thrown into jail in 1963, millions were upset. When he was released from prison in August 1966, there was jubilations. Now, the federal commissioner of finance, Ojugo, who had collected cocoa money and spent it wisely in the 1950s, was asking people to yield part of their pay to a government they distrusted. There was no point listening to him. People began to badmouth Ojugo, but these utterances were far less acidic than those meant for Irunmu.

There was a massive rejection of the government's decision to go ahead with tax collection. By July 1, everybody was to have paid his tax, and no one must belong to the Agbekoya, now proscribed by Irunmu. Those who fixed the deadline did not fully understand the mood of the people. Fearing a steep decline in revenues, the government needed the money. It resorted to asking chiefs and kings to appeal to the people to pay, promising them their own cut. Some kings, such as the *Soun* of Ogbomoso, were bold enough to make the appeal. The *Soun* became a target, just like anyone else who asked that taxes be paid. In February and March, tax collectors behaved quite lawlessly, especially in the cities outside of our control. They would stop taxis and buses and demand tax papers. They ran after adults, as if they had committed serious criminal offenses. If a person was arrested, they beat him like a serial killer and then locked him up for days. His relatives were forced to pay not only the tax but also the money to release him from his cell and various forms of bribes.

Underground activities followed previous patterns with new additions. A combative wing developed and decided to go on the attack. It argued that since the police did not shoot protesters in the legs but in the chests, subsequent encounters must be about who killed who first. When it was told not to be so extreme but merely to harass and scare the police, its members refused. The rebel group also decided to include tax collectors on the hit list. While the original strategy was to prevent them from collecting taxes, and terrify them to the point of not visiting villages, the rebel group felt it was now necessary to eliminate them. What the Ayoola Commission report did was to negatively impact and further radicalize the movement.

When Ojugo and his associates suggested that the collection system should be improved, the farmers said he was living in faraway Lagos and did not know what he was talking about. Tax collection was no longer possible, to say nothing of being improved upon. The tax collectors who harassed the poor men on the streets belonged to a gang, a brutal cabal, with a vast network of tentacles that they themselves did not fully understand. The tax collectors had not succeeded in school, but they did not want to be farmers. They were unhappy with themselves and unhappy with those who had stayed in school as well as with those who had stayed in the villages to cultivate the farmlands. They had lost the opportunity of either calling—they could no longer return to school, and they had been thrown out of the villages. For some reason, they were bad men, no different from thugs, both in their official capacity and also in a private capacity, who used violence and commissions from tax collection to augment their pay.

"Mighty one," the collector would tell his boss, "leave the job to your boys." What job? The job of beating up people, and using wooden sticks and clubs to hit them on the legs, back, and head? Broken bones and blood had no meaning to them. They hated themselves and those they beat. They saw those whom they beat, the men staying in regular jobs, as telling them that they were unsuccessful. Many of these tax collectors were employed as low-level workers in local governments, getting their jobs because they had served as party thugs, or knew a councilor in one way or another. When they were sent to the streets to demand receipts, there was something in it both for them and for those who sent them:

They could victimize the innocent, using the proxy power of their faceless masters. When an adult male provided his tax receipt and when a market woman showed evidence of a levy payment, the collectors were sad. You wondered why they should be sad that a fellow citizen was honest. There was nothing in it for them. What they wanted was for you to have paid your taxes but to have then forgotten to carry your receipt with you. Women turned their brassieres into temporary wallets, putting their tax receipts there so they would not forget them. A receipt must be produced on the spot. Failure to do so enabled collectors to confiscate belongings and intimidate or use violence on the presumed tax defaulters.

In our eyes, the tax collectors were fronting for city officials, and the state government could not remove them from the streets or curb their excesses. What the government failed to do, violence would achieve. Unknown to the government, the months of April, May, and June were used to replenish our supplies for war. Food supplies had become low because of men's withdrawal from the farms. Many were complaining of lack of money, not even a cent in their pockets. It was necessary to let them do some odd jobs to rebuild their finances and meet some urgent commitments. Medicine and charm supplies had also fallen low, and more secret work was needed.

When council officials were exuberant, they met with an immediate answer, as in the case of Ila Orangun on May 5, where the war took the life of a prominent titled chief, the Elemona (Chief Atoyebi), who was angrily clubbed to death. The king, known as the Orangun, fearing for his life, fled the city for an unknown destination. He was already marked for assassination, authorized by the leadership of the unit based there. Someone must have told him to flee, and he did so, leaving behind his crown, beads, flywhisks, leather sandals, and all the paraphernalia of kingship. Two days preceding the planned attack, word reached us at Ibadan that he would be presented with an *aroko,* a strange "gift" comprising seven parrot eggs. This was a dire coded message in more ways than one. The figure seven in that instance meant an expression of grave displeasure, that something terrible would be visited upon the recipient within seven days. The eggs reinforced the message—a bad smell oozed out of their broken shells. William Ayẹni Ariwajoye, the king, must have interpreted the *aroko* very well and planned a careful exit. He saved his life, but his palace was attacked.

The king deserved no sympathy. He was told by the movement that no one would pay taxes, but the government, always promising the kings and chiefs a cut from the collection, asked him to pressure his people to pay their rates and taxes. In collaboration with the divisional officer, the king sent word around that not only did he want the people to pay, he also wanted them to do so in front of his palace. Private messages were sent to the king, telling him not to pursue this course of action. He was even given a way to back off: He should tell the government that his people would pay if those in other parts of the region did the same. He refused. On May 5, tables were set up in front of the palace for tax collection. The king and his chiefs had arranged for their allies to pay.

There were no longer any fools in the land. As people gathered to pay, an army of anti-tax warriors pounced on them with whips, clubs, bows and arrows, machetes, and guns. Those who did not run experienced what such dangerous weapons could do to their bodies. One tax collector was made to remove all his clothes, and was beaten like a goat; another lost his life to the mob. The angry mob moved next to the palace, which was immediately attacked. "Kill the king," they sang angrily, as they ransacked the palace. The sprawling compound was empty of living souls, who had all fled. The palace was set on fire. Thereafter, the warriors moved to the city, attacking the police stations and council offices, all of which were badly damaged, losing all their doors and windows. Many houses were damaged. The entire city was deserted, with close to half of the population running away in panic to their farms and villages and to neighboring cities. This flight had propaganda value: When the people who had run away from Ila Orangun reported what they heard or saw, the king and chiefs in other places learned not to make the mistake of asking anyone to pay rates and taxes. By May 7, when lorry loads of "anti-riot policemen" arrived, the warriors had disbanded and melted into the remaining population, wearing regular clothing. Many of them used secret paths to begin their journey to Ibadan to file their reports.

The various movements agreed to resume violent actions on July 1 but left the specific details to local military commanders in different zones, allowing them to express their anger and disturb the public peace in any way they thought fit. The purpose of decentralizing was actually to make it far more complicated for the state security and police apparatus to mobilize against us. If we operated in different places, the police would be spread so thin as to become ineffective. This was brilliant in terms of attaining results, but also a recipe for disaster since unit military commanders tended to have other ambitions and scores to settle. It was also difficult to evaluate progress and results and to summon meetings. What they agreed to was to meet at a secret location on Sunday, July 6. Friday was sometimes used as a day on which to pause, to allow a number of people to show up in mosques where members of the movement could collect information on what the people and government were thinking, and to make pretenses that they were not part of any opposition movement.

On July 1, thousands marched out of Akanran (as well as from the villages of Moniya and Idi Ayunre on the way to separate battles) with the aim of destroying local government offices, attacking anyone they found in them, and preventing the collection of levies and taxes. The date was significant. The state government had chosen it as the deadline for all to pay.

June had seen an intensification of collection and harassment. The radio reported long lines of willing citizens paying their taxes in various places such as Akure, Idanre, Ondo, and Ibadan. The announcements would even report the amounts collected: for example, that £21,474 16s 3d had been collected by the Ibadan City Council in the last week. Tax collectors, assisted by policemen, stayed at the entrances to the city, to collect money forcibly from those returning from their farms. Fear of arrest and detention forced a large number of city dwellers to rush to the council offices to pay. Not carrying a receipt could lead to being beaten and treated like a criminal, and when people were prosecuted, the judge would impose a minimum prison term of two months with hard labor.

The announcement of the deadline enraged the movements, as it was seen as a way to ridicule them and show the public they had failed. In addition, the government announced that on the same day, July 1, taxes would be collected by force in what was called a "tax raid." This time around, as it was announced, it would be a "full-scale raid," which meant that tax collectors and police would work together. The central organization of the Agbekoya, the umbrella movement, decided that it would now be a "full-scale" response. This was a war—no more no less— with the state and the movement about to clash.

We did. I was part of the Akanran contingent. We marched out, intending to move in the direction of the city. A surprise awaited us. The government had anticipated this and had fully mobilized its own forces. Over two hundred fully armed police officers and additional mobile "anti-riot" police had been sent to await us. This was a deadly force in number—and also one armed with modern guns and ammunition. They could kill well over five thousand within a few hours. The goal was to prevent us from reaching the city, where we would merge with a much bigger crowd. The other goal might have been to enable the governor to tell his boss in Lagos that he was in full control of the situation.

The government was probably calculating that it had the force to stop us. Without any intermediary or peacemaker, the war started as soon as both sides laid eyes upon one another. Guns fired: the dane guns of the rebels against the modern guns of the regular police and the mobile police (aka "Kill and Go"). Retreat on both sides. Pursuit in retreat: first on both sides, but later by just one. Advance forward. Sporadic gunshots, loud noises. Wailing and crying. Pandemonium. If you fell, you would be crushed to death. Teargas was fired, producing smoke all over the place. Run to get kerosene to wash it out of your eyes and nostrils. Deafening noises. Curses. Calamities. Injuries and death. The regular police and the mobile police began to run to their vehicles. Their drivers sped off. Those left behind began to run into the bushes, running for their dear lives. Five police lorries could not be moved, as the drivers were unable to reach their vehicles. The lorries were set on fire. More smoke and the cover of clouds. Charms lay all over the ground, falling from the bodies of warriors in action or in retreat. The battle was fierce, and the regular and mobile police were routed.

Who shot first? The police and the government claimed that we did; we claimed the opposite. The shots occurred within seconds of one another. How many died? The police claimed they lost three men and a senior officer and that they killed scores of us. For days later, over a dozen corpses lay on the ground covered with leaves. We claimed that we killed over a dozen police officers. How many were injured? The police claimed more than a dozen of them were injured, but we claimed that none of them actually escaped without incurring one form of injury or another, from losing an eye to a finger.

Akanran, Ogunmakin, and the nearby villages were deserted, as previously planned, as we knew that the army would come for revenge, killing innocent women and children. They did come, and they stayed for a few days, collecting abandoned weapons and discarded charms as evidence of their success. Two innocent farmers who came back were characterized as spies and "rebel leaders" and were later paraded in public as criminals. Maybe the soldiers thought we would be so stupid as to send a member of our group as a spy. Almost a thousand people were gathered in different villages and in the city, including nursing mothers and aging adults who could not even walk quickly, much less run. The police had a list of criminal charges but none based on investigations.

Everybody believed the charms had delivered success, and even the police used this to explain their defeat. Our charms became the narrative of the movement, protest, and war. Then and now, it is the charms that people remember. Soldiers and high-ranking officers in the federal army in faraway Biafra were sending friends and family members to look for our charm makers. The demand was high, the requests were limitless. Some wanted *afeeri* (the force to make you invisible before an enemy), *ayeta* (the force to repel a bullet), *egbe* (the force to make you disappear and transport you from one place and land to another in nanoseconds), *okigbe* (the power to neutralize a machete cut), or *kanako* (the force to shrink distances so that a ten-mile journey would become a one-mile journey).

Charlatans began to profit, selling fake charms to eager buyers with money. Nigeria was about to discover its might: New charlatan intellectuals emerged from all corners, saying that with the potency of our charms, the end of apartheid in South Africa was in sight. We could will development to happen, asking juju to supply electricity here and water there. The charm that glued the uniform of a police officer to his body could also be deployed to produce water in pipes as well as electricity from trees. The rebels had now made charms and magic part of the very core of modernity itself. Charms had fully reclaimed the African past. Today, the belief in charms has grown much stronger, using what we did as evidence, and it forms the very core of contemporary Nollywood movies: Without the insertion of supernatural power, witchcraft, and juju into the narratives, the very basis of the Nigerian movie industry would collapse. So, too, would Christianity, especially Pentecostalism; witness a new beginning if the power of juju is removed, as many prayers were directed at overcoming the consequences of juju.

On the part of the state, reports of the encounter needed to be controlled. The sizable police forces, including the "mobile police" force, the equivalent of the military, had been routed. The government must never admit this. The head of the police was put to shame. He, too, must not admit it. The military battalion at Ibadan was humiliated. It must not admit this. The power of the police and that of their guns had been crushed. They took refuge in one answer: the potency of our charms. In the eyes of the state government, its enemies were behind it all, so-called powerful politicians who wanted to bring down the government.

The police lost in all the other towns and villages, with one-third of the state completely paralyzed. In Ogbomoso, sixty miles northeast of Ibadan, the attack was again directed at the king, who was regarded as too pro-government. The attack on February 12 became a mock trial. The king survived that one, and he even appealed to his people, using the language of mutual love and blaming the problem on corrupt officials. In late June, he bestowed a chieftaincy title on one of his citizens, Colonel Benjamin Adekunle (aka Scorpion), a ruthless soldier who terrified his enemies in the Biafran war. The king even granted an interview, in which he stated that the ongoing rebellions would not let him flee his palace, in spite of the pleadings of his wife and children. Neither the king nor his family members heard the grumblings and rumblings, nor did they interpret them well enough to have an exit plan in place.

On Wednesday, July 2, 1969, protesters descended on the palace, catching everyone by surprise. With shouts of displeasure, violence followed, leading to the massive destruction of buildings. The palace was set on fire, and everything was gone. So also the cars and houses of some chiefs were set ablaze. The inhabitants of the palace fled. Instead of asking the king to commit suicide, the older way of requesting mandatory abdication, his life was now to be terminated by violence. He tried to run for his life, seeking refuge in the house of a loyal chief. The pursuit was fierce. His host, fearing for his own life, released him to the mob. He was treated worse than a common criminal, as his body was dragged through the street and he was hacked to death, and then his legs and head were cut off. This was a very gruesome end for Oba Olajide Olayode Laoye 11, too brutal, unprecedented. The level of bitterness and anger directed at him was intense and so publicly expressed that his head and legs were displayed in different parts of the city. Someone put his head in a bag and ran away with it, another abominable act.

Five of his chiefs suffered a similar fate, in addition to two innocent people, the king's wife and child, the latter being stepped upon by the crowd. The flow of traffic was disrupted; the entrances to the highway that connected the city to others were blocked; and telephone communication was cut off. The rebels and a combined team of soldiers and police engaged in an intense battle, with heavy casualties on both sides. The city was thrown into confusion, and thousands fled to the bush and the neighboring cities, especially to Ilorin. As they did so, they spread the news of a rebellion bigger than it actually was and about the loss of hundreds of lives. This not only marked an escalation of the conflict, but revealed clear evidence of a nation in decline. Pro-government voices called the violent protests an act of treason and wanted collective punishment imposed on the entire city; that is, they wanted close to a million people to be declared guilty and to be punished accordingly. But it is the finger that commits a sin that a king cuts off; when a king cuts off all the fingers, the punishment has exceeded the crime.

The government panicked. It mobilized its military troops and sent

The king of Ogbomoso,
Oba Olajide Olayode
Laoye 11, 1969. Ministry of
Information, Ibadan.

them in lorry loads to Ogbomoso on Thursday, July 3. As the troops patrolled the city, the government claimed credit for the fact that the city was calm and things were under control. Yet troops could not have done much, as the protesters had disbanded, and hundreds became faceless, disappearing into their various compounds, pretending they had not participated in the violence. Arrests followed; the police carried out predawn swoops seizing innocent people, arresting them based on false information.

As the Ogbomoso wing melted away and mingled with the public, its members also began to regroup and sent a delegation to Ibadan. On July 6, a decision was taken by the movement based at Ibadan to escalate the war by targeting policemen. This was not a decision that was taken in ignorance of its full implications: Many lives were now to be lost. In all previous encounters, even when the intention of the demonstrators was to draw attention to our cause, the police had been unfriendly. They were quick to discharge teargas, to beat people, and to use live bullets. It

Parts of the Palace of the Soun destroyed during the tax riot at Ogbomoso, 1969. Ministry of Information, Ibadan.

was no longer enough to go after council officials; those who were protecting them became enemies as well. After July 6, it became movement policy to attack policemen in uniform, and the police received an order to attack and shoot us as well. The public and the police had become mortal enemies. The smart policemen who lived in barracks refused to carry out their routine patrols. Those who lived in volatile areas and in the precincts of the city refused to report for work at their stations. When the police were forced to work by superior authorities, they removed their uniforms and became civilians. Policemen denied their occupations and were afraid for their lives.

People died on both sides. As there were plans in place for the quick removal of the dead, the government knew little of the casualties or the number they had killed. It was not in our best interest to reveal the number of the injured and dead. To be sure, we too can never know the numbers, since there was no compilation of the figures of the dead for all the towns and villages. Morale would have been damaged if we produced constant updates on the dead and the injured. The strong belief in the efficacy of protective charms would have also declined. However, by not

**Chief Adeoye Adisa, Commissioner for Information and Home Affairs in charge of local councils and villages—a formidable politician with deep historical connections to the city. Ministry of Information, Ibadan.**

revealing the consequences of police brutality, especially the injuries and deaths the police caused, we denied the members of the public key information they needed on the state of the war and also provided cover for the government to keep misbehaving.

In the third week of July 1969, the government enraged us further. It asked members of the public to contribute funds to aid the dependents of the police and council officials who had died in the rebellion, and who were in dire need of money to enable them to eat, live in good houses, and pay for their children's education. Collection points were set up throughout the state. We saw this as yet further evidence of how much we were despised. The useless government did not care about us and our own families, only about the children of those who wanted to kill us. Our people created new units to monitor the collection and those giving money: first, to ensure that no one who professed membership in any of the anti-government movements donated any money, as this would be a gesture of betrayal; second, to get the list of all donors and target them for destruction; and third, to undertake counter-propaganda, arguing that the donations would be stolen, just as tax money was being stolen.

Forgetting that many of our members could not read newspapers, the government launched a massive propaganda effort, using the media to describe protesters as dangerous rioters. It leveled various allegations against us. We refused to pay our taxes. We took the law into own hands. Participation in the rebellion became a treasonable offence, and the government was entitled to use ruthless brutality to suppress it. If any of our members was caught, any part of his body could be cut off. Since policemen had been killed, to be arrested was to be visited with the most severe punishments. We were fighting at the wrong time, when the nation was at war, thus diverting attention away from winning the war against Biafra. The rebellion then became an expression of opposition to the war, yet another instance of treason. As the supporters of the government insisted, any of us who was caught must be given the gravest punishment.

We were "enemies of the people": These were the words used repeatedly by Adeoye Adisa, the commissioner for Home Affairs and Information. He had ridden on our backs to obtain his powerful appointment. He claimed to represent us. He claimed to be the leader of what was now a banned political party that got our votes. He was sent by Irunmu to speak to the farmers, to sue for peace. Those he claimed to be representing were now the enemies. In Adisa's view, the governor was our friend, the head of state our father. Now enjoying his job, with a good car, a police escort, and contracts to award, he must not offend Irunmu, whom he kept praising for his military decisiveness. He was not afraid of anarchists, declared the commissioner, and he asked us to go back to where we belonged: our villages and farms.

The government began to write its own history of the movement and the rebellion, the history that you now find in its archives based at Ibadan. I have looked at those papers, especially those in the Ministry of Information. The contents are astonishing for their arrogance, deception, and lies. Lies are never the opposite of truth, and not all lies are bad either, as a lie that fixes is better than a truth that destroys. But even the truths in those papers are sometimes the equivalent of bad and ugly lies. The notion that we had no brains, none at all, was clearly communicated. We were incapable of thinking of a rebellion, much less of organizing one. We did not understand the inner workings and intricacies of a government and the process of collecting money and spending it. These were the statements made on the radio and in the newspapers that now fill the archives. Those who were never with us began to explain us, first to themselves and later to us. Those who knew not a single fact began to create facts. Not that we did not also create our own facts. But history, the why and how of it, began to be written for us. It was urgent to the government and its supporters to find the people who were manipulating us, us the dumb.

Those who were behind our war, they said, were among them as politicians and in the secretariat. They were those who did not want Nigeria to win the war against Biafra. They mentioned Julius Nyerere of Tanzania, who supported the secession. Julius had never been to Ibadan; should the people be given the opportunity to see and speak with him, they would have wanted him to talk about his own cooperative society that was giving land and seeds to the farmers. We were told that the cooperatives in Tanzania, Russia, and Cuba were better than ours. We would not have discussed Biafra with Julius, the man with a funny set of teeth.

The story changed. It was no longer Julius but Ojukwu's emissaries who had penetrated our rank and file. So, another round of stories was circulated by the ministry men, some seeking favor with the military, assuring them that they knew the real enemies. The reason they made up the ugly stories was clear: If Ojukwu was to win the war, he must destabilize the West. He must have sent many men to the villages, giving them money to cause trouble. He must have promised the farmers to double the price of cocoa and to pay off their loans. He was successful, as the rebellion brought chaos to the land. Ojukwu's problem was that he did not cash in on it, for he should have marched west with his army and taken over Ibadan and Lagos to extend his Republic. We had done our own part.

Angry former politicians who had been kicked out by the military wanted to be compensated. A few were, like Adisa the commissioner and Ojugo, who became the prime minister in Lagos. Those who were not compensated became very angry and desperately wanted revenge. They did not have guns and could not go and fight the soldiers, but they had people, us poor people, whom they could use to fight their battle. In the government's eyes, it was these bitter men who went from one village to another to deceive us, to misinterpret the policies and intentions of the good government. The politicians, spreading their foul propaganda, wanted to revive the conflicts between Ojugo and Bamu and were preparing to take over power from the military when party politics returned. We were reminded of the decree in place that proscribed political parties and declared that allowing clandestine political activities was a treasonable offense. If politicians could be policed, the government argued,

Irunmu with the king of Ikire (the Alakire), inspecting damaged council buildings in the town of Ikire, 1969. Ministry or Information, Ibadan.

they would not be able to incite us to disturb the peace. The "tax drive," the name the government gave to running after the poor farmers, was made difficult because politicians who wanted to bring down the government had told the disgruntled elements, the name they called us, to fight. These politicians must be hounded.

The motivations attributed to us and the explanation given for our mission reached our ears. Rather than crumbling, the movements became larger. One member would introduce three new recruits, another would bring five. Some movements introduced the idea of membership cards and initial fees and monthly payments. This divided old from new members. Building trust was far more complicated than ever before. Discipline was an issue, as some members began to act with less moral conviction than others.

Innocent people were being arrested and tortured by the police. In the government's view, such arrests demonstrated power and confidence. With jubilation, the number of arrests was announced over the radio: Sixty rioters were arrested yesterday at Iyana Ofa, and twenty were arrested today at Olodo. They were called "suspects," and put in

A damaged council office, Ikire, 1969. Ministry of Information, Ibadan.

police cells and prisons. Those in prisons, without being charged for any offence, were treated as hardened criminals; those in police custody were locked up in impregnable rooms with iron doors.

The month of July was very tough and rough. The government was unable to arrest any member of the movement at Akanran on July 1. The security forces had been defeated and forced to retreat. They usually arrested the innocent, as well as making surprise attacks on villages late in the evenings. Several charms in households would be confiscated, for the police to show to the public as evidence of their work, and this was reported in the newspapers of the time, the *West African Pilot*, the *Nigerian Tribune*, and the *New Nigerian*, all of which treated the protests as headline news. Even the confiscation of charms was treated as a major achievement. Irunmu was going about calling farmers "stupid," wondering why they could not ask their chiefs and kings to appeal to him for help.

Skirmishes were hard for us to control. A group of young men harassed market women in different places and seized their wares. Many of us were horrified. Could they be our members? It was difficult

A damaged council office, Ikire, 1969. Ministry of Information, Ibadan.

to answer the question. Could they have been planted by the police to cause division and discredit us? It was possible, but we did not know. Or could we have been corrupted by new members who did not share the vision of the collective progressive group? The government took to the courts, to see whether the judiciary could do what the police had been unable to. Many people, mainly innocent people, were now being arrested and threatened with legal action. There were massive arrests at Moniya after the July 1 battle, as well as at Ogbomoso after the king was killed. On July 11, a magistrate sentenced 115 men to a total of 230 years, about 2 years per person. Many more were awaiting prosecution. Some among them died in custody. The use of the judiciary to intimidate us created a legal challenge. The government had made up its mind to prosecute those who had been arrested and asked the judges to impose the maximum punishment, from long-term imprisonment to the death sentence. Arrests were being made at various locations and cities, notably at Ibadan, Ede, and Ogbomoso. Threats of more arrests were always being made.

We had to decide on our response to the judicial attack. Our first problem was how to isolate members from non-members when both were being arrested and tried. It was easy for the police to arrest innocent people in order to give the government the idea that they were doing their job. We had sympathy for the innocent people, but also resented them for not joining us to take up arms. We eventually decided that where a member was on trial, even if lumped with non-members, we would throw our weight behind the case.

A second complication we needed to address was the survival of the family members of those on trial, locked up in prison at Agodi and elsewhere. This was a serious problem as there were usually no savings for the family to survive on during the prolonged incarceration. In the hot spots, farm work had been suspended, and women and children relocated to safe havens. The movement decided to order members to supply free food to affected families. The families would be fed, and every month, a delegation would be sent to check on their well-being. A token amount of £1 would be offered to them. We realized that the group had limited sources of money and that to impose an unbearable levy on members would lead to internal fragmentation; so it was decided that contributions would be voluntary. A new unit emerged, and it was very successful as people donated money.

Part of the money donated was meant to cover the legal fees of those undergoing trial. Here was yet another complication. Hiring and paying lawyers would risk exposing some members to bad lawyers, wanting to curry favor with the government, who might mislead them or trick them into betraying other members. A decoy was created. We would use the government-appointed cooperative societies in the city as a front. Intermediaries between the cooperative societies and us would operate at night; in order to confuse the co-ops and lawyers we resolved not to use the same people over and over again. Whenever we were summoned to a meeting by city lawyers, we would promise to attend but would not show up, or we would show up when we were not expected.

We also came up with a strategy to trick the city lawyers. They were media conscious and had political ambitions. They wanted power in order to steal cocoa money. As the military was always calling itself a transitional government, promising to go back to the barracks as soon as the war ended, many of these lawyers and politicians were meeting in secret to form political associations. They needed us more than we needed them. We compiled a list of these lawyers and carefully used some of them who were willing to represent our members for no fee or for only a nominal payment, as in the case of the complicated murder trials at Ogbomoso where the government was bent on executing those who had killed the king.

The case at Ede was well managed. The police, in collaboration with the Timi, arrested almost seventy people following the one-day battle in December 1968. Many of those arrested had actually done nothing wrong, but the authorities wanted to use the case to intimidate others. The government dragged the case on until July 1969, knowing well that the families of the accused would be ruined. On July 16, the magistrate trying the accused men at Osogbo, frustrated by the lack of any direct evidence linking them to the case, decided to use a different approach. The arrested men had been coached to say only one thing: "We did not know of what the government was accusing us, and we were not even at Ede on December 19." Even if they had been at Ede, the government had to use fake witnesses to establish the fact. The magistrate asked those who had brought the case to withdraw the charges. They had gone to court to say that those arrested were the ones who destroyed their properties. Not only could they not prove this, but even if the magistrate pronounced the accused guilty, there would be no monetary compensation for the complainants. The accused were men who could not even be asked to pay £1. The only option would be to send them to prison. In releasing them, the magistrate appealed to them to pay the levies and taxes, to be good citizens, never again to engage in riots and in violent actions that damaged property, and not to join the Agbekoya. As not all the charges had been dismissed, the government promised to exercise its right to re-arrest them. The judiciary was unable to resolve a social crisis.

The coordinated and sporadic acts of rebellion made the Western State harder to govern. When people woke up in the morning, they did not know what to expect. The government had promised the public that some of our members, when arrested, would be executed by firing squad. People who had anticipated death were not afraid of being shot. The protesters were not afraid of the police, the mobile police, or the army. In our view, the government had ears that did not listen, eyes that could not see, and a nose that could not smell. Our activities were interpreted in only one way: as sabotage—sabotage directed against the state and federal government; sabotage against the civil war. Even Ojugo was saying the same: that his own political opponents were behind it.

In mid-July, the state government attempted a new trick: It would allow the payment of tax in installments. This was presented to the public as a kind government gesture designed to lighten the burden on poor people. We did not buy this propaganda and had to counter it through an extensive network of whispering not only to explain our side of the story but to ridicule the government. It worked. At an initial meeting to discuss our strategy, the strategist was Mr. Saberedowo—"one who converts the needle to money"—a nickname that referenced his occupation as a tailor, only that "Mr." must always be added to his name. If you failed to do so, he would remind you he was Mr. Saberedowo and not Saberedowo, as if the name without the Mr. would be ordinary. But he was also a farmer. To me, he was a mediocre tailor and a mediocre farmer: His farms were always badly kept, with weeds overrunning his crops. One year, his cornfields grew very well, but he had no time to harvest them until the cobs were burned by the heat and damaged by insects. After Pasitor sent me to him so that he could at least hire someone as a laborer to help harvest his crops, he was full of gratitude, gave me some coins as a gift, and said "*ona po*"—the "roads" are too many, and traveling on them is endless—an idiomatic way of saying that his attention was always too divided, that his tasks were too many and difficult to coordinate, and that time moved too quickly.

When Mr. Saberedowo opened his mouth on July 13, many were not eager to listen. It turned out, however, that he understood the government and his peers. "You cannot pay little by little," he said, basing his argument on the long period when most farmers could not have savings of any more than £3. It was only at the time of the harvest, around August to October, that they had slightly more money in their pockets. There was heavy farm work to do from May to July, and little to sell. The long dry season was a period of penury for many, when they acquired many things on credit, later having to pay creditors triple the principal in the difficult months of November to April. Mr. Saberedowo was not telling us anything new, but he said that many might believe that tax payment by installment was not difficult and that those protesters who refused the offer were extremists. In a compromise, he reduced the strategy to one element: There were three months in a year, not twelve, when people had money. Our strategy and propaganda came to be called *osu meta* (three months). We would now say that council clerks and ministry men had twelve months, but we had just three. We rejected installment payments and succeeded in winning over public opinion.

Mr. Saberedowo suggested that we must pressure the self-employed to link the calculation of their own income with the harvest period, which was correct as they also made more money when the farmers made most of theirs. The government put pressure on those in the city to pay by installments since they were generating income on a daily basis. To qualify for payment by installments, the city's self-employed had to be assessed as earning an income of £200 a year and must maintain a bank account. They could pay their taxes in nine to twelve installments deducted from their accounts. Mr. Saberedowo convinced his peers that this was a trick to over-assess the self-employed, as it was not they, but the assessors, who determined their projected incomes. His first suggestion was for us to fight the tax assessors. This was easy since many of the self-employed were already part of us and would not even allow the assessors to come near them. Mr. Saberedowo's second suggestion was to ask them not to put all their earnings in a bank that the government could always access. Their maximum deposit should be £10 per month so that their maximum income appeared as £120 a year, far less than the assessors were saying. And they must keep withdrawing money every month so that the amounts in the bank did not look like savings. This became another successful strategy. The government's plan to collect taxes by installments collapsed. Mr. Saberedowo had his moment of fame.

On August 14, the Ibadan coordinating units agreed to conduct another massive strike. They took the public by surprise in the early morning, marching out in the villages of Iyana Ofa, Akanran, Egbeda, and Akufo. The council offices that were still standing were attacked and damaged. The guard at Iyana Ofa, headquarters of the Ibadan North West District Council, was killed and all the records destroyed. Hundreds of files were set on fire. The city was overwhelmed.

Schoolchildren, more for excitement than politics, flocked to the streets in the thousands, joining us, carrying leaves of peace to indicate their support. They knew what was going on. Schoolchildren knew far more than their parents were willing to admit, from sex to politics, from morality to crime. I knew the day when Adegoke Adelabu died in a car accident and the news reached Ibadan, followed by pandemonium, which also took me to the streets throwing stones at nothing and standing by burning tires. I was five years old. I knew about the elections of

1959 and those who rigged them. I heard whispers of what they would do. I was six. I could tell you about Ibadan's celebration of Nigeria's independence in 1960, and how we marched to the stadium to celebrate. I was seven.

The question is not whether schoolchildren knew, but how much they knew and how they got the information. I have always known a lot, about the marijuana that grew in farms in the bush, about the adulterous men who sneaked into the corners of compounds—and the adulterous women who joined them. We knew which girls in the area were promiscuous. We knew the families who ate well and those who did not. We were the first to know the son whose affliction with leprosy the parents were trying to hide. Our communication networks were faster than those of adults. Adults generally waited until the evening to circulate information, and they did so with caution, sometimes telling themselves not to tell the women. We were like cell phones, using our quick legs to relay information from one boy to another, boy to girl, girl to girl. It was rapid, efficient, and effective. If a boy, imitating adults, kissed a girl and one saw them, the news spread all through our network quickly.

Just as the boy and girl who kissed got into the information circuit, so too did the news about politics. We picked up the information from adults. Whether they were playing *ayo* (a board game) or drinking palm wine, there was always a boy there who would hear the conversation and plug it into the fast-flowing traffic of an efficient information network. Do not bring a mistress into the house, as we would know; actually we were the first to know, and we would tell. We imitated adults and began to talk like them. We became polygamists before we had our first date and married our first wife. Boys never embellished stories, as you would get into trouble if you did. And never say what you did not hear or report what you did not see. Accuracy and honesty were not negotiable and were treated as sacrosanct.

The schoolboys and girls would know about the ongoing rebellion from the radio, from the television, and from listening to adult conversations. The schoolboys could read newspapers. There were public libraries in a few places, and there were occasional mobile libraries. As the schoolchildren trooped out of their classrooms on August 14, the teachers and headmasters lost control. The headmasters would be afraid of being punished, removed from their posts, or transferred many miles away from their families. Schools would be reorganized, and teachers would be blamed for losing control. Teachers were maligned all the time. Commissioners, high-ranking civil servants, and even the governor lectured them. Usually the lowest paid in the salary structures, teachers had begun to lose the prestige they had enjoyed in the colonial era. To date, teaching remains one of the most undesirable jobs.

Definitely fearing that the government would go after them, the schoolteachers and headmasters went after the schoolchildren. I saw teachers pursuing some into the streets, grabbing their shirts by the collar and tearing their clothing by accident. The few who were caught were asked to kneel down on small rocks and were lashed. Men of the movement, either in anger or frustration or to broaden the fight, did what they had been warned never to do: They attacked the teachers and headmasters. The news of the attack spread like wildfire. Like the police officers, hundreds of teachers fled to the bush. All the schools were deserted. Thugs joined in the mayhem, invading schools to loot them of their small items, erasers and pencils, notes and gongs. Some took chairs, perhaps to use as firewood.

Invading schools was like invading the governor's mansion. This was what it was all about. I was there when two schools were invaded. One of the invasions was led by a man called Asoroko, which was a nickname used to describe his personality and character: "difficult to encounter." Asoroko's name warned you not to mess with him; if you confronted him, you were in trouble; if he confronted you, you were in trouble. His name warned you to see him and run. During the day, his look terrified, as if he carried a hammer to hit you on the head. At night, he was deadly, acquiring the power of the devil. His eyes were reddish, not from lack of sleep but from sniffing *asa*, ground tobacco mixed with natron. *Asa* by itself was as potent as snuff. I tried it once, putting it in my left nostril. The impact was immediate as I began to sneeze, water running from my eyes. My head felt like I was high. Asoroko added other nicotine-derived plants to his *asa*. Behind his back, we called what he added to his snuff *igbo*, "Indian hemp," better known as marijuana. Indian hemp was always available to a few who were dependent on it, kept in their pouches and pockets. Asoroko added his own peculiarity to hemp use. If people smoked hemp, he never did. It was just alleged that he combined it with *asa*. What he did was unusual: He would not only use *asa* as snuff, but would put it in his ears and eyes. A moment after he did this, you should try not to say anything, as one wrong word and Asoroko would attack you.

When Asoroko saw teachers running after the boys and girls who wanted to support us, he showed his true self. He took out a small sachet, opened it, and used his snuff. He bent backwards and drained the rest into his eyes. He jumped up several times, and used his machete to hit the ground in the most frightening manner. "*O ya!*" he commanded us to move, but not to head in the direction we had planned, rather toward the school. He was calling the teachers traitors, agents of the government. What he could not do to their bosses, the commissioner and governor, he would do to them. Shouting "*Petepete ada,*" which was meant to turn the machete into a tool of spanking instead of cutting, he went after the teachers to beat those unable to run. *Petepete ada* was painful—there would be no blood but the severe pain of being hit with metal. The headmaster, who was being introduced to Asoroko for the first time, received a raw deal: Asoroko asked him to hop like a frog. The headmaster, in the eyes of Asoroko, was the military governor. He rejoiced over the victory.

By the time the tally was taken, many teachers had been beaten in many schools, with no fewer than twenty who ended up in the hospital. One died, and this was announced over the radio. Two were permanently injured. What happened to the others? There were no records. The government turned on the teachers, inflicting its own injuries and draconian punishments on many of them. Some were accused of not stopping the students from joining us. Others were reported for clapping for the protesters, cheering them on. The police actually arrested more than thirty teachers and threw more than a dozen in jail. Those in jail came from the villages of Egbeda, Jago, Koroboto, and Gbadegun, where the teachers were smart enough to support us. Since they lived in the households of farmers, some were already privy to what was going on and actually participated in some strategic meetings. The problem though was that they had to be monitored as they could betray us. They were in a bind: If they knew our secrets and did not tell the government, they were committing treason, according to a decree already put in place by the federal government; if they revealed our secrets and we found out, they had to run for their lives. Saving those in jail involved our circulating the propaganda that the teachers were innocent and knew nothing. The politicians saw pleading for their release as scoring one or two points.

By September 29, 1969, eighty-three primary schools had been shut down, and more than two hundred teachers had been relocated. No more schools at Akufo, Egbeda and Akanran, as all these areas were considered too dangerous. Their teachers would be redeployed, was the official instruction broadcast over the radio. The headmasters must now report on a daily basis to the Local Schools Board in the city, where benches awaited them so they could sit all day. The teachers and head-masters would be paid, an assurance that cocoa money was still available, even if cocoa farmers "chose" not to benefit from it.

If the government thought that closing down the schools would serve as punishment to the farmers, it had again miscalculated. Keeping the students in school was a better way of keeping the peace. In any case, the farmers who wanted their children to stay in school did so by moving them elsewhere, to schools in the city. Most of the protesting parents had actually struggled hard to prevent their children from joining them. All the students knew that their fate and future were very much tied to cocoa. Their parents did not want them to become farmers, warning them that life on the farms led to poverty. A future disaster was now in the making, where farmers' children were being disconnected from the farms. With the students at home, anti-government lessons spread, producing one of the most cynical generations in history. If you run into any of those kids today, now adults in their fifties and sixties, you will find a consistent expression of anti-establishment views, the visceral notion that government is useless and that political leaders only steal money.

In September, the government's insistence that it would embark on tax raids met with the resolve of protesting warriors to keep the violence going. In the government's view, taxes must be paid if the local govern-ments were not to collapse and if essential services were to be provided. The state government kept insisting that local councils were the ones that needed the money, and we kept insisting that the taxes were not being used to provide services but ended up in private pockets. State violence was needed to collect money; terrorism was needed to prevent it. The state and councils were notorious for their inability to account for what they had collected. To collect taxes even in the city now, the govern-ment had to use armed policemen: When guns were needed to demand tax receipts, the contract between the government and its people had broken down.

In the month of September, the official announcements told the pub-lic that more than sixty people had been killed, comprising policemen, civilians, and "rioting farmers." This figure was patently misleading. They were counting the dead that were picked up and taken to the mor-tuary. This was not the right way to count, as they should have known. Muslims did not make it to the mortuary but to their graves within hours. In places where our struggles were particularly intense, there were very many Muslims. Unknown to the government, we had set up our own burial arrangements, the mourning, the consolation, and the donations.

No one had any permanent insurance. God would take care of your children, just as He had taken care of you. Christians, like Pasitor, had also begun to imitate the Muslims. Were they to die, they were not to be taken to the mortuary. The police had already revealed their brutal side by hounding the injured who were taken to the hospital, from where some were taken to cells for torture. Pasitor instructed me on what to do were he to die, describing the location of the plot of land where he was to be buried. There was no going back on the rebellion, and there would be no negotiations with the government.

CHAPTER 10

# The Fall of Agodi

✦ ✦ ✦

On Tuesday, September 16, 1969, the rebellion achieved an unimaginable feat: We stormed Agodi Prison, the most dreaded prison in the state, broke its gates open, and freed all the prisoners. This would also be my second-to-last direct participation in a war that was now a year old and had taken a heavy toll on me, setting me back in life and making any possible plans for a future career almost impossible to imagine. My mind was in constant turmoil. I had suicidal dreams and, in one instance, attempted suicide in a dream, thwarted by weak decking made of planks that had been degraded by time and termites. The noose was well made, the chair well positioned, and the hook in the middle. The planks collapsed on me, crashed into a room, and left me to deal with dust rather than death. There would always be time to die and multiple routes to the end of life. Agodi and the preparation for it brought action, with the probable end of freedom—or of life itself.

I had known Agodi as far back as 1963. All schoolchildren knew about Agodi—if not its location its significance. Agodi, *ewon*, and *ewa* meant the same thing to us: the location of confinement, bringing with it the loss of freedom and severe sanctions. We knew Agodi as a prison, which had crept into the routine of conversation as one of the three terrifying words to describe a wish—a place one must never enter in an entire lifetime—and as a curse—the place where one's enemy should end up. Agodi was a British creation, part of a new prison system designed to maintain the colonial order and its new laws and, later, to detain those whom the military regimes saw as "enemies." Prisons made available cheap labor to build rail lines, cut lawns, and clean the streets.

People prayed to avoid prison. An ex-convict, an *elewon*, must never return to his place of birth. He could not get a wife; if he had one already, he should expect divorce. No one wanted to be associated with an *elewon* in any form or manner; and it was shameful for his children, who acquired a negative nickname such as *omo baba elewon* (son of an ex-convict); his wife, *iyawo elewon* (wife of a convict); or his brother, *aburo elewon*. Even if an *iyawo elewon* offered her body for free sex, she must add money to the deal to succeed.

Thus, it was better for an *elewon*, on being released, to relocate to another city, usually to places like Kaduna or Kano in the far north where no one would recognize him, or even further away, as far away as Sokoto in the northwest corner of the country or Maiduguri in the northeast. Nigeria did not have or use identity cards or birth certificates, making it easier for an *elewon*, if he liked, to change his name from Samson to Ibrahim, that is, from a Christian to a Muslim, or from Sulaiman to Jacob, from a Muslim to a Christian. All he needed was to find a job in the informal economy and become part of the crowd. From Maiduguri, the *elewon* could move further east to Darfur in the Sudan, leaving behind him a memory known to no one on earth but himself. He would now become "born again," living a new life with success or failure known to new associates, but the tragedy of the past would be known to him alone. Such was his fate: unforgiven, cruel, traumatic, and tragic, in spite of the redeeming possibility offered by the disguise of relocation. The future that awaited him was disastrous: at best, that of a common laborer. Or perhaps he would return to criminal activities and find a network he could join, and end up in a prison in a foreign land and be lost forever. He disappeared into the very margins of society, with a lost past that was beyond discovery and a present that was beyond redemption.

Never call a person an *elewon*. It would be a bad joke, if this was the intention. Sometimes we did so anyway, when a peer offended us, and we expected what followed such an act of deliberate provocation: a fight, verbal and physical—rough, extreme, tough, and deadly. The prison, *ewon*, the location, provided a sleeping place and three meals, not decent but merely enough to keep the person alive. Cockroaches and bedbugs were the usual companions, with mosquitoes parading the place at will. The prison was filthy, and living in it was as bad as living in the worst refuse dump. When an adult was misbehaving, doing or intending things of a criminal nature, others would tell him that he would *"fewon lo'gba,"* that is, that his time, future, leisure, and pleasure would be defined by the space of confinement, and he would be forgotten, erased from memory, condemned forever. Never joke that an adult would "*fewon lo'gba*"; never say that someone would ever find himself confined at Agodi.

I could walk to Agodi from Ode Aje in less than an hour. I did so too many times, first to see the dreaded place and then to pass by it on the way to a motor park, the Muslim praying ground called "Yidi," and the various small stores that were close to it. As this area grew, it became one of the mega-trading areas in West Africa where you could get anything you wanted, from motor parts to body parts, from a pin to a truck. My mother died in one of the stores there in the 1980s, forcing me back to Agodi and the constant trauma and violence that defined this place for me. The narration of the very last, fatal encounter between my mother and Sango, the god of thunder and lightning, has to wait until another season; it binds Agodi and myself permanently in time and pain. Agodi and I will wait until the next world before we part company.

My first encounter with Agodi, both the place and the prison, came in February 1963. Mid-morning at Ode Aje, I saw, for the very first time in my life, seventeen men wearing white uniforms, shirts, and short knickers made of low-quality *teru*, the fabric of the poor, the lowest grade of cotton, sometimes used for linings. Ahead of them was a man wearing a better uniform, a brown khaki shirt and long pants, a green beret, and black shoes. He had a foot-long wooden baton, called a *kondo*, which he either held or kept attached by a leather string to the right side of his waist, where his right hand could immediately grab it when needed. At the rear was another man wearing a similar uniform, holding handcuffs and a leather whip.

"Who are those?" I asked.

"*Elewon*," someone answered. They were prisoners, the first ones I would see in body and flesh, not at Agodi but on the streets. The better-dressed men at the front and rear were the *oga elewon*—the bosses of the prisoners, officially called the "wardens" but commonly "warders." Although it came with an income, *oga elewon* was not a good job, neither then nor now. Only a minimal level of education was needed in those days to apply for the short training; the completion of elementary school, one or two years in high school, and the ability to speak some "half-English." The *oga elewon* would get a wife, with no problem. With small raises after promotion from one level to another, he could gather some money to send his children to a poor school. The *oga elewon* had no influence in the neighborhood where he lived, but he regarded himself as far ahead of full-time farmers working on smallholdings. He, too, was a farmer, going to his farm in the village so he could generate his own food supply and sell the surplus, while he was also assured of a regular income at the end of the month. His smattering of English gave him some boasting rights—he could even claim to have seen Irunmu and the ministry men, and he could read newspapers and circulate both true and false information.

If the *oga elewon* had little influence in his neighborhood, unlike the tax collectors, *akoda*, and tax estimators, he had tremendous power over the *elewon* on the streets where I saw them and at Agodi where they were kept. He used his baton on the *elewon*'s heads, also beating them on the back, shoulders, and other parts of the body. The whip could be used on the body, and it routinely was. If the *elewon* was asked to bend down, and he was slow to comply, the whip would prompt immediate obedience. The handcuffs were there to immobilize a recalcitrant, to remove the stubbornness from his head, and to limit both the physical capabilities of his legs and the violence in his speech. The *oga elewon* was a cruel man, so cruel that he could beat an *elewon* so badly that he would be taken to the Adeoyo hospital. Whether it was true or not, we all believed the *oga elewon* could kill any *elewon* and that nothing would happen to him or his job. One thing was clear: The *elewon* got to Agodi because the police and judges believed he did not belong in society, and to keep him there, they needed someone much tougher than he was. As the saying goes, *elewon loga*, that is, the hardened *elewon* had a master, and this was the *oga elewon*, one who himself had the toughness of a criminal, only he was biding his time, waiting to commit a serious crime for which the judge would impose a prison sentence on him. But *oga elewon* did commit crimes; it was just that they did not see the whipping and clubbing of prisoners as crimes but as punishment meted out to miscreants and the unfit. Just as one cattle herder uses only a stick to lead over a dozen cows, so too could one *oga elewon* use a baton to herd the *elewon*. Cows and *elewon* have been deprived of their ability to escape; if the cow wanders away, he wanders back. The *elewon*, even with agility and speed, could not just take to the streets in his white uniform. There was nowhere to run to, no bush to hide in, no house to enter. The uniform was a badge of captivity, the dress of humiliation, the identity of shame. On those streets, it was better for the prisoners to behave like cows and obey the herder with the stick. If they resisted, which was not impossible given their terrible conditions, it was not in public, and I had no way of knowing or seeing it.

When I saw the *elewon* on the streets in February 1963, I saw them at least once a week. It was a kind of parade, to remind everyone, children and adults alike, of the fate that awaited them if they chose to *fewon lo'gba*. The constant parades of prisoners on major streets produced consistency in prayers, expressed on a daily basis, never to go to prison. Instead, it was better to commit suicide.

That a free person wanted to cut his life short instead of being a prisoner or even being threatened with a prison sentence was itself tied to two compelling notions that drove many people: guilt and shame. Many tried to avoid doing things that would either make them feel guilty or put them to shame. Guilt could come from transgressions, the violation of the "ten commandments" of culture: thou shall not sleep with other men's wives; thou shall not steal; thou shall not borrow money and not repay; thou shall not betray trust; thou shall not lie; thou shall not have sex with thy father's younger wife (not uncommon since she was not regarded as your stepmother!), and so on. Prison was a confirmation that someone was guilty of something. Parading prisoners was done to put them to shame, to announce that they were guilty and that you and I deserved to know who they were and to ridicule them.

And we did. As the *elewon* walked through the streets in single file, you would hear people saying that death was better than shame. My mates and I would talk of how we would rather commit suicide than be sent to jail and paraded on the streets. If suicide were not possible, we would have to mobilize and kill the *oga elewon* and escape. "Where would you escape to?" This was a good question. For, on the very first day of your new life in prison, you would first lose your clothes, shoes, wristwatch, wallet, and all your other possessions. When the *elewon* were paraded on the streets, they did so barefoot, as yet another form of punishment. In that tropical land, where the intense sun cooks the ground, the prisoners' feet would cook slowly as they walked, and cook much faster when they were asked to stand still. Thank God for small mercies: The *oga elewon* had no use for grilled feet.

In March 1963, I decided to follow the *oga elewon* and the prisoners as they marched through the streets toward the west. I told no one before leaving the house, running to the other side of the street, with the prisoners to my left and the road dividing us. They all kept walking until they reached the public library, a small building surrounded by an unkempt lawn with overgrown weeds. The two *oga elewon* brought out machetes from storage and gave one each to the prisoners. They began to cut the grass. As they did so, it appeared as if their tongues became loose with the temporary freedom. The prisoners mocked one another, telling stories, talking loudly, yelling, sharing jokes, and even singing. I found out what I wanted to know—where the prisoners were being marched to—and I returned home. I was later to find out that the prisoners were not only being humiliated on the streets but also being used as cheap labor.

On another occasion, I followed them in the opposite direction, that is, to the east of the house, to their very abode, the dreaded Agodi Prison. There was a medium-sized front entrance, which the prisoners used to enter into their house of pain. I knew all the external features of this notorious prison, front, back, and sides. I had no wish to follow them inside; to do so would be a curse and would lead to devastating jokes. Associating oneself with Agodi was not a good idea. There were those with regular business there, such as the *oga elewon*, food vendors, visiting relatives, and experts in crime economy making money from supplying marijuana.

Six years later, I would enter Agodi Prison. And had I been caught while doing so, I would have been its tenant for a decade or so and been paraded on the very street where I first saw the *elewon*. No one, other than those who planned the invasion of Agodi, can ever know the details. None of the media of the time or the archival sources I have read understood anything; they do not even come close. Most of the reports of the Agodi invasion, in the official documentation, are inaccurate or of very limited value. I can confirm, without any fear of contradiction, that all academic writings based on those files are relying on misleading evidence. In 1988, I found myself grimacing at a conference when someone was reporting his research on the Agodi episode; then I went into my room to quench my anger with a flood of beer. Here is what they got right: that we attacked Agodi sometime between 6 and 9 a.m., but they did not even know the reason why we chose the day and time. Eyewitness accounts said they saw guns, machetes, clubs, cudgels, and charms, but they did not know the scale or the magnitude of the planning.

For now, I can reveal no more than snippets, for the full retelling awaits its own moment of reckoning. Attacking Agodi was a suicidal operation. Yet we were left with no choice if the movement was not to collapse. You could walk from Agodi to the governor's mansion, which was heavily guarded twenty-four hours a day. There was a police station less than five minutes away. There was a heavily armed military police station, and a barracks some miles away at Eleyele, with ruthless soldiers able to reach Agodi in about twenty minutes. There was a military mess with armed soldiers less than ten minutes away. There was even a widespread rumor that the trigger-happy soulless officer Olusegun Obasanjo might be in town. The roads were not congested. The multitude of our fighters with their dane guns and charms would be killed like flies. There was no large civilian population to use as human shields. Agodi was an almost impossible mission. To even contemplate it was insane.

Yet it had to be done. Many mentioned the names of our active members who were at Agodi. The fear of what our fellow members in prison would be going through and thinking was the driving force for some to take the risk of freeing them. We had to fight for them and figure out how to release them. We could not do so through the legal process. A decree was already in place allowing the military government to arrest and detain anyone for as long as the authorities wanted, and no judge had the power to free them. Hundreds, many of whom were innocent, along with vulnerable women who had taken no part in the rebellion, were in various detention cells. No formal charges had been laid against them, as the police kept conducting investigations but found no evidence other than the broad allegation that they had taken part in "demonstrations." To be caught with a machete, which you carried whenever you were going to a farm, was the only evidence the police needed to justify your arrest. The investigations were never concluded, since there was actually nothing to investigate. Of the twenty-eight publicized names of those arrested in relation to the July battle at Akanran, none was actually there! These men were arrested on account of state violence, and we had to free them with violence. They were put in prison to punish them for their opposition to the government, to warn the free that they too would be silenced if they committed any affront to authority, and to use Agodi to break the backbone of the strong.

The families of the inmates, our fellow rebels, were already devastated. Those who sought freedom and wanted to rejoin their anguished families might talk and betray the rest of us. The meager award of £1 per visit to a distressed family would be nothing compared to what Irunmu and his boys could give to them in order to extract information. Our disgrace was imminent, just a matter of time. We must unite the husbands and fathers, the breadwinners, with their families.

We were all walking along *bebe ewon* (the edges of prison) as sworn friends. We knew that those who had become the *elewon*, tarnished and disgraced, would be paraded on the streets, mocked by adults and schoolchildren. They would be served *ewa* (beans that usually contained pebbles and dirt). When you cooked for the *elewon*, you did not bother to clean the beans, to sift the seeds from the pebbles, dust, and pesticides. Prison food vendors cooked two sets of meals, the cleaner and tastier meals for the *oga elewon,* who were actually stealing the food since they had been paid and were not entitled to free meals, and the dirty, ill-prepared meals for the *elewon.* Food rations were generally small, to remind the *elewon* of their loss of freedom but creating problems of malnutrition and infection. An *elewon* was not entitled to a good night's sleep. The grass-filled mattresses were bug-infested. Each cell was small, and the common toilet facilities were terrible. Bathrooms were treated as optional. Why would farmers struggling for improved living standards fall to no standard at all? Being poor and struggling to overcome poverty was not a crime to justify becoming an *elewon.*

The reasons why our friends and colleagues became *elewon* were irrelevant. What mattered was their identity. There were two thousand reasons to end up at Agodi, from the legitimate one of committing a crime to the bad luck of wrongful allegations, or, as in our case, to fighting for justice. An *elewon* was an *elewon:* This was a fact, not about the reason for becoming an *elewon,* but about imprisonment itself. An *elewon* was always an *elewon,* even after serving his sentence. It was a permanent condition of his definition of being, immutable, unchanging, fixed, and frozen in time. Our associates were now *elewon,* and we had become the friends of *elewon.* The friends of an *elewon,* as a category, were bad—guilty by association. A friend of an *elewon* was an *elewon,* only the friends were not wearing uniforms. Pasitor, a friend to many *elewons,* lost sleep over it, wondering what they had done wrong. "Those who were full," he would say, were trying to "shrink their stomachs," and "those who were hungry were faking bloated stomachs." He did not know why Irunmu and many ministry men were not the ones at Agodi but living big on the wealth created by his *elewon* friends.

He transferred his agonies to me. He was becoming sad and depressed. I was not. I was concerned and worried about him. He was not much of a talker, while I could speak until tomorrow. When Pasitor was sad, he would lose his appetite, which gave me a double ration to consume, especially beef. Adults got the biggest pieces of beef in the pot of stew, and the children got the thumb-sized pieces. Pasitor's meat was the first thing I would pounce upon when he asked Abiodun—his favorite name for me—to grab his leftovers. Pasitor introduced me to leftovers, a habit I have retained until now, unable to throw away food even when I sense that maggots are preparing to compete with me for it. I will look at food that is already a week old and tell myself that my stomach is a sewer. A good stomach never disappoints; it protests only when it is fed food from five-star restaurants.

Pasitor was not alone in the agony of our group over the members incarcerated at Agodi. Our leader, the *kakanfo*, too, was worried. All the preliminary meetings came to one conclusion: Invading Agodi was not possible. But a combination of luck and circumstances produced a new line of thinking. Information about the prison came from a former farm laborer at Elepo, named Jakobu, who had not paid his tenancy fees; when Jakobu had been exploited and humiliated, his absentee land-lord schemed to send him to Agodi in 1965. Pasitor revealed to me all his efforts to fight for Jakobu's release. Regaining his freedom, Jakobu became a loyal member of the Agbekoya from its very inception, work-ing in the communication relay team and also fighting as a foot soldier. It was Jakobu who knew the prison well enough to be able to describe the place.

We got to know that there were two major doors that had to be bro-ken down, the giant front door that led into an open space and another door that led to most of the cells. The doors to the individual cells were usually left unlocked. The walls, built with fourteen-by-eighteen-inch bricks, were too thick to break, unless you used a heavy machine to drill holes in order to gradually chip them into bits and pieces. We had nei-ther the machine nor the time. We could not enter through the windows in the short time that would be available to us. Jakobu said that breaking down the two doors within two minutes or so was the only smart option. The entire operation must take no longer than ten minutes.

Thanks to Jakobu, the giant among ants, we began to learn more and more about the internal arrangements of the prison. It was both filthy and overcrowded, a sort of storage facility in which to put away human cargo. Buckets for urine and feces were placed close to the water needed for drinking and cleaning. The prisoners were forced to work inside the prison, making their uniforms and those of the *oga elewon*—not with the idea of transmitting tailoring skills but as a part of the punishment, using the prisoners as cheap labor for necessary work. Jakobu told us that the *oga elewon* were also engaged in small trade on the side. Their relations had small stores outside the prison, selling cigarettes, bread, sardines, milk, and marijuana, all to the prisoners. The *oga elewon* encouraged the prisoners to buy from their relatives. Jakobu said that those traders were valuable in providing information on movements, but they would do so only if they could be led to cheaper sources of marijuana. Making more profits from marijuana would open their mouths. They would talk about the doors, the locks, the keys, the activities of the *oga elewon*, and much more, without knowing what we intended to do with the answers.

Jakobu was of the opinion that although there were guns in the prison, he was not sure the *oga elewon* knew how to use them. He had never seen them near the guns, had not even seen them touch the guns, instead always using their whips and batons to beat the prisoners. Their mouths, uttering harsh obscenities, were their guns. With the insights from Jakobu and the information gleaned from the small traders supplying items to Agodi, we were better equipped with the details that informed our decision to attack the prison.

Maximum force would have to be used to break down Agodi's main door. We had discussed two possibilities with regard to the main door when we realized that the door was made of wood. The first was to set it on fire with kerosene, but this would create complications arising from smoke. The second was to break it down. The carpenters and bricklayers had recommended that the side frames be hit with heavy chunks of wood to create a hole in the middle or that the gate be bypassed by creating a manhole entrance into the prison yard. If we chose to penetrate through the front door, it had to be broken down in less than two minutes, if possible in seconds. We rehearsed the scenario that we hoped would ensure this. Those inside the prison walls had weapons with which to fight back, and to give them time would result in many deaths for us. The prison officials must be taken by surprise. As we planned, when they heard a bang on the door, they would not reach for their guns, but would go to check what was going on. And before they could reach for their guns, we would have attacked and overpowered them. The plan was to use younger folks with energy and those who could run in case they were pursued. Exit options were in place if escape was needed. It was not good for thugs to join us here, as they would complicate the plans with diversions.

As it turned out, the plan provided a script that was enacted without any hitch. We left the secret locations at which we had stayed all night in the bush. Between 8:30 and 9 a.m., when we could see well, we stormed the prison. The telephone lines were cut within seconds. These had previously been located, and the men knew exactly what to do with the visible cables dangling from poles without any sense of order. The entrance door was taken down in less than twenty seconds, with heavy multiple hits by men who had prepared well for this job. The officials were indeed stunned and taken by surprise. The danger they were trained to handle was a riot on the inside—to contain the prisoners—but not an attack from the outside. The reports they later gave, now in the archives, made it clear that they never expected what happened, and the speed of events was so fast that they recognized not a single person. In the very inaccurate official documents, fifty "armed thugs" were said to have been responsible, when far more people had been used just as spies in the days preceding the attack.

While the attack on Agodi was the primary goal, the secondary goal was to severely destabilize the city at multiple points in order to confuse the government and to prevent the police and army from moving quickly in pursuit of fleeing rebels and liberated prisoners. It was clear that the federal army would be called, and they would shoot to kill. Since attacking a prison was more than criminal, making arrests would not be the goal of angry policemen and soldiers; they would seek people to kill. "Unknown soldiers," as these killers were called when civil society asked for an investigation, had the right to kill "unknown people," who would be dumped in unmarked graves. History could be murdered by the state. Everyone understood this.

We had to create panic in the city and give ourselves enough time to escape. The pursuit would be immediate and ferocious, with soldiers in fast-moving trucks pursuing untrained rebels on foot. The soldiers' guns would discharge bullets with a rapidity that would fell hundreds, and their trucks would crush people as in meat grinders. These soldiers just wanted to kill anyway, as this was the main purpose for their recruitment and service. Killing boosted their credentials and chances of promotion. Those who had not been sent to Biafra had received training that hadn't been put to use, useless soldiers who had not taken anyone's life.

While the attack on Agodi was very successful, there were heavy casualties on both sides, with seven dead. Two *oga elewon* were fatally wounded, and another died five days later. An assistant superintendent of the police also lost his life. He wanted to use his gun but was overpowered. Two angry men at whom the gun had been pointed reacted angrily and brutally used their machetes on him. We did not plan only to take our members from prison and drive them away in a lorry. All the freed prisoners could make their own decisions. Our members knew we were there for them. As we retreated to the bush paths, they followed us, wearing regular clothes. Many escaped in different directions. These were tough men who knew what to do with freedom without their prison uniforms.

Four hundred prisoners regained their freedom. We did not know that the number was so large until the government released the number of prisoners on the run. The prison had been holding 485 inmates, the majority of whom were male. Only about 60 refused to escape. We did not know the number left behind or why they made such a choice until we heard it over the radio. The politicians serving jail terms on corruption charges stayed behind. The former finance minister of Western Nigeria, Oba C. D. Akran, and another powerful politician, Prince Adeleke Ademiluyi, a former chairman of the Western Nigeria Development Corporation, refused to leave. They knew that Irunmu or his boss, Gowon, the young man who had become the country's president, would eventually release them in one of the new year's addresses when the government granted state pardons to a number of prisoners whose names were closely guarded. Stealing small amounts of money was enough to make a man end up at Agodi, but stealing large amounts from government coffers was not. Akran and Ademiluyi were in jail not because they were the most corrupt, but because they must have behaved arrogantly to the new men in power who railroaded them to jail. When a thief calls another thief a thief, the confrontation must be about something other than thievery, like greed or jealousy.

Politicians are a funny lot. Both of the powerful men thought we were their thugs and followers who had come to release them. One assumed that his followers were angry at the government and had mobilized to release him. In or out of prison, many of these politicians were delusional, exaggerating the support their followers had for them. Those who went to them for one favor or another usually lavished praises on them, prayed for them, and exaggerated their contributions to society. At the prison, one angry farmer pushed Ademiluyi aside like a common man, lampooning him and others like him for bringing the farmer to a state of rebellion. "*Eyi kii se ise oba*"—this is not a government mission, the farmer told the politician: The pestle belongs to the mortar, the long wooden spoon belongs to the pot, and the crook belongs to the prison. As the farmer made clear, in that encounter of less than one minute, we were there for the just and the innocent.

A number of prisoners were able to locate where their clothes and property were kept, and they hurriedly removed their attire of disgrace and put on the dress of freedom. Those who could not locate their clothes fled in their prison uniforms, but we gave them *agbada* (big robes) that they wore on top.

To disorient the brutalizing state police and army, we sent scores of our people to many other locations. They were to do small things that halted traffic and created diversions and to send signals about our motives that people needed time to discern. They were to burn tires, sing anti-government songs, scare parents to keep their children from going to school, and terrify the police into removing their uniforms and hiding. Courts and offices were forced to shut down. Thugs and high school students would join in, as they always did in all rebellions, since they had their own motives. So too would thousands of adults who were angry for one reason or the other. They had no jobs; they did not have enough money; they were not doing as well in life as they had expected; and the politicians and soldiers had failed them. By 9:30 a.m., the city was already in a panic. Those who had gone to work early had closed their stores; thousands stayed indoors, looking out at the chaos in the streets. The arterial roads that connected two big markets at Gege, where people made bulk purchases of foodstuffs, and the Ogunpa Motor Park, the hub for intercity transportation, were abandoned; shoppers fled, and store owners closed their stores to avoid being looted by thugs.

The newly liberated prisoners joined in the attacks that followed. A list of houses to be destroyed had been compiled, houses built with stolen money; an order had been given to destroy them and damage the property inside. The attacks were carried out by hundreds of angry people who delighted in throwing stones and imposing mortal curses. The houses of city council officials living at Agugu, south of Agodi, were destroyed and set on fire. Council officials were thrown into panic. Those in the most powerful and most corrupt council, of Mapo, shut down their offices and ran away. As stories filtered back to us, we heard of landlords who had council staff as tenants asking them to relocate temporarily elsewhere, to go into hiding, or to run to Lagos.

Thousands of people jubilated over the burning of houses, the destruction of property, and the rebels' control of the streets. They were waiting for more action, thinking this would trigger a revolution of some sort, not just the fall of the incumbent government but a new orientation of politics that would put people first. Many were not happy that criminals had been set free along with the innocent at Agodi, but they blamed the government for having lumped good men with bad. Their idea of justice was affronted at the punishment of the innocent and the just.

The boldness of the contingent that operated at Iyaganku police station was first rate. Here was the location of one of the largest police forces in the entire city, if not in the entire state. With sprawling offices and barracks, Iyaganku was an intimidating police zone. Our target was the court, not the police station. Our members from Moniya, north of the city, had been arrested and put on trial. They had a court proceeding on September 16, already having been taken from their cells to appear before the judge. The instruction was to attack the court and capture them by force, even if they were handcuffed. The police with the keys would be captured along with them. Iyaganku turned out to be a much easier operation than anticipated. As soon as the judge and police heard gunshots, they fled. Court officials and litigants ran; the "rioters"—the media's name for those on trial—also ran, but to join their colleagues who had come to free them. Someone remembered to enter the judge's office and chamber to steal all the files. This would be the end of the case if there were no duplicate files. This was not the age of computers with multiple backups! A thief being charged on that day won the lottery. He escaped, never to be found again. Iyaganku was closer to Dugbe and Gbagi, the biggest markets in the city. The markets closed in panic as the news of the gunshots at Iyaganku spread. If the court near the police station could not be protected, who were they to brave the onslaught?

When No Baga, the leader of the Iyaganku operation, later reported his activities, he received a standing ovation. In the view of a braggart, the ovation would have enhanced his stature. Incidentally, No Baga is still alive, and the only story he loves telling with relish is the story of this operation, although he is now a politician making shady deals. Whenever I ask him why the turnaround, from rebel to dealmaker, his answer is, "Man must wack something," "wack" being broken English for "eat." No Baga, who wanted to "wack" a judge in 1969, is now "wacking" state funds. Money is much tastier than a judge's flesh!

The government was discredited. While we received masses of condemnation as "thugs," leaders of opinion wondered why law-enforcement agencies had not been able to detect our plans The government had lost control. It imposed a one-week curfew, from 6 p.m. to 7 a.m., to halt the movement of people. The inspector general of police in Lagos, the country's capital, rushed to Ibadan to discuss the matter in private with his senior officers. The head of state, Major-General Gowon, vowed to involve more soldiers and policemen, giving instructions that surveillance should be increased. The "riots" became a top issue on the agenda of the Federal Supreme Military Council, next to the ongoing civil war. We can never know what they discussed, but it certainly involved the decision to use the full force of the army to destroy us. "We will crush it," became the slogan of Irunmu, the inspector general of police, and of the head of state. An order was given to dismiss policemen who had retreated during any of our attacks, as hundreds of them had, and twenty-four of them were sacked in September. They weren't paid to die! Everyone was now about to shoot his arrow into the sky, but not all had the means to protect their heads.

Politicians began to weigh in. They had all sown thorns and were worried about not reaping flowers. They were accused of stealing goats but

**Colonel Olusegun Obasanjo. Photograph taken in the 1970s, Ministry of Information, Ibadan.**

were still bold enough to serve goat meat for dinner. Some suggested the removal of Irunmu and the appointment of a non-Yoruba administrator or interim governor. This suggestion represented a loss of confidence in Irunmu. Some believed our movement was being sponsored to fragment the region and create additional states. Some believed that we wanted the military to leave government immediately after the war, which we could do only by causing trouble. Well, we wanted exploitation to end; we wanted to see the benefits of taxation; and we did not endorse corruption. Where the politicians acquired their own motives, one must ask them. Ojugo, using his office as prime minister and keeping in mind his political ambition to become the head of state, began a process of reconciliation with us. He, too, was already getting into trouble, being accused of wanting to topple the government. He even believed that politicians opposed to his party were aiding and abetting us. By the end of September, we were no longer troublemakers but allies he could cultivate, as he pleaded to Irunmu to grant all our requests.

None of these would stop the rebellion, and various battles followed for about six weeks. As long as the cat is alive, the mouse does not get close enough to lick its nose. Indeed, on September 19, there was another battle at the village of Elesin, close to Akanran, with the police gunning down twenty people there. Both sides had become determined to shoot the other to death. In the case of Egbeda on September 21, there was a six-hour fight involving the rebels and the combined forces of the army and the police, leading not only to the death of twenty-four people at the hands of the police but also to the arrest and torture of over two hundred men. Our men captured an inspector of police and a constable and kept them for a long time, feeding them well with a regular supply of palm wine. The next day at Oba, near Abeokuta, the palace was burned down, and two policemen were fatally injured. At Omi Adio, not far from Oba, the gun battle was intense, especially on September 23, with over a dozen policemen badly injured, and the police, too, in fury, shot to kill as many as they could. On September 29 at Owode, close to Abeokuta, another prolonged battle was fought, in the course of which all the government offices and two private houses were destroyed. The police and army now knew how to rout our forces; use maximum firepower. It was no longer a "riot" but a "rebellion," justifying its destruction and requiring the army to destroy it. It would not be easy for either side.

However, the government could not admit its powerlessness and had to find a way to save face. Kings and chiefs in Ibadan and other cities were afraid, fearing attacks. The king of Ibadan, Oba Salawu Aminu, began to sleep in different, secret locations. By late September, he was already calling on the governor to stop all tax raids. His chiefs joined him in seeking the suspension of tax collection. The media and the educated citizenry also began to pressure the government to modernize tax collection. An articulate group warned the federal government to keep an eye on the Western State, whose government was incompetent to deal with dissidents. Ojugo changed his mind; he ditched the government and began to support us. Various associations began to appeal for the end of bitterness, for both sides to "cool off."

Restoring order and preventing further political degeneration were now far more important than tax collection. Signs began to emerge that the government was in trouble. Two of its commissioners from Ibadan, Dr. Omololu Olunloyo, the commissioner for education, and Chief Adeoye Adisa, in charge of Home Affairs, composed a joint letter which they sent to Oba Salawu Aminu on September 21, seeking an end to the rebellion. We interpreted this action of prominent members of the state government in writing the letter, which Irunmu must have approved of, as a clear signal that reliance on the army and police had failed the government. Copies of the letter were reproduced and sent to all the branches of our movement to boost morale. Olunloyo and Adisa wanted an end to armed conflict, especially an end to the clashes between us and the police. The *olubadan* was begged to call a meeting of all the religious leaders, village heads, and prominent citizens to discuss the reasons for the rebellion and to find solutions. This was an open admission of the failure of the Ayoola Commission, with all its expenditure and testimonies. It was no longer Irunmu who was called upon to act. It was now the civil authority under the *olubadan* that was charged with getting the farmers to lay down their arms, to stop the bloody fighting between citizens and the security forces. King Aminu was now basking in the glory of being a peace mediator, trying to arrange a meeting between Irunmu and the poor farmers, behaving like an aged father holding a meeting with a younger son.

The first major personal consequence of the rebellion was about to hit me. The meeting between Aminu and Irunmu was yet to be fixed, if it would be at all, before another calamity struck on September 23, this time triggered by angry officials who wanted revenge. I do not know what was in the officials' minds or what their plans were, but I saw what they did, and I understood why. With Akanran under constant surveillance and spies routinely visiting the village, our central command had shifted to another village, Akufo, in Ibadan North West District, twelve miles from the city. Akufo had participated in the July 1 rebellion, driving away those suspected of being pro-government, and killing one person who was accused of leaking war plans to the police. I relocated with Pasitor to Akufo, but I was sent on constant errands to the city to receive and deliver private messages. If Akanran's strategy had been to take the war to the city, Akufo was expecting the police and the army to invade us. In order to prevent this, Akufo called for an entirely new planning strategy: Retain the idea of a surprise invasion of the city again, a strategy that had been well developed, while expecting an attack on us in the village. Beating us in the city was next to impossible as we had human shields. The majority of city dwellers, except in the new areas containing the university, the railway, and government workers, were hostile to the police and the government. They would gladly hide a fleeing farmer-rebel.

If Akufo was to be able to withstand an attack, it could not rely solely on dane guns. Modern guns, like the ones the police and army were using, were now available to us. Contractors who supplied the federal forces were probably stealing guns and bullets, which were then sold to various people in underground markets. Soldiers and policemen looking for extra money were also stealing guns and bullets from their various depots. Akufo had some small access to such modern guns, not enough but adequate to create a frontline. The commanders ordered the building of trenches from which members of the movement could shoot and defend the village. The movement was now benefiting from techniques made available courtesy of the Nigeria-Biafra war. Soldiers returning home from the Biafra war front, boasting about their prowess and conquests, were connecting with Akufo to give valuable training to our men. Charms and modern guns came together at Akufo.

Before the new strategy could be put into practice, disaster struck on September 23. We were awoken by heavy gunfire in the morning, around 7 a.m. It was totally unexpected. The police and the soldiers, in large numbers, had planned a surprise attack of their own. The humiliation at Agodi and Iyaganku was apparently too much for them to bear. They were not interested in the peace initiative between the king and the governor, only in revenge.

They were surprised by how fast we were able to respond after the initial chaos. A ten-hour battle ensued with the police and soldiers always gaining the upper hand. We lost 112 men; we were unable to carry away the corpses of about 30 of them. The next day the media reported that 30 rebels had been killed. Not so, this was the number lying dead on the ground that the police counted as their trophies. As dead bodies were being carried away, and children and women were fleeing, the police were in pursuit of us—performing the incredible feat of following us deeper into the bush for nearly seventeen miles. We were completely routed. We wounded several policemen, but killed only one. Five more of our own were killed. One hundred seventeen to one was a disaster. We were in trouble, trying to deal with the bodies, to console hundreds of family members.

The battle of Akufo had been unceasing, and it was the most brutal in the series of skirmishes. The police described it as their "toughest operation." Both sides shot at one another until 4 p.m., when our side ran out of bullets and gunpowder and had to disperse. The police pursued us, shooting randomly, aiming not at legs but at the upper parts of our bodies. They wanted to kill, not to maim or arrest. The trenches had to be abandoned; if the police came nearer to us, they would just shoot at the heads and chests of the men in the trenches. To survive, our men had to avoid being shot at close range. They were smart to run. The ability to retreat in warfare was not cowardice by any means but an act of wisdom in itself, since the men who were saved could live to fight another day. Countless dane guns and charms were left behind as our men ran. When the bush is set on fire, birds and grasshoppers run without bidding farewell to one another.

Pasitor was hit twice, mainly because he was too old to run. He fell to the ground in a pool of blood. When I came near him, he told me to keep running, not to stop. "Keep running," he kept saying. Gunshots followed me, but I kept running, to the north, toward a village known as Omi Adio, where, unknown to me, another brutal police team was conducting a major operation. Isola ran, remembering the river full of scorpions and snakes, the riverbank with its crocodiles, the forest full of vipers. It took long agonizing hours to walk to Ibadan, but immediately I had to return to Akufo, to learn what had happened to Pasitor. Maybe he was lucky, maybe the police had carried away the injured and taken them to the hospital.

He was dead, his body decaying by the third day. Pasitor had set fire to his father's house and could not even wait to inherit the wreckage. There were other dead bodies around him. Death has no cure. I broke down: I was mad and sad. I looked into the skies, bad vultures were hovering! My enemies were no longer the police but the vultures; they would have to eat me along with Pasitor. I recovered very quickly. My brain was working imaginatively. I dipped into Pasitor's pocket, took out his wallet, made up of a piece of cloth, like a small sack. I took all his money and the money I found on two other corpses. The village was deserted. I walked to the road that linked Ibadan with Abeokuta, about a quarter of a mile away. Brave traders had gathered to sell food items by the roadside. I needed help. Dead bodies had to be removed. They did not know about them, they confessed, or they would have already done so. The women called on their men for support. Two men followed me back to the village and suggested that we look for more men to dig graves, pray, and bury the bodies. Very kind people, they prayed, insulted the government, and cursed the police that had killed Pasitor and the others. They asked me to wait while they gathered additional men and looked for religious leaders as well as tools with which to dig.

But before we started preparing for the burial, a lorry pulled up, bringing the Reverend Oladimeji of Jago Anglican Church, who had to look for members of his church. He saw Pasitor and broke down in tears. He had known him as a junior church worker. He prayed and asked me what to do. I told him the instructions Pasitor had given me to bury him by the side of his mud house at Gbenla in the city. On September 26, he was buried after a short service on the site. I left before the grave was filled in and did not partake of the meal that had to be served. My teeth would not have been able to grind the food. May Pasitor continue to find the rewards of the afterlife even greater than his amazing worldly deeds. This was no time for deep thinking or long mourning—both can be left to await darker days although the memory and its emotional pain are constantly there. It is not true, I can assure you, that time heals.

There were just no resources to deal with this crisis, to bury all the men, to assist their families, to keep their children in school. The vengeance of the police also brought another disaster: They were able to capture well over three hundred people with their surprise tactics, as fleeing people fell into their net. The federal government became involved, ordering the permanent detention of all of those who had been captured. Not all were arrested at Akufo or Omi Adio, as the police went after innocent people going to their farms or villages between Abeokuta and Ibadan. Even those on their way to attend church services were taken for rebels and arrested. In the days that followed, the police were raiding villages, arresting anyone they found, and more and more people fled, leaving all the small villages deserted, leaving only goats and hens to live in them. Once the villages were deserted, regrouping became a challenge. Those arrests allowed the police to declare that they were in full control of the situation and the rebellion had been quashed.

Then came some luck for us, the saving grace that we needed very badly. Church leaders began to complain, especially as innocent members of the Anglican Church were arrested. The Anglican bishop of Ibadan, the Right Reverend S. O. Odutola, went on the radio and petitioned the governor to release his church members. The advantage of this was that no one knew the difference between warriors and church members. The government could not offend the Anglican Church.

Anger was on the rise, as the excesses of the police generated bad publicity. Warriors were now presented as defenseless. Meanwhile, the movement had not been defeated and was bracing for its own counteraction. A contingent of the Agbekoya was mobilized just one day after the raids at the village of Obafemi with a decision to attack police stations and to kill any policeman found on the streets. Most of the police posts in Ibadan and some parts of Abeokuta districts were closed, as finding officers willing to man them was impossible.

The Western State was perceived as ungovernable. Governors of other states began to call on the federal government to intervene, saying that Irunmu lacked the political skill to handle the rebellion. This was an indictment that could lead to his removal as governor. Irunmu's credibility was now on the line. Rumors spread that he was a lazy governor, given to excessive drinking and womanizing instead of doing his job. He was labeled the "Owambe governor," one who found excuses to leave his work to enjoy the pleasures of dancing and drinking, discarding his military uniform to wear expensive lace, and lavishing state money on cheap girls. The failure to handle us had now been magnified to embrace the limitations of his own leadership, to say nothing of the flaws in his character. If we had been defeated at Akufo, Irunmu's image, too, was now badly damaged in the eyes of the public. People were calling for his removal as governor, and a newspaper editorial asked Gowon to replace him as soon as possible. Chiefs and city landlords were feeling the loss of income from villages and farmlands, and they, too, began to call for an end to tax raids and collections.

Prominent politicians were eager to end the worsening crisis that Irunmu and his administration were unable to solve. The federal government was also thinking of a non-military solution. The movement refused to grant audience to discredited politicians. On October 5, Ojugo came to a village, some six miles from Ibadan, to meet the Agbekoya delegation led by Tafa Adeoye, now openly known as the leader and described in flattering terms as "Generalissimo" and "Field Commander," and his assistant, Folarin Idowu. It was a secret meeting, which made Irunmu nervous, as Ojugo was intervening without his permission. Ojugo paid another visit on October 15. Others followed, arranging secret meetings, swallowing their previous words that we were hooligans and now recognizing us as those aggrieved by injustice. Irunmu quickly arranged his own secret meeting, and he received a friendly audience as his demeanor was gentle and humble; he called himself a "friend," "son," and "servant." Their suggestions were becoming positive, all along the lines of what we had presented in our petitions as far back as 1968.

However, October would be like September if the government did not change its course. The riots would not stop in Ibadan and its surrounding villages. The government could not mobilize force sufficient to stop the rebellion. The police forces were no longer adequate and knew they could be attacked at any time. The toll was heavy in lives, injuries, damage to property, school cancellations, and threats to public spaces. The traditional authorities were discredited: One king had been beaten very badly and another killed. A palace had been set on fire, and many houses had been damaged. The Agodi Prison had been successfully attacked, and the prisoners liberated. Plans were in place to attack other prisons. Teachers were failing to report for work in schools located in villages and city edges. The taxes were even harder to collect, and those being collected could not be used for development purposes. The primary purpose of government was now in question if it could not guarantee peace or maintain law and order. The daily language of politics was chaos; many believed that society was in chaos and turbulence. Christian preachers saw the end of the world as now really in sight, and were using the language of gloom and doom.

By mid-October, fearing that more troubles were around the corner, the government changed its views and tactics. It ordered the release of hundreds of people who had been charged with unlawful assembly. In Moniya alone, a village that had known no peace for months, over two hundred were released; so also were all those arrested at Akanran for "riot offences," and another four hundred fourteen at Abeokuta. The collection of taxes was suspended. In a dramatic reversal, the government did what it had been asked to do a year earlier. On October 14, it began to change the way it spoke, using kinder words, and announcing new rules on taxes and fees.

First, the flat tax rate was to be reduced. This met a key demand from individuals who believed that they were being asked to pay too much, that the burden was unrealistic. People were happy when they heard this on the radio. Those who had been forced to pay the old rate were to be compensated for their overpayment by paying less in the following year. Irrespective of income, all those without regular wages in the formal sector would now pay £2 instead of the previous minimum of £3.5s. The urban workers making a living from their trade were happy and thanked the farmers for saving them. The barbers and tailors would now get to keep more of their income, while the tradesmen could declare no income. We won: The rebellion was worth it.

Second, there would be no more tax raids. All those in jail, detention, and prison over "tax riots" were to be released, including those already convicted. Call this amnesty. So the joke was, if the government forgave us, we would not forgive the government. We won: The rebellion was worth it.

Third, more cocoa money would come into the pockets of those who collected the seeds. At last! The government did not say how much would reach the producers, but the marketing board had already been instructed to review the prices for the new season and to pay the producers 50 percent more. As this would affect the revenues of the federation, the Central Bank was equally drawn into the equation, to review the earnings based on cocoa. All levels of government had been taking their cut from the cocoa. The government knew that if the prices were not adjusted in favor of the farmers, the secretariat would be set on fire. We won: The rebellion was worth it.

Fourth, the fees that local councils had been collecting, some without authorization and some of which the council bosses had been putting in their pockets, were abolished. The two most notorious fees were the market fees and the motor park fees. The market fees were taxes on women. To own a stall in the market, you paid a fee, which was sensible if it was the council that had built the stall. But this was a stall you had built with your own money. If you asked your daughter to take some of your items from the store and hawk them in the market, a council officer could arrest her for not paying a fee. If you traded on the street, fees were demanded. Many did not understand what an imposition it was to ask a woman selling twelve oranges in a small basket to pay a market fee. Not all the taxes and fees collected reached the council offices; after collecting the motor park fees, the police would still collect bribes. Inspectors, motor park officers, and market masters, their grandiose titles useful only to steal money, were prevented from visiting all rural areas in the state. "No special rates shall be levied," the radio announced repeatedly, "on the people where no corresponding services are provided, save with the active consent of the people concerned." We won: The rebellion was worth it.

Fifth, local government officials and ministry men would no longer visit the villages. More jubilation. People had grown to hate the tax collectors, and the cooperative officers who collected bribes promising to support the award of loans. Inspectors of cocoa produce, who were meant to ensure the proper harvesting and drying of cocoa, had become rogues. Some brought bags with them to collect bribes from farmers in cocoa, which they later sold to produce buyers. After a farmer had worked hard and kept all the rules, his Grade A cocoa could be converted to Grade B by the inspector who went behind the backs of the farmers to share the difference with buyers. Sanitary inspectors were also stopped from going to the villages. Called *wolewole*, the inspectors were tasked with providing the public with lessons on the importance of getting and using clean water, having a good drainage system, and clearing mosquitoes from pools. What did they do? They extended their power even to going inside people's houses, inspecting their kitchens, looking at their pots for fresh meat to eat. Muslims repeated that the sanitary inspectors even had the effrontery to look at women in purdah, asking them to unveil themselves to see if they had washed their faces. The inspectors always fought with market women. They accused palm wine sellers of mixing the wine with bad water, confiscated it, but then drank it, sometimes in the presence of people. From the lowly to the middling, local government staff converted encounters with villagers and farmers into power: They claimed the power to insult; the power to ask for money from the poor; and the power to take free food, palm wine, and game. We won: The rebellion was worth it.

Sixth, the business of the district councils in the Ibadan area would no longer be conducted in the villages but at Ibadan itself until a new arrangement was put in place. This was to prevent the opening of local government councils that would instigate more violence. Local government would be reorganized. We won: The rebellion was worth it.

Seventh, it was now time to check the contents of the fat stomachs of council workers. District councils would have to be probed. The government had been forced to recognize the massive corruption in the councils. The assets of council workers would be checked, and their sources of income investigated. How did a junior officer making so little have a house in the city? How was he able to buy a car? With what income was he supporting three wives, three mistresses, and nine children? The villagers had known the answer all along, and now the state government wanted to spend cocoa money to learn the simple truth about graft and theft. Irunmu directed that all corrupt council men should be sacked. We won: The rebellion was worth it.

The councils would also be reorganized, with individuals appointed to advisory committees. This was rather vague, as these appointed individuals would not be those like Leku or Pasitor, but city politicians and produce buyers, although the promise was that farmers, too, would be included. Regarding this re-organization, in the long term, change in a barber's shop was all we got: The more things change, the more they stay the same. Another rebellion was needed to change political behavior. As to representation and accountability, we lost: The rebellion was a waste.

# CHAPTER 11

# Esu at the Crossroads

✦ ✦ ✦

It is time to end the detour in the story of my life. I am now too wet to fear the rain. If the beginning starts with Ogun, the god of iron, it now must end with Esu, the god of the crossroads. Esu requires no introduction, the mighty trickster god who is both short and tall, black and red, kind and cruel, wise and foolish, generous and stingy. Esu is the fierce god who can hit a rock until it breaks open and bleeds. Esu can support or disturb order and plans: He allows you to make all your plans, which he can then sabotage as you are boasting that everything is set and fixed. If you want cold water, Esu will give you hot to test your capacity for endurance, making you wait for the hot to turn cold before you can drink. If you are fully ready to move forward, Esu may decide to upset your plans so that you must reconsider whether to stay still or move backward. Esu may rupture your destiny and change your fate, as he chose to change mine. If you see the right path, Esu will lead you in a different direction, neither wrong nor right. Well, Esu is telling you that if you do not know where you are going, all roads will take you there, but you will not always remember where you are coming from. If you know where you are going, doubts will lead you in a wrong direction. If you live big today, eating as much meat as you want with your food, Esu will smile, as you may, by this time tomorrow, be consuming bones like a dog, so far removed from your big wardrobe that you begin to wear rags.

Standing up,
Esu cannot look into the pot on the floor.
Lying down,
Esu's head hits the roof.

Esu, as I close a part of my life, I invoke your name, not in vain, but in a respectful salutation. For I remember that my father and mother live in heaven whose address is known to you but not to me. A mailman cannot take a letter to the next world. Esu, I need you to link me with their abode and to carry my wishes and supplications to them. Thy glory is big, thy will be done! Do not turn me, the wise, into the foolish one. Wisdom and knowledge do not reside in my head but in yours. Esu, you are wiser than me—do not ask me to go to the goat to become wise; just give me a word, which is enough for the wise; and do not let me associate the growth of beard with wisdom, like someone that I know, so that a goat is not counted as wise. I take your chick as a gift so that hens may follow. I do not know your mistakes, Esu, and your weaknesses are hidden from me. Do not take my two eyes to be replaced by one large one since two small eyes can see better than one big one. If a man considers himself the most wise and refuses advice, Esu will encourage him to marry his mother. Let my words be well received, and accept my positive goals and meditations.

From 1970 onward, Esu was now set to do his work on us and the space we lived in, the space with the elegant name "Nigeria," whose meaning the majority of "Nigerians" do not know. Esu, the mighty one, had now made up his mind to turn right into wrong, wrong into right. The trickster god wanted to take his own revenge and to show his sinister side. We were about to be punished because we had not remembered to make sacrifices to Esu on that day when we honored Ogun and gave him his best food. For Esu must always receive the first portion of any sacrifice as a form of appeasement so that wishes and prayers can come true. I do not know why they forgot to give a portion to Esu on October 15, 1968.

Just as I was not there at the beginning, I was not there at the end. I volunteered to use my head to break open the coconut, and I was not expected to eat any piece of it. I was only in the middle, which I have faithfully reported to you. My eyes did not see the beginning of this rebellion, and my ears only listened to its end. Many years ago when the eyes were located in the knees, the mouth was always complaining about the nose, the rubbish that it contained, the noisy sneeze, the mucus. The nose was always quiet, absorbing the insult, until one day it could take it no more and opened up to tell the mouth what it thought: If I describe what goes inside you and what comes out of you, all would know that you are the worst part of the body, worse than the anus that at least is dignified enough not to receive rubbish but to release it. You, the mouth, you take and release rubbish. What I want to end with is the rubbish that the nose is able to smell; the contents that the mouth sends to the stomach, later released by the anus that again disturbs the nose. The mouth now wants to release its hidden contents to confirm what the nose says of it. My mouth wants to report what the eagle eyes began to see, what the ears began to hear, what the nose smelled.

Esu was breaking his pact with Ogun—if the god of iron wanted more wars, Esu was sabotaging his wish along with the sacrifices to him. Esu was the intermediary between all the gods, goddesses, and God. He could refuse to deliver an errand, and he could sabotage all prayers, all sacrifices. Esu began to enter many villages and market centers, telling them not to fight anymore, that their sacrifices to Ogun were being wasted. The people began to erect small poles carrying white flags in their main entrances. Market women began to carry leaves on market days. Leaves and flags were the *aroko* of peace and surrender: If the police came, they would meet no warriors; if the tax collectors visited, they would cooperate, giving them some figures when the police asked the size of their income. "Just fake the figures," the women told themselves, "the world hates the truth." A hundred years earlier, the flags and leaves would also have meant that they were ready to pay tribute and be enslaved—their spirits were already broken; their valor crushed; and their bravery now turned to cowardice. Flags and leaves meant that the cause was no longer worth dying for. Human beings just got tired, and they might surrender, meekly, to reduce the sufferings of the moment. In the nineteenth century, after your town had been set on fire and you escaped, scrounging for food, living in this cave today and on that hill tomorrow, on the day you were unlucky enough to be captured, your spirit might be broken, and you might care no more.

Esu can turn a man of God into a man of Satan, and a man of Satan into a man of God. If a god boasted too much about his power, Esu could humiliate the god so that when people offered their sacrifices, supplications, and prayers, they would receive no positive results. Satan, by being humble, could wear a smiling face, work positively, and get rewarded. Esu removed tax collectors from our roads and markets, sending them to offices where they quietly sat down and lamented their lost incomes.

The Satans were gone, and they became purified into temporary saints. Esu then put the farmers in their place, as Satans who had to be put to work, and the former saints became the new Satans.

By 1970, the stories that circulated were no longer about evil tax collectors but about corrupt farmers who were collecting taxes from their fellow farmers and small traders. The farmers, previously warlords, were setting up roadblocks to ask fellow farmers to produce receipts. Hens were beginning to lay duck eggs. They were raiding markets, asking women to produce evidence of payment to local governments. As a woman paid, she would say, "Baba Tawa," well done, and another woman would compliment her, "Alhaji Musibau," we salute you. These words were meant to deride the new tax/toll collectors, a signal that the women knew these men as former rebels now tormenting them. And before the lorry moved forward, carrying the former rebels, Iya Hidiatu Alaso, who was carrying some textiles to sell in the village, would smile, in a manner loaded with meaning, and greet all of them, thanking them for their services to the community. As the lorry moved forward, the women would begin their mockery, with Iya Hidiatu Alaso starting the conversation with a long, insulting cry of "*sioooo.*"

The woman sitting next to her, Iya Suratu Onisu, who dealt in the yam trade, would launch her own vigorous attack and revel in it. Iya Suratu Onisu would adjust her position in her seat in such a way as to shake the woman to her left and the other to the right. She would cough, not an ordinary cough, but one so loud that you had to turn to look and greet her. After the greeting, the usual "*e pele,*" she would slap one palm against the other, as if she wanted to clap. But no, she was not clapping but signaling that she had something to say in a lampooning spirit.

She would pause, all eyes now upon her. She would adjust her shoulders, and begin with a command: "Hear me."

Having gained their full attention, no one listening to any other besides her, including the rascally Kondo, she would say, "There is the biggest wonder in town, the unbelievable wonder."

The other women would ask: "What is this?"

Suratu Onişu would become excited: "It was that useless man we just passed, Alhaji Musibau."

Curious women would demand to know more. "He wanted to make me his concubine!"

Ten responses would follow: "Does he not know that you are married?"

"The dog with four wives already at home?"

"An Alhaji without a job who lives on fake tickets?"

"What a silly man; if his is the only one penis left in this world, it will not be for my vagina."

After he had been fully abused, a woman would end with a summary: "The Iyaganku policeman is better than Alhaji Musibau." This was the same Musibau who had been part of the contingent that attacked the Iyaganku police station a year before, now become worse than the policemen he had attacked.

The farmers stopped lorries and asked the drivers, the victims of victory, to pay levies, and they collected bribes on top. The farmers had been corrupted. The government asked for a flat rate of £2; the farmers were asking for more and pocketing the difference. The farmers who had fought council officials, objecting to the way the state was using their cocoa money, had now become their own officials in an illegitimate "government" accountable to no one. Those who were not paying their tax, Tafa was to declare on the radio, were saboteurs who did not want Irunmu to succeed. He and the faithful farmers were loyal to the government and had direct access to the officials to express their legitimate grievances.

Esu decreed an end to the collective power and unions of farmers and the urban poor. While we had started with one or two powerful movements without even any address at which we could receive a letter, Esu had splintered us into many organizations, each with confused agendas and with leaders looking for nothing but money. A crack in the wall allows the lizard to enter. Former friends became mortal enemies. From the high level of trust of 1968, the level sank to low and zero: As all lizards lie down, no one knows which of them is suffering from stomachache. The organizations had addresses and leaders whose faces were known. Some began to call themselves the Western State Farmers' Union, with a secretariat in the city. Another called itself the Reformed Agbekoya Movement, with a Western-educated president and secretary. Farmers with pens! All now had lawyers who collected money from them. Some of these lawyers were adding affiliation with the old Agbekoya to their credentials. Even Chief Mojeed Agbaje, who had previously claimed to have nothing to do with our rebellion, now said he was a strong member, an insider. Sure, Tafa Adeoye was instructed to speak with some lawyers in 1969 when it was thought that dialogue could resolve the conflict, but no lawyer knew of the plans, the anger, the spontaneity of thousands marching on places and palaces. Poor Muslims, abused as illiterates and as poor men when the rebellion started, were abused again for stupidity, allowing themselves to become objects of manipulation when the rebellion was nearing its end.

The government chose to recognize whichever organizations it liked, usually those that agreed with its own goals. The reformed organizations began to meet not with the farmers at Akanran but with the ministry men in the secretariat. Tafa and others went to the Executive Council chambers to see Irunmu. They were given tea and biscuits before the meeting and pounded yam and beef after the meeting. They ate. The governor gave them brown envelopes containing money, and they took the envelopes. Tafa even promised to cooperate with the governor to deal with the bad eggs in the union. Our leader had now become the policeman assisting Irunmu, who was now in a position to upset the cook and eat his dinner on time. Tafa wanted to befriend a leper but avoid his handshake.

The farmers' bosses were settling down to some level of comfort. They identified themselves as leaders, operating as a stream that does not remember its source. One would steal, and the other would watch for him as he did so. Friends and colleagues in a cemetery, where only the dead knew the way of the dead. A snail does not know how to bite a tortoise—only a tortoise knows how. Tafa now had a large and fanciful American car with a driver and a retinue of staff members to maintain. With money from Irunmu and from politicians looking for support, he was even able to build an impressive three-story house. He was behaving like a chief as people milled around him. He even opened his own office in the city. Fearing for his safety, he converted some of the previous rebels into personal security guards. He even wanted to expand his harem, so he took two additional wives. He was no longer wearing a war uniform but a flowing *agbada*, and spending time entertaining a large retinue of followers. His house became a tourist attraction, with visitors ranging from those who wanted to see a former hero to those seeking charms. When former members of the movement expressed disappointment and began to rail against him, he appealed to Irunmu and the police to hunt them down. Tafa's activities not only fragmented the movement, but led to its collapse. Many now wanted to become like Tafa, who had made money by mediating between the farmers and the government.

Tafa had now split his firewood to warm himself twice: first as the leader of the rebels and second as the representative of poor farmers to the government. In the first warmth, we all felt the pain of hard work that it brought; in the second, Tafa became the baby in the womb who does not feel the smoke and heat in its mother's kitchen and cooking pot.

**Photograph of Tafa Adeoye, a celebrity figure, taken in late 1969 or early 1970. Ministry of Information, Ibadan.**

The politicians corrupted Tafa and many other prominent leaders. Very cleverly, the politicians became cats who used their paws to cover their claws so that they could pretend to be friends of the rats. The jackal borrows the lamb's skin to catch the sheep. The politicians were smiling, white teeth that did not represent purity of heart. Ojugo had visited Tafa on October 5. He even visited again, on October 15. On this day, the calm representatives of farmers from six districts met with Ojugo and some other political leaders aligned with the banned Action Group. For Tafa and others, this was a once-in-a-lifetime achievement: for the leader of the Yoruba, as his unofficial title proclaimed him to be, to visit for a second time. Ojugo's message was to ask the rebels to support the government, to use their dane guns to shoot wild game instead of humans, to allow schools to open, and to go back to their farms.

Ojugo came to Tafa and other elders in the form of a snake charmer. It was difficult to get to our leaders, real and fake, for we had cut down big trees to block the roads. To get to the real leader, you would have

The "civilian" face of Tafa Adeoye at a public meeting. The pocket of his garb contained charms. Photograph taken in 1970. Ministry of Information, Ibadan.

to figure out how to sidetrack twelve big trees—Iroko, the biggest and proudest trees of all. To reach Tafa's place, you should be prepared to deal with six of them. For the war strategy had been to block the roads in such a way that police vehicles could never get through. A helicopter, yes; police and army vehicles, no. Tafa's base could only be attacked from the air. Ojugo walked ten miles, climbing over fallen trees to see Tafa. By that time, Akanran had gone: Houses were already destroyed, men and women had migrated elsewhere, the church and school had closed down. Ojugo behaved like Irunmu, telling them that the rebellion was over, as if he was the one who had declared its beginning. "Enough is enough," he told small crowds whenever he saw villagers. He invoked the Yoruba saying: If something makes you angry, and you are not angry, you are a bastard; if they appeal to you, and you refuse to accede, you are a bastard. We had become the bastards who were not listening to the government. Tafa listened, and he later moved to the city, to begin his fall from grace to grass, until he ended his life in humiliation. Tafa grew

Tafa Adeoye with one of his wives and loyalists. Notice his flywhisk, which was credited with tremendous magical powers. Ministry of Information, Ibadan.

taller than his father and began to see his father as his peer, and, as his beard grew longer, it began to claim the same age as the eyebrows. He began to disconnect, forgetting that he who eats alone dies alone.

The visits by politicians were the beginning of Tafa's downfall. For Tafa did not know that Ojugo, the vice chairman of the Federal Executive Council and the leader of the Yoruba, came to him wearing a garb borrowed from Esu. Ojugo was not satisfied with being vice chairman but was totally obsessed with becoming Number One. The trouble in the Western State meant that Ojugo had no control over his own people. And there was a growing movement to create more states, to break the Western State into smaller states, which indeed was done in later years, meaning that the basis of his power would be weakened unless the big North was also broken into more smaller units. Ojugo had already lost the Igbo in the East forever, after his bitter rivalry with Kikiwe, being accused of starving the Igbo during the war, a charge that translated into the proposition that war is not supposed to be nasty. There was even the very trivial charge that he had asked the Igbo to stop eating their number-one delicacy, "stock fish." This is a nutrient-deficient codfish from Norway, its valuable oil removed, dried into solid rock and sold

**Tafa Adeoye, now loyal to Irunmu, endorsing a new tax receipt. Ministry of Information, Ibadan.**

as a waste product to Africans. As insignificant as this request was, it was like asking an Ibadan man to stop eating his not-so-nice-looking *amala* made of yam and then asking him for his vote. Ojugo had also lost the Hausa and Fulani in the North, for, they believed, he did not think they were civilized and educated enough. They already had a sufficient number of turban-wearing headmasters with gentle words coming from their mouths and harsh mischief hidden in their bellies. Ojugo was left with his own people, and the rebellion was a political nuisance to him.

The almighty Esu had changed the brains of Tafa and his associates from bright to dull, their energies from positive to negative. As their

Various propaganda photographs of the governor, Adeyinka Adebayo, intended to show that peace had returned and that the farmers "loved" him. Ministry of Information, Ibadan.

chicken didn't want to scratch the soil before it ate, the governor was now able to abuse and insult them, and they said, "Thank you, sir." Tafa said in March 1970 that the farmers were being misled by politicians who wanted to destroy them. In a twist of fate, Tafa dictated a petition that he delivered to Irunmu when he visited Tafa at his village of Fada. Speaking as the leader of six Ibadan districts, Tafa reported two powerful commissioners, Prince Alade Lamuye in charge of Local Government and Chieftaincy Affairs and Adeoye Adisa of Home Affairs and Home Information, to Irunmu, asking that they should be dismissed. Other names were added, all of whom, according to Tafa, were those responsible for the war, for misleading him, and for causing the rift between the farmers and the government. He was yet to kill a lion but was already talking about how to share it. Young women were asked to dance to honor Irunmu, who, in delight, blamed the rebellion on the devil. Irunmu's dog could now bark and bite at the same time; it could put a bone in its mouth and bark as well; and it could eat the bone hung around its neck. On September 16, 1970, Irunmu, realizing that Tafa's power was gone and his base had collapsed, made his best move ever: He had Tafa arrested and thrown into detention, taken far away to the northern city of Jos, where no relatives or friends could visit him; he released him many months later in March 1971 to return to a life of obscurity and disgrace. Dirty water, Irunmu seemed to be asserting, can extinguish a fire.

Esu changed the key products in the villages and farms. When I traveled to Elepo to check on Pasitor's farm, what I saw would pass for one of the wonders of the world. Grown along with various crops was marijuana, not in small hidden pots as in previous years, but in acres upon acres. I looked in all directions; it was marijuana. The next-door village, called Agbo, was founded by my ancestors, leaving my father extensive inherited land. Everything was overgrown with marijuana, not growing as a weed but cultivated. I had to ask what possessed them, why Esu was asking them to do this. They were consistent in their answer, as if they had all memorized it:

*B'o se to ko si mo*
*B'o se gba l'o ku.*

They were telling me that surviving was no longer a matter of doing the right thing, being just, or being ethical, but a matter of solving the problems at hand. The end justifies the means: If the problem was about obtaining money, any product that produced the money was good

enough. In other words, survival was to be ensured by any means necessary. The world was being reborn, away from that which was right, based
on ethical principles of living, to that which was pragmatically expedi-
ent. Honest workers, religious people, and responsible householders
were beginning to supplement cocoa with marijuana. The demand
had expanded exponentially because of the civil war, rising truancy in
schools, youth disenchantment, and the massive expansion of the Nigerian army. Hundreds of new-generation traders, mainly men, were raiding the villages for marijuana. A few years earlier, these traders would
have been stoned to death, lambasted for encouraging illegal trade and
moral lapses. Not any more. If the "ministry men" and council officers,
with Irunmu as their boss, could be terrible, why should the farmers be
virtuous and moral? The moral fabric of society was being altered. Young
men were being discouraged from farm work, asked to go to the city to
learn how to fix bicycle tires, while more and more women were roasting plantains and corn by the roadside. You now began to see more and
more men loafing in the early hours of the morning, refusing to work.

Esu was imposing his curse on cocoa and the farmers. For Esu can
take what you have and keep it for himself or give you something else.
Esu even, through trickery, entered the palace of a great king, set it on
fire, ruined the king, and took his place as the new king with a new palace hurriedly built for him while the people were still in mourning. Esu
showed that impatience could ignite fire and an empty sack could stand
upright.

A new source of wealth had now opened up for Nigeria: crude oil. It
was discovered in the late 1950s, and extraction began in the 1960s, with
most of the initial proceeds used to finance the civil war. The amount of
revenue the oil could produce was not too clear at that time. As it became
clearer when the war ended, the country found it no longer needed the
cocoa and its farmers. Ever since, cocoa and the farmers have been useless to the government. To reap money from cocoa required patience;
with oil, it was instant. Oil did not need thousands of people to produce
it. It was not found in Ibadan but far away in the Niger Delta, which many
could not even locate on the map. Money from there now began to feed
the Yoruba people. They could complain as much as they wanted that
the money was not enough, but it was not their money, not the product
of their sweat—it just came to them because they had the good fortune
to be part of Nigeria. Without cocoa, there could be no rural protest,
and so ours was the last. Esu, who led us to fight over cocoa, then led us
to a new set of conflicts over oil. What you now need to control is politics

in the federal capital of Abuja, to gain the power to distribute oil revenues and grant the licenses to extract oil.

Esu was clever in turning the oil money into more of a curse than a blessing. Most of the oil money, Esu divined, would go to waste—some stolen, some set on fire, and some spent on useless projects. Oil money would create *idamu*, that is, a crisis that could not be resolved. This showed itself in the idea that the oil produced too much money and that Nigeria did not know what to do with it. Short of setting it on fire, it has been used to destroy communities, destroy farms and villages, and damage the work ethic. The country has become a man with only a shirt confronting the winter, a crab that leaves its house to inhabit a dried-up stream. The more the country spends, the less anything works. The managers of the oil money love themselves more than the owners of the oil—men who kill strangers in the dark, not realizing that these are their brothers and sisters. As the strangers fight back, they are like chickens with weak beaks pecking at rocks. The managers' hens keep getting drunk, forgetting that there is a bigger bird called the hawk. The managers keep running after their own shadows and will later be communicating with their dead predecessors. Our own chicken may have to await the eagle's funeral to feel safe.

Esu found jobs for idle hands. By 1973, four of the men at Akanran had been arrested for the most serious crime in the land: armed robbery. The most notorious armed robber of the decade, by the name of Oyenusi, was found at Agugu and publicly executed in Lagos. I am sure I ran into him once or twice. Two were executed at Ibadan, at Eleyele, where I went to see if it was at all possible to ask them what had happened. No one could get close. The military, entrenched in corruption and stealing such enormous amounts of money, was making a public display of small-time robbers, entertaining the population with public executions. This military was trying to distance its own behavior from the behavior of these robbers, lecturing from higher moral ground. Some of the robbers had once been very decent men, extremely hardworking, with a profound sense of morality. Thus, the question I have asked myself for many years is what drove them to what they did.

Some answers. In 1960, if you were a civilian and not a hunter, looking for game in the forest and the forest reserves, you would not have seen a gun, much less touched one. The hunters had the dane guns we later used, manufactured in large numbers. You could shoot only once before reloading, and reloading took time. The firepower of the gun was dependent on the powder you fed into it. It was originally introduced to West Africa by Danish traders, and so it became known as a "dane gun." By 1960, it had become obsolete, not even part of international trade anymore. Local blacksmiths as far back as a hundred years earlier had known how to make it. You could use the dane gun to kill a rabbit, guinea fowl, grass cutter, or even to shoot antelopes and deer. When you loaded this gun, it was for the purpose of killing these small animals; it would not kill the bigger ones. They could be wounded and walk away. Human beings were accidentally shot too, but many survived. Your bullets would be wasted if aimed at an elephant. To aim at bigger mammals, you needed to put more powder and heavier pellets into the narrow barrel. A loud noise was produced by the gun, *o tun ku* (there is more!), followed by small amounts of smoke. If those animals had known that the cry of *o tun ku* was no more than mere boasting, they would have advanced to challenge the hunter who would have to run since he could not reload his gun.

Modern guns were originally confined to the army and police. There were not many of them. In 1960, you were unlikely to see soldiers on the streets. They lived in the barracks and came out during parades. You began to see more of them after the first coup. You would see the police but not with guns. They carried only batons. By 1970, you would see soldiers and police with guns on major roads. They would even stop you and point their guns at you if you did not stop.

These guns began to circulate in the underground economy. They made it to Akufo, where our movement purchased some. Discharged soldiers stole guns. Policemen stole guns as well. The ugly trees were now producing sour fruits. And those who stole began to sell. Stories began to circulate in neighborhoods about men who had guns, stories told to warn people to be careful near some houses as the owner could blast off your head.

Guns and marijuana made a potent combination. The soldiers who served in the war were the worst. Some of our former foot soldiers in the rebellion, who had once relied on dane guns, now also began to gain access to the better guns, and some were also growing marijuana.

The charms that had been prepared for the rebellion were to be put to other uses. Criminals began to seek charms, as rebels and soldiers had before. They sought charms to enable them to steal and disappear, as well as the charms needed to withstand the police in a shootout. And when the police failed to arrest a notorious criminal, everyone attributed it to the right charms. Stories abound about robbers who were shot many times and did not die; about those arrested and locked up in cells who disappeared into thin air; about male criminals who were able to turn into beautiful women and ultimately walk away; and even about a charm used to confuse a judge who, on the day of judgment, would read a verdict of guilty as not guilty.

It was obvious that many were disappointed with the outcome of the rebellion: It did not lead to any enhancement in the standard of living; living costs had gone up; and the military had failed the nation. There was now more money in the cities, as more and more oil money was flowing. Young men were driving cars. And those young men who saw themselves as failures or who had no credible jobs saw a way out: crime.

*B'o se to ko si mo*
*B'o se gba l'o ku.*

Esu was leading many men to ask the wrong questions: Why bother to fight the government when you could use a gun to rob fellow citizens of their possessions? Why waste valuable time thinking about solutions to serious development questions when you could enrich yourself? The answer, taking care of yourself and caring nothing about the rest of society, has become the theory of survival in Nigeria, based not on religion or culture but on the ethics of self-enrichment and security: The big man builds a big house with his own big generator, big borehole, big security fence, big dogs. The only thing he cannot control is the road that leads to his abode, which unfortunately for him also brings criminals to his house.

An extensive regional economy concerned with the dispersal of stolen goods developed, such that stolen items at Ibadan could make it to Cotonou in the Republic of Benin or Accra in Ghana. The market for stolen items expanded and flourished. Men and women specialized in the lucrative underground economy. Cars, televisions, and jewelry became the most sought-after items. When a car was stolen, within hours, it could be reduced to pieces, never to be recovered. The pieces would find their way to flourishing spare-parts stores. Or the car could be repainted within hours, given a new number plate, as well as new engraved engine numbers. Off it went to the Republic of Benin.

Stealing a car was far more lucrative than looking after cocoa trees and seeds. There was no need to wait for the harvest. There was no need to take loans from greedy moneylenders. Guns and marijuana were put to use in the underground economy. Fast living abounded in the cities—drinking most of the time in the company of cheap women with bleached skins. These were women who did not know who had made them pregnant, and who would throw their newborn babies into a dump so they could return to a nightclub. The society that produced these women who wasted their lives was also the society that paid the pastors and the imams to crucify them in weekly sermons.

"Just accept Jesus, the widow's husband," the pastor would proclaim, and "your vagina will no longer be a dustbin." But it was far more complicated than that: Before the women could put food in their mouths, their vaginas must first be fed.

Imported lace fabric from Switzerland became the new status symbol, replacing the locally hand woven *ofi*. The lace redefined the notion of success—to wear it was to announce one's arrival in a new world. Irunmu had more than a few lace outfits. Thieves used some of their money to buy lace. Popular music, especially the juju of Ebenezer Obey and King Sunny Ade, captured the moment with their focus on praise singing and slavish flattery of those with money. Successful men, that is, those with money, were now attaining the attributes of gods—one can strike you with thunder as Sango, and another can inflict you with smallpox like Sanponna. "Londoners," those with the money to go abroad, were the new Ogun, the pathfinders who could reach anywhere created by God. These men, as the musicians of the time were singing, were bigger than Ogun. In future years, they would live up to their reputation, building houses that the gods could not have contemplated. They fulfilled society's expectation of reproduction through voluptuous women who gave them as many children as they wanted. As they could not eat more salt than the poor, they took to the consumption of beef. The more meat they ate, the more respect they had. Since none of them could consume an entire cow, there came a point at which the respect had to stop.

Babs Foluso, a most decent human being in 1968, but executed by firing squad in 1973, was illustrative of the new era in history. He was led before the firing squad wearing his lace and looking downcast like a goat about to be slaughtered. Five years earlier, Foluso had been an ally to be trusted and could not even hit anyone with a club. He was too comfortable in his own skin, too polite. He was so trusted by our movement that he served, for ten months, in the capacity of Ojise Ogun ("errand boy of war matters")—entrusted with money to be carried and secret information to be delivered to multiple locations. He was no Judas Iscariot! Foluso betrayed no one and stole not a cent. What he was later killed for was far less than the money with which he had been entrusted. He was elevated to the rank of Onise Iku (the errand boy of death), with its insignia of office the Opa Iku (the staff of death). In older Yoruba wars, the Onise Iku delivered the unpleasant message of announcing an impending war, and the insignia was to forewarn people that they should prepare to die. In a redefined role, Foluso was to move from one branch to another to say that proposals to end the rebellion were not acceptable, as he did after the Ayoola Commission submitted its report, and that people should prepare for more fighting. All that was in 1968 and 1969.

His arrest, short trial, and death sentence came as a shock to many of us, but the state was able to put a gun in his hands at a crime site. Some days, I would think he had committed the heinous crime, bowing to the command of Esu and the demon in his body. Some other days, I would think he had been set up, as Esu possessed the policeman who accused him of armed robbery. His son is now a successful professor of chemistry, if this is any consolation to the dead or the living. When I pressured the son to review the files of the case, we discovered that they were not to be found, not even the trace of a single sheet of paper. All there is now is the newspaper report of his ending—the photographs of his fallen body pumped with bullets.

There was a tragic side to this new delight in killing armed robbers. One or two persons who were shot had not killed anyone or committed any other crime. They were arrested on the streets either because the police were looking for people to take the place of criminals or they appeared too rough. The police were in collusion with men of the under-world. Everyone knew this. When a criminal was arrested, he could be released back to the streets. The police would grab an innocent person who was given the name of the criminal and locked up. Such was the fate of Kobomoje, who smoked lots of hemp, got arrested, and was charged with armed robbery. Such men had no money to hire the services of attorneys. Their families and friends deserted them, with no one willing to testify to their characters or defend their integrity. When I tried to tell people that I thought Foluso, who had been turned into a celebrity armed robber, was probably innocent, everyone, including my mother, asked me never to say that I had ever met him. Such was the fate of such men, whether innocent or not: By the time the police put the stamp of armed robbery on you, your wife would take all the children back to her father's house and your name would be erased from memory. By the time you appeared in court, you had been so humiliated, so badly beaten up that you barely remembered your own name. When the judge read the charge and asked whether you were guilty, you just answered yes because death was more comfortable than living. A house falls together with its roof.

Esu had also possessed Buoda Gebu, so that he would recruit more converts and wage a relentless war on Ogun and other gods and goddesses who were now being forced into exile. The Muslims joined the Christians to seek an end to the old cultural order. All forms of indigenous worship were to be attacked with extreme verbal warfare of a new kind. The Orisa would be treated as enemies, far worse than witches and wizards, with stones and cudgels to kill all the gods and goddesses who the Muslims and Christians could recognize. Yoruba Christians with Western education, serving as schoolteachers, began to present the Orisa as useless, spurring irrelevant pagan practices, corrupting religion. The Yoruba began to leave behind a major component of their past and their moral fabric. Esu would take his vengeance on them for as they were leaving the past behind, the birth of the present was spawning miscarriages and abortions.

Why would Esu use Buoda Gebu and his followers to destroy what they had inherited when they could have lived together side-by-side and complemented one another? Perhaps Esu's work is still unfolding, and he may still perform one of his tricks on those churches and mosques. Nothing is beyond Esu, as one myth affirms. Perhaps you have not heard what Esu did to two best friends, how this divine trickster set the two on the path of conflict and violence. When the going was good, the two friends did everything together: They ate the same food, wore the same clothes, married twin sisters, and the one could not be seen without the other. They loved one another dearly, and they used to boast about their friendship, far stronger than Buoda Gebu's romance with Jesus Christ. They became the very model of friendship and were even boasting that they would be friends for life and die on the same day.

Esu knew of this great friendship and heard of their boasting. He smiled gently, touched his long forehead, admired his phallic symbols, and hatched his plans. Esu hates the absolute and abhors all definitive conclusions. He was expecting a sacrifice to be made to him, and nothing came. Esu sprang into action: He put on a cap made of two colors; one side was white and the other red. He went to the farm where the two best friends were doing their work. As the friends were talking facing one another on the bush path, Esu walked in between them, even saying hello as he walked ahead. He was wearing his fanciful cap, so beautiful that it could not escape notice.

As he left, one of the friends said, "I loved Esu's red cap."

"What do you mean by red? He was wearing a white cap."

"Are you calling me a blind man or a forgetful character?"

"Yes, you must be blind and stupid if you did not know the difference between red and white."

More arguments ensued, and they began to exchange blows. Word reached the village that the two best friends, the acclaimed perfect model of friendship, had exchanged blows and bruises. The great friendship collapsed. Look no further for an explanation: Esu had shown his cap made of two colors. Both described what they saw, but neither could see both colors. Esu then appeared to mediate and end the conflict, showing his two-sided cap. His mischief was noted, but the damage had been done.

Esu, the miracle worker, could at least bring those myths that made Ode Aje a laboratory of culture back to the schools. Esu should now mislead those schoolteachers into thinking that myths are no more than literature, like Greek myths. Esu, possess the schoolchildren with the mythology of the Yoruba past so that they can talk back to Buoda Gebu and his followers. When I remember Buoda Gebu, I also remember the song I sang for a performance in December 1965:

Who stole my brain?
*Lenle lenle n lere o; lenle lenle*
He wears a long beard and a long gown
*Lenle lenle n lere o; lenle lenle*
He carries a strange book with his left hand
*Lenle lenle n lere o; lenle lenle*
He holds a big bell with the right
*Lenle lenle n lere o; lenle lenle*
Who stole my heart?
*Lenle lenle n lere o; lenle lenle*
Who stole my charms, my power?
*Lenle lenle n lere o; lenle lenle*

We never supplied the answer, but at the end of the song, the audience did: witches. Not so, but we agreed anyway. Today, I would disagree and supply a different answer: Buoda Gebu and Alhaji Ajagbemokeferi did.

You have not met this Alhaji before. He was also new to me. He was tall and elegant, and he moved to Ibadan in late 1969. Some said he came from Kano; others said Ilorin; and some others said he came from a compound in the city. They called him Fulani because he was light in complexion. He called himself Ajagbemokeferi, "someone who yells at pagans." When a man proclaims himself to be a saint, be warned. He went about the city saying he had an army ready to fight all the pagans, all the masquerades, and he was already successfully building up an army of followers to accomplish his mission. He would not fight the Christians for now, he assured us, but he would do so in the second stage of the battle. His language was harsh. His book was the Quran. His open revival meetings were conducted in several spots, and he had a "translator" who repeated everything he said, even when you already understood it. Money came as donations, but also as gifts from places far and near, far more than would be needed for him to build a road in the sky. His messages were designed to prepare the ground for a jihad, which came later, when he led his formidable force to attack the pagans and their masquerades. So confident was the Arab in town that he spoke as if he could move the moon. Here was a cat able to chase many dogs who began to see himself as a tiger. Irunmu, who pursued us with guns, left Alhaji alone. Alhaji's wings kept growing, and he made himself taller by wearing a high turban. The moment of regrets and agony would come later, but the warning period was long.

Esu could be funny; interesting, too. He was blessing Ajagbemokeferi and Buoda Gebu in their missionary endeavors. And they truly prospered. Both became foxes setting up a tribunal to try chickens. As both were killing "paganism," Esu was busy spreading the worldview of "paganism." Belief in *oogun* (charms, medicine) refused to go away. When an Aladura like Buoda Gebu was successful, it was attributed to his use of charms to lure followers to him. When Ajagbemokeferi claimed to have the power to perform miracles, people said it was *oogun*. Witches increased in number, and so, too, did witch hunters. They all continued to flourish until the Nollywood films of the 1990s and beyond began to reveal their locations, power, and machinations. Buoda Gebu's angels, in popular imagination, became real beings one could see and describe, whom God would send to you to tell you the location of hidden treasure. The mighty Esu himself began to appear every day, everywhere among both the lowly and the mighty. Esu was being blamed for all the failed coups and counter-coups that occurred after 1970. Esu could take it—the blood of the executed armed robbers became his new elixir, as he shared the blood tonic with Ogun.

I needed to cry more, so declared Esu who believed that my agonies were not enough, my sufferings too miniscule, and my traumas too few.

On Friday, December 12, 1969, Leku sent for me. Her first statement was a blow: "My time is up: I want to go home!" People of her age, according to a strong belief, actually knew when to die. They would begin to communicate it as a premonition. Sometimes, they would be conversing with their dead relatives. Or, we would accuse them of losing their coherence and memory. The phrase "eating the tongue" could be used to describe their meaningless statements. When you gave them food, they would eat little and say they were saving the rest for the journey they were embarking upon. They would ask you whether you saw the woman who died three years ago. When the elderly began to "eat the tongue," you needed to look at your savings and start to make funeral arrangements. If you needed blessings, this was the time to collect them. If you needed to stake a claim on a piece of land, this was the time to let the elderly transfer it to you, as there were no written wills.

Then Leku told me that I was the only one she wanted to tell. For a woman who did not like to talk, she gave a long speech, almost an hour nonstop—telling an incredible autobiography; the time is not yet ripe enough to retell it. She punctuated her speech by puffing and putting more tobacco in her pipe. She gave me the pipe and asked me to inhale it three times. I did. She held on firmly to my head, asking me to swallow the smoke instead of releasing it. I did. She said certain things that I will always remember. She told me what to do with her stuff and stores. She asked me to take some soap and go to the stream with flowing water to wash with it, in the early hours of the morning. I must do so within twenty-four hours of her death. She told me the reason for this, a reason I will share in later years. Finally, she licked an *agbalumo* seed, asked me to open my mouth, put it in my mouth as if it were a kiss, but not the kiss of two lips touching in a romance, and asked me to lick it. The *agbalumo* is a seed that grows inside a pod, much smaller than a cocoa pod. In looking for an English word for it, I found that *agbalumo* is called the "white star apple." The tree on which it grows carries the Latin name of *Chrysophyllum albidum*, which has several varieties that do well in tropical weather. Like cocoa, the seed has a creamy taste, and when licked, it is revealed as a very beautiful, hard seed that one can play with. Schoolchildren used it to practice counting numbers, among other things. After seven days, I was instructed, I must go and bury the seed at a location she specified. I still know the location and what I should not do with the site. Then she recited incantations that would allow me always to overcome all adversities, so that no matter how hard the struggle, the other person would lose. She gave me a long list of instructions about key aspects of life. Then, she brought out three bowls whose contents I did not recognize. She asked me to choose one. I did, and she said that my fate was sealed, irrevocable. She did not tell me the details of the fate, but she told me the ultimate punishment for attempting to deviate from it. There is a dreadful component, tormenting even to remember. She warned that what I would later call mistakes and accidents would be part of the journey, as those mistakes and accidents were built into the fate, in part to ward off negative forces and people. She asked me to look away from her and told me I must never see her again, must never attend her funeral, and must never see her grave. And she uttered her last words, slowly as a command:

*Ohun ti o ba se di asegbe*
Any act that you execute is sealed, unassailable

This concluded her speech and rituals, ending with those powerful words telling me that whatever I do, which she never specified, is unquestionable, permanently irreversible. I could even wear a grass robe and move new fire. The next day, Leku died at dawn. Farewell, Iya Leku. I await Leku's permission to say more. The time will come.

> The Iya-hun of many mysteries
> Odor of smoke and of the numinous fire
> Enclosed in a closet of snakes and scorpions
> Dark leather belts on minuscule buttocks
> Closed eyes that see far beyond common sight
> Weak limbs that run faster than a hunted hare
> Feeble fingers that cut like knives
> The wisdom of the deep jungle and of the township,
> The tempting grain that even a fowl must not dare to swallow
> A tall tree once attempted to fall and crush Iya-hun,
> Ka-ka, it cracked, and crashed almost, then . . . it stopped mid-way
> Iya-hun, the crafty smith, turned the tree into an umbrella
> That protects and secures the eye of the earth,
> Where the three knuckles of time meet
> The solo sun that beats cowardly men and their manhoods!
> The mindboggling moon, daughter of the wild spirit
> The restless One that shuttles between
> The crypts of heaven and earth.
> When Iya-hun arrived on earth,

She had ten heads, twenty starry eyes
And with them, she sees the four corners of the earth, at once,
Holds dialogue with heaven and earth at once,
Eats with one mouth, drinks with another,
And vomits all she had in her womb with the tenth mouth
Her small body is resting in a corner,
But her heads sleep in a dozen other places:
Today at the foot of a mighty rock
Tomorrow at the ocean's deep
Ten big heads balanced on the frail body
Of a chameleon that leaps and never sleeps.
Iya-hun carries the bag of the world's wisdom with her left hand,
With her right hand she holds the calabash of life,
The only being that inhabits the sky in company of birds;
In the waters she makes her abode with crocodiles and whales;
A tether that enters the ground not once, and not twice, but at will!
In the sky, Iya-hun is fed by the birds; in the waters by the whales;
And underneath the ground by half-human, half-animal gnomes.

That I no longer can see Leku does not mean that she cannot see me. My tears are invisible, like the cries and tears of the fish hidden by the water in which it lives. I should stop crying in the rain and wait for a drier season.

I was now a few days short of turning seventeen—on January 1, 1970. I needed a job to support myself. A bird in the sky must always have its mind on the ground. For months, I had gone to the bottom of the river to pick stones, and I was now fully wet, narrowly escaping being drowned. I had consumed too many sour fruits, and my teeth were set on edge. That I washed my cloth in hot water does not mean that I could avoid using the sun to dry it. I had assumed that because I had two legs I could climb two trees at the same time. I was one of two birds tied together with four wings that could not fly. I was like the plant in the strong wind: I blew down in one moment and rose up again in the next. Both today and tomorrow were my great companions. Whether you wait or not, tomorrow will come, leaving you to wonder about today. The ostrich and the giraffe, with their long necks, cannot see what will happen tomorrow.

I had previously registered as an external candidate for the Ordinary Level of the General Certificate Examinations of the University of London. I had given this a first stab in 1968, and I passed all the subjects whose examinations I had the time to attend. With one eye, I had been preparing minimally for this examination, spending more time on chemistry and biology, which required separate examinations on laboratory work. I had no access to any laboratory, but I figured out, after studying the examination pattern for ten years, that one could memorize the terminology, understand the steps, and reach the right conclusions. Thus, I understood the outcome of adding different chemicals. The biology practical was far simpler, at least for me, as all I needed to do was memorize the entire contents of a 212-page book. That book and others, I had to steal, raiding the library of Lagelu Grammar School a few miles away from Ode Aje: A man climbs a thorny tree not because he is bold but because he needs to survive. There was a huge mountain in my path, and I could not sit down wishing for it to disappear. I must get up, climb it to the top, descend to the valley, hit the road to gather the firewood to warm my body in old age, and use my legs to ensure that my pocket is never empty.

With two eyes, I could have prepared far more thoroughly, as the examination days were fast approaching. I could use only one eye, as I needed a job in order to be able to eat. I had grown used to taking care of myself since the age of fourteen. The GCE exam I took and passed at the end of 1968, when my mates were still in Class Three of high school and I had already dropped out, actually qualified me for a job in the secretariat, but I hated this place so much that I would rather die of hunger than work there. I needed to pass in one more subject to qualify for admission to a university, but going to one was neither in my thoughts nor in my dreams. In April 1968, I had entered on a crash course in bricklaying and masonry, but I was never paid as an apprentice, and I quit. I also started a small school of my own, called "home lessons," to coach primary school students in the evenings. A morning session developed for people like Moses, high school truants who converged at my place, whom I also began to teach a variety of subjects, from the Yoruba language to chemistry. Some of these boys are now successful men, and we had a happy reunion in July 2012. It occurred to me that I could return to any of my two previous occupations.

Walking about on the morning of December 23, wondering what next to do, I reached the popular abattoir some three miles from Ode Aje. I stopped to observe:

Three men had tied a powerful rope to two ankles of a hefty cow. Following a signal, they pulled on the rope to fell the unsuspecting cow. Before it could regain its balance, they used the rope to bind three of its legs together so that no matter how hard it struggled, it could no longer stand erect or even crawl. It was crying, begging for sympathy from its tormentors, eyes wide open looking at the knife. As it was busy struggling, as if it knew that death was around the corner, the man wielding the sharp knife came closer and bent down. Only Muslims could slaughter cows for sale—the prayer they offered cleansed the animal for all to eat; without that prayer, one would be consuming a cursed animal. After a short prayer seeking forgiveness from Allah for the sin he was knowingly committing, he cut the cow's neck open and blood gushed out. Professional butchers descended on the dead cow, cutting it into pieces with competence and elegance. The parts were divided up, and the dealers took the portions they had paid for. It was time to move the flesh and bones to streets and markets. Boys of my age, working either solo or with a leader, worked on commission to sell the beef in open wooden trays or covered wooden boxes carried on their heads, which they hawked around the city, stopping for customers who called them. I could do this job, learning to be a butcher and selling meat for a fee, earning enough to take care of myself for the time being, and promote the alliance between my hands and my mouth. I approached a meat dealer, and I got the job in an instant. I had been standing with a crowd for months, but I now needed to stand on my own. Isola, onward! The most violent of winds cannot force a river to flow backwards. Hope, as good as it was, could only deliver breakfast but would not promise an excellent dinner.

It is not all that the eyes see that the mouth must reveal. I can keep writing, telling you what I did in high school before my involvement in this unprecedented rebellion or what I did afterwards, but I am now exhausted, and I need to sleep. Not everyone who says good night will say good morning. Good night, not goodbye. If I wake up, fully rested, I will say more.

# Acknowledgments

✦ ✦ ✦

Let me start off on a depressing note. October 2009 started with peace and joy and ended in trauma and pain. On October 17, 2009, Bisola, my daughter, got married to Colemar, and everything was bright and promising. A week later, I flew to Buenos Aires in Argentina to give a couple of public lectures. In the afternoon of the second day, a calamity struck that affected the writing and completion of this memoir.

More for convenience than addiction, the laptop is now part of the makeup of my career. As with its predecessor, *A Mouth Sweeter Than Salt*, I stole time to write this book, doing so while waiting to catch flights, flying to many destinations, and staying in many hotel rooms. Thus, my laptop contains lecture notes and creative works, notably poems, which I compose away from my desktop computer, on which I do most of my work at home. From time to time, I back up the items on the laptop to an external drive that stays at home. The contents of my desktop and of my laptop are not the same, and the backups are also kept separate.

In Buenos Aires, the guide who came to pick me up at the hotel asked me not to leave any valuables in my room. I took my bag, with the laptop, and I was surprised to find my external drive in it, accidentally packed with the luggage. I told my guide that I would like to return the external drive to the room, and she assured me that it was safer with me. That afternoon at lunch, a set of professional thieves raided our five-star restaurant and took everything. Within a few minutes, all our computers and wallets along with our bags were gone. Gone forever, and with them three of my manuscripts, countless poems, and the first version of this memoir. I had yet to share the drafts, as I always do, and I had no one to turn to to recover any of the lost items. I usually give my writings to five friends and colleagues for comments but not until I am sure that they are close to completion. I was writing the memoir as a secret project, to present it as a surprise to family and friends, allies, and foes. The entire draft of the memoir was gone, together with the backup. It was as if my hope was gone, too; but it retained a life that could, with time, revive hope in itself.

Completing the remaining five weeks of lectures to close the fall semester was a big challenge. I had no alternative lecture notes. My morale was too low for me to be able to write. I was not depressed, as I hardly ever suffer depression, or perhaps I do not know what depression and stress are all about. It is the soft face that acne attacks; stress leaves alone the strong-willed. I lost all interest in writing. I took to heavy drinking, starting as early as nine o'clock in the morning; and I consumed large amounts of carbohydrates to make me fall asleep. I was thinking of alternative careers. History writing was gone, I promised myself. This memoir would not happen, I announced to listening ears.

Dr. Vik Bahl, with whom I spoke regularly about my trauma, came on a rescue mission with his Indian Hinduism to replace my Yoruba Sango. A professor of English literature turned himself into a psychologist. He sent me a statue of Saraswati, the goddess of knowledge and creativity (art, music, science), and on December 2, 2009, he conducted a ceremony of revival with me, Chief, his cooperative client:

Devi, I invoke you this morning to introduce you to Toyin Falola and him to you. Here is Toyin/Isola, an African, a Yoruba, who has seemingly defied the laws of what is possible on earth. What he has achieved and how he has served others will continue to bear fruit and to be a material and inspirational force for what is good and just.

Chief, Mother Saraswati is one of the great lights in Hinduism. She was born from the great creative force of the god Brahma [something like the Yoruba Olodumare], yet her beauty was such that she had to elude his lustful desires and to calm the potential chaos and turmoil of his own power. Saraswati is the goddess of knowledge and wisdom, uninterested in lavish adornments. It is she who transforms our baser energies and instincts into the higher good, into peace and purpose. She looks "upon the past as pure experience . . . without anger or resentment"; she is "a dispassionate historian."

Saraswati Mata, I have never regarded Falola as an ordinary man.

I have called him a god. Hinduism teaches us that we all have divinity within, and some are graced with the capacity to have full realization of their divinity, and they are called to earth to guide others with their light, their example, and their teachings.

Chief, whether or not you are a god does not concern us here today, but we do know that you keep company with your own gods. Let us invite them to join us today, to help us create this divine meeting of the minds and spirits of two ancient and exalted continents and traditions. Let them welcome Saraswati and be welcomed by her. I would invite Ogun. Chief, whom would you like to invite?

Saraswati Devi, the world, as always, is big and small. As each Indian has traveled out of India, she and he have taken you with them. As Africans have left the continent, they have taken their gods with them. Falola has traveled like the snail to America, but we need to more comprehensively internationalize him! Devi, tell Falola that his work is not done. You must invite him to meditate with you, to listen for you and all the other divinities, including his own, so that your message, your purpose and your strength may be renewed in his heart and in his muscles. Let us invite him to India so that he can sing and dance and laugh with us. Let us learn from him and let us teach him what we know.

Chief, whatever obstacles there may be to your work, I am too small to fathom them, and too small to fix them. Your secrets and mysteries are greater than I am. Yet I know that they are not too big for the gods since they are of the gods.

We ask humbly, with all earnestness, from all of the divine spirits assembled here this morning, to remove whatever obstacles there may be on Falola's path. The purpose of the gods, even in their mischief, is too important to be lost or squandered. Give Falola the guidance and grace to renew his focus, to renew your divine vision, and to take on again the mantle that had been bestowed upon him at birth.

I will close now with a recitation of the Gayatri mantra in Sanskrit, one of my earliest memories and memorized prayers:

Chief, may you know peace and rest, may you always keep the company of the gods, and may you always find a way to return to your own greatest Self, where you will be the "monarch of the realm of permanent amazement."

After the ceremony, he asked Chief to take a topic and begin to write on it. Before I could protest, he said, "Chief, let us now work together and write for one hour. One suggestion is that you write a chapter from your memoir, either a new chapter or one of the ones that was lost, but you can write anything else as well, as long as it is not administrative work!" I chose to write about Vik himself, choosing the title "Vik Bahl: A Meditation on Migration." A fine tree bears juicy fruits. Within his timeframe, I wrote four single-spaced pages. This began the process of recovery, thanks to Saraswati! What Vik did was to remake my emotions, telling me that for a bird to learn to fly it must first learn to leave its nest.

But Saraswati chose to delay the writing of this memoir. I had to write my teaching notes, then a series of public lectures, then a one-thousand-page official history of Ibadan, then a book on the African Diaspora. Saraswati then gave her blessing in 2013 for me to start and complete this memoir. Following a most unusual method, I am rewriting, from memory, the very first version that was lost. Other than checking that a few dates are correct, everything is from the reconstruction of the lost memoir.

The living assisted me in speaking about the dead. Let me thank them before it is too late, before the soil and land demand their complementary meals. Dr. Michael Afolayan showed so much excitement after reading each chapter, and his kind words never wore out his tongue. His prodding created a trance that produced abundant words. A friend at hand, Michael reminds me, is much better than a relative who lives on another planet. Thanks to Michael, I did not behave like a cow without a tail to be mocked by flies.

Dr. Vik Bahl has a way of smuggling himself into all my books with good advice, sometimes forgetting that what you do with advice is to pass it on to others. To Seema Bahl, Mama Ayo of Seattle, I would like to pass on a piece of advice, this time not given to me by Vik: A smile is the strongest weapon to win all battles. Keep smiling, to overcome the trauma that life visits on us. To Ayo, growing in the womb of capitalism, may he always realize that laziness makes the bed for hunger to sleep on. Little boy, never ambush a big crocodile when you play close to the river. To you and me, your family and mine, may misfortune never get close to us.

I thank Dr. Aderonke Adesanya for her abiding interest, reading each chapter as if consuming the favorite Ijebu meal, the *ikokore,* made of soft yam and fish. May her moon continue to shine while she doesn't deceive herself that it can be compared to daylight. E. C. Osondu, winner of the Cain Prize in 2009 for his short story "Waiting," discussed various titles with me. I need not introduce Osondu: A good diviner does not need to advertise his business. Drs. Shennette Garrett-Scott, Ann O'Hear, and

Jessica Achberger read the manuscript with the eyes of historians. No one can hear the sound of a broken drum: May the glory of these three women continue to be proclaimed, loud and clear. Professor Ademola Dasylva waited for the last sentence to offer his comments as a sage. When the cock crows at dawn may he not blame the night for being too short. To all others whom I cannot mention or I have forgotten, forgive me, only know that the sun should share in the shame and blame when the sea dries up.

In revisiting the official documentation on the late 1960s, I have to thank many officials in various ministries and the governor's office, as well as those in the Nigerian National Archives at Ibadan. Saheed Aderinto, while here in Austin as a graduate student, assisted in collecting some of the newspaper items on the rebellion. May he know that a vast ocean exists beyond the stream in his village. When his lion becomes old, may it not become a toy for little flies. Other than to check some facts, figures of casualties as reported by the police, and dates and to see how the events were reported on the government side, I do not rely in this personal history on any of these documents. Relying on those documents is like buying a goat because of its voice and thinking that white teeth can prevent bad breath.

To the survivors and descendants of those who participated in one way or another in the personal history narrated here, the memory will surely bring back the pain. The descendants must remember that if the fly on the top of the wine glass boasts that it is drunk, what will the one deep inside the glass say? I have always been the fly deep inside the glass. We all must know that injustice and peace, like night and day, never live together. The anger may linger but work on its bitter roots and not the emotions. If you go to the forest as hunters without sharpening your spears, the lions and the tigers will turn you into food. Nigerians have to stop buying a monkey that lives on a tree, hang their bags where their hands can reach, stop catching the frog by the tail, and stop blaming their poor dance on the drums. Small men and women need to know that no matter how small the pepper is, it produces a sharp taste; and that their leaders and big men cannot stand on their heads and can only run with their legs. Unite: If many cattle unite, the lion will lie down. Stop the ovation for the big men: When you beat the drums for the madman to dance, you are no better than the madman. Unite: A finger cannot carry a load to the head, a finger cannot extract a thorn from the foot, and a finger cannot remove lice from the head. Unite: If the left hand washes the right hand, and the right washes the left, both become clean. Unite! On this errand of change, send no one but yourself. Be unafraid: A dead man will not arrange his own funeral.

To all the members of my nuclear family who have not been told this aspect of my life, hopefully, they will learn one or two lessons. My own life is drawing to a close: A ripe fruit cannot hang forever on a branch. My ways are fixed; it is now too late for me to become left-handed. The baton must pass: A fruit does not fall too far from the tree that produces it. When an old man exposes himself, walking naked in the marketplace, it is his children who will be ashamed, not he. As Bisola, Dolapo, and Toyin develop new families, remember that you all must walk behind a big elephant so that you do not get drenched with dew; keep a green tree branch in your heart for birds to find a place to sing; plant seeds when others do so that you can all harvest at the same time; the eye and the eyeball must never fight; and if all spiders' webs unite, they can tie up an elephant. No matter how excellent a dancer is, sooner or later, he will yield the floor to others.

Made in the USA
Coppell, TX
03 February 2021